THE NEW
PALGRAVE

FINANCE

D1243600

THE NEW PALGRAVE

FINANCE

EDITED BY
JOHN EATWELL · MURRAY MILGATE · PETER NEWMAN

W·W·NORTON

NEW YORK · LONDON

ISBN 0-393-02732-5

ISBN 0-393-95857-4   {PBK.}

W. W. Norton & Company, Inc.
500 Fifth Avenue
New York, NY 10110

W. W. Norton & Company, Ltd.
37 Great Russell Street
London WC1B 3NU

Printed in Hong Kong

1   2   3   4   5   6   7   8   9   0

Contents

Acknowledgements   vi

General Preface   vii

Preface   xi

Finance	Stephen A. Ross	1
Financial intermediaries	James Tobin	35
Agency costs	Clifford W. Smith, Jr.	53
Arbitrage	Philip H. Dybvig and Stephen A. Ross	57
Arbitrage pricing theory	Gur Huberman	72
Asset pricing	Thomas E. Copeland and J. Fred Weston	81
Louis Bachelier	Benoit B. Mandelbrot	86
Backwardation	Masahiro Kawai	89
Capital asset pricing model	M.J. Brennan	91
Continuous-time stochastic models	Robert C. Merton	103
Continuous-time stochastic processes	Chi-Fu Huang	110
Dividend policy	James A. Brickley and John J. McConnell	119
Efficient market hypothesis	Burton G. Malkiel	127
Financial markets	Nils H. Hakansson	135
Futures markets, hedging and speculation	David M. Newbery	145
Futures trading	H.S. Houthaker	153
Gearing	J.S.S. Edwards	159
Hedging	Gregory Connor	164
Interest rates	Jonathan E. Ingersoll, Jr.	172
Intertemporal portfolio theory and asset pricing	Douglas T. Breeden	180
Mean-variance analysis	Harry M. Markowitz	194

Contents

Option pricing theory	Jonathan E. Ingersoll, Jr.	199
Options	Robert C. Merton	213
Organization theory	Thomas Marschak	219
Portfolio analysis	Nils H. Hakansson	227
Present value	Stephen F. LeRoy	237
Retention ratio	A. Cosh	243
Stochastic optimal control	A.G. Malliaris	246
Takeovers and the Stock Market	Alan Hughes and Ajit Singh	252
Term structure of interest rates	Burton G. Malkiel	265
Contributors		271

Acknowledgements

The following contributors (articles shown in parentheses) acknowledge support from public bodies or permission to reprint copyright material:

Gur Huberman (Arbitrage Pricing Theory), support from the National Science Foundation and the Center for Research in Security Prices.

Alan Hughes and Ajit Singh (Takeovers and the Stock Market), material previously published in *Contributions to Political Economy*, (1987) vol. 6, 74–85, London: Academic Press Ltd.

General Preface

The books in this series are the offspring of *The New Palgrave: A Dictionary of Economics*. Published in late 1987, the *Dictionary* has rapidly become a standard reference work in economics. However, its four heavy tomes containing over four million words on the whole range of economic thought is not a form convenient to every potential user. For many students and teachers it is simply too bulky, too comprehensive and too expensive for everyday use.

By developing the present series of compact volumes of reprints from the original work, we hope that some of the intellectual wealth of *The New Palgrave* will become accessible to much wider groups of readers. Each of the volumes is devoted to a particular branch of economics, such as econometrics or general equilibrium or money, with a scope corresponding roughly to a university course on that subject. Apart from correction of misprints, etc. the content of each of its reprinted articles is exactly the same as that of the original. In addition, a few brand new entries have been commissioned especially for the series, either to fill an apparent gap or more commonly to include topics that have risen to prominence since the dictionary was originally commissioned.

As *The New Palgrave* is the sole parent of the present series, it may be helpful to explain that it is the modern successor to the excellent *Dictionary of Political Economy* edited by R.H. Inglis Palgrave and published in three volumes in 1894, 1896 and 1899. A second and slightly modified version, edited by Henry Higgs, appeared during the mid-1920s. These two editions each contained almost 4,000 entries, but many of those were simply brief definitions and many of the others were devoted to peripheral topics such as foreign coinage, maritime commerce, and Scottish law. To make room for the spectacular growth in economics over the last 60 years while keeping still to a manageable length, *The New Palgrave* concentrated instead on economic theory, its originators, and its closely cognate disciplines. Its nearly 2,000 entries (commissioned from over 900 scholars) are all self-contained essays, sometimes brief but never mere definitions.

Apart from its biographical entries, *The New Palgrave* is concerned chiefly with theory rather than fact, doctrine rather than data; and it is not at all clear how theory and doctrine, as distinct from facts and figures, *should* be treated in an encyclopaedia. One way is to treat everything from a particular point of view. Broadly speaking, that was the way of Diderot's classic *Encyclopédie raisonée* (1751–1772), as it was also of Léon Say's *Nouveau dictionnaire d'économie politique* (1891–2). Sometimes, as in articles by Quesnay and Turgot in the *Encyclopédie*, this approach has yielded entries of surpassing brilliance. Too often, however, both the range of subjects covered and the quality of the coverage itself are seriously reduced by such a self-limiting perspective. Thus the entry called '*Méthode*' in the first edition of Say's *Dictionnaire* asserted that the use of mathematics in economics 'will only ever be in the hands of a few', and the dictionary backed up that claim by choosing not to have any entry on Cournot.

Another approach is to have each entry take care to reflect within itself varying points of view. This may help the student temporarily, as when preparing for an examination. But in a subject like economics, the Olympian detachment which this approach requires often places a heavy burden on the author, asking for a scrupulous account of doctrines he or she believes to be at best wrong-headed. Even when an especially able author does produce a judicious survey article, it is surely too much to ask that it also convey just as much enthusiasm for those theories thought misguided as for those found congenial. Lacking an enthusiastic exposition, however, the disfavoured theories may then be studied less closely than they deserve.

The New Palgrave did not ask its authors to treat economic theory from any particular point of view, except in one respect to be discussed below. Nor did it call for surveys. Instead, each author was asked to make clear his or her own views of the subject under discussion, and for the rest to be as fair and accurate as possible, without striving to be 'judicious'. A balanced perspective on each topic was always the aim, the ideal. But it was to be sought not *internally*, within each article, but *externally*, between articles, with the reader rather than the writer handed the task of achieving a personal balance between differing views.

For a controversial topic, a set of several more or less synonymous headwords, matched by a broad diversity of contributors, was designed to produce enough variety of opinion to help form the reader's own synthesis; indeed, such diversity will be found in most of the individual volumes in this series.

This approach was not without its problems. Thus, the prevalence of uncertainty in the process of commissioning entries sometimes produced a less diverse outcome than we had planned. 'I can call spirits from the vasty deep,' said Owen Glendower. 'Why, so can I,' replied Hotspur, 'or so can any man;/ But will they come when you do call for them?' In our experience, not quite as often as we would have liked.

The one point of view we did urge upon every one of *Palgrave*'s authors was to write from an historical perspective. For each subject its contributor was asked to discuss not only present problems but also past growth and future prospects. This request was made in the belief that knowledge of the historical development of any theory enriches our present understanding of it, and so helps to construct better theories for the future. The authors' response to the request was generally so positive that, as the reader of any of these volumes will discover, the resulting contributions amply justified that belief.

John Eatwell
Murray Milgate
Peter Newman

Preface

Over the last few decades economics has become, at least in one respect, increasingly unified. Subjects of empirical interest that were previously mainly descriptive and diverse in character – labour economics, industrial organization, economic demography – have become striking examples of *applied* economics, in which methods drawn from the central core of value theory are imaginatively used to penetrate mere appearance. This unifying trend can be seen even in the study of international trade and public finance, where in neither case was the gap between analytical and empirical investigation ever so wide as it was elsewhere.

As evident from its now fashionable name of *financial economics*, the same trend has also been at work in the subdiscipline historically known as *finance*. Forty years ago primarily the province of business specialists who dealt descriptively with 'corporate finance' and 'stock markets', today it is a coherent branch of applied economics that among its other tools makes brilliantly perceptive use of value theory in order to understand the real workings of financial markets. Consider, for example, its deployment of arbitrage arguments in such famous papers as those of Modigliani–Miller (1958) on corporate financial structure and Black–Scholes (1973) on options pricing. As Stephen Ross has remarked, the change wrought by those arguments was so great that pre-1958 precepts about the relative roles of debt and equity in corporate financial planning have about them the air of phlogiston, in comparison with the Lavoisier-like insights of Modigliani–Miller.

How finance evolved into its present impressive state seems never to have been told with any degree of precision. To adapt a remark by Arrow about Gossen, the subject has its Gregor Mendel in Louis Bachelier, a French mathematician who in 1900 published his extraordinary thesis on speculation, which not only pioneered the theory of pricing of derivative securities but also anticipated important developments in the theory of stochastic processes, notably in Einstein's treatment of Brownian motion.

Thereafter progress in financial fundamentals seems to have been slow and confined essentially to lonely and mainly empirical workers such as Alfred Cowles and Holbrook Working. But soon after World War II the revival of expected utility theory and the invention of mathematical programming combined to spark off the modern portfolio theory of Markowitz and Tobin. Progress then accelerated rapidly, both in further work on portfolio analysis and its aggregation to capital asset pricing models by Lintner, Mossin, Sharpe and others, and in the evolution of the work of Cowles and Working into the full-fledged Efficient Market Hypothesis (EMH), regarding which one of its more ardent proponents claims that 'No proposition in any of the sciences is better documented' (Michael Jensen, *Journal of Economic Perspectives* (1988), 26).

Even if one takes the last assertion *cum grano salis* as the lively expression of a natural enthusiasm, still the achievements of modern finance theory are remarkable and not without influence on the main body of economics itself, as in the well-attested role of the EMH in the development of the 'new classical macroeconomics'. It is rather surprising, therefore, to find that unlike such modern subdisciplines as Beckerian labour economics and game-theoretic industrial organization, finance has not yet been closely integrated into the ordinary economics curriculum. This slow progress may be traceable to the sociological division of teaching between economics departments and business schools, or perhaps to the idea that financial assets are not genuinely economic 'commodities'. Whatever the reason, a process of natural evolution (to which this volume may modestly contribute) should soon ensure that a broad understanding of financial economics becomes part of the standard equipment of any well-trained economist.

The Editors

Finance

STEPHEN A. ROSS

Finance is a subfield of economics distinguished by both its focus and its methodology. The primary focus of finance is the workings of the capital markets and the supply and the pricing of capital assets. The methodology of finance is the use of close substitutes to price financial contracts and instruments. This methodology is applied to value instruments whose characteristics extend across time and whose payoffs depend upon the resolution of uncertainty.

Finance is not terribly concerned with the problems that arise in a barter economy or, for that matter, in a static and certain world. But, once the element of time is introduced, transactions develop a dual side to them. When a loan is made, the amount and the terms are recorded to insure that repayment can be enforced. The piece of paper or the computer entry that describes and legally binds the borrower to repay the loan can now trade on its own as a 'bearer' instrument. It is at the point when debts were first traded that capital markets and the subject of finance began.

The study of finance is enriched by having a large body of evolving data and market lore and some powerful and, at times, competing intuitions. These intuitions are used to structure our understanding of the data and the markets which generate it. The modern tradition in finance began with the development of well-articulated models and theories to explore these intuitions and render them susceptible to empirical testing.

While the subject of finance is anything but complete, it is now possible to recognize the broad outlines of what might be called the neoclassical theory. In the discussion which follows we will group the subjects under four main headings corresponding with four basic intuitions. The first topic is efficient markets, which was also the first area of finance that matured into a science. Next come the twinned subjects of return and risk. This leads naturally into option pricing theory and the central intuition of pricing close substitutes by the absence of arbitrage. The principle of no arbitrage is used to tie together the major subfields

1

of finance. The fourth section looks at corporate finance from its well-developed form as a consequence of no arbitrage to its current probings. A short conclusion ends the essay.

The word efficient is too useful to be monopolized by a single meaning in economics. As a consequence, it has a variety of related but distinct meanings. In neoclassical equilibrium theory efficiency refers to Pareto efficiency. A system is Pareto efficient if there is no way to improve the well being of any one individual without making someone worse off. Productive efficiency is an implication of Pareto efficiency. An economy is productively efficient if it is not possible to produce more of any one good or service without lowering the output of some other.

In finance the word efficiency has taken on quite a different meaning. A capital market is said to be (informationally) efficient if it utilizes all of the available information in setting the prices of assets. This definition is purposely vague and it is designed more to capture an intuition than to state a formal mathematical result. The basic intuition of efficient markets is that individual traders process the information that is available to them and take positions in assets in response to their information as well as to their personal situations. The market price aggregates this diverse information and in that sense it 'reflects' the available information.

The relation between the definitions of efficiency is not obvious, but it is not unreasonable to think of the efficient markets definition of finance as being a requirement for a competitive economy to be Pareto efficient. Presumably, if prices did not depend on the information available to the economy, then it would only be by accident that they could be set in such a way as to guarantee a Pareto efficient allocation (at least with respect to the commonly held information).

If the capital market is competitive and efficient, then neoclassical reasoning implies that the return that an investor expects to get on an investment in an asset will be equal to the opportunity cost of using the funds. The exact specification of the opportunity cost is the subject of the section on risk and return, but for the moment we can observe that investing in risky assets should carry with it some additional measure of return beyond that on riskless assets to induce risk averse investors to part with their funds. For now we will defer the measurement of this risk premium, and simply represent the opportunity cost by the letter 'r'.

In much of the early empirical work on efficient markets no attempt was made to measure risk premia, and the opportunity cost of investing was set equal to the riskless rate of interest. This can be justified either by assuming that there are risk neutral investors who are indifferent to risk (or, as we shall see, by assuming that the asset's risk is diversified away in large portfolios). Whatever the rationale, to focus on the topic of efficient markets rather than on the pricing of risk, we will let r be the riskless interest rate.

If R_t denotes the total return on the asset – capital gains as well as payouts – over a holding period from t to $t + 1$, then the efficient markets hypothesis (EMH) asserts that

$$E(R_t | I_t) = (1 + r_t),$$ (1)

where E is the expectation taken with respect to a given information set I_t, that is available at time t (and that includes r_t). An alternative formulation of the basic EMH equation is in terms of prices. For an asset with no payouts, since

$$R_t \equiv p_{t+1} / p_t,$$

we can rewrite (1) as

$$E(p_{t+1} | I_t) = (1 + r_t) p_t,$$ (2)

or, equivalently, discounted prices must follow the martingale,

$$\frac{1}{(1 + r_t)} E(p_{t+1} | I_t) = p_t.$$

The EMH is given empirical content by specifying the information set that is used to determine prices. Harry Roberts (1967) first coined the terms which have come to describe the categories of information sets and, concomitantly, of efficient market theories that are employed in empirical work. Fama (1970) subsequently articulated them in the form which we now use. These categories describe a hierarchy of nested information sets. As we go up the hierarchy from the smallest to the biggest set (i.e. from coarser to finer partitions) we are requiring efficiency with respect to increasing amounts of information. At the far end of the spectrum is strong-form efficiency. Strong-form efficiency asserts that the information set, I_t, used by the market to set prices at each date t contains all of the available information that could possibly be relevant to pricing the asset. Not only is all publicly available information embodied in the price, but all privately held information as well.

A substantial notch down from strong-form efficiency is semistrong-form efficiency. A market is efficient in the semistrong sense if it uses all of the publicly available information. The important distinction is that the information set, I_t, is not assumed to include privately held information, i.e. information that has not been made public. Making this distinction precise is possible in formal models but categorizing information as publicly available or not can be subjective. Presumably, accounting information such as the income statements and the balance sheets of the firm is publicly available, as is any other information that the government mandates should be released such as the stock holdings of the top executives in the firm. Presumably too, the true but unrevealed intention of a major stockholder would fall into the category of private information. In between these extremes is a large grey area.

The tendency in the empirical literature has been to take a purist's view of semistrong efficiency, and to adopt the position that if the information was in the public domain then it was available to the public and should be reflected in prices. This ignores the cost of acquiring the information, but the intuitive justification for this position is that the costs of acquiring such public information are small compared to the potential rewards. Thus, while the government-mandated and publicly reported trades of the top executives require a bit more effort to obtain in a timely fashion than some average of their past holdings, such trades, when reported, would fall squarely within the realm of publicly available information under the semistrong version of the EMH.

If the asset is traded on an organized exchange, then of all the information that is clearly available to the public, none is as accessible and cheap as its past price history. At the bottom of the ladder in the efficiency hierarchy, weak-form efficiency requires only that the current and past price history be incorporated in the information set. If there is empirical validity to the EMH then, at the very least, the market for an asset should be weak-form efficient, that is, efficient with respect to its own past price history.

Empirical testing. The empirical implications of efficiency with respect to a particular information set are that the current price of the asset embodies all of the information in that set. Since the categories of information sets are nested, rejection of any one type, say, weak-form efficiency, implies the rejection of all stronger forms.

For example, according to weak-form efficiency, the current price of an asset embodies all of the information contained in the past price history. This implies that,

$$E(R_t | R_{t-1}, R_{t-2}, \ldots) = (1 + r_t), \qquad (3)$$

or, in price terms,

$$E(p_{t+1} | p_{t-1}, \ldots) = (1 + r_t)p_t.$$

The most dramatic consequence of the EMH and certainly the one that receives the most attention from the public, is that it denies the possibility of successful trading schemes. If, for example, the market is weak-form efficient, then an investor who makes use of the 'technical' information of past prices can only expect to receive a return of the opportunity cost $(1 + r_t)$. No amount of clever manipulation of the past information can improve this result.

As a test of weak-form efficiency, then, we could test (although not as a simple regression) the null hypothesis that

$$H_0 : E(p_{t+1} | p_t, p_{t-1}) = \beta_0 + \beta_1 p_t + \beta_2 p_{t-1}, \qquad (4)$$

where

$$\beta_0 = 0,$$

$$\beta_1 = (1 + r_t)$$

and

$$\beta_2 = 0$$

The important feature of this hypothesis is that it tells what information does *not* play a role (given r_t), namely the lagged price, p_{t-1}. If the coefficient β_2 should prove to be statistically significant, then this would constitute a rejection of the weak-form EMH.

The other empirical implication of the EMH that is often cited as a defining characteristic is that an efficient price series should 'move randomly'. The precise meaning of this in our context is that price changes should be serially uncorrelated.

Consider the serial covariance between two adjacent rates of return,

$$\text{cov}(R_{t+1}, R_t) \equiv E([R_{t+1} - E(R_{t+1})][R_t - E(R_t)]). \tag{5}$$
$$= E(R_{t+1}[R_t - E(R_t)])$$
$$= E(E(R_{t+1}|R_t)[R_t - E(R_t)]).$$

In equation (5), since we have not specified the information set with respect to which the expectations are to be taken, they are unconditional expectations. Under weak-form efficiency, the information set will contain the past rates of return. Suppose that the (expected) opportunity cost, e.g. the interest rate r, is independent of past returns on the asset or that changes are of a second order of magnitude. This would occur, for example, if we held r_t constant at r. In such a case, since weak-form efficiency implies that I_{t+1} contains R_t, we have

$$E(R_{t+1}|R_t) = E[E(R_{t+1}|I_{t+1})|R_t]$$
$$= E[(1 + r_{t+1})|R_t] \tag{6}$$
$$= E(1 + r_{t+1}),$$

the unconditional expectation of next period's opportunity cost. Putting (5) and (6) together yields,

$$\text{cov}(R_{t+1}, R_t) = E(1 + r_{t+1})E[R_t - E(R_t)] = 0. \tag{7}$$

which is to say that rates of return are serially uncorrelated.

Tests of the EMH are legion and by and large they have been supportive. The early tests were essentially tests of the inability of trading schemes or of the random walk nature of prices, which implies that actual rates of return are serially uncorrelated. While the EMH does not imply that prices follow a random walk, such a price process is consistent with market efficiency. Alternatively, unable to specify closely the opportunity cost, some of the early tests took refuge in the view that it must be positive, which leads to a submartingale model for prices,

$$E(p_{t+1}|I_t) \geqslant p_t. \tag{8}$$

The lack of a specification of the opportunity cost characterizes the early tests (see Cowles (1933), Granger and Morgenstern (1962) and Cootner (1964), and see Roll's (1984) study of the orange juice futures market for a modern example of such a test). Following Fama (1970), the literature shifted to a concern for specifying the opportunity cost and, in this sense, empirical tests became joint tests of the EMH and of the correct specification of the opportunity cost and its attendant theory.

In terms of the information hierarchy, the general message that emerged from the testing is that the market does appear to be consistent with weak-form efficiency. Tests of stronger forms of efficiency, though, have produced mixed results. Fama, Fisher, Jensen and Roll (1969) introduced a new methodology to test semistrong efficiency and applied it to stock splits. They observed that the residuals from a simple regression of a stock's returns on a market index would measure the portion of the return that was not attributable to market movements. By adding the residuals over a period of time, the resulting cumulative residual measures the total return over that period that is attributable to nonmarket movements. If a stock splits, say, 2 for 1, then under semistrong efficiency its price should split in proportion, i.e., halve for a 2 for 1 split. Using this 'event study' approach, Fama, Fisher, Jensen and Roll verified that stock split data was consistent with semistrong efficiency. The event study methodology they introduced and the use of cumulative residuals (averaged over firms) has become the standard method for examining the impact of information on stock returns.

By contrast with their supportive findings, Jaffé (1974), for example, found that a rule based on the publicly released information about insider trades produced abnormal returns. These results and others like them (see the section on *Risk and Return* below) have been much debated and no final verdict on the matter is likely.

Recently a more interesting empirical challenge to the EMH has come from a different tack. Shiller (1981) has argued that the traditional statistical tests that have been employed are too weak to examine the EMH properly and, moreover, that they are misfocused. Shiller adopts the intuitive perspective that if stock prices are discounted expected dividends, then they ought not to vary over time as much as actual dividends. He argues that since the price is an expectation of the dividends and future price, what actually occurs will be this expectation *plus* the error in the forecast and should be more variable than the price. This leads him to formulate statistical tests of the EMH based on the volatility of stock prices which are claimed to be more powerful than the traditional (regression based) tests.

An alternative view has been taken by critics of this perspective, notably Kleidon (1986), Flavin (1983) and Marsh and Merton (1986). These critics have taken issue with Shiller's specification of the statistical tests of volatility and, more importantly, with his basic intuition. In particular, they contend that the single realization of dividends and prices that is observed is only one drawing from all of the random possibilities and that the price is based on the expectation taken over all of these possibilities. A little bit of information, then, can have an important influence on the current price. Furthermore, they argue that when the smoothing of dividends and the finite time horizon of the data samples are taken into account, volatility tests do not reject the EMH. The testing of the EMH is taking a new direction because of this work, but, at present, the results are still mixed.

Less cosmic in scope, but perhaps more worrisome is the discovery by French and Roll (1985) that the variance per unit time of market returns over periods when the market is closed (for example, from Tuesday's close to Thursday's close when the market was closed on Wednesday because of a backlog of paperwork) is many times smaller than when it is open. It is difficult to reconcile this result with the requirement that prices reflect information about the cash flows of the assets, unless the generation of fundamental information slows dramatically when the market closes – no matter why it is closed.

Theoretical formulations. The attempts to formalize the EMH as a consistent, analytical economic theory have met with less success than the empirical tests of the hypothesis. The theory can be broken into two parts. The first part is neoclassical and is largely formulated in terms of models in which investors share a common information set. Such models focus on the intertemporal aspects of the theory and the changing shape of the information set.

It has long been recognized that a competitive economy with a single risk neutral investor would lead to the traditional efficient market theories with respect to the information set employed by that investor. More interestingly, Cox, Ingersoll and Ross (1985a), and Lucas (1978) have developed intertemporal rational expectations models each of which is consistent with certain versions of the efficient market theories.

There is, however, an important sense in which these models fail to capture the essential intuition of efficient markets. In informationally efficient markets, prices communicate information to participants. Information possessed by one investor is communicated to another through the influence – however microscopic – that the first investor has on equilibrium prices. In models where investors have homogeneous information sets such information transfer is irrelevant.

A variety of attempts have been made to develop models of financial markets which can deal with such informational issues, but the task is formidable and a satisfactory resolution is not now in hand. This work parallels that of the neoclassical rational expectations view of macroeconomics. This is no accident since the rational expectations school of macroeconomics was very clearly influenced by the intuition of efficiency in finance. The original insight that prices reflect the available information lies at the heart of rational expectations macroeconomics. In this latter work aggregate prices, for example, not only provide the terms of trade for producers, they also inform producers about the aggregate state of production in the economy.

Perhaps the principal difficulty is that models with fully rational investors tend to break down. As investors apply the full scope of their analytical and reasoning talents, the result is an equilibrium in which they lack the incentive to engage in trade. (See Grossman, 1976; Grossman and Stiglitz, 1980; Diamond and Verrecchia, 1981; Milgrom and Stokey, 1982; and Admati, 1985.) The only way out of this bind seems to be to add a discomforting element of irrationality – or

7

an alternative motive for trade from an equilibrium, such as insurance – to the model.

To understand this point, consider a risk-averse individual trading in a market where he or she receives information signals about the ultimate value of the asset being traded and where it is common knowledge that all investors are in the same position. That is not to say that all investors have the same information, rather, it only means that they all begin with the same information, have the same view of the world (Bayesian priors), and then receive signals from the same sort of information generating mechanism. In such a market, the offer to trade on the part of any one investor communicates information to other investors. In particular, it tells them that the individual, based upon his or her information, will be improved by the trade. If all investors are rational they will all feel similarly bettered by trade. But, if the market had been in an equilibrium prior to the receipt of new information, and if it is common knowledge that trade balances, then in the new equilibrium not all of them can be improved. This contradiction can only be resolved by having no further trade upon the receipt of information.

To put the matter in an equivalent form, consider an investor who possesses some special information. Presumably, it is by trading that this information is incorporated into the market price. The above argument implies that the mere announcement of a wish to trade results in a change in prices with no profits for the investor since none will trade at the original prices. If information is costly to acquire and impossible to profit from, then why bother? In other words, if the price reflects the available information possessed by the individual participants, then why gather information if one only needs to look at the price?

The resolution of this dilemma can take many forms, and research will proceed by altering the assumptions that lead to this result. For example, we can drop the assumption about a common prior and let investors come to the markets with different a priori beliefs. We could also drop the assumption that all investors are perfectly rational and introduce 'noisy' traders. Lastly, we could drop efficiency and complete markets or integrate insurance motives in other ways.

All of these approaches are being explored but we must leave this discussion with the theory that underlies the incorporation of asymmetric information into securities prices in an unsettled state. The traditional theory that prices reflect the available information is well understood with a representative individual. The theory with asymmetric information is not well understood at all. In short, the exact mechanism by which prices incorporate information is still a mystery and an attendant theory of volume is simply missing.

To conclude, the efficient market paradigm is the backbone of much of financial research and it continues to guide a large body of theoretical and empirical work. Its usefulness is beyond question, but its fine structure is not. In a sense, like much of economics, it remains a central intuition whose analytical representations seem less compelling than the insight itself. This presents more of a problem for theory than for empirical work, but the empirical side is also not without challenge. Although the evidence in support of the efficiency of capital markets is widespread, troublesome pockets of anomalies are growing and the power of the traditional methodology to test the theory is being seriously questioned. Nevertheless, there is currently no competitor for the basic intuition of efficient markets and few insights have proven as fruitful.

The theory of efficient markets leads inexorably to the second central intuition in finance, the trade-off between risk and return. It has long been recognized that risk-averse investors require additional return to bear additional risk. Indeed, this insight goes back to the earliest writings on gambling and it is as much a definition of risk aversion as it is a description of risk-averse behaviour. The contribution made by finance has been to translate this observation into a body of intuition, theory and empirics on the workings of the capital markets.

The intuition that in a competitive market higher return is accompanied by higher risk owes at least as much to Calvin as it does to Adam Smith, but, in large part of the development of capital market theory has been an attempt to explain risk premia, the difference between expected returns and the riskless interest rate. The foundations for the models that would first explain risk premia and that would become the workhorses of financial asset pricing theories were laid by Hicks (1946), Markowitz (1959) and Tobin (1958). These authors developed a rigorous micromodel of individual behaviour in a 'mean variance' world where investment portfolios were evaluated in terms of their mean returns and the total variance of their returns. They justified focusing on these two distributional characteristics by assuming either that investors had quadratic von Neumann–Morgenstern utility functions or that asset returns were normally distributed. In such a world, investors would choose mean variance efficient portfolios, i.e., portfolios with the highest mean return for a given level of variance. This observation reduced the study of portfolio choice to the analysis of the properties of the mean variance efficient set. Building on their work, Sharpe (1964), Lintner (1965) and Mossin (1966), all came to the fundamental insight that this micromodel could be aggregated into a simple model of equilibrium in the capital markets, the capital asset pricing model or CAPM.

The Mean Variance Capital Asset Pricing Model (CAPM). In neoclassical equilibrium models, an investor evaluates an asset in terms of its marginal contribution to his or her portfolio. The decision to alter the proportion of the portfolio invested in an asset will depend on whether the cost of doing so in terms of risk is greater or less than the benefit in expected return. An individual in a personal equilibrium will find the cost at the margin equal to the benefit.

We will assume that a unit addition of an asset to the portfolio can be financed at an interest rate of r. In a mean variance model the net benefit of adding an asset to a portfolio is the additional expected return it brings, E, less the cost of financing it. Such a change, Δx, will augment the expected return on the portfolio, E_p, by the risk premium of the asset, i.e. by the difference between the expected return on the asset, E_i, and the cost of the financing, r,

$$\Delta E_p = (E_i - r)\Delta x. \tag{9}$$

The marginal cost, in terms of risk, of an increase in the holding of an asset is the addition to the total variance of the portfolio occasioned by an increase in the holding of the asset. To compute this increase, let v denote the variance of returns on the current portfolio, let $\text{var}(i)$ stand for the variance of asset i's returns, let $\text{cov}(i, p)$ denote the covariance between the return of asset i and that of the portfolio, p, and let Δx be the addition in the holding of asset i.

The variance of the portfolio after adding Δx of asset i will be,

$$v + \Delta v = v + 2\Delta x \, \text{cov}(i, p) + (\Delta x)^2 \, \text{var}(i),$$

which means the change in the variance is given by

$$\Delta v = (\Delta x) \, \text{cov}(i, p) + (\Delta x)^2 \, \text{var}(i),$$

and for a small marginal change, Δx, this approximates,

$$\Delta v \approx 2(\Delta x) \, \text{cov}(i, p).$$

The marginal rate of transformation between return and risk, then, is given by

$$\text{MRT} = \frac{\Delta E_p}{\Delta v} = \frac{(E_i - r)\Delta x}{2(\Delta x) \, \text{cov}(i, p)} = \frac{(E_i - r)}{2 \, \text{cov}(i, p)}. \tag{10}$$

An investor will be in a personal equilibrium when this trade-off is equal to his or her personal marginal rate of substitution between return and risk. But, if the portfolio p is an optimal one for the investor then it must also have a trade-off between return and risk that is equal to the investor's marginal rate of substitution, and this permits us to use it as a benchmark. Consider, then, the alternative possibility of changing the portfolio position not by changing the amount of asset i being held, but rather by changing the amount of the entire portfolio p being held, again financing the change by an alteration in the holding of the riskless asset. This is equivalent to leveraging the portfolio of risky assets and altering the amount of the riskless asset so as to continue to satisfy the budget constraint. Such a change will produce a trade-off between return and risk exactly analogous to the one examined above:

$$\text{MRS} = \frac{E_p - r}{2 \, \text{var}(p)}, \tag{11}$$

where we have written this as the marginal rate of substitution, MRS. Since in equilibrium all of the marginal rates of transformation must equal the common marginal rate of substitution, putting these two equations together we have,

$$E_i - r = (E_p - r)\beta_{ip}, \tag{12}$$

where

$$\beta_{ip} \equiv \frac{\text{cov}(i, p)}{\text{var}(p)}, \tag{13}$$

the regression coefficient of the returns of asset i on the returns of portfolio, p. Equation (12) is the famous security market line equation, the SML. It describes the necessary and sufficient condition for a portfolio p to be mean variance efficient. It also provides a clear statement of the risk premium, asserting that it is proportional to the asset's beta, β_{ip}.

The insight of Sharpe, Lintner and Mossin was the observation that the SML and the mean variance analysis could be aggregated almost without change to a full equilibrium in the capital market. If we assume that all individuals have the same information and, therefore, see the same mean variance picture, then each individual's efficient portfolio will satisfy equation (12). Since the SML equation is linear in the portfolio holding, p, we can simply weight each individual's equation by the proportion of wealth that individual holds in equilibrium, and add up the individual SML's. The result will be an SML equation for the aggregate portfolio, m, that is the weighted average of the individual portfolios. In equilibrium, the weighted average of all of the individual portfolios, m, is the market portfolio, i.e., the portfolio of all assets held in proportion to their market valuation. In other words, each asset i, must lie on the SML with respect to the market,

$$E_i - r = (E_m - r)\beta_{lm}, \qquad (14)$$

which means that the market portfolio, m, is a mean variance efficient portfolio.

The geometry of the mean variance analysis is illustrated in Figure 1. The set

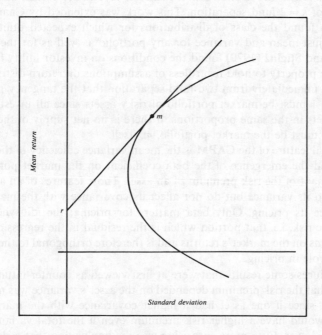

Figure 1

of mean variance efficient portfolios maps out a mean variance efficient frontier in the mean standard deviation space of Figure 1. Each investor will pick some point on this frontier and that point will be associated with a mean variance efficient portfolio that is suitable for the investor's particular degree of risk aversion. All such portfolios will themselves be portfolios of just two assets: the riskless asset, r, and a common portfolio, p, of risky assets. This fortunate simplification of the individual portfolio optimization problem is referred to as two fund separation. It implies that the only role for individual preferences lies in choosing the appropriate combination of the risky portfolio, p, and the riskless asset, r. As a consequence, when we aggregate, the market risk premium, $(E_m - r)/\text{var}(m)$, will be an average of individual measures of risk aversion.

Black (1972) showed that two fund separation would still hold in the mean variance model even if there were no riskless asset. In such a case he found that an efficient portfolio orthogonal – the 'zero beta portfolio' – to the market portfolio could be found, and that all investors would be able to find their optimal portfolios as combinations of m and this zero beta portfolio. In the above development of the CAPM we can simply let r be the expected return on a zero beta portfolio.

The necessary and sufficient conditions on return distributions for them to have this two fund separation property – for any concave utility function – were established by Ross (1978a). Ross characterized the class of distributions whose efficient frontier, i.e. the set of portfolios that *some* investor would choose, was spanned by k funds, and showed that it extended beyond the normal distribution in the case of $k = 2$ fund separation. This work was extended by Chamberlain (1983), who found the class of distributions for which expected utility was a function of just mean and variance for any portfolio as well as for the efficient ones. Cass and Stiglitz (1970) found the conditions on investor utility functions for a similar property to hold regardless of assumptions on return distributions.

It follows immediately from two fund separation that the tangency portfolio, p, in Figure 1 must be market portfolio of risky assets since all investors hold all risky assets in the same proportions. If there is no net supply of the riskless asset then p must be the market portfolio, m, itself.

The central feature of the CAPM is the mean variance efficiency of the market portfolio and the emergence of the beta coefficient on the market portfolio as the determinant of the risk premium of an asset. Those features of an asset that contribute to its variance but do not affect its covariance with the market will not influence its pricing. Only beta matters for pricing; the idiosyncratic or unsystematic risk, i.e. that portion which is the residual in the regression of the asset's returns on the market's returns and is therefore orthogonal to the market, playing no role in pricing.

This produces some results that were at first viewed as counter-intuitive. The older view that the risk premium depended on the asset's variance was no longer appropriate, since if one asset had a higher covariance with the market than another, it would have a higher risk premium even if the total variance of its returns were lower. Even more surprising was the implication that a risky asset that was uncorrelated with the market would have no risk premium and would be expected to have the same rate of return as the riskless asset, and that assets that were inversely correlated with the market would actually have expected returns of less than the riskless rate in equilibrium.

These results for the CAPM were supposedly explicated by the twin intuitions of diversification and systematic risk. There could be no premium for bearing unsystematic risk since a large and well diversified portfolio (i.e. one whose asset proportions are not concentrated in a small subset) would eliminate it – presumably by the law of large numbers. This would leave only systematic risk in any optimal portfolio and since this risk cannot be eliminated by diversification, it has to have a risk premium to entice risk averse investors to hold risky assets. From this perspective it becomes clear why an asset that is uncorrelated with the market bears no risk premium. One that is inversely correlated with the market actually offers some insurance against the all pervasive systematic risk and, therefore, there must be a payment for the insurance in the form of a negative risk premium.

There is nothing wrong with this intuition, but it does not fit the CAPM very well. The residuals from the regression of asset returns on the market portfolios are orthogonal to the market but they could be highly correlated with each other. In fact, they are linearly dependent since when they are weighted by the market proportions they sum to zero. This means the law of large numbers cannot be used to insure that large portfolios of residuals other than the market portfolio will be negligible. But, if that is the case, then the residuals could capture systematic risks not reflected in the market portfolio.

The CAPM was the genesis for countless empirical tests (see, e.g., Black, Jensen and Scholes, 1972; and Fama and MacBeth, 1973). The latter paper developed the most widely used technique. The general structure of these tests was the combination of the efficient market hypothesis with time series and cross section econometrics. Typically some index of the market, such as the value weighted combination of all stocks would be chosen and a sample of firms would be tested to see if their excess returns, $E - r$, were 'explained' in cross-section by their betas on the index, i.e., whether the SML was rejected.

Roll (1977b, 1978) put a stop to this indiscriminate testing by calling into question precisely what was being tested. Roll's critique had two parts. First, he argued that the tests were of very low power and probably could not detect departures from mean variance efficiency. His central point, though, began by noting that tests of the CAPM were tests of the implications of the statement that the *entire* market portfolio was mean variance efficient, and were not simply tests of the efficiency of some limited index such as could be formed from the stock market. The essential role played by the market portfolio in the CAPM had been stressed by others; Ross (1977b) had shown the equivalence between the CAPM and the mean variance efficiency of the market portfolio. (Ross (1976a) had also shown that in the absence of arbitrage there was always some efficient portfolio.) Roll went beyond this simple observation, though, by stressing the essential point that the market portfolio is unmeasurable. This called into question the entire cottage industry of testing the CAPM and all of the uses to which the theory had been put, such as performance measurement.

Intertemporal models. In the aftermath of Roll's critique, attention was turned to alternative models of asset pricing and the intertemporal nature of the theory became more important. Two separate strands of development can be traced. One essentially followed the lines of the CAPM and developed the intertemporal versions of it, the ICAPM. Merton (1973a) pioneered in this. Using continuous time diffusion analysis, Merton showed that the CAPM could be generalized to an intertemporal setting. Most interestingly, though, he demonstrated that if the economic environment was described by a finite dimensional vector of state variables, x, and if asset prices were exogenously specified random variables, then a version of the SML would hold at all moments of time with the addition to the risk premium of a linear combination of the betas between the assets' returns and each of the state variables, x_i.

Ross (1975) developed a similar intertemporal extension of the CAPM, but Ross's model simplified preferences in order to close the model with an intertemporal rationality constraint and to study equilibrium price dynamics. Along the lines being developed in the modern literature on macroeconomics, intertemporal rationality and the efficient market theory required that the distribution of prices be determined endogenously. A discrete time Markov model with this feature was presented in Lucas (1978) and a full rational expectations general equilibrium in continuous time was developed in Cox, Ingersoll and Ross (1985a).

Cox, Ingersoll and Ross (1985b) applied their model to analyse and resolve some longstanding questions in the theory of the term structure of interest rates. The theory of the term structure is one of the most important subfields of finance, and the bond markets were one of the first areas where the EMH was applied. In an efficient market, ignoring risk aversion, forward rates should be (unbiased) predictors of future spot rates, and many early theories and tests of the EMH were formulated to examine this proposition (see e.g. Malkiel, 1966). Roll (1970) integrated the EMH with the CAPM and used the resulting framework to examine empirically liquidity premia in the bond markets; the work of Cox, Ingersoll and Ross (1985b) can be considered as the logical extension of his analysis to a rational intertemporal setting.

Merton's model was simplified markedly by Breeden (1979), who showed that if investors had intertemporally additive utility functions, then Merton's ICAPM and its version of the SML could be collapsed back into a single beta model, the Consumption Beta model, with all assets being priced, i.e., having their risk premiums determined, by their covariance with aggregate consumption (see also Rubinstein (1976)). If we think of returns as relative prices between wealth today and in future states of nature, then optimizing individuals will set their marginal rates of substitution between consumption today and in future states equal to the rates of return. With continuous asset prices and additive utility functions, indirect utility functions are locally quadratic in consumption and this implies that consumption plays the role of wealth in the static CAPM. This work led to a variety of attempts to measure the ability of betas on aggregate consumption to explain risk premia (see e.g. Hansen and Singleton, 1983).

Arbitrage Pricing Theory (APT). A separable but related strand of theory is the Arbitrage Pricing Theory (APT) (see e.g. Ross, 1976a, 1976b). The CAPM and the Consumption Beta model share the common feature that they explain pricing in terms of endogenous market aggregates, the market portfolio and aggregate consumption, respectively. The APT takes a different tack.

The intuition of the CAPM (or of the Consumption Beta model) is that idiosyncratic risk can be diversified away leaving only the systematic risk to be priced. Idiosyncratic risk, though, is defined with reference to the market portfolio as the residual from a regression of returns on the market portfolio's returns. Since no further assumptions are made about the residuals, contrary to intuition a large diversified portfolio that differs from the market portfolio will not in general have insignificant residual risk. The exception is the market portfolio, but then the intuition that diversification leads to pricing by the market portfolio is circular at best.

The APT addresses this issue by assuming directly a return structure in which the systematic and idiosyncratic components of returns are defined a priori. Asset returns are assumed to satisfy a linear factor model,

$$R_i = E_i + \sum_j \beta_{ij} f_j + \varepsilon_i, \qquad i = 1, \ldots, n, \qquad (15)$$

where E_i is the expected return, f_j is a demeaned exogenous factor influencing each asset i through its beta on the factor, β_{ij}, and ε_i is an idiosyncratic mean zero term assumed to be sufficiently uncorrelated across assets that it is negligible in large portfolios. An implication of the factor structure is that the ε terms become negligible in large well diversified portfolios and, therefore, such portfolios approximately follow an exact factor structure,

$$R_i \approx E_i + \sum_j \beta_{ij} f_j, \qquad (16)$$

where i now denotes the ith well diversified portfolio. In an Arrow–Debreu state space framework, equation (16) can be interpreted as a restriction on the rank of the state-space tableaux.

An exact factor structure implies that there will be arbitrage unless the expected return on each portfolio is equal to a linear combination of the beta coefficients,

$$E_i - r = \sum_j \lambda_j \beta_{ij}, \qquad (17)$$

where λ_j is the risk premium associated with the jth factor, f_j. This equation is the APT version of the SML in the CAPM.

The APT is consistent with a wide variety of equilibrium models (including the CAPM if there is a factor structure) and it has been the object of much theoretical and empirical attention. In a sense, the APT can be thought of as a snapshot of any intertemporal model in which the factors represent innovations in the underlying state variables. This means that a rejection of the APT would imply a fairly wide ranging rejection of attempts to model asset markets with a finite set of state variables.

The original theoretical development of the APT (Ross, 1976a, 1976b) showed formally that if preferences are continuous in the quadratic mean, then the returns on a sequence of portfolios which require no wealth cannot converge to a positive return with a zero variance. This, in turn, implies that the sum of squared deviations from exact APT pricing is bounded above. These results were simplified by Huberman (1982) and extended by Ingersoll (1984) and Chamberlain and Rothschild (1983), all of whom side-stepped the issue of preferences by simply assuming that there could be no sequences converging to an arbitrage situation of a positive return with no variance. By contrast, Dybvig (1983) makes assumptions on preferences and aggregate supply to obtain a tight bound on pricing. His simple order of magnitude calculation is evidence that the pricing error is too small to be of practical significance.

By modelling the capital market explicitly as responding to innovations in exogenous variables, the APT is immediately intertemporally rational. By contrast with the CAPM and the Consumption Beta models which price assets in terms of their relation with a potentially observable and endogenous market aggregate (wealth for the CAPM and consumption for the Consumption Beta models), the APT factors are exogenous, but unspecified. Much empirical work is now underway to determine a suitable set of factors for representing systematic risk in a factor structure and to examine if they price assets successfully. (For example, see Roll and Ross, 1980; Brown and Weinstein, 1983; and Chen, Roll and Ross, 1986.)

The lack of an a priori specification for the factors has been the focus of criticism of the testability of the APT by Shanken (1982). Shanken argues that since the factors are not pre-specified, the intuitive, derivation of the APT given above can be used to verify the APT falsely even when it does not hold, and that to prevent this some equilibrium model, such as that proposed by Connor (1984), must be used. Shanken emphasizes that his critique applies not to the theory of the APT, but rather to the way in which it has been tested. Dybvig and Ross (1985) dispute his arguments, stressing that Shanken wants to test the theory including its assumptions and approximations rather than take the positive approach of testing the model's conclusions.

Empirical testing of asset pricing models. Since Roll's critique, the methodology for testing asset pricing models has changed. There has been a retreat from testing a model per se to an explicit view that what is being tested is not the CAPM, for example, but rather whether the particular index being used for pricing is mean variance efficient. This change of focus has led to a more formal approach to the statistics of testing. Ross (1980) developed the maximum likelihood test statistic for the efficiency of a given portfolio and pointed out the analogy between this and the mean variance geometry, and Gibbons (1982) showed that the test of efficiency could be conducted by the use of seemingly unrelated regressions. These results have been extended by others (for example, Kandel (1984) and Jobson and Korkie (1982)), and Gibbons, Ross and Shanken (1986) have developed and exploited an exact small sample test of the efficiency of a given index in the presence of a riskless asset. Similar tests of the APT have not yet been developed, and to date much of the testing of the APT has focused on comparisons between the APT and pricing using the value weighted index (see e.g. Chen, Roll and Ross, 1986).

The most important empirical finding in asset pricing, though, has been the discovery of a wide array of phenomena that appear to be inconsistent with nearly any neoclassical model. Consider, first, the secular effects. Asset returns fall, on average, over the weekend and rise during the week (see French, 1980). Similarly, it has been found that asset returns behave differently in the first half of the month than they do in the second. The most attention, though, has been lavished on the 'small firm effect'. It appears that the average returns on small firms exceed those on large firms no matter what theory of asset pricing is used to correct for differences in the risk premium between these two categories of assets. Furthermore, the bulk of the return difference is concentrated in the first few days of January. Indeed, on average, returns in January appear to be abnormally large for all stocks (see e.g. Keim, 1983 or Roll, 1981, 1983).

Potentially these sorts of anomalies can be explained by secular changes in risk premia – perhaps due to secular patterns in the release of information – but their persistence and magnitude make them serious challenges to all the asset pricing models. When evidence of this sort appears difficult to explain by any pricing model it calls into question the efficient market hypothesis itself. Tests of an asset pricing model are usually joint tests of both market efficiency and the pricing model; rejecting a wide enough range of such models is tantamount to rejecting efficiency itself.

SUBSTITUTION AND ARBITRAGE: OPTION PRICING

The APT is the child of one of the central intuitions of finance: namely, that close substitutes have the same price. This intuition reached fruition in the path breaking paper by Black and Scholes (1973) on option pricing. Since then the theory has found myriad applications and has been significantly extended (see, for example, Merton (1973b), Cox and Ross (1976a, 1976b), Rubinstein (1976), Ross (1976c), Ingersoll (1977), Cox, Ross and Rubinstein (1979) and Cox, Ingersoll and Ross (1985a)). The Black–Scholes model employed stochastic calculus, but a simpler framework for option pricing was presented by Cox, Ross and Rubinstein (1979) that retained its essential features and was more flexible for computational purposes. We will briefly outline this binomial approach and show its connections to the major theoretical features of option pricing.

The Binomial Model. The binomial model begins with the assumption that the price of a stock, *S*, follows a proportional geometric process:

$$S(t+1) = \begin{cases} aS(t) \text{ with probability } \pi \\ bS(t) \text{ with probability } 1 - \pi. \end{cases} \tag{18}$$

In addition to the stock there is also a riskless bond with a return of $1 + r$. The basic problem of option pricing theory is to determine the value of a derivative security, i.e., a security whose payoff depends only upon the value of an underlying primitive security, the stock in this case.

Let $C(s, t)$ denote the value of the derivative security as a function of the price of the stock and the time, t. Since its value depends only upon the movement of the stock – a result that is sometimes derived as a function of other attributes such as its value at the end of some period – it will also follow a binomial process:

$$C(S, t+1) = \begin{cases} C(aS, t) \text{ with probability } \pi \\ C(bS, t) \text{ with probability } 1 - \pi. \end{cases} \tag{19}$$

The time $t + 1$ values are illustrated in Figure 2. At any moment of time the information structure branches into relevant states, state a and state b, defined by whether the stock goes up by a or b. As the figure is drawn, $a > 1 + r > b$, and clearly $1 + r$ must lie between a and b to prevent the stock or the bond dominating. At this point there are two separate approaches to the analysis. The first is in the spirit of the original Black–Scholes model.

Suppose that at time t we form a portfolio of the riskless bond and the stock with α dollars invested in the stock and $1 - \alpha$ dollars invested in the bond. We

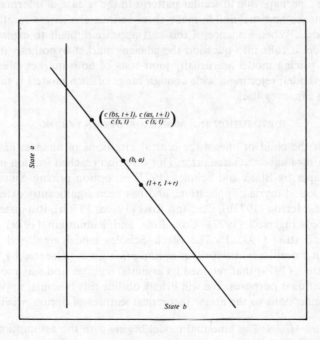

Figure 2

will choose the investment proportion so that the return on the portfolio coincides with the return on the derivative security in state b. This means choosing α so that

$$\frac{C(bS, t+1)}{C(S,t)} = \alpha b + (1-\alpha)(1+r), \tag{20}$$

which implies that

$$\alpha = \frac{(1+r) - C(bS, t+1)/C(S,t)}{(1+r) - b}. \tag{21}$$

But, since the portfolio's return matches that of the derivative security in state b, it must also match it in state a. If it did not, then either the portfolio or the derivative security would dominate the other, which would be an arbitrage opportunity. In other words, we must have,

$$\frac{C(aS, t+1)}{C(S,t)} = \alpha a + (1-\alpha)(1+r). \tag{22}$$

Putting these two equations together produces a difference equation which is satisfied by the value of the derivative security,

$$\pi^* C(aS, t+1) + (1-\pi^*)C(bS, t+1) - (1+r)c(S,t) = 0, \tag{23}$$

where

$$\pi^* \equiv \frac{(1+r) - b}{a - b}. \tag{24}$$

Perhaps the most remarkable feature of this equation is that it does not involve the original probabilities for the process, π, but rather is a function of what are called the martingale probabilities, π^*.

To solve this difference equation for the value, C, of a particular derivative security we would need only to append the contractual boundary conditions that define it. For example, a European call option is specified to have the value $\max(S-E, 0)$, at a specified future date, T, where E is its exercise price. Such an option gives the holder the right – but not the obligation – to buy the stock for E at time T. The dual security is a European put option which gives the holder the right, but again not the obligation, to sell the stock for E at time T. The problem is more difficult if the derivative security is of the American variety which means that the holder may exercise it any time up to and including the maturity date T and need not wait until T.

Soon after the Black–Scholes paper, Merton (1973b) examined a variety of option contracts and showed how extensive was the range of the technique. Notably, Merton was able to derive a number of qualitative results on option pricing that were relatively independent of the particular process being modelled. For example, he showed that an American call option on a stock that pays no dividends will never be exercised before its maturity date and, therefore, will have the same value as a similar European call. He also demonstrated that put/call parity, i.e. the equivalence between the positions of holding the stock and a put option and holding a bond and a call option, was not generally valid for American options. Ross (1976c) showed that the literature's emphasis on puts and calls was not misplaced since any derivative security could be composed of puts and calls.

A second approach to the valuation problem in our simple example illuminates why the original probabilities played no role in the analysis. Figure 2 displays what is essentially a two-state Arrow–Debreu model. In such a model if there are two pure contingent claims contracts paying one dollar in each state, then all securities can be valued as a function of their values, q_a and q_b. It follows, then, that any two securities which are not linearly dependent will span the space just as two pure contingent claims would and they can be used to value all securities in the space.

In our example, the value of the bond is 1 and it must satisfy,

$$1 = q_a(1+r) + q_b(1+r), \tag{25}$$

and the value of the stock must satisfy,

$$S = q_a(aS) + q_b(bS),$$

or

$$1 = q_a a + q_b b. \tag{26}$$

Solving these two equations we can find the implicit values of the state contingent claims,

$$q_a = \frac{(1+r)-b}{(1+r)(a-b)},$$

and

$$q_b = \frac{a-(1+r)}{(1+r)(a-b)}. \tag{27}$$

Notice that these prices do not depend on the original probability, π, since they are derived from the values of the stock and the bond. Whatever influence the probability, π, has on values is already reflected in the returns on the stock and the bond, and the derivative security value will just be a function of the implicit state prices. Using these prices, it is readily verified that the difference equation for the value of the derivative security, equation (23), is the same as,

$$q_a C(aS, t+1) + q_b C(bS, t+1) = C(S, t). \tag{28}$$

Geometrically, this means that the point,

$$\{[C(bS, t+1)/C(S,t)], [C(aS, t+1)/C(S,t)]\},$$

we plot on the same line as the return points for the bond and the stock, $(1+r, 1+r)$ and (b, a). For a call option the point will be as drawn in Figure 2 indicating that the call is more volatile than the stock.

Notice from (24) and (27) that

$$\pi^* = (1+r)q_a,$$

which means that the state space price can be interpreted as the discounted martingale probability. It is this interpretation that ties together the Cox and Ross (1976a) risk neutral approach to solving option pricing problems and the general theory of the absence of arbitrage.

Cox and Ross (1976a) argued that since the difference equation that emerged for solving option pricing problems made no explicit use of any preference information, the resulting solution must also be independent of preferences. For example, then, the resulting solution must be the same as that which would obtain in a risk neutral world. In such a world, the state probabilities must be such that the expected returns on all assets are the same,

$$\pi^* a + (1-\pi^*)b = 1+r,$$

where the solution for the probability, π^*, is the same martingale probability defined above. For a European call option, then, the solution will be

$$C(S,t) = \frac{1}{(1+r)^{T-t}} E^*[\max(S_T - E, 0)]$$

$$= \frac{1}{(1+r)^{T-t}} \sum_{j \geq \ln[E/Sb^{-(T-n)}]/\ln(a/b)} (\pi^*)^j$$

$$\times (1-\pi^*)^{T-t-j}(Sa^i b^{T-t-j} - E), \tag{29}$$

where E^* is the expectation with respect to the martingale probabilities, π^* and $(1-\pi^*)$. It is easily verified that (29) is the solution to the difference equation (23) subject to the boundary condition,

$$C(S,T) = \max(S-E, 0).$$

Contrast this formula with the original Black–Scholes formula for the value of a call option in a continuous time diffusion model,

$$C(S,t) = SN(d_1) - e^{-r(T-t)}N(d_2), \tag{30}$$

where $N(\cdot)$ is the standard cumulative normal distribution function and,

$$d_1 \equiv \frac{\ln(S/E) + r(T-t) + \frac{1}{2}\sigma^2(T-t)}{\sigma\sqrt{(T-t)}},$$

and

$$d_2 \equiv d_1 - \sigma\sqrt{(T-t)}.$$

Equation (30) is the solution to the Black–Scholes option pricing differential equation,

$$\tfrac{1}{2}\sigma^2 S^2 C_{ss} + rSC_s - rC = -C_t, \tag{31}$$

subject to the boundary condition,

$$C(S, T) = \max(S - E, 0).$$

The Black–Scholes differential equation (31) is derived from an analogous hedging argument to that for the binomial model, applied to the continuous lognormal stock process,

$$dS/S = \mu \, dt + \sigma \, dz,$$

where z is a standard Brownian motion. In fact, as the time interval between jumps converges to zero and the jump sizes shrink appropriately, the binomial converges to the lognormal diffusion and its option pricing solution will converge to that for the lognormal diffusion. Notice, too, that in analogy with the binomial whose solution does not depend upon the state probabilities, the Black–Scholes option price (30) is independent of the expected return on the stock, μ.

The most interesting comparative statics result from these models is the observation that call or put option values increase with increasing variance, σ^2. This is a consequence of these options being convex functions of the terminal stock value, S_T (Cox and Ross, 1976b).

The general theory of arbitrage. All of the above analysis can be tied together by the general theory of arbitrage. Under quite general conditions, it can be shown that the absence of arbitrage implies the existence of a linear pricing rule that values all of the assets (see e.g., Ross, 1976a, 1978b; Harrison and Kreps, 1979). In a static model with m states of nature, this means the existence of implicit state prices, q_j, such that $q_j > 0$, and such that any asset with payoffs of x_j in the states of nature will have the value,

$$p = \sum_j q_j x_j. \tag{32}$$

The intertemporal extension of this result is most neatly displayed in terms of the martingale expectation used above. The absence of arbitrage now implies the existence of a martingale measure such that, with obvious notation,

$$p = E^* \left\{ \exp\left[-\int_0^T r(s) \, ds \right] x_T \right\}.$$

This theory permits us to tie together not only the basic results of option pricing, but also our previous analysis of asset pricing models. For example, applying it to the exact factor model,

$$R_i = E_i + \sum_j \beta_{ij} f_j, \tag{16}$$

yields the APT,

$$1 = E^*(R_i) = E^*\left(E_i + \sum_j \beta_{ij} f_j\right)$$

$$= \frac{1}{(1+r)}\left[E_i + \sum_j \beta_{ij} E^*(f_j)\right],$$

or

$$E_i = (1+r) + \sum_j \lambda_j \beta_{ij},$$

where

$$\lambda_j \equiv -E^*(f_j).$$

Similarly, in a mean variance framework the martingale analysis can be used to prove that there is always a portfolio whose covariances are proportional to the excess returns on each asset. In other words, the absence of arbitrage implies the existence of a mean variance efficient portfolio (see Ross, 1976a; Chamberlain and Rothschild, 1983).

Empirical testing. Perhaps because the option pricing theory works so well, it has generated a surprisingly small empirical literature. Some early tests, for example, Black and Scholes (1973) and Galai (1977), focused on whether the models could be used to generate successful trading rules and found that any success was easily lost to transactions costs. Most interestingly, MacBeth and Merville (1979) found that the option formulas tended to underprice 'in the money' options and overprice 'out of the money' options, but Geske and Roll (1984) have argued that this effect disappears with a reformulation of the statistics.

Given a theory that works so well, the best empirical work will be to use it as a tool rather than to test it. Chiras and Manaster (1978), for example, show that implicit volatilities, i.e. variances computed by inverting the option formulas to obtain variance as a function of the quoted option price, have strong predictive power for explaining future realized stock variances. Patell and Wolfson (1979) use the implicit variances to examine whether stock prices are more volatile around earnings announcements.

These efforts should increase; options and option pricing theory give us an opportunity to measure directly the degree of anticipated uncertainty in the markets. Financial press terms such as 'investor confidence' take on new meaning when they can actually be measured.

This does not mean, however, that there are no important gaps in the theory. Perhaps of most importance, beyond numerical results (see, for example, Parkinson, 1977; or Brennan and Schwartz, 1977), very little is known about most American options which expire in finite time. The American call option on a stock paying a dividend or the American put option are both easily solved in the infinite maturity case since the optimal exercise boundary is a fixed stock value independent of time (Merton, 1973b; Cox and Ross, 1976a, 1976b). If dividends occur at discrete points, then if the call is exercised prematurely it will only be optimal to do so just prior to a dividend payment. This permits a recursive approach to the solution of this finite maturity option (see Roll, 1977a; Geske,

1979). But, with continuous payouts, surprisingly little is known about the exercise properties of either of these options in the American case.

Despite such gaps, when judged by its ability to explain the empirical data, option pricing theory is the most successful theory not only in finance, but in all of economics. It is now widely employed by the financial industry and its impact on economics has been far ranging. At a theoretical level, we now understand that option pricing theory is a manifestation of the force of arbitrage and that this is the same force that underlies much of neoclassical finance.

THE WHOLE IS THE SUM OF THE PARTS – CORPORATE FINANCE

The use of arbitrage as a serious tool of analysis coincided with the beginning of the modern theory of corporate finance. In two seminal papers on the cost of capital, Modigliani and Miller (1958, 1963) argued that the overall cost of capital and, therefore, the value of the firm would be unaffected by its financing decision. Specifically, using arbitrage arguments, Modigliani and Miller showed that the debt/equity split would not alter a firm's value and they then argued that with the investment decision held constant, the dividend payout rate of the firm would also not affect that value. These two irrelevance propositions defined the study of corporate finance in much the same way that Arrow's Impossibility Theorem defined social choice theory. At one and the same time they propounded an irreverent theory whose central feature was the irrelevance of the topic under study. This challenge, to weaken in a useful way the assumptions of their analysis, has guided research in this area ever since.

The Modigliani–Miller analysis. Since the Modigliani–Miller (henceforth MM) irrelevance propositions are developed from the absence of arbitrage, they are quite robust to alternative specifications of the economic model. To derive the Modigliani–Miller propositions we will employ the no arbitrage theory above. Consider a firm which will liquidate all of its assets at the end of the current period, and let x denote the random liquidation value of the assets. Assume that the firm has debt outstanding with a face value of F and that the remainder of the value of the firm is owned by the stockholders who have the residual claim after the bondholders.

At the end of the period, if x is large enough the stockholders will receive $x - F$ and if x falls short of F they will receive nothing. Formally, then, the terminal payment to the stockholders is

$$\max(x - F, 0),$$

which will be recognized as the terminal payment on a call option. In other words – in a tribute to the ubiquitous nature of option pricing theory – the stockholders have a call option on the terminal value of the firm, x, with an exercise price equal to the face value of the debt, F. The bondholders can claim the entire assets if x is not sufficient to cover the promised payment of F, which means that they will receive,

$$\min(x, F).$$

The current value of the firm, V, is defined to be the value of all of the outstanding claims against its assets which in this case is the value of the stocks, S, and the bonds, B. Using the no arbitrage analysis, we find that (ignoring discounting),

$$V \equiv S + B$$
$$= E^*[\max(x - F, 0)] + E^*[\min(x, F)]$$
$$= E^*[\max(x - F, 0) + \min(x, F)]$$
$$= E^*(x),$$

which is independent of the face value, F, of the debt and, therefore, independent of the relative amounts of debt and equity. This verifies the first of the MM irrelevance propositions.

To verify the irrelevance of value to the dividend payout, consider a firm about to pay a dividend, D. The current, pre-dividend, value of the stock is $p^-(D)$ and by the no arbitrage martingale analysis this is given by,

$$p^-(D) = E^*[D + p^+(D)] = D + E^*[p^+(D)],$$

where $p^+(D)$ is the ex-dividend price. If the investment policy of the firm has been fixed, then the only impact that the current dividend payout can have on the stockholders is through its alteration of the cash in the firm. This means that changing the dividend to, say $D + \Delta D$, would necessitate a change in current assets of $-\Delta D$. From the first MM proposition the mode of financing this change in the dividend will be irrelevant to the determination of the firm's value and to simplify the analysis we will assume that it is financed by riskless debt. At an interest rate of r this would entail, say, a perpetual outflow from the firm of $r\Delta D$. Again applying the analysis and letting x_{t+s} be the cash flow at time $t + s$ given that a dividend of D is paid now, we have,

$$p^+(D + \Delta D) = E^*\left[\int_0^\infty e^{-rs}(x_{t+s} - r\Delta D)\, ds\right]$$
$$= E^*\left(\int_0^\infty e^{-rs}x_{t+s}\, ds\right) - E^*\left(\int_0^\infty e^{-rs}r\Delta D\, ds\right)$$
$$= p^+(D) - \Delta D.$$

Thus, we have the irrelevance proposition,

$$p^-(D + \Delta D) = E^*[(D + \Delta D) + p^+(D + \Delta D)]$$
$$= D + \Delta D + E^*[p^+(D + \Delta D)]$$
$$= D + \Delta D + E^*[p^+(D)] - \Delta D$$
$$= D + E^*[p^+(D)]$$
$$= p^-(D).$$

The MM results were startling to those who had worked in corporate finance and had taken it for granted that the way in which a firm was financed affected its value. To understand the importance of the MM results for the most practical of problems; recall that the original impetus for the study of corporate finance was the determination of the firm's opportunity cost for investments, ρ. For a marginal investment, financed by the issuance of debt and equity, the cost of capital, ρ, also known as the weighted average cost of capital, WACC, would be the weighted average cost of the debt, r, and the cost of equity, k,

$$\rho = (S/V)k + (B/V)r, \tag{33}$$

(where we have ignored tax effects).

If debt is riskless, then r is the interest rate on such debt and k, the cost of equity, will be the return required by investors for the risk inherent in the stock. Presumably k could be found by appeal to one of the asset pricing models discussed above.

Now it is tempting to think, for example, that if $k > r$, then an increase in debt relative to equity will lower ρ. If this goes too far, debt will become risky and as r rises there will be a unique optimal debt/equity ratio, $(B/S)^0$, that minimizes the cost of capital, ρ. This would be the discount rate to use for present value calculations and it would maximize the value of the firm. This was the traditional analysis of the leverage decision before MM.

By the MM theorem, though, value, V, is unaffected by leverage. This means that ρ is unaltered, since the total (expected) return to the stockholders and the bondholders, $Sk + Br$, is unaltered [see Equation (33)]. In terms of the WACC, then, as the leverage (B/S) is increased by the substitution of debt for equity, the cost of equity changes.

$$k = \rho + (B/S)(\rho - r),$$

but not the WACC.

Spanning arguments. The efforts to elude these results and to develop a meaningful theory of corporate finance have taken many forms. First, it has been argued that the analysis itself contains a hidden and critical assumption, namely that the pricing operator is independent of the corporate financial structure. The alternative is that the change in the debt/equity decision, for example, will also change the span of the marketed assets in the economy and, consequently, the operator used for pricing will change. The simplest such example would be a single firm in a two-state world. If the firm is an all equity firm and if there are no other traded assets, then individuals cannot adjust their consumption across the states of nature and must split it according to the equity payoff. If this firm now issues debt the two securities will span the two states of nature and complete the market. This, in turn, will generally alter pricing in the economy.

While this argument has generated a large literature, the problem of the determination of the corporate financial structure and the value of the firm is primarily a microeconomic question and it is difficult to believe that it will be resolved or even illuminated by assuming that firms have some monopoly power that enables them to alter pricing in the capital markets. At the microlevel the MM propositions are unlikely to be seriously affected by such general equilibrium arguments.

At the microlevel, too, the intuition behind the MM propositions and its conclusions is so robust as to be daunting. Consider the following argument. According to MM there can be no optimal, i.e. value maximizing, financial structure since value is independent of structure. Suppose that there was an optimal, say, debt/equity ratio, $(B/S)^0$. Any departure from this target $(B/S)^0$, however, could not lower the firm's value since it would immediately afford an arbitrage opportunity to buy the total firm at its lowered value and refinance it in the optimal target propositions, $(B/S)^0$. (This somewhat facetious argument gets the point across, but it really means that we have not fully specified the rules of the game, e.g., who moves first, what happens when no one moves, etc.)

Signalling models. A more promising route which formally exploits incomplete spanning, but does not argue that the pricing operator itself is altered by any one firm changing its financial structure, makes use of the theory of asymmetric information and signalling (see Ross, 1977a; Leland and Pyle, 1977; and Bhattacharya, 1979). If the managers of the firm possess information that is not held by the market then the market will make inferences from the actions of the firm and, in particular, from financial decisions. Changes in its financial structure or its dividend policy will alter investors' perceptions of its risk class and, therefore, its value. While the operator, $E^*(\cdot)$ does not change, the perception of the distribution of the firm's cash flow does. In an effort to maximize their value, firms will take actions, such as taking on high debt to equity ratios, which can be imitated by lesser firms only at a prohibitive cost. This will distinguish them from lesser firms that the uninformed market erroneously puts into the same class with them. In this fashion, a hierarchy of firm risk classes will emerge, and, in equilibrium, firms will signal their true situations and investors will draw correct inferences from their signals.

All of this has a nice ring to it, but the nagging question that remains is why firms use their financial decisions to accomplish all of this information transfer. Financial changes are cheap, but even cheaper might be guarantees or, for that matter, a system of legislation. These issues remain unresolved, but it is difficult to think that much will be explained by theories that argue that firms take on more debt just to show the world that 'they can do it'. There is a limit to macho-finance.

Taxes. Another line of attack has been to introduce more 'imperfections', especially taxes, into the models. Modigliani and Miller originally had noted that the presence of a corporate tax meant that firms would have an incentive to issue additional debt. Since interest payments on debt are excluded from corporate taxes, substituting debt for equity permits firms to pass returns to investors with a lowered tax cut to the government. At the limit, firms would be all debt if the tax authorities still recognized such debt payments as excludable from taxable corporate income. Presumably, the only brake to this expansion would be the real costs of dealing with the inevitable bankruptcies of high debt firms. This is logically possible, but at the expense of reducing corporate finance to the study of the tradeoff between the tax advantages of debt and the costs of bankruptcy.

Miller (1977) found a more profound brake to this tendency to increase debt. He argued that while the firm could lower its taxes by increasing its debt, the ability of investors to defer or offset capital gains implies that they pay higher taxes on interest income than on the returns from equities. With a rising tax schedule, an equilibrium is possible in which the marginal investor has a tax differential between ordinary income and equity returns that exactly offsets the firm's corporate tax advantage to debt. In such an equilibrium, investors in a higher tax bracket than the marginal investor would purchase only equity (or non-taxed bonds such as municipals for US investors) and those in lower tax brackets would purchase corporate bonds. There would be an equilibrium amount of debt for the corporate sector as a whole, but not for any individual firm (assuming the absence of inframarginal firm tax schedules).

Miller's analysis led to a large literature on the impact of taxes on pricing. Black and Scholes (1974) had made a related argument for the absence of a tax effect on dividends, arguing that stocks with relatively higher yields should not have higher gross returns to compensate investors for the additional tax burden since companies would then just cut their dividends to increase the stock price. Black and Scholes verified their results empirically, but, using a different methodology, Litzenberger and Ramaswamy (1982) found that gross returns were higher for stocks with higher dividends. Whether the supply side or the demand side dominates remains undecided.

Whatever the resolution of this and similar debates, the equilibrium tax argument initiated by Miller has changed much of the analysis of these issues. Miller and Scholes (1978), for example, argue that by employing a number of 'laundering' devices individuals can dramatically cut their taxes. Their conclusion that, in theory, taxes should be much lower than they appear to be in practice, focuses attention on the role played by informational asymmetries and the related costliness of using techniques such as investing through tax exempt intermediaries.

Agency models. The emphasis on informational asymmetries has been the cornerstone of an alternative approach to corporate finance, agency theory. Wilson (1968) and Ross (1973) developed agency models in which one party, the agent (e.g. a corporate manager) acts on behalf of another, the principal (e.g. stockholders). Jensen and Meckling (1976), building on the agency theory and on Williamson's (1975) transaction cost approach, argue that corporate finance can be understood in terms of the monitoring and bonding costs imposed on stockholders and managers by such relations. The manager qua employee has an incentive to divert firm resources to his own benefit. Jensen and Meckling refer to the loss in value in restraining this incentive as the (equilibrium) agency cost of the relation.

28

To some extent this conflict can be resolved ex ante by the indenture agreements and covenants in financial contracts, but the cost of doing so rises with the monitoring requirements. Myers (1977), for example, has studied the implications for investment policy of the conflict between the stockholders and the bondholders. Stockholders own a call option on the assets of the firm and the value of a call increases with the variance of the asset value. Conversely, such increases will come at the expense of the bondholders. Ex ante indenture agreements can limit the ability of management and stockholders to take on additional risk, but the more precise the limits the costlier it is to write, observe and enforce them.

These trade-offs are the intuition and subject matter of the agency approach to corporate finance, but to date it is more a collection of intuitions than a well-articulated theory. The agency approach has pointed in some intriguing directions, but it fares poorly if judged by asking what it is that would be a counter observation or count as evidence against it. To the contrary, no phenomenon seems beyond the reach of 'agency costs' and at times the phrase takes on more of the trappings of an incantation than an analytical tool. The role of asymmetric information in corporate finance and in explaining the managerial and financial forces at work in the firm is self evident, but it remains fertile ground for theory.

Empirical evidence. The early empirical work examined the relation between the corporate financial structure and other characteristics of the firm. Hamada (1972), for example, studied whether the beta of a firm's equity was related to the beta of the firm's assets as would be predicted by the cost of capital, equation (33). There continues to be empirical work on these issues, but the attention of empiricists has shifted to the arena of corporate control.

A boom in merger and acquisition activity in the late 1970s and through to the present time has brought some striking and unexplained empirical regularities. On average, shareholders in firms that are the targets of tender offers gain significantly from such offers while the rewards to bidders are still ambiguous (Jensen and Ruback, 1983). For unsuccessful tenders the target firms appear to average an eventual loss and the bidders may, too. These results and the discrepancy between targets and bidders have been the object of close scrutiny.

If firms realize such abnormal gains as targets, and if it reflects the release of information about the value of their underlying assets, then that raises the question of why they were not priced correctly to begin with. On the other hand, if the returns for successful targets reflect synergies rather than simply a revaluation of their assets, why does the bidder get so little? Several game theoretic and bidding models have been built in an attempt to explain these results (see, e.g., Grossman and Hart, 1980), but a consensus has yet to emerge. Furthermore, some of the important empirical issues, such as whether bidders actually gain or lose on average remain unresolved.

Conclusion. For corporate finance, like the other major areas of finance, the neoclassical theory is now well established, but, like the other areas, the inadequacy of the neoclassical analysis is pushing researchers to begin the challenging but promising exploration of theories of asymmetric information. This work holds out the hope of explaining some of the deeper mysteries of finance that have eluded the neoclassical theory, from the embarrassing plethora of anomalies in capital markets to the basic questions of financial structure.

Perhaps the feature that truly distinguishes finance from much of the rest of economics is this constant interplay between theory and empirical analysis. The test of these new approaches will be decided less by reference to their aesthetics and more by their usefulness in explaining financial data. At the height of the subject, these two criteria become one.

BIBLIOGRAPHY

Admati, A. 1985. A noisy rational expectations equilibrium for multi-asset securities markets. *Econometrica* 53(3), May, 629–57.

Bhattacharya, S. 1979. Imperfect information, dividend policy and the 'Bird in the Hand' fallacy. *Bell Journal of Economics and Management Science* 10(1), Spring, 259–70.

Black, F. 1972. Capital market equilibrium with restricted borrowing. *Journal of Business* 45(3), July, 444–55.

Black, F. and Scholes, M. 1972. The valuation of option contracts and a test of market efficiency. *Journal of Finance* 27(2), May, 399–417.

Black, F. and Scholes, M. 1973. The pricing of options and corporate liabilities. *Journal of Political Economy* 81(3), May–June, 637–54.

Black, F., Jensen, M. and Scholes, M. 1972. The capital asset pricing model: some empirical tests. In *Studies in the Theory of Capital Markets*, ed. M. C. Jensen, New York: Praeger.

Black, F. and Scholes, M. 1974. The effects of dividend yield and dividend policy on common stock prices and returns. *Journal of Financial Economics* 1(1), May, 1–22.

Breeden, D.T. 1979. An intertemporal asset pricing model with stochastic consumption and investment opportunities. *Journal of Financial Economics* 7(3), September, 265–96.

Brennan, M.J. and Schwartz, E.S. 1977. The valuation of American put options. *Journal of Finance* 32(2), May, 449–62.

Brown, S. and Weinstein, M. 1983. A new approach to testing asset pricing models: the bilinear paradigm. *Journal of Finance* 38(3), June, 711–43.

Cass, D. and Stiglitz, J. 1970. The structure of investor preferences and asset returns, and separatability in portfolio selection: a contribution to the pure theory of mutual funds. *Journal of Economic Theory* 2(2), June, 122–60.

Chamberlain, G. 1983. Funds, factors and diversification in arbitrage pricing models. *Econometrica* 51(5), September, 1305–23.

Chamberlain, G. and Rothschild, M. 1983. Arbitrage, factor structure and mean-variance analysis on large asset markets. *Econometrica* 51(5), September, 1281–304.

Chen, N., Roll, R. and Ross, S.A. 1986. Economic forces and the stock market. *Journal of Business* 59, July, 383–403.

Chiras, D.P. and Manaster, S. 1978. The information content of option prices and a test of market efficiency. *Journal of Financial Economics* 6(2–3), June–September, 213–34.

Connor, G. 1984. A unified beta pricing theory. *Journal of Economic Theory* 34(1), October, 13–31.

Cootner, P. (ed.) 1964. *The Random Character of Stock Market Prices*. Cambridge, Mass.: MIT Press.

Cowles, A. 1933. Can stock market forecasters forecast? *Econometrica* 1, July, 309–24.

Cox, J.C., Ingersoll, J. and Ross, S.A. 1985a. An intertemporal general equilibrium model of asset prices. *Econometrica* 53(2), March, 363–84.

Cox, J.C., Ingersoll, J. and Ross, S.A. 1985b. A theory of the term structure of interest rates. *Econometrica* 53(2), March, 385–407.

Cox, J.C. and Ross, S.A. 1976a. The valuation of options for alternative stochastic processes. *Journal of Financial Economics* 3(1–2), January–March, 145–66.

Cox, J.C. and Ross, S.A. 1976b. A survey of some new results in financial option pricing theory. *Journal of Finance* 31(2), May, 383–402.

Cox, J.C., Ross, S.A. and Rubinstein, M. 1979. Option pricing: a simplified approach. *Journal of Financial Economics* 7(3), September, 229–63.

Diamond, D. and Verrecchia, R. 1981. Information aggregation in a noisy rational expectations economy. *Journal of Financial Economics* 9(3), September, 221–35.

Dybvig, P. 1983. An explicit bound on deviations from APT pricing in a finite economy. *Journal of Financial Economics* 12(4), December, 483–96.

Dybvig, P. and Ross, S. A. 1985. Yes, the APT is testable. *Journal of Finance* 40(4), September, 1173–88.

Fama, E. F. 1970. Efficient capital markets: a review of theory and empirical work. *Journal of Finance* 25(2), May, 383–417.

Fama, E.F., Fisher, L., Jensen, M. and Roll, R. 1969. The adjustment of stock prices to new information. *International Economic Review* 10(1), February, 1–21.

Fama, E.F. and MacBeth, J. 1973. Risk, return and equilibrium: empirical tests. *Journal of Political Economy* 81(3), May–June, 607–36.

Flavin, M. 1983. Excess volatility in the financial markets: a reassessment of the empirical evidence. *Journal of Political Economy* 91(6), December, 929–56.

French, K. 1980. Stock returns and the weekend effect. *Journal of Financial Economics* 8(1), March, 55–69.

French, K. and Roll, R. 1985. Stock return variances, the arrival of information and the reaction of traders. ULCA Working Paper.

Galai, D. 1977. Tests of market efficiency of the Chicago Board Options Exchange. *Journal of Business* 50(2), April, 167–97.

Geske, R. 1979. A note on an analytical valuation formula for unprotected American call options on stocks with known dividends. *Journal of Financial Economics* 7(4), December, 375–80.

Geske, R. and Roll, R. 1984. Isolating the observed biases in call option pricing: an alternative variance estimator. UCLA Working Paper, April.

Gibbons, M. 1982. Multivariate tests of financial models: a new approach. *Journal of Financial Economics* 10(1), March, 3–27.

Gibbons, M., Ross, S.A. and Shanken, J. 1986. A test of the efficiency of a given portfolio. Stanford University Working Paper No. 853.

Granger, C.W.J. and Morgenstern, O. 1962. Spectral analysis of New York stock market prices. Econometric Research Program, Princeton University, Research Memorandum, September.

Grossman, S.J. 1976. On the efficiency of competitive stock markets where traders have diverse information. *Journal of Finance* 31(2), May, 573–85.

Grossman, S.J. and Hart, O. 1980. Takeover bids, the free-rider problem, and the theory of the corporation. *Bell Journal of Economics and Management Science* 11(1), Spring, 42–64.

Grossman, S.J. and Stiglitz, J. 1980. The impossibility of informationally efficient markets.

American Economic Review 70, June, 393–408.

Hamada, R.S. 1972. The effect of the firm's capital structure on the systematic risk of common stocks. *Journal of Finance* 27(2), May, 435–52.

Hansen, L. and Singleton, R. 1983. Stochastic consumption, risk aversion and the temporal behavior of asset returns. *Journal of Political Economy* 91(2), April, 249–65.

Harrison, J.M. and Kreps, D.M. 1979. Martingales and arbitrage in multiperiod securities markets. *Journal of Economic Theory* 20(3), June, 381–408.

Hicks, J.R. 1946. *Value and Capital.* 2nd edn, London: Oxford University Press.

Huberman, G. 1982. A simple approach to arbitrage pricing theory. *Journal of Economic Theory* 28(1), October, 183–91.

Ingersoll, J. 1977. A contingent-claims valuation of convertible securities. *Journal of Financial Economics* 4(3), May, 289–322.

Ingersoll, J. 1984. Some results in the theory of arbitrage pricing. *Journal of Finance* 39(4), September, 1021–39.

Jaffé, J. 1974. The effect of regulation changes on insider trading. *Bell Journal of Economics and Management Science* 5(1), Spring, 93–121.

Jensen, M.C. and Meckling, W.H. 1976. Theory of the firm: managerial behavior, agency costs and ownership structure. *Journal of Financial Economics* 3(4), October, 305–60.

Jensen, M.C. and Ruback, R.S. 1983. The market for corporate control: the scientific evidence. *Journal of Financial Economics* 11(1–4), April, 5–50.

Jobson, J.D. and Korkie, B. 1982. Potential performance and tests of portfolio efficiency. *Journal of Financial Economics* 10(4), December, 433–66.

Kandel, S. 1984. On the exclusion of assets from tests of the mean variance efficiency of the market portfolio. *Journal of Finance* 39(1), March, 63–73.

Keim, D. 1983. Size-related anomalies and stock return seasonality: further empirical evidence. *Journal of Financial Economics* 12(1), June, 13–32.

Kleidon, A. 1986. Variance bounds tests and stock price valuation models. *Journal of Political Economy* 94(5), October, 953–1001.

Leland, H. and Pyle, D. 1977. Informational asymmetries, financial structure and financial intermediation. *Journal of Finance* 32(2), May, 371–87.

Lintner, J. 1965. The valuation of risk assets and the selection of risky investments in stock portfolios and capital budgets. *Review of Economics and Statistics* 47, February, 13–37.

Litzenberger, R. and Ramaswamy, K. 1982. The effect of dividends on common stock prices: tax effects or information effects? *Journal of Finance* 37(2), May, 429–43.

Lucas, R.E., Jr. 1978. Asset prices in an exchange economy. *Econometrica* 46(6), November, 1429–45.

MacBeth, J. and Merville, L. 1979. An empirical examination of the Black–Scholes call option pricing model. *Journal of Finance* 34(5), December, 1173–86.

Malkiel, B. 1966. *The Term Structure of Interest Rates: Expectations and Behavior Patterns.* Princeton: Princeton University Press.

Markowitz, H.M. 1959. *Portfolio Selection: Efficient Diversification of Investments.* New York: Wiley.

Marsh, T. and Merton, R.C. 1986. Dividend variability and variance bounds tests for the rationality of stock market prices. *American Economic Review* 76(3), June, 483–98.

Merton, R.C. 1973a. An intertemporal capital asset pricing model. *Econometrica* 41(5), September, 867–87.

Merton, R.C. 1973b. Theory of rational option pricing. *Bell Journal of Economics and Management Science* 4(1), Spring, 141–83.

Milgrom, P. and Stokey, N. 1982. Information, trade and common knowledge. *Journal of*

Economic Theory 26(1), February, 17–27.

Miller, M.H. 1977. Debt and taxes. *Journal of Finance* 32(2), May, 261–75.

Miller, M.H. and Scholes, M. 1978. Dividends and taxes. *Journal of Financial Economics* 6(4), December, 333–64.

Modigliani, F. and Miller, M.H. 1958. The cost of capital, corporation finance, and the theory of investment. *American Economic Review* 48, June, 261–97.

Modigliani, F. and Miller, M.H. 1963. Corporate income taxes and the cost of capital. *American Economic Review* 53, June, 433–43.

Mossin, J. 1966. Equilibrium in a capital asset market. *Econometrica* 34(4), October, 768–83.

Myers, S. 1977. Determinants of corporate borrowing. *Journal of Financial Economics* 5(2), November, 147–75.

Parkinson, M. 1977. Option pricing: the American put. *Journal of Business* 50(1), January, 21–36.

Patell, J.M. and Wolfson, M.A. 1979. Anticipated information releases reflected in call option prices. *Journal of Accounting and Economics* 1(2), August, 117–40.

Roberts, H. 1967. Statistical versus clinical prediction of the stock market. Unpublished manuscript, CRSP, Chicago: University of Chicago.

Roll, R. 1970. *The Behavior of Interest Rates: An Application of the Efficient Market Model to U.S. Treasury Bills.* New York: Basic Books.

Roll, R. 1977a. An analytic valuation formula for unprotected American call options on stocks with known dividends. *Journal of Financial Economics* 5(2), November, 251–8.

Roll, R. 1977b. A critique of the asset pricing theory's tests. *Journal of Financial Economics* 4(2), March, 129–76.

Roll, R. 1978. Ambiguity when performance is measured by the securities market line. *Journal of Finance* 33(4), September, 1051–69.

Roll, R. 1981. A possible explanation of the small firm effect. *Journal of Finance* 36(4), September, 879–88.

Roll, R. 1983. The turn-of-the-year effect and small firm premium. *Journal of Portfolio Management* 9(2), Winter, 18–28.

Roll, R. 1984. Orange juice and weather. *American Economic Review* 74(5), December, 861–80.

Roll, R. and Ross, S.A. 1980. An empirical investigation of the arbitrage pricing theory. *Journal of Finance* 35(5), December, 1073–103.

Ross, S.A. 1973. The economic theory of agency: the principal's problem. *American Economic Review* 63(2), May, 134–9.

Ross, S.A. 1975. Uncertainty and the heterogeneous capital good model. *Review of Economic Studies* 42(1), January 133–46.

Ross, S.A. 1976a. Return, risk and arbitrage. In *Risk and Return in Finance*, ed. I. Friend and J. Bicksler, Cambridge, Mass.: Ballinger.

Ross, S.A. 1976b. The arbitrage theory of capital asset pricing. *Journal of Economic Theory* 13(3), December, 341–60.

Ross, S.A. 1976c. Options and efficiency. *Quarterly Journal of Economics* 90(1), February, 75–89.

Ross, S.A. 1977a. The determination of financial structure: the incentive signalling approach. *Bell Journal of Economics and Management Science* 8(1), Spring, 23–40.

Ross, S.A. 1977b. The capital asset pricing model (CAPM), short-sale restrictions and related issues. *Journal of Finance* 32(1), March, 177–83.

Ross, S.A. 1978a. Mutual fund separation in financial theory – the separating distributions.

Journal of Economic Theory 17(2), April, 254–86.

Ross, S.A. 1978b. A simple approach to the valuation of risky streams. *Journal of Business* 51(3), July, 453–75.

Ross, S.A. 1980. A test of the efficiency of a given portfolio. Paper presented to the World Econometrics Meetings. Aix-en-Provence.

Rubinstein, M. 1976. The valuation of uncertain income streams and the pricing of options. *Bell Journal of Economics and Management Science* 7(2), Autumn, 407–25.

Shanken, J. 1982. The arbitrage pricing theory: is it testable? *Journal of Finance* 37(5), December, 1129–40.

Sharpe, W. 1964. Capital asset prices: a theory of market equilibrium under conditions of risk. *Journal of Finance* 19, September, 425–42.

Shiller, R. 1981. Do stock prices move too much to be justified by subsequent changes in dividends? *American Economic Review* 71(3), June, 421–36.

Tobin, J. 1958. Liquidity preference as behavior towards risk. *Review of Economic Studies* 25, February, 65–86.

Williamson, O.E. 1975. *Markets and Hierarchies: Analysis and Antitrust Implications.* New York: Free Press.

Wilson, R.B. 1968. The theory of syndicates. *Econometrica* 36(1), January, 119–32.

Financial Intermediaries

JAMES TOBIN

The tangible wealth of a nation consists of its natural resources, its stocks of goods, and its net claims against the rest of the world. The goods include structures, durable equipment of service to consumers or producers, and inventories of finished goods, raw materials and goods in process. A nation's wealth will help to meet its people's future needs and desires; tangible assets do so in a variety of ways, sometimes by yielding directly consumable goods and services, more often by enhancing the power of human effort and intelligence in producing consumable goods and services. There are many intangible forms of the wealth of a nation, notably the skill, knowledge and character of its population and the framework of law, convention and social interaction that sustains cooperation and community.

Some components of a nation's wealth are appropriable; they can be owned by governments, or privately by individuals or other legal entities. Some intangible assets are appropriable, notably by patents and copyrights. In a capitalist society most appropriable wealth is privately owned, more than 80 per cent by value in the United States. Private properties are generally transferable from owner to owner. Markets in these properties, *capital markets*, are a prominent feature of capitalist societies. In the absence of slavery, markets in 'human capital' are quite limited.

A person may be wealthy without owning any of the assets counted in appropriable *national wealth*. Instead, a personal wealth inventory would list paper currency and coin, bank deposits, bonds, stocks, mutual funds, cash values of insurance policies and pension rights. These are paper assets evidencing claims of various kinds against other individuals, companies, institutions or governments. In reckoning personal *net worth*, each person would deduct from the value of his total assets the claims of others against him. In 1984 American households' gross holdings of financial assets amounted to about 75 per cent of their net worth, and their net holdings to about 55 per cent (Federal Reserve, 1984). If

35

the net worths of all economic units of the nation are added up, paper claims and obligations cancel each other. All that remains, if valuations are consistent and the census is complete, is the value of the national wealth.

If the central government is excluded from this aggregation, *private net worth* – the aggregate net worth of individuals and institutions and subordinate governments (included in the 'private' sector because, lacking monetary powers, they have limited capacities to borrow) – will count not only the national-wealth assets they own but also their net claims against the central government. These include coin and currency, their equivalent in central bank deposit liabilities, and interest-bearing Treasury obligations. If these central government debts exceed the value of its real assets, *private net worth* will exceed national wealth. (However, in reckoning their net worth, private agents may subtract something for the future taxes they expect to pay to service the government's debts. Some economists argue that the subtraction is complete, so that public debt does not count in aggregate private wealth (Barro, 1974) while others give reasons why the offset is incomplete (Tobin, 1980). The issue is not crucial for this essay.)

OUTSIDE ASSETS, INSIDE ASSETS AND FINANCIAL MARKETS

Private net worth, then, consists of two parts: privately owned items of national wealth, mostly tangible assets, and government obligations. These *outside* assets are owned by private agents not directly but through the intermediation of a complex network of debts and claims, *inside* assets.

Empirical magnitudes. For the United States at the end of 1984, the value of tangible assets, land and reproducible goods, is estimated at $13.5 trillion, nearly four times the Gross National Product for the year. Of this, $11.2 trillion were privately owned. Adding net claims against the rest of the world and privately owned claims against the federal government gives private net worth of $12.5 trillion, of which only $1.3 trillion represent outside financial assets. The degree of intermediation is indicated by the gross value of financial assets, nearly $14.8 trillion; even if equities in business are regarded as direct titles to real property and excluded from financial assets, the outstanding stock of inside assets is $9.6 trillion. Of these more than half, $5.6 trillion, are claims on financial institutions. The $9.6 million is an underestimate, because many inside financial transactions elude the statisticians. The relative magnitudes of these numbers have changed very little since 1953, when private net worth was $1.27 trillion, gross financial assets $1.35 trillion ($1.05 excluding equities) and GNP was $0.37 trillion (Federal Reserve, 1984).

Raymond Goldsmith, who has studied intermediation throughout a long and distinguished career and knows far more about it than anyone else, has estimated measures of intermediation for many countries over long periods of time (1969, 1985). Here is his own summary:

The creation of a modern financial superstructure, not in its details but in its essentials, was generally accomplished at a fairly early stage of a country's economic development, usually within five to seven decades from the start of modern economic growth. Thus it was essentially completed in most now-developed countries by the end of the 19th century or the eve of World War I, though somewhat earlier in Great Britain. During this period the financial interrelations ratio, the quotient of financial and tangible assets, increased fairly continuously and sharply. Since World War I or the Great Depression, however, the ratio in most of these countries has shown no upward trend, though considerable movements have occurred over shorter periods, such as sharp reductions during inflations; and though significant changes have taken place in the relative importance of the various types of financial institutions and of financial instruments. Among less developed countries, on the other hand, the financial interrelations ratio has increased substantially, particularly in the postwar period, though it generally is still well below the level reached by the now-developed countries early in the 20th century.

Goldsmith finds that a ratio of the order of unity is characteristic of financial maturity, as is illustrated by the figures for the United States given above (1985, pp. 2–3).

Goldsmith finds also that the relative importance of financial institutions, especially non-banks, has trended upwards in most market economies but appears to taper off in mature systems. Institutions typically hold from a quarter to a half of all financial instruments. Ratios around 0.40 were typical in 1978, but there is considerably more variation among countries than in the financial interrelations ratio. The United States, at 0.27, is on the low side, probably because of its many well-organized financial markets (1985, Table 47, p. 136).

The volume of gross financial transactions is mind-boggling. The GNP velocity of the money stock in the United States is 6 or 7 per year; if intermediate as well as final transactions for goods and services are considered, the turnover may be 20 or 30 per year. But demand deposits turn over 500 times a year, 2500 times in New York City banks, indicating that most transactions are financial in nature. The value of stock market transactions alone in the United States is one third of the Gross National Product; an average share of stock changes hands every nineteen months. Gross foreign exchange transactions in United States dollars are estimated to be hundreds of billions of dollars every day. 'Value added' in the financial services industries amounts to 9 per cent of United States GNP (Tobin, 1984).

Outside and inside money. The outside/inside distinction is most frequently applied to money. *Outside money* is the monetary debt of the government and its central bank, currency and central bank deposits, sometimes referred to as 'base' or 'high-powered' money. *Inside money,* 'low-powered', consists of private deposit obligations of other banks and depository institutions in excess of their holdings of outside money assets. Just which kinds of deposit obligations count as 'money' depends on definitions, of which there are several, all somewhat arbitrary. Outside money in the United States amounted to $186 billion at the end of 1983, of which

37

$36 billion was held as reserves by banks and other depository institutions; the remaining $150 billion was held by other private agents as currency. The total money stock M1, currency in public circulation plus checkable deposits, was $480 billion. Thus inside M1 was $294 billion, more than 60 per cent of the total.

Financial markets, organized and informal. Inside assets and debts wash out in aggregative accounting; one person's asset is another's debt. But for the functioning of the economy, the inside network is of great importance. *Financial markets* allow inside assets and debts to be originated and to be exchanged at will for each other and for outside financial assets. These markets deal in paper contracts and claims. They complement the markets for real properties. Private agents often borrow to buy real property and pledge the property as security; households mortgage new homes, businesses incur debt to acquire stocks of materials or goods-in-process or to purchase structures and equipment. The term *capital markets* covers both financial and property markets. *Money markets* are financial markets in which short-term debts are exchanged for outside money.

Many of the assets traded in financial markets are promises to pay currency in specified amounts at specified future dates, sometimes conditional on future events and circumstances. The currency is not always the local currency; obligations denominated in various national currencies are traded all over the world. Many traded assets are not denominated in any future monetary unit of account: equity shares in corporations, contracts for deliveries of commodities – gold, oil, soy beans, hog bellies. There are various hybrid assets: preferred stock gives holders priority in distributions of company profits up to specified pecuniary limits; convertible debentures combine promises to pay currency with rights to exchange the securities for shares.

Capital markets, including financial markets, take a variety of forms. Some are highly organized auction markets, the leading real-world approximations to the abstract perfect markets of economic theory, where all transactions occurring at any moment in a commodity or security are made at a single price and every agent who wants to buy or sell at that price is accommodated. Such markets exist in shares, bonds, overnight loans of outside money, standard commodities and foreign currency deposits, and in futures contracts and options for most of the same items.

However, many financial and property transactions occur otherwise, in direct negotiations between the parties. Organized open markets require large tradable supplies of precisely defined homogeneous commodities or instruments. Many financial obligations are one of a kind, the promissory note of a local business proprietor, the mortgage on a specific farm or residence. The terms, conditions and collateral are specific to the case. The habit of referring to classes of heterogeneous negotiated transactions as 'markets' is metaphorical, like the use of the term 'labour market' to refer to the decentralized processes by which wages are set and jobs are filled, or 'computer market' to describe the pricing and selling of a host of differentiated products. In these cases the economists' faith is that the outcomes are 'as if' the transaction occurred in perfect organized auction markets.

FINANCIAL ENTERPRISES AND THEIR MARKETS

Financial intermediaries are enterprises in the business of buying and selling financial assets. The accounting balance sheet of a financial intermediary is virtually 100 per cent paper on both sides. The typical financial intermediary owns relatively little real property, just the structures, equipment and materials necessary to its business. The equity of the owners, or the equivalent capital reserve account for mutual, cooperative, nonprofit, or public institutions, is small compared to the enterprises' financial obligations.

Financial intermediaries are major participants in organized financial markets. They take large asset positions in market instruments; their equities and some of their liabilities, certificates of deposit or debt securities, are traded in those markets. They are not just middlemen like dealers and brokers whose main business is to execute transactions for clients.

Financial intermediaries are the principal makers of the informal financial markets discussed above. Banks and savings institutions hold mortgages, commercial loans and consumer credit; their liabilities are mainly checking accounts, savings deposits and certificates of deposit. Insurance companies and pension funds negotiate private placements of corporate bonds and commercial mortgages; their liabilities are contracts with policy-holders and obligations to future retirees. Thus financial intermediaries do much more than participate in organized markets. If financial intermediaries confined themselves to repackaging open market securities for the convenience of their creditors, they would be much less significant actors on the economic scene.

Financial businesses seek customers, both lenders and borrowers, not only by interest rate competition but by differentiating and advertising their 'products'. Financial products are easy to differentiate, by variations in maturities, fees, auxiliary services, office locations and hours of business, and many other features. As might be expected, non-price competition is especially active when prices, in this case interest rates, are fixed by regulation or by tacit or explicit collusion. But the industry is by the heterogeneous nature of its products monopolistically competitive; non-price competition flourishes even when interest rates are free to move. The industry shows symptoms of 'wastes of monopolistic competition'. Retail offices of banks and savings institutions cluster like competing gasoline stations. Much claimed product differentiation is trivial and atmospheric, emphasized and exaggerated in advertising

Financial intermediaries cultivate long-term relationships with customers. Even in the highly decentralized financial system of the United States, local financial intermediaries have some monopoly power, some clienteles who will stay with them even if their interest rates are somewhat less favourable than those elsewhere. Since much business is bilaterally negotiated, there are ample opportunities for price discrimination. The typical business customer of a bank is both a borrower and a depositor, often simultaneously. The customer 'earns' the right for credit accommodation when he needs it by lending surplus funds to the same bank when he has them. The same reciprocity occurs between credit unions and mutual savings institutions and some of their members. Close ties frequently develop between a financial intermediary and non-financial businesses whose sales depend on availability of credit to their customers, for example between automobile dealers and banks. Likewise, builders and realtors have funded and controlled many savings and loan associations in order to facilitate mortgage lending to home buyers.

Financial intermediaries balance the credit demands they face with their available funds by adjusting not only interest rates but also the other terms of loans. They also engage in quantitative rationing, the degree of stringency varying with the availability and costs of funds to the intermediary. Rationing occurs naturally as a by-product of lending decisions made and negotiated case by case. Most such loans require collateral, and the amount and quality of the collateral can be adjusted both to individual circumstances and to overall market conditions. Borrowers are classified as to riskiness and charged rates that vary with their classification.

United States commercial banks follow the 'prime rate convention'. One or another of the large banks acts as price leader and sets a rate on six-month commercial loans for its prime quality borrowers. If other large banks agree, as is usually the case, they follow, and the rate becomes standard for the whole industry until one of the leading banks decides another change is needed to stay in line with open-market interest rates. Loan customers are rated by the number of half-points above prime at which they will be accommodated. Of course, some applications for credit are just turned away. One mechanism of short-term adjustment to credit market conditions is to stiffen or relax the risk classifications of customers, likewise to deny credit to more or fewer applicants. Similar mechanisms for rationing help to equate demands to supplies of home mortgage finance and consumer credit.

THE FUNCTIONS OF FINANCIAL MARKETS AND INTERMEDIARY INSTITUTIONS

Intermediation, as defined and described above, converts the outside privately owned wealth of the economy into the quite different forms in which its ultimate owners hold their accumulated savings. Financial markets alone accomplish considerable intermediation, just by facilitating the origination and exchange of inside assets. Financial intermediaries greatly extend the process, adding 'markets' that would not exist without them, and participating along with other agents in other markets, organized or informal.

What economic functions does intermediation in general perform? What do inside markets add to markets in the basic outside assets? What functions does institutional intermediation by financial intermediaries perform beyond those of open markets in financial instruments? Economists characteristically impose on themselves questions like these, which do not seem problematic to lay practitioners.

Economists start from the presumption that financial activities are epiphenomena, that they create a veil obscuring to superficial observers an underlying reality which they do not affect. The celebrated Modigliani–Miller theorem (1958), generalized beyond the original intent of the authors, says so. With its help the sophisticated economist can pierce the veil and see that the values of financial assets are just those of the outside assets to which they are ultimately claims, no matter how circuitous the path from the one to the other.

However, economists also understand how the availability of certain markets alters, usually for the better, the outcomes prevailing in their absence. For a primitive illustration, consider the functions of inside loan markets as brilliantly described by Irving Fisher (1930). Each household has an intertemporal utility function in consumptions today and at future times, a sequence of what we now would call dated 'endowments' of consumption, and an individual 'backyard' production function by which consumption less than endowment at any one date can be transformed into consumption above endowment at another date. Absent the possibility of intertemporal trades with others, each household has to do its best on its own; its best will be to equate its marginal rate of substitution in utility between any two dates with its marginal rate of transformation in production between the same dates, with the usual amendments for corner solutions. The gains from trade, i.e., in this case from auction markets in inter-household lending and borrowing, arise from differences among households in those autarkic rates of substitution and transformation. They are qualitatively the same as those from free contemporaneous trade in commodities between agents or nations.

The introduction of consumer loans in this Fisherian model will alter the individual and aggregate paths of consumption and saving. It is not possible to say whether it will raise or lower the aggregate amount of capital, here in the sense of labour endowments in the process of producing future rather than current consumable output. In either case it is likely to be a Pareto-optimal improvement, although even this is not guaranteed *a priori*.

Similar argument suggests several reasons why ultimate savers, lenders, creditors prefer the liabilities of financial intermediaries not only to direct ownership of real property but also to the direct debt and equity issues of investors, borrowers and debtors.

Convenience of denomination. Issuers of securities find it costly to cut their issues into the variety of small and large denominations savers find convenient and commensurate to their means. The financial intermediary can break up large-denomination bonds and loans into amounts convenient to small savers, or combine debtors' obligations into large amounts convenient to the wealthy. Economies of scale and specialization in financial transactions enable financial intermediaries to tailor assets and liabilities to the needs and preferences of both lenders and borrowers. This service is especially valuable for agents on both sides whose needs vary in amount continuously; they like deposit accounts and credit lines whose use they can vary at will on their own initiative.

Risk pooling, reduction and allocation. The risks incident to economic activities take many forms. Some are nation-wide or world-wise – wars and revolutions, shifts in international comparative advantage, government fiscal and monetary policies, prices and supplies of oil and other basic materials. Some are specific to particular enterprises and technologies – the capacity and integrity of managers, the qualities of new products, the local weather. A financial intermediary can specialize in the appraisal of risks, especially specific risks, with expertise in the gathering and interpretation of information costly or unavailable to individual savers. By pooling the funds of its creditors, the financial intermediary can diversify away risks to an extent that the individual creditors cannot, because of the costs of transactions as well as the inconvenience of fixed lumpy denominations.

According to Joseph Schumpeter ([1911] 1934, pp. 72–4.), bankers are the gatekeepers – Schumpeter's word is 'ephor' – of capitalist economic development; their strategic function is to screen potential innovators and advance the necessary purchasing power to the most promising. They are the source of purchasing power for investment and innovation, beyond the savings accumulated from past economic development. In practice, the cachet of a banker often enables his customer also to obtain credit from other sources or to float paper in open markets.

Maturity shifting. A financial intermediary typically reconciles differences among borrowers and lenders in the timing of payments. Bank depositors want to commit funds for shorter times than borrowers want to have them. Business borrowers need credit to bridge the time gap between the inputs to profitable production and their output and sales. This source of bank business is formally modelled by Diamond and Dybvig (1983). The bank's scale of operations enables it to stagger the due dates of, say, half-year loans so as to accommodate depositors who want their money back in three months or one month or on demand. The reverse maturity shift may occur in other financial intermediaries. An insurance company or pension fund might invest short-term the savings its policy-owners or future pensioners will not claim for many years.

Transforming illiquid assets into liquid liabilities. Liquidity is a matter of degree. A perfectly liquid asset may be defined as one whose full present value can be realized, i.e., turned into purchasing power over goods and services, immediately. Dollar bills are perfectly liquid, and so for practical purposes are demand deposits and other deposits transferable to third parties by check or wire. Liquidity in this sense does not necessarily mean predictability of value. Securities traded on well organized markets are liquid. Any person selling at a given time will get the same price whether he decided and prepared to sell a month before or on the spur of the moment. But the price itself can vary unpredictably from minute to minute. Contrast a house, neither fully liquid nor predictable in value. Its selling proceeds at this moment are likely to be greater the longer it has been on the market. Consider the six-month promissory note of a small business proprietor known only to his local banker. However sure the payment on the scheduled date, the note may not be marketable at all. If the lender wants to realize its value before maturity, he will have to find a buyer and negotiate. A financial intermediary holds illiquid assets while its liabilities are liquid, and holds assets unpredictable in value while it guarantees the value of its liabilities. This is the traditional business of commercial banks, and the reason for the strong and durable relations of banks and their customers.

SUBSTITUTION OF INSIDE FOR OUTSIDE ASSETS

What determines the aggregate liabilities and assets of financial intermediaries? What determines the gross aggregate of inside assets generated by financial markets in general, including open markets as well as financial intermediaries? How can the empirical regularities found by Goldsmith, cited above, be explained?

Economic theory offers no answers to these questions. The differences among agents that invite mutually beneficial transactions, like those discussed above, offer opportunities for inside markets. Theory can tell us little *a priori* about the size of such differences. Moreover, markets are costly to operate, whether they are organized auction markets in homogeneous instruments or the imperfect 'markets' in heterogeneous contracts in which financial intermediaries are major participants. Society cannot afford all the markets that might exist in the absence of transactions costs and other frictions, and theory has little to say on which will arise and survive.

The macroeconomic consequence of inside markets and financial intermediaries is generally to provide substitutes for outside assets and thus to economize their supplies. That is, the same microeconomic outcomes are achievable with smaller supplies of one or more of the outside assets than in the absence of intermediation. The way in which intermediation mobilizes the surpluses of some agents to finance the deficits of others is the theme of the classic influential work of Gurley and Shaw (1960).

Consider, for example, how commercial banking diminishes the need of business firms for net worth invested in inventories, by channelling the seasonal cash surpluses of some firms to the contemporaneous seasonal deficits of others. Imagine two firms A and B with opposite and complementary seasonal zigzag patterns. A needs $2 in cash at time zero to buy inputs for production in period 1 sold for $2; the pattern repeats in 3, 4, ... B needs $2 in cash at time 1 to buy inputs for production in period 2 sold for $2 in period 3, and so on in 4, 5, ... In the absence of their commercial bank, A and B each need $2 of net worth to carry on business; from period to period each alternates holding it in cash and in goods-in-process. Between them the two firms always are holding $2 of currency and $2 of inventories. B enters the bank and lends A half the $2 he needs to carry his inventory in period 1; A repays the loan from sales proceeds the next period, 2; the bank now lends $1 to B, ... A and B now need only $1 of currency; each has on average net worth of $1.50–$2 and $1 alternating; as before they are together always holding $2 of inventories. Moreover, with a steady deposit of $2 from a third party, the bank could finance both businesses completely; they would need no net worth of their own. The example is trivial, but commercial banking proper can be understood as circulation of deposits and loans among businesses and as a revolving fund assembled from other sources and lent to businesses.

As a second primitive example, consider the effects of introducing markets that enable risks to be borne by those households more prepared to take them. Suppose that of two primary outside assets, currency and tangible capital, the return on the latter has the greater variance. Individuals who are risk neutral will hold all their wealth (possibly excepting minimal transactions balances of currency) in capital as long as its expected return exceeds the expected real return on currency. If these more adventurous households are not numerous and wealthy enough to absorb all the capital, the expected return on capital will have to exceed that on currency enough to induce risk-averse wealth-owners to hold the remainder. In this equilibrium the money price of capital and its mean real return are determined so as to allocate the two assets between the two kinds of households. Now suppose that the risk-neutral households can borrow from the risk-averse types, most realistically via financial intermediaries, and that the latter households regard those debts as close substitutes for currency, indeed as inside money if intermediation by financial intermediaries is involved. The inside assets do double duty, providing the services and security of money to those who value them while enabling the more adventurous to hold capital in excess of their own net worth. As a result, the private sector as a whole will want to hold a larger proportion of its wealth in capital at any given expected real return on capital. In equilibrium, the aggregate capital stock will be larger and its expected return, equal to its marginal productivity in a steady state, will be lower than in the absence of intermediation.

Intermediation can diminish the private sector's need not just for outside money but for net worth and tangible capital. These economies generally require financial markets in which financial intermediaries are major participants, because they involve heterogeneous credit instruments and risk pooling. In the absence of home mortgages, consumer credit and personal loans for education, young households would not be able to spend their future wages and salaries until they receive them. Constraints on borrowing against future earnings make the age-weighted average net non-human wealth of the population greater, but the relaxation of such liquidity constraints increases household welfare. Financial intermediaries invest the savings of older and more affluent households in loans to their younger and less wealthy contemporaries; otherwise those savings would go into outside assets. Likewise insurance makes it unnecessary to accumulate savings as precaution against certain risks, for example the living and medical expenses of unusual longevity. It is an all too common fallacy to assume that arrangements that increase aggregate savings and tangible wealth always augment social welfare.

DEPOSIT CREATION AND RESERVE REQUIREMENTS

The substitution of inside money for outside money is the familiar story of deposit creation, in which the banking system turns a dollar of base or 'high-powered' money into several dollars of deposits. The extra dollars are inside or 'low-powered' money. The banks need to hold only a fraction k, set by law or convention or prudence, of their deposit liabilities as reserves in base money. In an equilibrium in which they hold no excess reserves their deposits will be a multiple $1/k$ of their reserves; they will have created $(1-k)/k$ dollars of substitute money.

A key step in this process is that any bank with excess reserves makes a roughly equal amount of additional loans, crediting the borrowers with deposits. As the borrowers draw checks, these new deposits are transferred to other accounts, most likely in other banks. As deposits move to other banks, so do reserves, dollar for dollar. But now those banks have excess reserves and act in like manner. The process continues until all banks are 'loaned up', i.e. deposits have increased enough so that the initial excess reserves have become reserves that the banks require or desire.

The textbook fable of deposit creation does not do justice to the full macroeconomics of the process. The story is incomplete without explaining how the public is induced to borrow more and to hold more deposits. The borrowers and the depositors are not the same public. No one borrows at interest in order to hold idle deposits. To attract additional borrowers, banks must lower interest rates or relax their collateral requirements or their risk standards. The new borrowers are likely to be businesses that need bank credit to build up inventories of materials or goods in process. The loans lead quickly to additional production and economic activity. Or banks buy securities in the open market, raising their prices and lowering market interest rates. The lower market rates may encourage businesses to float issues of commercial paper, bonds or stocks, but the effects of investment in inventories or plant and equipment are less immediate and less potent than the extension of bank credit to a business otherwise held back by illiquidity. In either case, lower interest rates induce other members of the public, those who indirectly receive the loan disbursements or those who sell securities to banks, to hold additional deposits. They will be acquiring other assets as well, some in banks, some in other financial intermediaries, some in open financial markets. Lower interest rates may also induce banks themselves to hold extra excess reserves.

Interest rates are not the only variables of adjustment. Nominal incomes are rising at the same time, in some mixture of real quantities and prices depending on macroeconomic circumstances. The rise in incomes and economic activities creates new needs for transactions balances of money. Thus the process by which excess reserves are absorbed entails changes in interest rates, real economic activity and prices in some combination. It is possible to describe scenarios in which the entire ultimate adjustment is in one of these variables. Wicksell's cumulative credit expansion, which in the end just raises prices, is a classic example.

Do banks have a unique magic by which asset purchases generate their own financing? Is the magic due to the 'moneyness' of the banks' liabilities? The preceding account indicates it is not magic but reserve requirements. Moreover, a qualitatively similar story could be told if reserve requirements were related to bank assets or non-monetary liabilities and even if banks happened to have no monetary liabilities at all. In the absence of reserve requirements aggregate bank assets and liabilities, relative to the size of the economy, would be naturally limited by public supplies and demands at interest rates that cover banks' costs and normal profits. If, instead of banks, savings institutions specializing in mortgage lending were subject to reserve requirements, their incentives to minimize excess reserves would inspire a story telling how additional mortgage lending brings home savings deposits to match (Tobin, 1963).

RISKS, RUNS AND REGULATIONS

Some financial intermediaries confine themselves to activities that entail virtually no risk either to the institution itself or to its clients. An open-end mutual fund or unit trust holds only fully liquid assets traded continuously in organized markets. It promises the owners of its shares payment on demand at their pro rata net value calculated at the market prices of the underlying assets – no more, no less. The fund can always meet such demands by selling assets it holds. The shareowners pay in one way or another an agreed fee from the services of the fund – the convenience and flexibility of denomination, the bookkeeping, the transactions costs, the diversification, the expertise in choosing assets. The shareowners bear the market risks on the fund's portfolio – no less and, assuming the fund is honest, no more. Government regulations are largely confined to those governing all public security issues, designed to protect buyers from deceptions and insider manipulations. In the United States regulation of this kind is the province of the federal Securities and Exchange Commission.

Most financial intermediaries do take risks. The risks are intrinsic to the functions they serve and to the profit opportunities attracting financial entrepreneurs and investors in their enterprises. For banks and similar financial intermediaries, the principal risk is that depositors may at any time demand payments the institution can meet, if at all, only at extraordinary cost. Many of the assets are illiquid, unmarketable. Others can be liquidated at short notice only at substantial loss. In some cases, bad luck or imprudent management brings insolvency; the institution could never meet its obligations no matter how long its depositors and other creditors wait. In other cases, the problem is just illiquidity; the assets would suffice if they could be held until maturity, until buyers or lenders could be found, or until normal market conditions returned.

Banks and other financial intermediaries hold reserves, in currency or its equivalent, deposits in central banks, or in other liquid forms as precaution against withdrawals by their depositors. For a single bank, the withdrawal is usually a shift of deposits to other banks or financial intermediaries, arising from a negative balance in interbank clearings of checks or other transfers to third parties at the initiative of depositors. For the banking system, as a whole, withdrawal is a shift by the public from deposits to currency.

'Withdrawals' may in practice include the exercise of previously agreed borrowing rights. Automatic overdraft privileges are more common in other countries, notably the United Kingdom and British Commonwealth nations, than in the United States. They are becoming more frequent in the United States as an adjunct of bank credit cards. Banks' business loan customers often have explicit or implicit credit lines on which they can draw on demand.

Unless financial intermediaries hold safe liquid assets of predictable value matched in maturities to their liabilities – in particular, currency or equivalent against all their demand obligations – they and their creditors can never be completely protected from withdrawals. The same is true of the banking system as a whole, and of all intermediaries other than simple mutual funds. 'Runs', sudden, massive and contagious withdrawals, are always possible. They destroy prudent and imprudent institutions alike, along with their depositors and creditors. Of course, careful depositors inform themselves about the intermediaries to which they entrust their funds, about their asset portfolios, policies and skills. Their choices among competing depositories provide some discipline, but it can never be enough to rule out disasters. What the most careful depositor cannot foresee is the behaviour of other depositors, and it is rational for the well-informed depositor of a sound bank to withdraw funds if he believes that others are doing so or are about to do so.

Governments generally regulate the activies of banks and other financial intermediaries in greater detail than they do nonfinancial enterprises. The basic motivations for regulation appear to be the following:

It is costly, perhaps impossible, for individual depositors to appraise the soundness and liquidity of financial institutions and to estimate the probabilities of failures even if they could assume that other depositors would do likewise. It is impossible for them to estimate the probabilities of 'runs'. Without regulation, the liabilities of suspect institutions would be valued below par in check collections. Prior to 1866 banks in the United States were allowed to issue notes payable to bearers on demand, surrogates for government currency. The notes circulated at discounts varying with the current reputations of the issuers. A system in which transactions media other than government currency continuously vary in value depending on the issuer is clumsy and costly.

The government has an obligation to provide at low social cost an efficient system of transactions media, and also a menu of secure and convenient assets for citizens who wish to save in the national monetary unit of account. Those transactions media and saving assets can be offered by banks and other financial intermediaries, in a way that retains most of the efficiencies of decentralization and competition, if and only if government imposes some regulations and assumes some residual responsibilities. The government's role takes several forms.

Reserve requirements. An early and obvious intervention was to require banks to hold reserves in designated safe and liquid forms against their obligations, especially their demand liabilities. Left to themselves, without such requirements, some banks might sacrifice prudence for short-term profit. Paradoxically, however, required reserves are not available for meeting withdrawals unless the required ratio is 100 per cent. If the reserve requirement is 10 per cent of deposits, then withdrawal of one dollar from a bank reduces its reserve holdings by one dollar but its reserve requirement by only ten cents. Only excess reserves or other liquid assets are precautions against withdrawals. The legal reserve requirement just shifts the bank's prudential calculation to the size of these secondary reserves. Reserve requirements serve functions quite different from their original motivation. In the systems that use them, notably the United States, they are the fulcrum for central bank control of economy-wide monetary conditions. (They are also an interest-free source of finance of government debt, but in the United States today this amounts to only $45 billion of a total debt to the public of $1700 billion.)

Last resort lending. Banks and other financial intermediaries facing temporary shortages of reserves and secondary reserves of liquid assets can borrow them from other institutions. In the United States, for example, the well-organized market for 'federal funds' allows banks short of reserves to borrow them overnight from other banks. Or banks can gain reserves by attracting more deposits, offering higher interest rates on them than depositors are getting elsewhere. These ways of correcting reserve positions are not available to troubled banks, suspected of deep-rooted problems of liquidity or solvency or both, for example bad loans. Nor will they meet a system-wide run from liabilities of banks and other financial intermediaries into currency.

Banks in need of reserves can also borrow from the central bank, and much of this borrowing is routine, temporary and seasonal. Massive central bank credit is the last resort of troubled banks which cannot otherwise satisfy the demands of their depositors without forced liquidations of their assets. The government is the ultimate supplier of currency and reserves in aggregate. The primary *raison d'être* of the central bank is to protect the economy from runs into currency. System-wide shortages of currency and reserves can be relieved not only by central bank lending to individual banks but by central bank purchases of securities in the open market. The Federal Reserve's inability or unwillingness – which it was is still debated – to supply the currency bank depositors wanted in the early 1930s led to disastrous panic and epidemic bank failures. No legal or doctrinal obstacles would now stand in the way of such a rescue.

Deposit insurance. Federal insurance of bank deposits in the United States has effectively prevented contagious runs and epidemic failures since its enactment in 1935. Similar insurance applies to deposits in savings institutions. In effect, the federal government assumes a contingent residual liability to pay the insured deposits in full, even if the assets of the financial intermediary are permanently inadequate to do so. The insured institutions are charged premiums for the service, but the fund in which they are accumulated is not and cannot be large enough to eliminate possible calls on the Treasury. Although the guarantees are legally limited to a certain amount, now $100,000, per account, in practice depositors have eventually recovered their full deposits in most cases. Indeed the guarantee seems now to have been extended *de facto* to all deposits, at least in major banks.

Deposit insurance impairs such discipline as surveillance by large depositors might impose on financial intermediaries; instead the task of surveillance falls on the governmental insurance agencies themselves (in the United States the Federal Deposit Insurance Corporation and the Federal Savings and Loan Insurance Corporation) and on other regulatory authorities (the United States Comptroller of the Currency, the Federal Reserve and various state agencies). Insurance transfers some risks from financial intermediary depositors and owners to taxpayers at large, while virtually eliminating risks of runs. Those are risks we generate ourselves; they magnify the unavoidable natural risks of economic life. Insurance is a mutual compact to enable us to refrain from *sauve qui peut* behaviour that can inflict grave damage on us all. Formally, an uninsured system has two equilibria, a good one with mutual confidence and a bad one with runs. Deposit insurance eliminates the bad one (Diamond and Dybvig, 1983).

One hundred per cent reserve deposits would, of course, be perfectly safe – that is, as safe as the national currency – and would not have to be insured. Those deposits would in effect *be* currency, but in a secure and conveniently checkable form. One can imagine a system in which banks and other financial intermediaries offered such accounts, with the reserves behind them segregated from those related to the other business of the institution. That other business would include receiving deposits which required fractional or zero reserves and were insured only partially, if at all. The costs of the 100 per cent reserve deposit accounts would be met by service charges, or by government interest payments on the reserves, justified by the social benefits of a safe and efficient transactions medium. The burden of risk and supervision now placed on the insuring and regulating agencies would be greatly relieved. It is, after all, historical accident that supplies of transactions media in modern economies came to be byproducts of the banking business and vulnerable to its risks.

Government may insure financial intermediaries loans as well as deposits. Insurance of home mortgages in the United States not only has protected the institutions that hold them and their depositors but has converted the insured mortgages into marketable instruments.

Balance sheet supervision. Government surveillance of financial intermediaries limits their freedom of choice of assets and liabilities, in order to limit the risks to depositors and insurers. Standards of adequacy of capital – owners' equity at risk in the case of private corporations, net worth in the case of mutual and other nonprofit forms of organization – are enforced for the same reasons. Periodic examinations check the condition of the institution, the quality of its loans and the accuracy of its accounting statements. The regulators may close an institution if further operation is judged to be damaging to the interests of the depositors and the insurer.

Legislation which regulates financial intermediaries has differentiated them by purpose and function. Commercial banks, savings institutions, home building societies, credit unions and insurance companies are legally organized for different purposes. They are subject to different rules governing the nature of their assets. For example, home building societies – savings and loan associations in the United States – have been required to keep most of their asset portfolios in residential mortgages. Restrictions of this kind mean that when wealth-owners shift funds from one type of financial intermediary to another, they alter relative demands for assets of different kinds. Shifts of deposits from commercial banks to building societies would increase mortgage lending relative to commercial lending. Regulations have also restricted the kinds of liabilities allowed various types of financial intermediary. Until recently in the United States, only banks were permitted to have liabilities payable on demand to third parties by check or wire. Currently deregulation is relaxing specialized restrictions on financial intermediary assets and liabilities and blurring historical distinctions of purpose and function.

Interest ceilings. Government regulations in many countries set ceilings on the interest rates that can be charged on loans and on the rates that can be paid on deposits, both at banks and at other financial intermediaries. In the United States the Banking Act of 1935 prohibited payment of interest on demand deposits. After World War II effective ceilings on savings and time deposits in banks and savings institutions were administratively set, and on occasion changed, by federal agencies. Under legislation of 1980, these regulations are being phased out.

The operating characteristics of a system of financial intermediaries in which interest rates on deposits of various types, as well as on loans, are set by free competition are quite different from those of a system in which financial intermediary rates are subject to legal ceilings or central bank guidance, or set by agreement among a small number of institutions. For example, when rates on deposits are administratively set, funds flow out of financial intermediaries when open market rates rise and return to financial intermediaries when they fall. These processes of 'disintermediation' and 're-intermediation' are diminished when financial intermediary rates are free to move parallel to open market rates. Likewise flows between differential financial intermediaries due to administratively set rate differences among them are reduced when they are all free to compete for funds.

A regime with market-determined interest rates on moneys and near-moneys has significantly different macroeconomic characteristics from a regime constrained by ceilings on deposit interest rates. Since the opportunity cost of holding deposits is largely independent of the general level of interest rates, the 'LM' curve is steeper in the unregulated regime. Both central bank operations and exogenous monetary shocks could be expected to have larger effects on nominal income, while fiscal measures and other shocks to aggregate demand for goods and services would have smaller effects (Tobin, 1983).

Entry, branching, merging. Entry into regulated financial businesses is generally controlled, as are establishing branches or subsidiaries and merging of existing institutions. In the United States, charters are issued either by the federal government or by state governments, and regulatory powers are also divided. Until recently banks and savings institutions, no matter by whom chartered, were not allowed to operate in more than one state. This rule, combined with various restrictions on branches within states, gave the United States a much larger number of distinct financial enterprises, many of them very small and very local, than is typical in other countries. The prohibition of interstate operations is now being eroded and may be effectively eliminated in the next few years.

Deregulation has been forced by innovations in financial technology that made old regulations either easy hurdles to circumvent or obsolete barriers to efficiency. New opportunities not only are breaking down the walls separating financial intermediaries of different types and specializations. They are also bringing other businesses, both financial and nonfinancial, into activities previously reserved to regulated financial institutions. Mutual funds and brokers offer accounts from which funds can be withdrawn on demand or transferred to third parties by check or wire. National retail chains are becoming financial supermarkets – offering credit cards, various mutual funds, instalment lending and insurance along with their vast menus of consumer goods and services; in effect, they would like to become full-service financial intermediaries. At the same time, the traditional intermediaries are moving, as fast as they can obtain government permission, into lines of business from which they have been excluded. Only time will tell how these commercial and political conflicts are resolved and how the financial system will be reshaped (*Economic Report of the President*, 1985, ch. 5).

PORTFOLIO BEHAVIOUR OF FINANCIAL INTERMEDIARIES

A large literature has attempted to estimate econometrically the choices of assets and liabilities by financial intermediaries, their relationships to open market interest rates and to other variables exogenous to them. Models of the portfolio behaviour of the various species of financial intermediary also involve estimation of the supplies of funds to them, and the demands for credit, from other sectors of the economy particularly households and nonfinancial businesses. Recent research is presented in Dewald and Friedman (1980).

Difficult econometric problems arise in using time series for these purposes because of regime changes. For example, when deposit interest rate ceilings are effective, financial intermediaries are quantity-takers in the deposit markets; when the ceilings are non-constraining or non-existent, both the interest rates and the quantities are determined jointly by the schedules of supplies of deposits by the public and of demands for them by the financial intermediary. Similar problems arise in credit markets where interest rates, even though unregulated, are administered by financial intermediaries themselves and move sluggishly. The prime commercial loan rate is one case; mortgage rates in various periods are another. In these cases and others, the markets are not cleared at the established rates. Either the financial intermediary or the borrowers are quantity-takers, or perhaps both in some proportions. Changes in the rates follow, dependent on the amount of excess demand or supply. These problems of modelling and econometric estimation are discussed in papers in the reference above. The seminal paper is Modigliani and Jaffee (1969).

BIBLIOGRAPHY

Barro, R. 1974. Are government bonds net wealth? *Journal of Political Economy* 82(6), November–December, 1095–117.

Dewald, W.G. and Friedman, B.M. 1980. Financial market behavior, capital formation, and economic performance. (A conference supported by the National Science Foundation.) *Journal of Money, Credit, and Banking*, Special Issue 12(2), May.

Diamond, D.W. and Dybvig, P.H. 1983. Bank runs, deposit insurance, and liquidity. *Journal of Political Economy* 91(3), June, 401–19.

Economic Report of the President. 1985. Washington, DC: Government Printing Office, February.

Federal Reserve System, Board of Governors. 1984. *Balance Sheets for the US Economy 1945–83*. November, Washington, DC.

Fisher, I. 1930. *The Theory of Interest*. New York: Macmillan.

Goldsmith, R.W. 1969. *Financial Structure and Development*. New Haven: Yale University Press.

Goldsmith, R.W. 1985. *Comparative National Balance Sheets: A Study of Twenty Countries, 1688–1978*. Chicago: University of Chicago Press.

Gurley, J.G. and Shaw, E.S. 1969. *Money in a Theory of Finance*. Washington, DC: Brookings Institution.

Modigliani, F. and Miller, M.H. 1958. The cost of capital, corporation finance and the theory of investment. *American Economic Review* 48(3), June, 261–97.

Modigliani, F. and Jaffee, D.M. 1969. A theory and test of credit rationing. *American Economic Review* 59(5), December, 850–72.

Schumpeter, J.A. 1911. *The Theory of Economic Development*. Trans. from the German by R. Opie, Cambridge, Mass.: Harvard University Press, 1934.

Tobin, J. 1963. Commercial banks as creators of 'money'. In *Banking and Monetary Studies*, ed. D. Carson, Homewood, Ill.: Richard D. Irwin.

Tobin, J. 1980. *Asset Accumulation and Economic Activity*. Oxford: Blackwell; Chicago: University of Chicago Press.

Tobin, J. 1983. Financial structure and monetary rules. *Kredit und Kapital* 16(2), 155–71.

Tobin, J. 1984. On the efficiency of the financial system. *Lloyds Bank Review* 153, July, 1–15.

Agency Costs

CLIFFORD W. SMITH, JR.

In the traditional analysis of the firm, profit maximization is assumed, subject to the constraints of a technological production function for transforming inputs into output. Optimum production solutions are characterized in terms of the equality between the ratio of marginal products of inputs and the ratio of input prices. While this analysis has provided valuable insights in understanding certain aspects of choices by firms, it completely ignores others having to do with the process through which the inputs are organized and coordinated. In essence, the traditional economic analysis treats the firm as a black box in this transformation of inputs into output. Rarely are questions raised such as: Why are some firms organized as individual proprietorships, some as partnerships, some as corporations and others as cooperatives or mutuals? Why are some firms financed primarily by equity and others with debt? Why are some inputs owned and others leased? Why do some industries make extensive use of franchising while others do not? Why do some bonds contain call provisions, convertibility provisions, or sinking fund provisions while others do not? Why are some executives compensated with salary while others have extensive stock option or bonus plans? Why do some industries pay workers on a piece-rate basis while others pay at an hourly rate? Why do some firms employ one accounting procedure while others choose alternate procedures? To answer such questions requires the economic analysis of contractual relationships. Agency Theory provides a framework for such an analysis.

An agency relationship is defined through an explicit or implicit contract in which one or more persons (the principal(s)) engage another person (the agent) to take actions on behalf of the principal(s). The contract involves the delegation of some decision-making authority to the agent. Agency costs are the total costs of structuring, administering and enforcing such contracts. Agency costs, therefore, encompass all contracting costs frequently referred to as transactions costs, moral hazard costs and information costs.

53

Jensen and Meckling (1976) break down agency costs into three components: (1) monitoring expenditures by the principal, (2) bonding expenditures by the agent, and (3) the residual loss. Monitoring expenditures are paid by the principal to regulate the agent's conduct. Bonding expenditures are made by the agent to help assure that the agent will not take actions which damage the principal or will indemnify the principal if the prescribed actions are undertaken. Hence, monitoring and bonding costs are the out-of-pocket costs of structuring, administering and enforcing contracts. The residual loss is the value of the loss by the principal from decisions by the agent which deviate from the decisions which would have been made by the principal if he had the same information and talents as the agent. Since it is profitable to invest in policing contracts only to the point where the reduction in the loss from non-compliance equals the incremental costs of enforcement, the residual loss is the opportunity loss when contracts are optimally, but incompletely enforced.

Jensen and Mecklin (1976) point out that agency problems emanating from conflicts of interests are common to most cooperative endeavours whether or not they occur in the hierarchical manner implied in the principal–agent analogy. But, with the elimination of the difference between principal and agent, the distinction between monitoring and bonding costs is also lost; so, total agency costs are out-of-pocket costs plus the opportunity cost or residual loss.

It is crucial to recognize that the contracting parties bear the agency costs associated with their interaction and therefore have incentives to structure contracts to reduce agency costs wherever possible. Within the contracting process, incentives exist for individuals to negotiate contracts specifying monitoring and bonding activities so long as their marginal cost is less than the marginal gain from reducing the residual loss. Specifically, the contracting parties gain from forecasting accurately the actions to be undertaken and structuring the contracts to facilitate the expected actions. For example, with competitive and informationally efficient financial markets, unbiased estimates of agency costs should be included in the prices of securities when they are initially offered (as well as at any future date). This mechanism provides incentives to structure contracts and institutions to lower agency costs. Hence, in the absence of the usual externalities, the private contracting process produces an efficient allocation of resources.

Jensen (1983) describes two approaches to the development of a theory of agency which he labels the 'positive theory of agency' and the 'principal–agent' literatures. Both approaches examine contracting among self-interested individuals and both postulate that agency costs are minimized through the contracting process; thus, both address the design of Pareto-efficient contracts. However the approaches diverge at several junctures. The principal–agent literature generally has a mathematical and non-empirical orientation and concentrates on the effects of preferences and asymmetric information (for example, Harris and Raviv, 1978; Holmstrom, 1979; Ross, 1973; and Spence and Zeckhauser, 1971). The positive agency literature generally has a non-mathematical and empirical focus and concentrates on the effects of the contracting technology and specific human or physical capital (for example, Fama and Jensen, 1983a, 1983b; Jensen and Meckling, 1976; Myers, 1977; and Smith and Warner, 1979).

The investigation of agency costs has provided a deeper understanding of many dimensions of complex contractual arrangements, especially the modern corporate form. One can better understand the variation in contractual forms across organizations by studying the nature of the agency costs in alternative contractual arrangements. For example, Fama and Jensen (1983a) examine the nature of residual claims and the agency costs of separation of management and riskbearing to provide a theory of the determinants of alternative organizational forms. They argue that corporations, proprietorships, partnerships, mutuals and non-profits differ in the manner they trade off the benefits of risk-sharing with agency costs.

Agency cost analysis has been employed to examine the choice of organizational structure in the insurance (Mayers and Smith, 1981, 1986) and thrift industries (Smith, 1982; and Masulis, 1986). It has also been employed to examine the determinants of the firm's capital structure (Jensen and Meckling, 1976; Myers, 1977); the provisions in corporate bond contracts (Smith and Warner, 1979); the determinants of corporate leasing policy (Smith and Wakeman, 1985) and franchise policy (Brickley and Dark, 1987); the incentives for the development of a hierarchical structure within organizations (Zimmerman, 1979; Fama and Jensen, 1983b); and the determinants of corporate compensation policy (Smith and Watts, 1982). Finally, the analysis of agency costs has played a central role in the development of a positive theory of the choice of accounting techniques (Watts and Zimmerman, 1986).

Agency analysis has also afforded a different perspective in assessing the implications of observed contractual provisions. For example, typical discussions of mortgage loan provisions suggest that escrow accounts and limitations on renting the property are included in the loan contract for the benefit of the lender. However, if there is competition among lenders, these benefits must be reflected in compensating differentials in other loan terms, such as lower promised interest rates. If in addition, the rates on other securities are not affected by changes in the terms of this contract, then all of the benefits of these convenants must ultimately accrue to the borrower, not the lender.

BIBLIOGRAPHY

Brickley, J.A. and Dark, F.H. 1987. The choice of organizational form: the case of franchising. *Journal of Financial Economics*.

Fama, E. and Jensen, M. 1983a. Agency problems and residual claims. *Journal of Law and Economics*, June, 327–49.

Fama, E. and Jensen, M. 1983b. Separation of ownership and control. *Journal of Law and Economics* 26, 301–25.

Harris, M. and Raviv, A. 1978. Some results on incentive contracts with applications to education and employment, health insurance and law enforcement. *American Economic Review* 68, 20–30.

Holmstrom, B. 1979. Moral hazard and observability. *Bell Journal of Economics* 10(1), 74–91.

Jensen, M. 1983. Organization theory and methodology. *Accounting Review* 58, 319–39.

Jensen, M. and Meckling, W. 1976. Theory of the firm: managerial behavior, agency costs and ownership structure. *Journal of Financial Economics* 3, 305–60.

Masulis, R. 1986. Changes in ownership structure: conversions of mutual savings and loans to stock charter. *Journal of Financial Economics*.

Mayers, D. and Smith, C. 1981. Contractual provisions, organizational structure, and conflict control in insurance markets. *Journal of Business* 54, 407–34.

Mayers, D. and Smith, C. 1986. Ownership structure and control: the mutualization of stock life insurance companies. *Journal of Financial Economics* 16.

Myers, S. 1977. Determinants of corporate borrowing. *Journal of Financial Economics* 5, 147–75.

Ross, S. 1973. The economic theory of agency: the principal's problem. *American Economic Review* 63, 134–9.

Smith, C. 1982. Pricing mortgage originations. *AREUEA Journal* 10, Fall, 313–30.

Smith, C. and Wakeman, L. 1985. Determinants of corporate leasing policy. *Journal of Finance*, July, 895–908.

Smith, C. and Warner, J. 1979. On financial contracting: an analysis of bond covenants. *Journal of Financial Economics*, June, 117–61.

Smith, C. and Watts, R. 1982. Incentive and tax effects of U.S. executive compensation plans. *Australian Journal of Management*, December, 139–57.

Spence, M. and Zeckhauser, R. 1971. Insurance, information, and individual action. *American Economic Review* 61, 119–32.

Watts, R. and Zimmerman, J. 1986. *Positive Accounting Theory*. Englewood Cliffs, NJ: Prentice-Hall.

Zimmerman, J. 1979. The costs and benefits of cost allocations. *The Accounting Review* 54, 504–21.

Arbitrage

PHILIP H. DYBVIG AND STEPHEN A. ROSS

An arbitrage opportunity is an investment strategy that gurantees a positive payoff in some contingency with no possibility of a negative payoff and with no net investment. By assumption, it is possible to run the arbitrage possibility at arbitrary scale; in other words, an arbitrage opportunity represents a money pump. A simple example of arbitrage is the opportunity to borrow and lend costlessly at two different fixed rates of interest. Such a disparity between the two rates cannot persist: arbitrageurs will drive the rate together.

The modern study of arbitrage is the study of the implications of assuming that no arbitrage opportunities are available. Assuming no arbitrage is compelling because the presence of arbitrage is inconsistent with equilibrium when preferences increase with quantity. More fundamentally, the presence of arbitrage is inconsistent with the existence of an optimal portfolio strategy for *any* competitive agent who prefers more to less, because there is no limit to the scale at which an individual would want to hold the arbitrage position. Therefore, in principle, absence of arbitrage follows from individual rationality of a single agent. One appeal of results based on the absence of arbitrage is the intuition that absence of arbitrage is more primitive than equilibrium, since only relatively few rational agents are needed to bid away arbitrage opportunities, even in the presence of a sea of agents driven by 'animal spirits'.

The absence of arbitrage is very similar to the zero economic profit condition for a firm with constant returns to scale (and no fixed factors). If such a firm had an activity which yielded positive profits, there would be no limit to the scale at which the firm would want to run the activity and no optimum would exist. The theoretical distinction between a zero profit condition and the absence of arbitrage is the distinction between commerce and simply trading under the price system, namely that commerce requires production. In practice, the distinction blurs. For example, if gold is sold at different prices in two markets, there is an arbitrage opportunity but it requires production (transportation of the gold) to take advantage of the opportunity. Furthermore, there are almost always costs to trading in markets (for example, brokerage fees), and therefore a form of costly production is required to convert cash into a security. For the purposes of this entry, we will tend to ignore production. In practical applications the necessity of production will weaken the implications of absence of arbitrage and may drive a wedge between what the pure absence of arbitrage would predict and what actually occurs.

The assertion that two *perfect* substitutes (e.g. two shares of stock in the same company) must trade at the same price is an implication of no arbitrage that goes under the name of the law of one price. While the law of one price is an immediate consequence of the absence of arbitrage, it is not equivalent to the absence of arbitrage. An early use of a no arbitrage condition employed the law of one price to help explain the pattern of prices in the foreign exchange and commodities markets.

Many economic arguments use the absence of arbitrage implicitly. In discussions of purchasing power parity in international trade, for example, presumably it is an arbitrage possibility that forces the spot exchange rate between currencies to equal the relative prices of common baskets of (traded) goods. Similarly, the statement that the possibility of repackaging implies linear prices in competitive product markets is essentially a no-arbitrage argument.

EARLY USES OF THE LAW OF ONE PRICE

The parity theory of forward exchange based on the law of one price was first formulated by Keynes (1923) and developed further by Einzig (1937). Let s denote the current spot price of, say, German marks, in terms of dollars, and let f denote the forward price of marks one year in the future. The forward price is the price at which agreements can be struck currently for the future delivery of marks with no money changing hands today. Also, let r_s and r_m denote the one year dollar and mark interest rates, respectively. To prevent an arbitrage possibility from developing, these four prices must stand in a particular relation.

To see this, consider the choices facing a holder of dollars. The holder can lend the dollars in the domestic market and realize a return of r_s one year from now. Alternatively, the investor can purchase marks on the spot market, lend for one year in the German market, and convert the marks back into dollars one year from now at the fixed forward rate. By undertaking the conversion back into dollars in the forward market, the investor locks in the prevailing forward rate, f. The results of this latter path are a return of

$$f(1 + r_m)/s$$

dollars one year from now. If this exceeds $1 + r_s$, then the foreign route offers a sure higher return than domestic lending. By borrowing dollars at the domestic rate r_s and lending them in the foreign market, a sure profit at the rate

$$f(1 + r_m)/s - (1 + r_s)$$

can be made with no net investment of funds,. Alternatively, if the foreign route provides a lower return, then by running the arbitrage in reverse, i.e., by selling dollars forward, borrowing against them and converting the resulting marks into dollars on the spot market, the investor will collect an amount which, when lent in the domestic market at the dollar interest rate, r_S, will produce more dollars than were sold forward.

Thus, the prevention of arbitrage will enforce the forward parity result,

$$(1 + r_S)/(1 + r_m) = f/s.$$

This result takes on many different forms as we look across different markets. In a commodity market with costless storage, for example, an arbitrage opportunity will arise if the following relation does not hold:

$$f \leqslant s(1 + r).$$

In this equation, f is the currently quoted forward rate for the purchase of the commodity, e.g., silver, one year from now, s is the current spot price, and r is the interest rate. More generally, if c is the up-front proportional carrying cost, including such items as storage costs, spoilage and insurance, absence of arbitrage ensures that

$$f \leqslant s(1 + c)(1 + r).$$

(We normally would expect these relations to hold with equality in a market in which positive stocks are held at all points in time, and perhaps with inequality in a market which may not have positive stocks just before a harvest. However, proving equality is based on equilibrium arguments, not on the absence of arbitrage, since to short the physical commodity you must first own a positive amount.)

The above applications of the absence of arbitrage (via the law of one price) share the common characteristic of the absence of risk. The law of one price is less restrictive than the absence of arbitrage because it deals only with the case in which two assets are identical but have different prices. It does not cover cases in which one asset dominates another but may do so by different amounts in different states. The most interesting applications of the absence of arbitrage are to be found in uncertain situations, where this distinction may be important.

THE FUNDAMENTAL THEOREM OF ASSET PRICING

The absence of arbitrage is implied by the existence of an optimum for any agent who prefers more to less. The most important implication of the absence of arbitrage is the existence of a positive linear pricing rule, which in many spaces including finite state spaces is the same as the existence of positive state prices that correctly price all assets. Taken together with their converses, we refer collectively to these results as the *Fundamental Theorem of Asset Pricing*. (In the past, the emphasis has been on the linear pricing rule as an implication of the absence of arbitrage. Adding the other result emphasizes why we are concerned with the absence of arbitrage in the first place.) We state the theorem verbally here; the formal meanings of the words and the proof are given later in this section.

Theorem: (Fundamental Theorem of Asset Pricing) The following are equivalent:

(i)   Absence of arbitrage
(ii) Existence of a positive linear pricing rule
(iii) Existence of an optimal demand for some agent who prefers more to less.

Beja (1971) was one of the first to emphasize explicitly the linearity of the asset pricing function, but he did not link it to the absence of arbitrage. Beja simply assumed that equilibrium prices existed and observed 'that equilibrium properties require that the functional q be linear', where q is a functional that assigns a price or value to a risky cash flow. The first statement and proof that the absence of arbitrage implied the existence of nonnegative state space prices and, more generally, of a positive linear operator that could be used to value risky assets appeared in Ross (1976a, 1978). Besides providing a formal analysis, Ross showed that there was a pricing rule that prices *all* assets and not just those actually marketed. (In other words, the linear pricing rule could be extended from the marketed assets to all hypothetical assets defined over the same set of states.) The advantage of this extension is that the domain of the pricing function does not depend on the set of marketed assets. We will largely follow Ross's analysis with some modern improvements.

Linearity for pricing means that the price functional or operator q satisfies the ordinary linear condition of algebra. If we let x and y be two random payoffs and we let q be the operator that assigns values to prospects, then we require that

$$q(ax + by) = aq(x) + bq(y),$$

where a and b are arbitrary constants. Of course, for many spaces (including a finite state space), any linear functional can be represented as a sum or integral across states of state prices times quantities.

To simplify proofs in this essay, we will make the assumption that there are finitely many states, each of which occurs with positive probability, and that all claims purchased today pay off at a single future date. Let Θ denote the state space,

$$\Theta = \{1, \ldots, m\},$$

where there are m states and the state of nature θ occurs with probability π_θ. Applying q to the 'indicator' asset e_θ whose payoff is 1 in state θ and 0 otherwise, we can define a price q_θ for each state θ as the value of e_θ;

$$q_\theta = q(e_\theta).$$

Now, if there were linearity, the value of any payoff, x, could be written as

$$q(x) = \Sigma_\theta q_\theta x_\theta.$$

Of course, this argument presupposes that $q(e_\theta)$ is well defined, which is a strong assumption if e_θ is not marketed.

We want to make a statement about the conditions under which all marketed assets can be priced by such a linear pricing rule q. We assume that there is a set of n marketed assets with a corresponding price vector, p. Asset i has a terminal payoff $X_{\theta i}$ (inclusive of dividends, etc.) in state of nature θ. The matrix $X \equiv [X_{\theta i}]$ denotes the state space tableau whose columns correspond to assets and whose rows correspond to states. Lowercase x represents the random vector of terminal payoffs to the various securities. An arbitrage opportunity is a portfolio (vector) η with two properties. It does not cost anything today or in any state in the future. And, it has a positive payoff either today or in some state in the future (or both). We can express the first property as a pair of vector inequalities. The initial cost is not greater than zero, which is to say that it uses no wealth and may actually generate some,

$$p\eta \leqslant 0, \tag{1}$$

and its random payoff later is never negative,

$$X\eta \geqslant 0, \tag{2}$$

(We use the notation that $\geqslant$ denotes greater or equal in each component, $>$ denotes $\geqslant$ and greater in some component, and $\gg$ denotes greater in all components. Note that writing the price of X_η as p_η for arbitrary η embodies an assumption that investment in marketed assets is divisible.) The second property says that the arbitrage portfolio η has a strict inequality, either in (1) or in some component of (2). We can express both properties together as

$$X_*\eta \equiv \begin{bmatrix} -p \\ X \end{bmatrix}\eta > 0. \tag{3}$$

Here, we have stacked the net payoff today on top of the vector of payoffs at the future date. This is in the spirit of the Arrow–Debreu model in which consumption in different states, commodities, points of time and so forth, are all considered components of one large consumption vector.

The absence of arbitrage is simply the condition that no η satisfies (3). A consistent positive linear pricing rule is a vector of state prices $q \gg 0$ that correctly prices all marketed assets, i.e. such that

$$p = qX. \tag{4}$$

We have now collected enough definitions to prove the first half (that (i)$\Leftrightarrow$(ii)) of the Fundamental Theorem of Asset Pricing.

Theorem: (First half of the Fundamental Theorem of Asset Pricing) There is no arbitrage if and only if there exists a consistent positive linear pricing rule.

Proof: The proof that having a consistent positive linear pricing rule precludes arbitrage is simple, since any arbitrage opportunity gives a direct violation of (4). Let η be an arbitrage opportunity. By (4),

$$p\eta = qX\eta,$$

or equivalently

$$0 = -p\eta + q(X\eta) = [1 \; q]X_*\eta.$$

By definition of an arbitrage opportunity (3) and positivity of q, we have a contradiction.

The proof that the absence of arbitrage implies the existence of a consistent positive linear pricing rule is more subtle and requires a separation theorem. The mathematical problem is equivalent to Farkas' Lemma of the alternative and to the basic duality theorem of linear programming. We will adopt an approach that is analogous to the proof of the second theorem of welfare economics that asserts the existence of a price vector which supports any efficient allocation, by separating the aggregate Pareto optimal allocation from all aggregate allocations corresponding to Pareto preferable allocations. Here we will find a price vector that 'supports' an arbitrage-free allocation by separating the net trades from the set of free lunches (the positive orthant).

The absence of arbitrage is equivalent to the requirement that the linear space of net trades defined by

$$s \equiv \{y | \text{for some } \eta, \; y = X_*\eta\}, \tag{5}$$

does not intersect the positive orthant $\mathscr{R}_+^{m+1} \equiv \{y | y \geqslant 0\}$ except at the origin, i.e., $S \cap \mathscr{R}_+^{m+1} = \{0\}$.

Since S is a subspace (and is therefore a convex closed cone), a simple separation theorem (Karlin, 1959, Theorem B3.5) implies that there exists a nonzero vector q_* such that for all $y \in S$ and all $z \in \mathscr{R}_+^{m+1}$, $z \neq 0$, we must have

$$q_* z > 0 \geqslant q_* y. \tag{6}$$

Letting z be each of the unit vectors in turn, the first inequality in (6) implies that q_* is a strictly positive vector.

Since S is a subspace, the second inequality in (6) must hold with equality for all $y \in S$. Define

$$q \equiv (q_{*2}, q_{*3}, \ldots, q_{*n}) / q_{*1}.$$

Since $q_* \gg 0$, likewise $q \gg 0$. Dividing the second equality in (6) (which we now know to be an equality) by q_{*1} and expanding using the definition of X_* [from (3)], we have that

$$0 = -p + qX,$$

or

$$p = qX,$$

which shows that q is a consistent positive linear pricing rule. $\qquad\square$

Before we can prove the second half of the pricing theorem, we need to define the maximization problem faced by a typical investor. In this problem, all we really need to assume is that more is preferred (strictly) to less, i.e. that increasing initial consumption or random consumption later in one or more states always leads to a preferred outcome. In fact, this is literally all we need: we do not need completeness or even transitivity of preferences, let alone a utility function representatuion or any restriction to a functional form. However, for concreteness, we will write down preferences using a state-dependent utility function of consumption now and in the future. The assumption that the investor prefers more to less is satisfied if the utility function in each state is increasing in consumption at both dates.

The state-dependent restriction implies that the maximization problem faced by a particular agent is the maximization of the expectation of the state dependent utility function $u_\theta(\cdot, \cdot)$ of initial wealth and terminal wealth, given initial wealth w_0 and the possibility of trading in the security market. Then the maximization problem faced by a typical agent is the unconstrained choice of a vector α of portfolio weights to maximize

$$\Sigma_\theta \pi_\theta u_\theta [w_0 - p\alpha, (X\alpha)_\theta].$$

The quantity $p\alpha$ is the price of the portfolio, and therefore $w_0 - p\alpha$ is the residual amount of the initial wealth available for initial consumption. The preferences of the agent are said to be increasing if each $u_\theta(\cdot, \cdot)$ is (strictly) increasing in both arguments. Saying the agent prefers more to less is just another way of saying that preferences are increasing.

Here is the rest of the proof of the Fundamental Theorem of Asset Pricing.

Theorem: (Second half of the Fundamental Theory of Asset Pricing) There is no arbitrage if and only if there exists some (at least hypothetical) agent with increasing preferences whose choice problem has a maximum.

Proof: If there is an arbitrage opportunity η, then clearly the choice problem for an agent with increasing preferences cannot have a maximum, since for every α,

$$\Sigma_\theta \pi_\theta u_\theta \{w_0 - p(\alpha + k\eta), [X(\alpha + k\eta)]_\theta\}$$

increases as k increases.

Conversely, if there is no arbitrage, by the first half of the Fundamental Theorem of Asset Pricing (proven earlier), there exists a consistent positive linear pricing rule q. Let $w_0 = 0$ and $\alpha = 0$. Consider the particular utility function

$$u_{*\theta}(c_0, c_1) \equiv -\exp[-(c_0 - w_0)] - (q_\theta/\pi_\theta)\exp(-c_1). \tag{7}$$

Each function $u_{*\theta}$ is strictly increasing and also happens to be strictly concave, infinitely differentiable and additively separable over time. Using $p = qX$, it is easy to show that this utility function satisfies the first order conditions for a maximum, which are necessary and sufficient by concavity. (Note: by a more complicated argument, it can be shown that the von Neumann–Morgenstern 'state independent' utility function $-\exp(-c_0) - \exp(-c_1)$ has a maximum, but the maximum will not necessarily be achieved at $\alpha = 0$.) □

As should be clear from the proof, it is not really important what class of preferences we use, so long as all agents having preferences in the class prefer more to less and the class includes the particular preferences used in the proof (which are additive over states and time, increasing, concave and infinitely differentiable).

Recent research on arbitrage, starting with Ross (1978) and Harrison and Kreps (1979), has focused on extending these results to more general state spaces in which there are many time periods and, more importantly, infinitely many states. In these spaces, deriving a positive linear pricing rule for marketed claims is still straightforward (you can prove the algebraic linearity condition and positively directly from the no arbitrage condition), but extending the pricing rule from the priced claims to all non-marketed claims requires some sort of extension theorem, such as a Hahn–Banach theorem. Obtaining a truly general result is complicated by the fact that the positive orthant is not typically an open set in these general spaces, and openness is a condition of the Hahn–Banach theorems. One part of the result that goes through in general is the implication that existence of an optimum implies existence of a linear pricing rule: so long as preferences are continuous in our topology, the preferred set will be open, and the linear pricing rule will be a hyperplane that separates the optimum from the preferred set.

ALTERNATIVE REPRESENTATIONS OF LINEAR PRICING RULES

There are many equivalent ways of representing a linear pricing rule. Which representation is simplest depends on the context. In one representation, the price is the expected value under artificial 'risk-neutral' probabilities discounted at the riskless rate. (The risk-neutral probability measure is also referred to as an equivalent martingale measure.) In another representation, the price is the expectation of the quantity times the state price density, which is the state price per unit probability. In yet another representation, the price is the expected value discounted at a risk-adjusted rate. The purpose of this section is to show the fundamental equivalence of these representations.

The motive for using a particular representation is usually found in the study of intertemporal models or models with a continuum of states. Nonetheless, we will continue our formal analysis of the single-period model with finitely many states, leaving the more general discussion of the merits of the various approaches until afterwards. Now, we have already seen the basic linear pricing rule representation. For any portfolio α,

$$p\alpha = qX\alpha$$
$$= \Sigma_\theta q_\theta (X\alpha)_\theta, \tag{8}$$

i.e. the sum across states of state price times the payoff.

The risk-neutral or martingale representation asserts the existence of a vector Π of artificial probabilities and a shadow riskless rate r such that

$$p\alpha = (1+r)^{-1}\Pi X\alpha$$
$$= (1+r)^{-1}E_\Pi(X\alpha), \tag{9}$$

i.e., the expectation E_Π of the payoff under the risk-neutral (martingale) probabilities Π, discounted at the riskless rate. It is easy to see the shadow riskless rate is equal to the riskless rate if one exists. The risk neutral approach is trivially equivalent to the positive linear pricing rule approach. Simply let

$$\Pi = q/\Sigma_\theta q_\theta \tag{10}$$

and

$$(1+r)^{-1} = \Sigma_\theta q_\theta. \tag{11}$$

For the converse, let

$$q = (1+r)^{-1}\Pi. \tag{12}$$

Therefore, the existence of a positive linear pricing rule is the same as the existence of positive risk-neutral probabilities. (The risk-neutral measure is equivalent to the original probability measure, i.e. Π has the same null sets as π. Here, that is simply the requirement that the list of states with positive probability is the same for both measures.)

A third approach emphasizes the role of the state price density, ρ_θ. In this case, the price is given by

$$p\alpha = \Sigma_\theta \pi_\theta \rho_\theta (X\alpha)_\theta$$
$$= E(\rho x \alpha). \tag{13}$$

To see that this is equivalent to the linear pricing rule, simply let

$$\rho_\theta = q_\theta/\pi_\theta, \tag{14}$$

or, conversely, let

$$q_\theta = \rho_\theta \pi_\theta. \tag{15}$$

Clearly, ρ is positive in all states if and only if q is.

We have shown the equivalence of these three approaches. This equivalence is stated in the following theorem.

Theorem: (Pricing Rule Representation Theorem) The following are equivalent:

 (i) Existence of a positive linear pricing rule
 (ii) Existence of positive risk-neutral probabilities and an associated riskless rate (the martingale property)
(iii) Existence of a positive state price density.

The remaining representation is that the value is equal to the terminal value discounted at a risk-adjusted interest rate r_a,

$$p\alpha = (1+r_a)^{-1}E(x\alpha). \tag{16}$$

While this might at first appear to be inconsistent with the other representations, the risk-adjusted rate r_a is typically proportional to the covariance of return

65

($= x\alpha/p\alpha$) with some random variable, and consequently solving this equation for $p\alpha$ yields a linear rule. (See Beja, 1971, and Rubinstein, 1976, for general results concerning pricing rules using covariances.) For example, in the Capital Asset Pricing Model,

$$r_a = r + \lambda \operatorname{cov}(x\alpha/p\alpha, r_m), \tag{17}$$

where r_m is the random return on the market and λ is the market price of risk. Solving these two equations for $p\alpha$, we obtain

$$p\alpha = (1 + r)^{-1} E[x\alpha\{1 - \lambda[r_m - E(r_m)]\}], \tag{18}$$

which is certainly linear in $x\alpha$. The subtle question is whether or not this is positive, and this hinges on whether the market return can get larger than $E(r_m) + 1/\lambda$ (Dybvig and Ingersoll, 1982). In any case, the important observation is that the basic form of the representation is linear even if verification of positivity depends on the exact form of the risk premium.

Now we return to the question of the comparative advantages of the various representations. The risk-neutral or martingale representation was first employed by Cox and Ross (1976a) for use in option pricing problems and was later developed more formally by Harrison and Kreps (1979) and a number of others. The risk-neutral representation is particularly useful for problems of valuation or optimization without reference to individual preferences, since under the martingale probabilities we can ignore risk altogether and maximize discounted expected value. In fact, for some problems, this approach tells us that risk-neutral results generalize immediately to worlds where risk is priced. However, this approach tends to be complicated when preferences are introduced, since von Neumann–Morgenstern (state independent) preferences under ordinary probabilities become state dependent under the martingale probabilities. As an aside, we note that in intertemporal contexts in which the interest rate is stochastic, the price is the risk-neutral expectation of the future value discounted by the rolled-over spot rate (which is stochastic).

The state price density representation (Cox and Leland, 1982, and Dybvig, 1980, 1985), is most useful when we want to look at choice problems. For von Neumann–Morgenstern preferences, the state price density is equal to the marginal utility of consumption, for some consistent positive state price density (Dybvig and Ross, 1982). (Note that if there is a non-atomic continuum of states, the state price density will typically be well-defined even though all primitive states have probability zero and state price zero.)

The representation of discounting expected returns using a risk-adjusted discount rate is most useful when we can get some independent assessment of the risk premium involved. Otherwise, it is needlessly complicated, since the price appears not only on the left-hand side of the equation but also in the denominator on the right-hand side. Discounting using a risk-adjusted rate is usually the method of choice for capital budgeting, since the risk adjustment is usually determined from comparables (e.g. from past returns on assets in similar firms). For capital budgeting, there may also be a pedagogical advantage that (so far) it has been easier to communicate to practitioners than the other methods. Furthermore, focusing on the risk adjusted discount rate sharpens the comparison of competing approaches (such as the Capital Asset Pricing Model and the dividend discount model).

It is useful to note how the various representations evolve over time. State prices are simply the product of state prices over subperiods. For example, for $t < s < T$, the state price of a state at T given the state at t is equal to the state price of the state at T given the state at s times the state price of the state at s given the state at t. (The state at s is determined by the state at T given the pervasive assumption of perfect recall, i.e. the assumption that the family of sigma-algebras is increasing. If we use some reduced specification of the state – as when looking at Markov processes – the state price is the product of the two, summed over all possible intermediate states.)

The martingale representation yields a price equal to the expected value under the martingale measure of the product of the terminal value times a discount factor that corresponds to rolling over shortest maturity default-free bonds. This representation makes particularly clear the interaction between term structure effects and other effects. If there is a significant term structure, the discount factor is random, and we cannot ignore the interplay between term structure risk and random terminal value unless the terminal value of the asset under consideration is independent of interest rates (under the martingale measure). If the terminal value is independent of interest rate movements, then the value of the asset today is the risk-neutral expected terminal value of the asset discounted at the riskless discount factor (which equals the risk-neutral expected discount factor from rolling over shorts).

The state price density has an evolution over time similar to that of the state price, namely the state price density over a long interval is the product of the state price density over short intervals. Since the state price density equals the state price divided by the probability, the ratio of the two evolutions gives us a relation involving only probabilities, which is Bayes' law.

Finally, the discounted expected value approach is more complicated than the others. The exact evolution over time depends on whether uncertainty is multiplicative, linear, a distributed lag, or whatever. This difficulty is usually overlooked in capital budgeting applications, which is probably not so bad in practice, given the imprecision of our estimates of risk premia and future cash flows.

MODERN RESULTS BASED ON THE ABSENCE OF ARBITRAGE

Most of modern finance is based on either the intuitive or the actual theory of the absence of arbitrage. In fact, it is possible to view absence of arbitrage as the one concept that unifies all of finance (Ross, 1978). In this section, we will try to provide a sample of how arbitrage arguments are used in diverse areas in finance. We will touch on applications in option pricing, corporate finance, asset pricing and efficient markets.

The efficient market hypothesis says that the price of an asset should fully reflect all available information. The intuition behind this hypothesis is that if the price does not fully reflect available information, then there is a profit opportunity available from buying the asset if the asset is underpriced or from selling it if it is overpriced. Clearly this is consistent with the intuition of the absence of arbitrage, even if what we have here is only an approximate arbitrage possibility, i.e. a large profit at little risk. Approximate arbitrage is always profitable to a risk-neutral investor. More generally, the issue is clouded somewhat by questions of risk tolerance and what is the appropriate risk premium. Happily, empirical violation of efficiency of the market (e.g. in event studies) is not significantly affected by the procedure for measuring the risk premium (Brown and Warner, 1980, 1985). Therefore, an empirical violation of efficiency is an approximate arbitrage opportunity that presumably would be attractive at large scale to many investors.

The Modigliani–Miller propositions tell us that in perfect capital markets, changing capital structure or dividend policy without changing investment is a matter of irrelevance to the shareholders. The original proofs of the Modigliani–Miller propositions used the law of one price and assumed the presence of a perfect substitute for the firm that was altering its capital structure. As an illustration of the Fundamental Theorem of Asset Pricing, Ross (1978) demonstrated that these propositions could be derived directly from the existence of a positive linear pricing rule.

To illustrate this argument, consider the proposition that the total value of the firm does not depend on the capital structure. The original argument assumed that there is another identical firm. If we change the financing of our firm, then the value of holding a portfolio of all the parts will give a final payoff equal to that of the identical firm, and must therefore have the same value under the law of one price. Alternatively, suppose that there exists a positive linear pricing rule q. Let x represent the total terminal value of a firm in a one period model and x_i the payoff to financial claim i on the assets of the firm. Then the sum of all the payoffs must add up to the total terminal value,

$$x = \Sigma_i x_i. \tag{19}$$

Using the positive linear operator, q, which values assets, we have that the value of the firm,

$$v \equiv \Sigma_i q(x_i)$$
$$= q(\Sigma_i x_i)$$
$$= q(x_i), \tag{20}$$

which is independent of the number or structure of the financial claims.

Note that both proofs make an implicit assumption that goes beyond what absence of arbitrage promises, namely that changing the capital structure of the firm does not change the way in which prices are formed in the economy. In the original proof this is the assumption that the other firm's price will not change when the firm changes its capital structure. In the linear pricing rule proof this is the assumption that the state price vector q does not change.

Another application of the absence of arbitrage is to asset pricing. The most obvious application is the derivation of the Arbitrage Pricing Theory (Ross, 1976a, 1976b). We will consider the special case without asset-specific noise. Assume that the mechanism generating the per dollar investment rates of return for a set of assets is given by

$$R_i = E_i + \beta_{i1} f_1 + \cdots + \beta_{ik} f_k, \qquad i = 1, \ldots, n, \tag{21}$$

where E_i is the expected rate of return on asset i per dollar invested and f_i is an exogenous factor. This form is an exact factor generating mechanism (as opposed to an approximate one with an additional asset specific mean zero term).

Applying the pricing operator, q, to equation (21) we have that

$$1 = q(1 + R_i)$$
$$= q(1 + E_i + \beta_{i1} f_i + \cdots + \beta_{ik} f_k)$$
$$= q(1 + E_i) + \beta_{i1} q(f_1) + \cdots + \beta_{ik} q(f_k)$$
$$= (1 + E_i)/(1 + r) + \beta_{i1} q(f_1) + \cdots + \beta_{ik} q(f_k),$$

which implies that

$$E_i - r = \lambda_1 \beta_{i1} + \cdots + \lambda_k \beta_{ik}, \tag{22}$$

where $\lambda_j \equiv -(1 + r)q(f_j)$ is the risk premium associated with factor j. Equation (22) is the basic equation of the Arbitrage Pricing Theory. We have derived it using absence of exact arbitrage in the absence of asset-specific noise. More general derivations account for asset-specific noise and use absence of approximate arbitrage.

The most important paper in option pricing, Black and Scholes (1973), is based on the absence of arbitrage, as is the whole literature it has generated. At any point in time, the option is priced by duplicating the value one period later using a portfolio of other assets, and assigning a value using the law of one price. We will illustrate this procedure using the binomial process studied by Cox, Ross and Rubenstein (1979). During each period, the stock price either goes up by 20 per cent or it goes down by 10 per cent and for simplicity we take the riskless rate to be zero. Assume that we are one period from the maturity of a call option with an exercise price of $100, and that the stock price is now $100 (the call is at the money).

How much is the option worth? To figure this out, we must find a portfolio of the stock and the bond that gives the same terminal value. This is the solution of two linear equations (one for each state) in two unknowns (the two portfolio weights). Explicitly, the terminal call value is the larger of 0 and the stock price less 100. In the good state, the stock value will be $120 and the option will be worth $20. In the bad state, the stock price will be $90 and the option will be worthless. If α_S is the amount of stock and α_B the amount of $100 face bond to hold in the duplicating portfolio, then we have that

$$20 = 120\alpha_S + 100\alpha_B$$

to duplicate the option value in the good state, and

$$0 = 90\alpha_S + 100\alpha_B$$

to duplicate the option value in the bad state. The solution to the two equations is given by

$$\alpha_S = 2/3$$
$$\alpha_B = -3/5$$

Therefore, each option is equivalent to holding 2/3 shares of stock and shorting (borrowing) 3/5 bonds. By the law of one price, the option value is the value of this portfolio, or $100\alpha_S + 100\alpha_B = 6\ 2/3$. In this context, we used arbitrage to value the option exactly. More generally, if less is known about the form of the stock price process, absence of arbitrage still places useful restrictions on the option price (Merton, 1973; Cox and Ross, 1976b).

An alternative to option pricing by arbitrage is to use a 'preference-based' model and price options using the first order conditions of an agent (Rubenstein, 1976). While using this alternative approach is very convenient in some contexts, the Fundamental Theorem of Asset Pricing tells us that we are not really doing anything different, and that the two approaches are simply two different ways of making the same assumption. The same point is true of the distinction some authors have made between the 'equilibrium' derivations of the Arbitrage Pricing Theory and the 'arbitrage' derivations: there is no substance in this distinction. One derivation may give a tighter approximation than another, but all derivations require similar assumptions in one form or another.

BIBLIOGRAPHY

Beja, A. 1971. The structure of the cost of capital under uncertainty. *Review of Economic Studies* 38, July, 359–68.

Black, F. and Scholes, M.S. 1973. The pricing of options and corporate liabilities. *Journal of Political Economy* 81(3), May–June, 637–54.

Brown, S. and Warner, J. 1980. Measuring security price performance. *Journal of Financial Economics* 8(3), September, 205–58.

Brown, S. and Warner, J. 1985. Using daily stock returns: the case of event studies. *Journal of Financial Economics* 14(1), March, 3–31.

Cox, J. and Leland, H. 1982. On dynamic investment strategies. *Proceedings, Seminar on the Analysis of Security Prices*, Center for Research in Security Prices, University of Chicago.

Cox, J. and Ross, S.A. 1976a. The valuation of options for alternative stochastic processes. *Journal of Financial Economics* 3(1/2), January/March, 145–66.

Cox, J. and Ross, S.A. 1976b. A survey of some new results in financial option pricing theory. *Journal of Finance* 31(2), May, 383–402.

Cox, J., Ross, S. and Rubinstein, M. 1979. Option pricing: a simplified approach. *Journal of Financial Economics* 7(3), September, 229–63.

Dybvig, P. 1980. Some new tools for testing market efficiency and measuring mutual fund performance. Unpublished manuscript.

Dybvig, P. 1985. Distributional analysis of portfolio choice. Yale School of Management, unpublished manuscript.

Dybvig, P. and Ingersoll, J., Jr. 1982. Mean-variance theory in complete markets. *Journal of Business* 55(2), April, 233–51.

Dybvig, P. and Ross, S. 1982. Portfolio efficient sets. *Econometrica* 50(6), November, 1525–46.

Einzig, P. 1937. *The Theory of Forward Exchange*. London: Macmillan.

Harrison, J.M. and Kreps, D. 1979. Martingales and arbitrage in multiperiod securities markets. *Journal of Economic Theory* 20(3), June, 381–408.

Karlin, S. 1959. *Mathematical Methods and Theory in Games, Programming, and Economics*. Reading, Mass.: Addison-Wesley.

Keynes, J.M. 1923. *A Tract on Monetary Reform*. London: Macmillan; New York: St Martin's Press, 1971.

Merton, R. 1973. Theory of rational option pricing. *Bell Journal of Economics and Management Science* 4(1), Spring, 141–83.

Ross, S.A. 1976a. Return, risk and arbitrage. In *Risk and Return in Finance*, ed. I. Friend and J. Bicksler, Cambridge, Mass.: Ballinger.

Ross, S.A. 1976b. The arbitrage theory of capital asset pricing. *Journal of Economic Theory* 13(3), December, 341–60.

Ross, S.A. 1978. A simple approach to the valuation of risky streams. *Journal of Business* 51(3), July, 453–75.

Rubinstein, M. 1976. The valuation of uncertain income streams and the pricing of options. *Bell Journal of Economics and Management Science* 7(2), Autumn, 407–25.

Arbitrage Pricing Theory

GUR HUBERMAN

The Arbitrage Pricing Theory (APT) is due to Ross (1976a, 1976b). It is a one period model in which every investor believes that the stochastic properties of capital assets' returns are consistent with a factor structure. Ross argues that if equilibrium prices offer no arbitrage opportunities, then the expected returns on these capital assets are approximately linearly related to the factor loadings. (The factor loadings are proportional to the returns' covariances with the factors.)

In his introductory remarks, Ross (1976a) makes a heuristic argument based on the preclusion of arbitrage. That paper's formal proof shows that the theory's asserted pricing relation is a necessary condition for an equilibrium in a market where certain types of utility maximizing agents are present. The subsequent work, which is surveyed below, follows either the 'no arbitrage' or the equilibrium, utility based, route.

The APT is a substitute for the Capital Asset Pricing Model (CAPM) in that both assert a linear relation between assets' expected returns and their covariances with other random variables. (In the CAPM the covariances are with the market portfolio's return.) These covariances are interpreted as measures of risks which an investor cannot avoid by diversification. The slope coefficients of the linear relation between the expected returns and the covariances are interpreted as risk premia.

A FORMAL STATEMENT. The APT assumes that investors believe that the $N \times 1$ vector of the single period random returns on capital assets r satisfies the generating model

$$r = E + Bf + e, \tag{1.1}$$

where r and e are $N \times 1$ vectors of random variables, f is a $K \times 1$ vector of random variables (factors), E is an $N \times 1$ vector and B is an $N \times K$ matrix. With no loss of generality normalize (1.1) to make $E\{f\} = E\{e\} = 0$, where $E\{\cdot\}$ denotes expectation. Thus, $E\{r\} = E$.

72

Restrictions on the diagonality of the covariance matrix $E\{ee'\}$ and on the relation between the eigenvalues of that covariance matrix and those of BB' are required for proofs of the APT. An additional customary assumption is that $E\{e|f\} = 0$, but this assumption is not necessary in some of the APT's developments (e.g. those of Ingersoll).

The number of assets N is assumed to be much larger than the number of factors K. In some models N approaches infinity and in some it is infinite. Thus, representation (1.1) applies to a sequence of capital markets; the first N assets in the $(N + 1)$st market are the same as the assets in the Nth market and the first N rows of the matrix B in the $(N + 1)$st market constitute the matrix B in the Nth market.

The APT asserts the existence of a $(K + 1) \times 1$ vector of risk premia u, an $N \times N$ positive definite matrix Z, and a constant a such that

$$(E - Cu)Z^{-1}(E - Cu) \leqslant a, \tag{1.2}$$

where the $N(K + 1)$ matrix $C = (i, B)$ and i is an $N \times 1$ column vector of 1's. The positive definite matrix Z is often the covariance matrix $E\{ee'\}$. If a risk-free asset is present in the investment universe under consideration then the first component of the vector of risk premia u is equal to the risk-free rate of return.

Exact arbitrage pricing obtains if (1.2) is replaced by

$$E = Cu. \tag{1.2'}$$

The interpretation of (1.2) is that each component of the vector E depends *approximately* linearly on the corresponding row of the matrix B. This linear relation is the same across assets. The approximation is better the smaller the constant a; if $a = 0$ the linear relation is exact and (1.2') obtains.

A portfolio v is an $N \times 1$ vector. The cost of the portfolio v is $v'i$, the income from it is $v'r$, and its return is $v'r/v'i$ (if its cost is not zero).

INTUITION. The intuition behind the model draws from the intuition behind Arrow–Debreu securities pricing. K fundamental securities span all possible future states of nature in an Arrow–Debreu model. Each asset's payoff can be described as the payoff on a portfolio of the fundamental K assets. In other words, an asset's payoff is a weighted average of the fundamental assets' payoffs. If market clearing prices allow no arbitrage opportunities, then the current price of each asset must equal the weighted average of the current prices of the fundamental assets.

The Arrow–Debreu intuition can be couched in terms of returns and expected returns rather than payoffs and prices. If the unexpected part of each asset's return is a linear combination of the unexpected parts of the returns on the K fundamental securities, then the expected return of each asset is the same linear combination of the expected returns on the K fundamental assets.

To see how the Arrow–Debreu intuition leads from the factor structure (1.1) to exact arbitrage pricing (1.2'), set the idiosyncratic terms on the right-hand side of (1.1), e, equal to zero. Translate the K factors on the right-hand side of

(1.1) into the K fundamental securities in the Arrow–Debreu model. Then (1.2′) follows immediately.

The presence of the idiosyncratic terms e in the factor structure (1.1) makes the model more general and realistic. It also makes the relation between (1.1) and (1.2′) more tenuous. Indeed, 'no arbitrage' arguments typically prove the weaker (1.2). Moreover, they require a weaker definition of arbitrage (and therefore a stronger definition of no arbitrage) in order to get from (1.1) to (1.2).

The proofs that lead from (1.1) to (1.2) augment the Arrow–Debreu intuition with a version of the law of large numbers. That law is used to argue that the average effect of the idiosyncratic terms is negligible. Here the independence of the e's is used. Indeed, the more one assumes about the (absence of) contemporaneous correlations among the e's, the tighter the bound on the deviation from (1.2′).

'NO ARBITRAGE' MODELS. Huberman (1982) formalizes the argument in the introduction of Ross (1976a). Huberman defines arbitrage as the existence of a subsequence of $N \times 1$ vectors w such that

$$w'i = 0, \tag{1.3a}$$

$$E\{w'r\} \text{ approaches infinity as } N \text{ approaches infinity}, \tag{1.3b}$$

$$\text{var}\{w'r\} \text{ approaches zero as } N \text{ approaches infinity}, \tag{1.3c}$$

where $\text{var}\{\cdot\}$ denotes variance.

Requirement (1.3a) is that for each N, the portfolio w is costless. Requirement (1.3b) is that the expected income associated with w becomes large as the number of assets increases. Requirement (1.3c) is that the risk (as measured by the income's variance) vanishes as the number of assets increases.

A sequence of capital markets offers no arbitrage opportunities if there is no subsequence $\{w\}$ of portfolios which satisfies (1.3). Huberman shows that if (1.1) holds, the covariance matrix $E\{ee'\}$ is diagonal for all N and uniformly bounded, and no arbitrage opportunities exist, then (1.2) holds with $Z = I$ and a finite bound a.

Ingersoll (1984) generalizes Huberman's result. He shows that (1.1), uniform boundedness of the elements of B and no arbitrage imply (1.2) with $Z = E\{ee'\}$, the covariance matrix of the idiosyncratic term e. A variant of Ingersoll's argument follows. Write the positive definite matrix Z as the product $Z = UU'$, where U is an $N \times N$ nonsingular matrix. Consider the orthogonal projection of the vector $U^{-1}E$ on the column space of $U^{-1}C$

$$U^{-1}E = U^{-1}Cu + g, \tag{1.4}$$

where $g'U^{-1}C = 0$, the $(K + 1)$-dimensional zero vector.

The position $w = U'^{-1}g$ (or kw, where k is a scalar) satisfies (1.3a) (because the first column of C is i). Compute $E\{kw'r\} = kg'g$ and $\text{var}\{kw'r\} = k^2g'g$. For $k = (g'g)^{-0.75}$, $E\{kw'r\} = (g'g)^{0.25}$ and $\text{var}\{kw'r\} = (g'g)^{-0.5}$. A violation of (1.2) implies that a subsequence of $\{g'g\}$ converges to infinity, which implies that (1.3) is satisfied by the costless positions $(g'g)^{-0.75}g$. A preclusion of (1.3) implies a bound on $g'g$. This last conclusion is equivalent to (1.2).

Stambaugh (1983) reconsiders the theory by assuming, in addition to the factor structure (1.1), that prices are set by investors who observe a vector of random variables y. The joint distribution of (r, y) is either multivariate normal or multivariate Student t. Thus, the factor structure (1.1) holds unconditionally but prices are set by investors who possess additional information. Stambaugh's distributional assumptions guarantee that the factor structure is maintained conditionally with the same matrix of factor loadings B as in the unconditional factor structure (1.1). This observation leads to an extension of the APT to a setting where investors have information about future returns (namely, they observe y) and it justifies tests of the APT which do not use that information.

Chamberlain and Rothschild (1983) employ Hilbert space techniques to study capital markets with (possibly infinitely) many assets. For two portfolios v and w they define the inner product $\langle v, w \rangle = E\{v'rw'r\}$. By the Riesz representation theorem both the expectation and the cost functional can be identified with inner products of unique members of the underlying Hilbert space. Chamberlain and Rothschild show that the minimum variance frontier (i.e., the set of portfolios whose return variance is minimal along all return variances of portfolios with the same expected return) in that space is generated by these two members of the space.

The preclusion of arbitrage implies the continuity of the cost functional in the Hilbert space. Letting $L(Z)$ equal the maximal eigenvalue of the limit covariance matrix $Z = E\{ee'\}$ and d equal the supremum of all ratios of expectation to standard deviation of the incomes on all costless portfolios with a non-zero weight on at least one asset, Chamberlain and Rothschild argue that (1.2) holds with $a = L(Z)d^2$ and with the identity matrix replacing Z in the left-hand side of (1.2) if asset prices allow no arbitrage profits.

A portfolio w is *well diversified* if var$\{w'e\} = 0$, i.e., the portfolio's return contains only factor variance. Chamberlain (1983) assumes that K is the dimension of the subspace (in the Chamberlain–Rothschild Hilbert space) of all portfolio sequences $\{w\}$ such that $w'w$ converges to zero. He assumes also that if v is a portfolio sequence such that $v'v$ converges to zero and the covariance $\text{cov}(v'r, w'r) = 0$ for all w in that subspace and all v in the sequence, then the variance var$(v'r)$ converges to zero. The first assumption is that all the factors can be represented as limits (in the Hilbert space norm) of traded assets and the second is that the variances of the incomes on any sequence of portfolios which are well diversified in the limit, and which are uncorrelated with the factors, converge to zero. With these additional assumptions Chamberlain provides explicit lower and upper bounds on the left-hand side of (1.2). He shows further that exact arbitrage pricing obtains if and only if there is a well diversified portfolio on the mean variance frontier.

UTILITY BASED ARGUMENTS. Connor (1984) shows that if the market portfolio is well diversified then every investor holds a well diversified portfolio (i.e. a $K + 1$

fund separation obtains; the funds are associated with the factors and with the risk-free asset which Connor assumes to exist). This and the first order conditions of any investor imply exact arbitrage pricing in a competitive equilibrium.

Connor and Korajczyk (1986) extend Connor's work to a model with investors with better information about returns than most other investors. The former class of investors is sufficiently small, so the pricing result remains intact and is used to derive a test of the superiority of information of the allegedly better informed investors.

Connor and Korajczyk (1985) extend the single period model of Connor to a multi-period model. They assume that the capital assets are the same in all periods, that each period's cash payoffs from these assets obey a factor structure, and that competitive equilibrium prices are set as if the economy had a representative investor who is an exponential utility maximizer. They show that exact arbitrage pricing obtains with time varying risk premia. (But, similar to Stambaugh (1983), with constant factor loadings.)

Chen and Ingersoll (1983) argue that if a well diversified portfolio exists and it is the optimal portfolio of some utility maximizing investor, then the first order conditions of that investor imply exact arbitrage pricing.

Dybvig (1983) and Grinblatt and Titman (1983) consider the finite asset case and provide explicit bounds on the deviations from exact arbitrage pricing. These bounds are functions of the per capita asset supplies, individual bounds on absolute risk aversion, variance of the idiosyncratic risk and the interest rate. To derive his bound, Dybvig assumes that the support of the distribution of the idiosyncratic term e is bounded below, that each investor's coefficient of absolute risk aversion is non-increasing and that the competitive equilibrium allocation is unconstrained Pareto optimal. To derive their bound, Grinblatt and Titman require a bound on a quantity related to investors' coefficients of absolute risk aversion and the existence of K independent costless well diversified portfolios.

All the utility based developments of the model require that the vector of conditional means $E\{e|f\} = 0$.

ARBITRAGE PRICING AND MEAN VARIANCE EFFICIENCY. The APT was developed as a generalization of the CAPM, which asserts that the expectations of assets' returns are linearly related to their covariances (or betas, which are proportional to the covariances) with the market portfolio's return. Equivalently, the CAPM says that the market portfolio is mean variance efficient in the investment universe containing all possible assets. If the factors in (1.1) can be identified with traded assets then exact arbitrage pricing, (1.2'), says that a portfolio of these factors is mean variance efficient in the investment universe consisting of the assets r.

Huberman and Kandel (1985b), Jobson and Korkie (1982, 1985) and Jobson (1982) note the relation between the APT and mean variance efficiency to propose likelihood ratio tests of the joint hypothesis that a given set of random variables are factors in the statistical model (1.1) and that (1.2') obtains.

Even when the factors are not traded assets, (1.2') is a statement about mean variance efficiency: Grinblatt and Titman (1987) suppose that the factor structure

(1.1) holds and a riskfree asset is available. They identify K traded assets such that a portfolio of them is mean variance efficient if and only if (1.2′) holds. The work of Grinblatt and Titman is extended by Huberman, Kandel and Stambaugh (1986) who characterize the sets of K traded positions with that property and show that these assets can be described as portfolios if and only if the global minimum variance portfolio has nonzero systematic risk. To compute these sets of assets one must know the matrices BB' and $E\{ee'\}$. If the latter matrix is diagonal, factor analysis produces estimates of it and of BB'.

The interpretation of (1.2′) as a statement about mean variance efficiency contributes to the debate about the testability of the APT. (Shanken (1982, 1985) and Dybvig and Ross (1985) discuss the APT's testability without mentioning that (1.2′) is a statement about mean variance efficiency.) The theory's silence not only about the factors' identities but also about their number renders any test of the APT a joint test of the pricing relation and the correctness of the factors. As a mean variance efficient portfolio always exists, one can always find 'factors' with respect to which (1.2′) holds.

The factor structure (1.1) imposes restrictions which, combined with (1.2′), provide refutable hypotheses about assets' returns. The factor structure suggests looking for factors with two properties: (i) their time series movements explain a substantial fraction of the time series movements of the returns on the priced assets, and (ii) the unexplained parts of the time series movements of the returns on the priced assets are approximately uncorrelated across the priced assets.

EMPIRICAL WORK. The APT has generated a good deal of empirical work, not all of it as good as it claims to be. Much more empirical work is likely to be written, and by the time this section appears in print, it may seem obsolete; hence its brevity.

The APT is a one period model which makes an assertion about moments of a probability distribution function. That function is held in investors' minds and is not directly observable. The empirical implementation of the model assumes that the observed time series of asset returns are samples from the population which obeys the distribution function assumed in the model. Furthermore, a period of the model is interpreted to be any period with which the researcher feels comfortable (e.g. a day, a week or a month). Hence a licence to use the time series of asset returns to estimate the moments of the probability function which is assumed to be held by investors.

Empirical work inspired by the APT typically ignores (1.2) and studies instead exact arbitrage pricing, (1.2′). It consists of two steps: an estimation of factors (or at least of the matrix B in (1.1)) and then a check to see whether exact arbitrage pricing holds. Thus, these works can be interpreted as joint tests that the matrix B is correctly estimated and that exact arbitrage pricing holds. Estimation of the factor loading matrix B entails at least an implicit identification of the factors.

Three approaches have been used to estimate the matrix B. The first consists of algorithmic analysis of the estimated covariance matrix of asset returns. For instance, Roll and Ross (1980), Chen (1983) and Lehman and Modest (1985a) use factor analysis and Chamberlain and Rothschild (1983) and Connor and Korajczyk (1985, 1986) recommend using principal component analysis.

Factor analysis is a statistically more efficient method to estimate the matrix B in (1.1) than principal component analysis. It is also more expensive computationally. Indeed, it is so expensive that nobody has factor analysed the full covariance matrix $E\{rr'\}$ which has the estimated covariances of all the stocks on the NYSE (let alone the AMEX too). Factor analysis is typically applied to small subsets of asset returns. Lehman and Modest (1985b) compare different methods of factor loading estimation and conclude that the best is maximum likelihood factor analysis which uses as many securities as possible (they have as many as 750 securities in the factor analysis).

The second approach consists of the researcher's staring at the estimated covariance matrix of asset returns and using his judgement to choose factors and subsequently estimate the matrix B. Huberman and Kandel (1985a) note that the correlations of stock returns of firms of different sizes are increasing with the similarity in size. Therefore they choose an index of small firms, one of medium size firms and one of large firms to serve as factors.

The third approach is purely judgemental in that the researcher uses primarily his intuition to pick factors and then estimates the factor loadings and checks if they explain the cross sectional variations in estimated expected returns (i.e., he checks (1.2′)). Chan, Chen and Hsieh (1985) and Chen, Roll and Ross (1986) select financial and macroeconomic variables to serve as factors. They include the derivatives of the following variables: the return on an index of the New York Stock Exchange, the short and long-term interest rates on US government debt, a measure of the private sector's default premium, the inflation rate, the growth rate of industrial production and the aggregate consumption rate.

The first two approaches are implemented to conform to the factor structure underlying the APT: the first approach by the algorithmic design and the second because Huberman and Kandel check that the factors they use indeed leave the unexplained parts of asset returns almost uncorrelated. The third approach is implemented without regard for the factor structure. Its attempt to relate assets' expected returns to the covariances of assets' returns with other variables is more in the spirit of Merton's (1973) intertemporal CAPM than in the spirit of the APT.

The empirical work cited above checks exact arbitrage pricing against a few alternatives: that the betas with the market are just as good in explaining the cross sectional variations of assets' mean returns (i.e. against the CAPM), and that other variables have marginal explanatory power above and beyond the factor loadings; these variables include firm size and the variance of the asset's return. Another test of the model, due to Brown and Weinstein (1983), checks the equality of the risk premia u across groups of assets.

By and large, the results support the APT except when it is tested against the alternative that small firms have higher mean returns than large firms even after differences in the factor loadings are accounted for. Results are mixed with respect to this alternative. Chen (1983), Chan, Chen and Hsieh (1985) and Chen, Roll and Ross (1986) and Huberman and Kandel (1985a) fail to reject the null hypothesis that factor loadings alone explain the cross sectional variations in assets' mean returns. Connor and Korajczyk (1985), Lehman and Modest (1985a) and Reinganum (1981) conclude the opposite. Before hastily interpreting this evidence as an overwhelming rejection of the APT, one must keep in mind that the competing model, the CAPM, fares even more poorly against the same alternative.

At the moment, then, the APT seems to describe the data better than competing models. It is wise to recall, however, that the purported empirical success of the APT may well be due to the weakness of the tests employed.

Which factors capture the data best? What are the relations among the factors which different researchers claim to have found? As any test of the APT is a joint test that the factors are correctly identified and that the linear pricing relation holds, we have within the APT's umbrella a host of competing theories. Each one accepts the APT but has its own factor identification procedure. The explosive number of factors and methods to construct them on the one hand, and the absence of a theory that interprets the factors and relates them to other aspects of economics on the other, leave us with a rich research agenda.

BIBLIOGRAPHY

Admati, A.R. and Pfleiderer, P. 1985. Interpreting the factor risk premia in the arbitrage pricing theory. *Journal of Economic Theory* 35, 191–5.

Brown, S. and Weinstein, M. 1983. A new approach to testing asset pricing models: the bilinear paradigm. *Journal of Finance* 38, 711–43.

Chamberlain, G. 1983. Funds, factors and diversification in arbitrage pricing models. *Econometrica* 51, 1305–23.

Chamberlain, G. and Rothschild, M. 1983. Arbitrage, factor structure, and mean variance analysis on large asset markets. *Econometrica* 51, 1281–304.

Chan, K.C., Chen, N. and Hsieh, D. 1985. An exploratory investigation of the firm size effect. *Journal of Financial Economics* 14, 451–71.

Chen, N. 1983. Some empirical tests of the theory of arbitrage pricing. *Journal of Finance* 38, 1393–414.

Chen, N. and Ingersoll, J. 1983. Exact pricing in linear factor models with infinitely many assets: a note. *Journal of Finance* 38, 985–8.

Chen, N., Roll, R. and Ross, S.A. 1986. Economic forces and the stock markets. *Journal of Business* 59, 383–403.

Connor, G. 1984. A unified beta pricing theory. *Journal of Economic Theory* 34, 13–31.

Connor, G. and Korajczyk, R.A. 1985. Risk and return in an equilibrium APT: theory and tests. Banking Research Center Working Paper 129, Northwestern University.

Connor, G. and Korajczyk, R.A. 1986. Performance measurement with the arbitrage pricing theory: a framework for analysis. *Journal of Financial Economics* 15, 373–94.

Dhrymes, P., Friend, I. and Gultekin, B. 1984. A critical reexamination of the empirical evidence on the arbitrage pricing theory. *Journal of Finance* 39, 323–46.

Dybvig, P.H. 1983. An explicit bound on deviations from APT pricing in a finite economy. *Journal of Financial Economics* 12, 483–96.

Dybvig, P.H. and Ross, S.A. 1985. Yes, the APT is testable. *Journal of Finance* 40, 1173–88.

Gehr, A., Jr. 1978. Some tests of the arbitrage pricing theory. *Journal of the Midwest Finance Association* 7, 91–106.

Grinblatt, M. and Titman, S. 1983. Factor pricing in a finite economy. *Journal of Financial Economics* 12, 495–507.

Grinblatt, M. and Titman, S. 1987. The relation between mean-variance efficiency and arbitrage pricing. *Journal of Business*.

Huberman, G. 1982. A simple approach to arbitrage pricing. *Journal of Economic Theory* 28, 183–91.

Huberman, G. and Kandel, S. 1985a. A size based stock returns model. Center for Research in Security Prices Working Paper 148, University of Chicago.

Huberman, G. and Kandel, S. 1985b. Likelihood ratio tests of asset pricing and mutual fund separation. Center for Research in Security Prices Working Paper 149, University of Chicago.

Huberman, G., Kandel, S. and Stambaugh, R. 1986. Mimicking portfolios and exact arbitrage pricing. Center for Research in Security Prices Working Paper 165, University of Chicago. *Journal of Finance* 42(1), March 1987, 1–11.

Ingersoll, J. 1984. Some results in the theory of arbitrage pricing. *Journal of Finance* 39(4), 1021–39.

Jobson, J.D. 1982. A multivariate linear regression test of the arbitrage pricing theory. *Journal of Finance* 37, 1037–42.

Jobson, J.D. and Korkie, B. 1982. Potential performance and tests of portfolio efficiency. *Journal of Financial Economics* 10, 433–66.

Jobson, J.D. and Korkie, B. 1985. Some tests of linear asset pricing with multivariate normality. *Canadian Journal of Administrative Sciences* 2, 114–38.

Lehman, B. and Modest, D. 1985a. The empirical foundations of the arbitrage pricing theory I: the empirical tests. Department of Economics Working Paper 291, Columbia University.

Lehman, B. and Modest, D. 1985b. The empirical foundations of the arbitrage pricing theory II: the optimal construction of basis portfolios. Department of Economics Working Paper 292, Columbia University.

Merton, R. 1973. An intertemporal capital asset pricing model. *Econometrica* 41, 867–87.

Reinganum, M. 1981. The arbitrage pricing theory: some simple tests. *Journal of Finance* 36, 313–22.

Roll, R. and Ross, S.A. 1980. An empirical investigation of the arbitrage pricing theory. *Journal of Finance* 35, 1073–103.

Roll, R. and Ross, S.A. 1984. A critical reexamination of the empirical evidence on the arbitrage pricing theory. *Journal of Finance* 39, 347–50.

Ross, S.A. 1976a. The arbitrage theory of capital asset pricing. *Journal of Economic Theory* 13, 341–60.

Ross, S.A. 1976b. Risk, return and arbitrage. In *Risk Return in Finance*, ed. I. Friend and J. Bicksler, Cambridge, Mass.: Ballinger.

Shanken, J. 1982. The arbitrage pricing theory: is it testable? *Journal of Finance* 37(5), 1129–240.

Shanken, J. 1985. A multi-beta CAPM or equilibrium APT?: a reply. *Journal of Finance* 40, 1189–96.

Stambaugh, R. 1983. Arbitrage pricing with information. *Journal of Financial Economics* 12, 357–69.

Asset Pricing

THOMAS E. COPELAND AND J. FRED WESTON

In the early 1950s Harry Markowitz developed a theory of portfolio selection which has resulted in a revolution in the theory of finance leading to the development of modern capital market theory (1952, 1959). He formulated a theory of investor investment selection as a problem of utility maximization under conditions of uncertainty. Markowitz discusses mainly the special case in which investors' preferences are assumed to be defined over the mean and variance of the probability distribution of single-period portfolio returns, but he also treated most issues developed more fully in the subsequent literature.

J. Tobin (1958) utilized the foundations of portfolio theory to draw implications with regard to the demand for cash balances. He also demonstrated that given the possibility of an investment in a risk-free asset as well as in a risky asset (or portfolio), an investor can construct a combined portfolio of the two assets to achieve any desired combination of risk and return. Subsequently, W. F. Sharpe, using one of the efficient methods for constructing portfolios discussed in the appendices to the Markowitz book (1959), developed what he called the 'diagonal model' in his dissertation under the direction of Markowitz, the results of which were later summarized in an article (1963). This represented another step towards general equilibrium models of asset prices developed almost simultaneously by Treynor (1965), Sharpe (1964, 1970), Lintner (1965a, b) and Mossin (1966, 1969). Important contributions were made by Fama (1971, 1976) and by Fama and Miller (1972).

These works resulted in the development of the relationship between return and risk summarized in what has been called the Security Market Line of the Capital Asset Pricing Model (CAPM).

$$E(R_j) = R_F + \left[\frac{E(R_M) - R_F}{\sigma_M^2} \right] \text{COV}(R_j, R_M). \qquad (1)$$

This equation says that the return required (*ex ante*) by investors on any asset is equal to the return, R_F, on a risk-free asset plus an adjustment for risk.

Alternatively, the risk adjustment can be defined as the market risk premium weighted by the risk of the individual asset normalised by the variance of market returns. This latter measure has been referred to as the beta measure (β) of the risk of an individual asset or security. $[\beta = \text{COV}(R_j, R_M)/\sigma_M^2]$ Leading synthesis papers on the CAPM are by Jensen (1972) and Rubinstein (1973).

The CAPM assumes that the market functions in a reasonably perfect way in the sense that: all individuals act as if they are price-takers of all relevant prices; all securities are perfectly divisible and can be sold both long and short without margin and/or escrow requirements; there are no transaction costs or taxes; and, as in nearly all useful economic theory, arbitrage opportunities are absent so that an appropriate one price law obtains. Individuals are assumed to be risk averse, expected utility maximizers. In that differential assessment of probabilities generally explains too much, it is usual (although not necessary for all purposes) to require that probability beliefs are homogeneous (Krouse, 1986). Subsequent work established that the main principles of the CAPM held up with the successive relaxation of the above assumptions (Black, 1972; Brennan, 1971; Lintner 1969; Mayers 1972, 1973; Merton 1973).

Roll's critique (1977) has had a major impact. His major conclusions are: (1) The only legitimate test of the CAPM is whether or not the market portfolio (which includes *all* assets) is mean-variance efficient; (2) If performance is measured relative to an index which is *ex post* efficient, then from the mathematics of the efficient set, no security will have abnormal performance when measured as a departure from the Security Market Line; (3) If performance is measured relative to an *ex post* inefficient index, then any ranking of portfolio performance is possible depending on which inefficient index has been chosen. The Roll critique does not imply that the CAPM is invalid, but that tests of the CAPM are joint tests with market efficiency and that its uses must be implemented with due care.

Three basic types of models of asset pricing have been most frequently employed. The simplest, called the *market model*, is based on the fact that returns on security j can be linearly related to returns on a 'market' portfolio, namely:

$$R_{jt} = a_j + b_j R_{Mt} + \varepsilon_{jt} \tag{2}$$

where ε_{jt} is the mean zero classical normally distributed error term. The market model assumes that the slope and intercept terms are constant over the time period during which the model is fit to the available data, a strong assumption.

The second model is the capital asset pricing theory. It requires the intercept term to be equal to the risk-free rate, or the rate of return on the minimum variance zero-beta portfolio, both of which may change over time. In its simplest form, the CAPM is written

$$R_{jt} - R_{Ft} = [R_{Mt} - R_{Ft}]\beta_{jt} + \varepsilon_{jt}. \tag{3}$$

Systematic risk, β_{jt}, is generally assumed to remain constant over the interval of estimation.

The third model is the empirical counterpart to the CAPM, referred to as the *empirical market line*

$$R_{jt} = \hat{\gamma}_{0t} + \hat{\gamma}_{1t}\beta_{jt} + \varepsilon_{jt}. \tag{4}$$

This formulation does not require that the intercept term equal the risk-free rate. No parameters are assumed to be constant over time. In contrast to the market model, which is a time series expression, both the intercept, $\hat{\gamma}_{0t}$, and the slope, $\hat{\gamma}_{1t} = (R_{Mt} - R_{Ft})$, are the estimates taken from cross-section data each time period (typically each month). The betas in (4) are (following Fama and MacBeth, 1973) calculated from the market model [equation (2)]. (See Copeland and Weston, 1983, chs 7 and 10.)

Empirical tests of the CAPM were conducted by Miller and Scholes (1972), Fama and MacBeth (1973) and Reinganum (1981), among others. Most of the studies use monthly total returns (dividends are reinvested) on listed common stocks.

Asset pricing models have been used to measure portfolio performance by mutual funds, pension fund advisers, etc., and in residual analysis of the impact of accounting reports, stock splits, mergers, etc. Some studies have used the market model to measure the error terms or residuals – positive or negative performance. However, the generally accepted procedure is first to calculate the β's from the market line [equation (2)]. Portfolios ranked by β's provide groupings to minimize errors in the measurement of variables problem. These portfolio betas are used to develop the parameters (intercept and slope terms) in equation (4) which is the empirical market line used to estimate the CAPM of equation (3). With estimates of the γ terms, the empirical market line can then be used to calculate 'abnormal' returns or residuals from predicted security returns.

The empirical tests of CAPM typically are conducted in excess return form. The equation in this form should have an intercept term not significantly different from zero, with a slope equal to the excess market portfolio return. The empirical tests have found an intercept term significantly above zero with a slope less than predicted. Thus the empirical securities market line is tilted clockwise implying that low beta securities earn more than the CAPM would predict and high beta securities earn less. But the main predictions of the CAPM of a positive market price for risk and a model linear in beta are supported.

The recognition that the market return alone might not explain all of the variation in the return on an asset or a portfolio gave rise to a multiple factor analysis of capital asset pricing. This more general approach formulated by Ross (1976b) was called the Arbitrage Pricing Theory (APT). Requiring only that individuals be risk averse, the APT has multiple factors and in equilibrium all assets must fall on the arbitrage pricing line. Thus the CAPM is viewed as a special case of the APT in which the return on the market portfolio is the single applicable factor.

Empirical work on the APT was performed by Gehr (1975), Roll and Ross (1980), Reinganum (1981) and Chen, Roll and Ross (1986). These studies use data on equity daily rates of return for the New York and American Stock Exchange listed stocks. The initial studies establish that other factors contribute to an explanation of required returns but did not identify them. Later studies suggest that economic influences such as unexpected changes in inflation rates, default premia (measured by the difference between high- and low-grade bond yields), and the term premium in interest rates (measured by the difference between yields on short- and long-term bonds) correlate highly with the identified explanatory factors.

The CAPM and APT have provided useful conceptual frameworks for business finance applications such as capital budgeting analysis and for measurement of the cost of capital. Although the CAPM has not been perfectly validated by empirical tests, its main implications are upheld: systematic risk (beta) is a valid measure of risk, the model is linear in beta, and the tradeoff between return and risk is positive. The earliest empirical tests of the APT have shown that asset returns are explained by three or possibly four factors and have ruled out the variance of an asset's own returns as one of the factors.

BIBLIOGRAPHY

Black, F. 1972. Capital market equilibrium with restricted borrowing. *Journal of Business* 45(3), July, 444–55.

Brennan, M.J. 1971. Capital market equilibrium with divergent borrowing and lending rates. *Journal of Financial and Quantitative Analysis* 6(5), December, 1197–205.

Chen, N.F., Roll, R. and Ross, S.A. 1986. Economic forces and the stock market. *Journal of Business* 59(3), July, 383–403.

Copeland, T.E. and Weston, J.F. 1983. *Financial Theory and Corporate Policy*. 2nd edn, Menlo Park, California: Addison-Wesley Publishing Company.

Fama, E.F. 1971. Risk, return, and equilibrium. *Journal of Political Economy* 79(1), January–February, 30–55.

Fama, E.F. 1976. *Foundations of Finance*. New York: Basic Books.

Fama, E.F. and MacBeth, J. 1973. Risk, return, and equilibrium: empirical tests. *Journal of Political Economy* 81(3), May–June, 607–36.

Fama, E.F. and Miller, M.H. 1972. *The Theory of Finance*, New York: Holt, Rinehart and Winston.

Gehr, A., Jr. 1975. Some tests of the arbitrage pricing theory. *Journal of the Midwest Finance Association* 7, 91–107.

Jensen, M.C. 1972. Capital markets: theory and evidence. *Bell Journal of Economics and Management Science* 3(2), Autumn, 357–98.

Krouse, C.G. 1986. *Capital Markets and Prices: Valuing Uncertain Income Streams*. New York: North-Holland Press.

Lintner, J. 1965a. Security prices, risk, and maximal gains from diversification. *Journal of Finance* 20, December, 587–616.

Lintner, J. 1965b. The valuation of risk assets and the selection of risky investments in stock portfolios and capital budgets. *Review of Economics and Statistics* 47, February, 13–37.

Lintner, J. 1969. The aggregation of investors' diverse judgments and preferences in purely competitive securities markets. *Journal of Financial and Quantitative Analysis* 4, December, 347–400.

Markowitz, H.M. 1952. Portfolio selection. *Journal of Finance* 7, March, 77–91.

Markowitz, H.M. 1959. *Portfolio selection: Efficient Diversification of Investments*. New York: Wiley.

Mayers, D. 1972. Non-marketable assets and capital market equilibrium under uncertainty. In *Studies in the Theory of Capital Markets*, ed. M.C. Jensen, New York: Praeger.

Mayers, D. 1973. Non-marketable assets and the determination of capital asset prices in the absence of a riskless asset. *Journal of Business* 46(2), April, 258–67.

Merton, R. 1973. An intertemporal capital asset pricing model. *Econometrica* 41(5), September, 867–87.

Miller, M. and Scholes, M. 1972. Rates of return in relation to risk: a re-examination of some recent findings. In *Studies in the Theory of Capital Markets*, ed. M.C. Jensen, New York: Praeger, 47–78.

Mossin, J. 1966. Equilibrium in a capital asset market. *Econometrica* 34, October, 768–83.

Mossin, J. 1969. Security pricing and investment criteria in competitive markets. *American Economic Review* 59, December, 739–56.

Reinganum, M.R. 1981. The arbitrage pricing theory: some empirical results. *Journal of Finance* 36(2), May, 313–22.

Roll, R. 1977. A critique of the asset pricing theory's tests: Part I. *Journal of Financial Economics* 4(2), March, 129–76.

Roll, R. and Ross, S. 1980. An empirical investigation of the arbitrage pricing theory. *Journal of Finance* 35(5), December, 1073–103.

Ross, S.A. 1976a. Options and efficiency. *Quarterly Journal of Economics* 90(1), February, 75–89.

Ross, S.A. 1976b. The arbitrage theory of capital asset pricing. *Journal of Economic Theory* 13(3), December, 341–60.

Rubinstein, M.E. 1973. A mean-variance synthesis of corporate financial theory. *Journal of Finance* 28(1), March, 167–81.

Sharpe, W. F. 1963. A simplified model for portfolio analysis. *Management Science* 9, January, 277–93.

Sharpe, W.F. 1964. Capital asset prices: a theory of market equilibrium under conditions of risk. *Journal of Finance* 19, September, 425–42.

Sharpe, W.F. 1970. *Portfolio Theory and Capital Markets*. New York: McGraw-Hill.

Tobin, J. 1958. Liquidity preference as behavior toward risk. *Review of Economic Studies* 25, February, 65–86.

Treynor, J.L. 1965. How to rate management of investment funds. *Harvard Business Review* 43, January–February, 63–75.

Louis Bachelier

BENOIT B. MANDELBROT

Bachelier was born in Le Havre, France, on 11 March 1870 and died in Saint-Servan-sur-Mer, Ille-et-Villaine, on 28 April 1946. He taught at Besançon, Dijon and Rennes and was professor at Besançon from 1927 to 1937.

The unrecognized genius is one of the stock figures of popular history, and it is also a platitude that many examples dissolve upon careful examination. But the story of Louis Bachelier is in perfect conformity to all the clichés. He invented efficient markets in 1900, sixty years before the idea came into vogue. He described the random walk model of prices, ordinary diffusion of probability – also called Brownian motion – and martingales, which are the mathematical expression of efficient markets. He even attempted an empirical verification. But he remained a shadowy presence until 1960 or so, when his major work was revived in English translation.

This major work was his doctoral dissertation in the mathematical sciences, defended in Paris on 19 March 1900. Things went badly from the start: the committee failed to give it the 'mention très honorable', key to a University career. It was very late, after repeated failures, that Bachelier was appointed to the tiny University of Besançon. After he had retired, the University Archives were accidentally set on fire and no record survives, not even one photograph. Here are a few scraps I have managed to put together.

We begin with the proverbial episode of the grain of sand, or the lack of a nail. Bachelier made a mathematical error that is recounted in a letter the great probabilist Paul Levy wrote me on 25 January 1964:

> I first heard of him around 1928. He was a candidate for a professorship at the University of Dijon. Gevrey, who was teaching there, came to ask my opinion. In a work published in 1913, Bachelier had defined Wiener's function (prior to Wiener) as follows: In each interval $[n\tau, (n + 1)\tau]$, he considered a function $X(t|\tau)$ that has a constant derivative equal to either $+v$ or $-v$, the

86

two values being equiprobable. He then proceeded to the limit $\tau \to 0$, keeping v constant, and claimed he was obtaining a proper function $X(t)$! Gevrey was scandalized by this error. I agreed with him and Bachelier was blackballed.

I had forgotten it when in 1931, reading Kolmogorov's fundamental paper, I came to 'der Bacheliers Fall'. I looked up Bachelier's works, and saw that this error, which is repeated everywhere, does not prevent him from obtaining results that would have been correct if only he had written $v = C\tau^{-1/2}$, and that, prior to Einstein [1905] and prior to Wiener [circa 1925], he has seen some important properties of the Wiener function, namely, the diffusion equation and the distribution of $\max_{0 < \tau < 1} X(\tau)$.

We became reconciled. I had written to him that I regretted that an impression, produced by a single initial error, should have kept me from going on with my reading of a work in which there were so many interesting ideas. He replied with a long letter in which he expressed great enthusiasm for research.

That Levy should have played this role is tragic, for his own career, also nearly foundered because his papers were not sufficiently rigorous for the mathematical extremists.

The second and deeper reason for Bachelier's career problems was the topic of his dissertation: 'Mathematical theory of speculation' – not of (philosophical) speculation on the nature of chance, rather of (money-grubbing) speculation on the ups and downs of the market for consolidated state bonds: 'la rente'. The function $X(t)$ mentioned by Levy stood for the price of *la rente* at time t. Hence, the delicately understated comment by Henri Poincaré, who wrote the official report on this dissertation, that 'the topic is somewhat remote from those our candidates are in the habit of treating'. One may wonder why Bachelier asked for the judgement of unwilling mathematicians (assigning a thesis subject was totally foreign to French professors of that period), but he had no choice: his lower degree was in mathematics and probability was taught by Poincaré.

Bachelier's tragedy was to be a man of the past and of the future but not of his present. He was a man of the past because gambling is the historical root of probability theory; he introduced the continuous-time gambling on *La Bourse*. He was a man of the future, both in mathematics (witness the above letter by Levy) and in economics. Unfortunately, no organized scientific community of his time was in a position to understand and welcome him. To gain acceptance for himself would have required political skills that he did not possess, and one wonders where he could have gained acceptance for his thoughts.

Poincaré's report on the 1908 dissertation deserves further excerpting:

The manner in which the candidate obtains the law of Gauss is most original, and all the more interesting as the same reasoning might, with a few changes, be extended to the theory of errors. He develops this in a chapter which might at first seem strange, for he titles it 'Radiation of Probability'. In effect, the author resorts to a comparison with the analytical theory of the propagation of heat. A little reflection shows that the analogy is real and the comparison legitimate. Fourier's reasoning is applicable almost without change to this problem, which is so different from that for which it had been created. It is regrettable that [the author] did not develop this part of his thesis further.

While Poincaré had seen that Bachelier had advanced to the threshold of a general theory of diffusion, he was notorious for lapses of memory. A few years later, he took an active part in discussions concerning Brownian diffusion, but had forgotten Bachelier.

Comments in a *Notice* Bachelier wrote in 1921 are worth summarizing:

1906: *Théorie des probabilités continues.* This theory has no relation whatsoever with the theory of geometric probability, whose scope is very limited. This is a science of another level of difficulty and generality than the calculus of probability. Conception, analysis, method, everything in it is new. 1913: *Probabilitiés cinématiques et dynamiques.* These applications of probability to mechanics are the author's own, absolutely. He took the original idea from no one; no work of the same kind has ever been performed. Conception, method, results, everything is new.

The hapless authors of academic *Notices* are not called upon to be modest, but Louis Bachelier had no reason for being modest. Does anyone know more about him?

SELECTED WORKS

1900. Théorie de la spéculation. *Annales de l'Ecole normale supérieure*, 3rd series, 17, 21–86. Trans. by A.J. Boness in *The Random Character of Stock Market Prices*, ed. P.H. Cootner, Cambridge, Mass.: MIT Press, 1967.

1901. Théorie mathématique des jeux. *Annales de l'Ecole normale supérieure*, 3rd series, 18, 143–210.

1906. Théorie des probabilités continues. *Journal des mathématiques pures et appliquées*, 6th series, 2(3), 259–327.

1910a. Les probabilités à plusieurs variables. *Annales de l'Ecole normale supérieure*, 3rd series, 27, 340–60.

1910b. Mouvement d'un point ou d'un système soumis à l'action des forces dépendant du hasard. *Comptes rendus de l'Académie des sciences* 151, 852–5.

1912. *Calcul des probabilités.* Paris: Gauthier-Villars.

1913. Les probabilités cinématiques et dynamiques. *Annales de l'Ecole normale supérieure*, 3rd series, 30, 77–119.

1924. *Le jeu, la change et le hasard.* Paris: E. Flammarion.

1937. *Les lois des grands nombres du calcul des probabilités.* Paris: Gauthier-Villars.

1938. *La spéculation et le calcul des probabilités.* Paris: Gauthier-Villars.

1939. *Les nouvelles méthodes du calcul des probabilités.* Paris: Gauthier-Villars.

Backwardation

MASAHIRO KAWAI

Using the language of the London Stock Exchange, 'backwardation' is a fee paid by a seller of stocks (or securities) to the buyer for the privilege of deferring delivery of them. Hence it means that the futures price (i.e. the current price for the future delivery) falls short of the spot price (i.e. the current price of immediate delivery). 'Contango', the reverse of backwardation, is a fee paid by the buyer who wants to postpone delivery, and means that the futures price exceeds the spot price. These terms may be extended to any futures transaction.

Keynes (1923, pp. 255–66; 1930, ch. 29) and Hicks (1946, pp. 130–40) advanced the theory of 'normal' backwardation; namely, the situation where the futures price of commodities is a downwardly biased prediction of the spot price at delivery time. Since normal backwardation is tantamount to the presence of a positive risk premium, hedgers as a whole take a short futures position of the commodities, and speculators as a group a long position. The theory of normal backwardation attempts to explain why hedgers tend to go short in futures.

Keynes and Hicks explained the existence of normal backwardation on technological grounds. That is, technological conditions in production and consumption (including demand activities by manufacturers who use the commodities as inputs) are such that producers must look much further ahead than consumers, because the former may already have committed themselves to production while the latter have a freer hand about acquiring the commodities. Thus there exists a greater desire to cover planned production (supplies) than to cover planned consumption (demands), and hedgers as a whole have a tendency to go short in futures. In order to persuade speculators to assume a matching long position, a positive risk premium has to be offered, hence a 'normal' backwardation.

Although this technological explanation is valid for typical commodity markets, it does not apply to all markets. Consider the following equilibrium conditions in the spot and futures markets at time 0:

$$Q_{0,0} + Z_{-1} = C_{0,0} + K_0 \text{ (Spot Market Equilibrium)}$$

$$Q_{0,1} + K_0 - C_{0,1} = Z_0 \text{ (Futures Market Equilibrium)}.$$

The variables Q, C, K and Z denote output supply, consumption, storage and futures speculation, respectively. The subscripts signify time; $Q_{t,s}$ (or $C_{t,s}$) is output or consumption planned at time t and actually supplied (or demanded) at time s, K_0 is the amount carried from time 0 to time 1, and Z_0 is the quantity of speculative futures contracts purchased (if $Z_0 > 0$, or sold if $Z_0 < 0$) at time 0 for time 1 delivery. In the case of typical commodities, Q, C, $K > 0$ and $Z \leqq 0$. (For more detailed discussions about the market equilibrium, see Kawai (1983).) The market clearing conditions yield:

$$Z_0 = Q_{0,1} + K_0 - C_{0,1} = C_{1,1} + K_1 - Q_{1,1}.$$

The arguments put forward by Keynes and Hicks assert that production is mostly planned and consumption is largely flexible so that $Q_{0,1} > C_{0,1}$ and $C_{1,1} > Q_{1,1}$. From this, $Z_0 > 0$ follows and there exists a 'normal backwardation' (or a positive risk premium). But when the adjustment cost of changing production is low and that of changing consumption high, such technological conditions may not be satisfied. Furthermore, in some markets (such as those for foreign exchange and financial instruments) the technological distinction between production (Q) and consumption (C) is unimportant and storage can be negative ($K < 0$); then, normal backwardation is not guaranteed. In essence, whether or not normal backwardation is generated depends on the nature of the commodities in question and is an empirical matter.

Considerable empirical effort has been devoted to detecting a positive or negative risk premium in various types of markets, with mixed result (see Peck, 1977). The 'efficient futures market hypothesis' (the hypothesis of no systematic risk premium combined with rational expectations) cannot be rejected for many markets, thus invalidating the theory of normal backwardation. In other markets, time-varying risk premia, positive or negative, have also been found.

BIBLIOGRAPHY

Hicks, J.R. 1946. *Value and Capital*, 2nd edn, London: Oxford University Press.

Kawai, M. 1983. Price volatility of storable commodities under rational expectations in spot and futures markets. *International Economic Review* 24(2), June, 435–54.

Keynes, J.M. 1923. Some aspects of commodity markets. *The Manchester Guardian Commercial, Reconstruction Supplement* 29, March. Reprinted in *The Collected Writings of John Maynard Keynes*, Vol. 7, London: Macmillan: New York: St. Martin's Press, 1971.

Keynes, J.M. 1930. *A Treatise on Money*, Vol. 2. London: Macmillan. Reprinted in *The Collected Writings of John Maynard Keynes*, London: Macmillan; New York: St. Martin's Press, 1971.

Peck, A.E. (ed.) 1977. *Selected Writings on Futures Markets*, Vol. 2. Chicago: Chicago Board of Trade.

Capital Asset Pricing Model

M.J. BRENNAN

Two general approaches to the problem of valuing assets under uncertainty may be distinguished. The first approach relies on arbitrage arguments of one kind or another, while under the second approach equilibrium asset prices are obtained by equating endogenously determined asset demands to asset supplies, which are typically taken as exogenous. Examples of the former range from the static arbitrage arguments which underlie the Modigliani–Miller theorem to the dynamic arbitrage strategies which are the basis for the Option Pricing Model: such arbitrage based models can only yield the price of one asset relative to the prices of other assets. The Capital Asset Pricing Model (CAPM) is an example of an equilibrium model in which asset prices are related to the exogenous data, the tastes and endowments of investors although, as we shall see below, the CAPM is often presented as a relative pricing model.

If they are to be of practical use, equilibrium asset pricing models must be parsimonious in their parameterization of asset demands. To date, this parsimony has been achieved only by a choice of assumptions which leads to universal portfolio separation: this is the property that the asset demand vector of every agent can be expressed as a linear combination of a set of basis vectors which may be thought of as portfolios or mutual funds. The distinguishing feature of the set of models which is collectively known as the CAPM is that each of the basis portfolios can be interpreted as the solution to a particular constrained portfolio variance minimization problem.

HISTORICAL PERSPECTIVE

The assumption that uncertainty about future asset returns can be described in terms of a probability distribution is at least as old as Irving Fisher (1906), although Hicks (1934b) appears to have been the first to suggest that preferences for investment could be represented as preferences for the moments of the probability distributions of their returns, and to propose that as a first approximation, preferences could be presented by indifference curves in mean-variance space. Other writers such as J. Marschak (1938) adopted a similar view, but it remained for von Neumann and Morgenstern (1947) to place the theory of choice under uncertainty on a rigorous axiomatic basis, and their expected utility theory is now an essential element of the financial economics paradigm.

The story of modern portfolio theory really begins, however, with the classic contributions of Markowitz (1952, 1958) who assumed explicitly that investor preferences were defined over the mean and variance of the aggregate portfolio return, related these parameters to the portfolio composition and the parameters of the joint distribution of security returns, and for the first time applied the principles of marginal analysis to the choice of optimal portfolios.

Both Markowitz and Tobin (1958) showed that mean variance preferences could be reconciled with the von Neumann/Morgenstern axioms if the utility function is quadratic in return or wealth. This assumption is objectionable since it implies negative marginal utility at high wealth levels. Tobin also showed, however, that mean-variance preferences could be derived by restricting the probability distributions over which choices are made to a two parameter family. After some initial confusion it was recognized that since portfolio returns are weighted sums of security returns, the two parameter family must be stable under addition, and the only member of the stable class with a finite variance is in the normal distribution. Subsequently Merton (1969) and Samuelson (1970) showed that mean-variance analysis is applicable for a broad class of continuous asset price processes if the trading interval is infinitesimal.

The major part of Tobin's analysis deals with the choice between a single risky asset and cash, but he demonstrated that nothing essential is changed if there are many risky assets, for they will always be held in the same proportions and can be treated as a single composite asset. This, the first separation theorem in

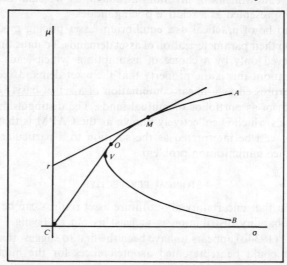

Figure 1

portfolio theory, is illustrated in Figure 1 which plots mean returns, μ, against the standard deviation, σ. In this figure the curved locus $AMOVB$ corresponds to the set of portfolios offering the lowest standard deviation for each level of mean return: the positively sloped segment is referred to as the efficient frontier, for points along it offer the highest μ for a given σ. In the absence of any riskless investment opportunities, risk averse mean-variance investors will select portfolios corresponding to the points at which their indifference curves in (μ, σ) space are tangent to the efficient frontier (Tobin shows that the indifference curves of risk averters will have the requisite curvature). Point C represents cash which has zero risk and return. By combining cash with the portfolio of risky assets corresponding to the tangency portfolio O, investors are able to attain the (μ, σ) combinations along the line segment CO, and all investors who find it optimal to hold cash will find it optimal to combine their cash with the same risky portfolio O; their portfolio decisions can be *separated* into the choice of the optimal combination of risky asset (O) and the choice of the cash/risky asset ratio.

Six years elapsed before the equilibrium implications of the Tobin Separation Theorem were exploited by Sharpe (1964) and Lintner (1965). The reason for delay was undoubtedly the boldness of the assumption required for progress, namely that all investors hold the same beliefs about the joint distribution of security returns. Nevertheless, this assumption of homogeneous beliefs, combined with the further assumption that all investors can borrow as well as lend at the riskless rate, r, leads to the powerful conclusion that all investors hold the same portfolio of risky assets, denoted by M in the figure. Then the only risky assets that will be held by investors in equilibrium are those contained in portfolio M, and M must be the market portfolio of all risky assets in the economy. This identification of the tangency portfolio M with the aggregate market portfolio is the essence of the Sharpe–Lintner CAPM.

The interest of this result derives from the restriction that it imposes on expected asset returns: the excess of μ_j, the expected return on any security j, over the risk free rate r, must be proportional to the covariance of the security return with the return on the market portfolio, σ_{jM}:

$$\mu_j - r = \theta_M \sigma_{jM} \qquad \text{for all } j \qquad (1)$$

where θ_M is a measure of aggregate risk aversion. The intuition behind this important result is that if investors are content to hold portfolio M, the marginal rate of transformation between risk and return obtained by borrowing to invest in a risky security must be the same for all risky securities. Frequently the unknown risk aversion parameter, θ_M, is eliminated and the relative pricing result is obtained:

$$\mu_j - r = \beta_j(\mu_M - r) \qquad \text{for all } j \qquad (2)$$

where μ_M is the expected return on the market portfolio and $\beta_j \equiv \sigma_{jM}/\sigma_{MM}$ is the 'beta' coefficient, which corresponds to the slope of the regression line relating the return on the security to the return on the market portfolio.

During the first half of the 1970s extensive progress was made in relaxing the strong assumptions underlying the original model, and new separation theorems and models were obtained. At the same time, extensive empirical investigations made possible by the development of new stock price data bases found results which were interpreted as favourable to the model. The model also has an influence on practical investment management and corporate finance.

A turning point was reached with the publication of a paper by Roll (1977); this argued that the market portfolio of the theory, which includes all assets, could never be empirically identified, and that therefore the CAPM, which simply asserts the efficiency properties of this portfolio, could never be empirically tested. This argument had substantial influence, and played a major role in shifting attention away from the CAPM to the newly emerging Arbitrage Pricing Theory of Ross (1976).

The CAPM is of great historical significance not only because it was the first equilibrium model of asset pricing under uncertainty, but also because it showed the importance of portfolio separation for tractable equilibrium models; and, being derivable from assumptions of either quadratic utility or normal distributions it revealed that the requisite separation properties could be obtained by restrictions either on preferences or on distributions. Cass and Stiglitz (1970) clarified the rather restrictive assumptions necessary for preference based separation, and equilibrium models based on this have been constructed, for example, by Rubinstein (1976). Ross (1978) has identified the distributional assumptions required for separation in the absence of restrictions on preferences, and the Arbitrage Pricing Theory is based on a generalization of his 'Separating Distributions'. Thus both preference-based and distribution-based models of capital market equilibrium are lineal descendants of the CAPM.

An unfortunate consequence of the one period nature of the CAPM was a concentration of attention on equilibrium rates of return, rather than on prices, which are the fundamental variables of interest. However, Merton (1973) placed the CAPM in an intertemporal context, and his necessary condition for equilibrium rates of return forms one cornerstone (the other being an assumption of rational expectations) for the Cox, Ingersoll and Ross (1985) partial differential equation for asset prices.

FORMAL MODELS

While a complete asset pricing model endogenizes the riskless interest rate as well as the prices of risky securities, the CAPM adds nothing new to the theory of interest rate determination and we shall simplify by taking the interest rate and current consumption decisions as given, concentrating our attention on portfolio decisions and the pricing of risky securities.

In considering the various versions of the CAPM we shall pay particular attention to the implied demands of investors. It will be seen that in all cases in which risks are freely traded, asset demands exhibit the separation property, and even when there are restrictions on trading as in the Mayers (1972) asset pricing model, an approximate separation property obtains.

The Sharpe–Lintner Model. Consider a setting in which each investor i $(i = 1, \ldots, m)$ is endowed with a fraction $\bar{z}_{ij}$ of security j $(j = 1, \ldots, n)$ and (a) investor utility is defined over the mean and variance of end of period wealth; (b) securities are traded in a competitive market with no taxes or transactions costs; (c) investors share homogeneous beliefs or assessments of the joint distribution of payoffs on the securities; there are no dividends; (d) there is an exogenously determined interest rate $r = R - 1$ at which investors may borrow or lend without default; (e) there are no restrictions on short sales.

Then define:

$\bar{P}_1$ expected end of period value of security j;

$\bar{P}_{j0}$ initial value of security j;

ω_{jk} covariance between end of period value of j and k;

$\bar{W}_i, S_i^2$ expectation and variance of end of period wealth of investor i;

$V_i(\bar{W}_i, S_i^2)$ utility of investor i with $V_{i1} \equiv \partial V_i / \partial \bar{W}_i > 0$, $V_{i2} \equiv \partial V_i / \partial S_i^2 < 0$.

The investor's decision problem may be written as

$$\max_{z_{ij}} V_i(\bar{W}_i, S_i^2) \tag{3}$$

$$\text{s.t.} \quad \bar{W}_i = \sum_j z_{ij} \bar{P}_{j1} - R \sum_j (z_{ij} - \bar{z}_{ij}) P_{j0} \tag{4}$$

$$S_i^2 = \sum_j \sum_k z_{ij} z_{ik} \omega_{jk}. \tag{5}$$

The first order conditions for an optimum are

$$V_{i1}(\bar{P}_{j1} - RP_{j0}) + 2V_{i2} \sum_k z_{ik} \omega_{jk} = 0, \qquad (j = 1, \ldots, n) \tag{6}$$

and the second conditions are satisfied by virtue of the assumption of risk aversion. Defining Ω^* as the variance covariance matrix $[\omega_{jk}]$ and using boldface type to denote vectors, the vector of fractional asset demands may be written

$$\mathbf{z}_i = \theta_i^{-1} \Omega^{*-1}(\bar{\mathbf{P}}_1 - R\mathbf{P}_0) \tag{7}$$

where $\theta_i^{-1} \equiv -V_{i1}/2V_{i2}$ is a measure of the investor's risk tolerance. Equation (7) is a statement of the Tobin Separation Theorem, that investor demands for risky assets differ only by a scalar multiple.

Market clearing requires that $\Sigma_i \mathbf{z}_i = \mathbf{1}$ where $\mathbf{1}$ is a vector of units. Then the equilibrium initial price vector is obtained by summing (7) over i and imposing the market clearing condition:

$$\mathbf{P}_0 = \frac{1}{R}\{\bar{\mathbf{P}}_1 - \theta_m \Omega^* \mathbf{1}\} \tag{8}$$

where $\theta_m \equiv (\Sigma_i \theta_i^{-1})^{-1}$. In this form the CAPM expresses equilibrium prices in terms of the exogenous variables, the distribution of end of period prices, investor risk aversion parameters and the interest rate, although it should be noted that in general the market risk aversion parameter θ_m will depend upon the endogenously determined distribution of wealth. This formulation corresponds to that of Lintner (1965) and emphasizes the one period nature of the model and the exogeneity of the end of period prices. However, the CAPM is most often written as a necessary condition for the equilibrium rates of return, although this obscures the distinction between endogenous and exogenous variables.

In what follows we shall work with the rate of return formulation; thus define $x_{ij} \equiv z_{ij} P_{j0}$, the amount invested in security j; $\mu_j \equiv \bar{P}_{j1}/P_{j0} - 1$, the expected rate of return and $\sigma_{jk} \equiv \omega_{jk}/P_{j0} P_{k0}$, the covariance of the rates of return between securities j and k. Making these substitutions in (4) and (5), the first order conditions (6) become

$$V_{i1}(\mu_j - r) + 2V_{i2} \sum_k x_{ik}\sigma_{jk} = 0, \qquad (j = 1, \ldots, n). \tag{9}$$

Then, defining Ω as the variance covariance matrix of rates of return, the vector of asset demands $\mathbf{x}_i$ may be expressed as

$$\mathbf{x}_i = \theta_i^{-1} \Omega^{-1}(\mu - r\mathbf{1}). \tag{10}$$

This is an alternative statement of the Tobin Separation Theorem and the portfolio $\Omega^{-1}(\mu - r\mathbf{1})\square$ corresponds to the point of tangency in figure 1. This portfolio itself may be decomposed into the two portfolios $\Omega^{-1}\mu$ and $\Omega^{-1}\mathbf{1}$. The former is the solution to the problem of finding the minimum variance portfolio of risky assets with a given expected payoff, and the latter is the solution to the problem of finding the global minimum variance portfolio of risky assets; these two portfolios plot at points O and V in the figure. As Merton (1972) has shown, the whole locus may be constructed from just these two portfolios.

Let V_m denote the aggregate market value of all assets in the market portfolio and let $\mathbf{v_m}$ denote the vector of market proportions. Combining the market clearing condition $\Sigma_i \mathbf{x}_i = V_m \mathbf{v_m}$ with (10) yields

$$\mu - r\mathbf{1} = \theta_m V_m \Omega \mathbf{v_m}. \tag{11}$$

This form of the CAPM expresses asset risk premia as proportional to the covariances of their returns with the returns on the market portfolio; this of course is no more than the condition for the market portfolio to correspond to the tangency point in figure 1. Equation (11) contains the market risk aversion parameter θ_m. This can be eliminated by premultiplying (11) by $\mathbf{v_m}$ and solving for $\theta_m = (\mu_m - r)/\sigma_m^2$, where μ_m and σ_m^2 are the expected return and variance of return on the market portfolio respectively. Then, substituting for θ_m in (11) we have the equation of the 'security market line':

$$\mu_j - r = \beta_j(\mu_m - r) \tag{12}$$

where $\beta_j \equiv \sigma_{jm}/\sigma_m^2$. In this form the CAPM is a relative pricing model which relates the risk premium on individual securities to the risk premium on the market portfolio. The proportionality factor, β_j, often referred to as the 'beta coefficient', is the coefficient from the regression of $\tilde{R}_j$, the return on security j, on $\tilde{R}_m$, the return on the market portfolio:

$$\tilde{R}_j = \alpha_j + \beta_j \tilde{R}_m + \tilde{e}_j \qquad (13)$$

where $\tilde{e}_j$ is an orthogonal error term. Taking expectations in the market model equation (13), the asset pricing equation (12) is seen to imply the restriction $\alpha_j = (1 - \beta_j)r$. This restriction, and the existence of a positive risk premium on the market portfolio, are the major empirical predictions of the Sharpe–Lintner model. They have been the subject of extensive empirical tests.

Taxes and restrictions on riskless transactions. The absence of short sales restriction is not critical to the Sharpe–Lintner model, since in equilibrium all investors hold the market portfolio, which does not involve short sales. The assumption is critical, however, for all the remaining models we shall consider which involve more than a single basis fund of risky securities.

Thus, following Black (1972) and Brennan (1970), assume that there are no opportunities for riskless borrowing or lending, and that each security pays pre-determined dividends which are taxed in the hands of the investor at the rate t_i $(i = 1, \ldots, m)$. Denoting the dividend yield by δ_j, and assuming that investor preferences are defined over the moments of after tax wealth, the first order conditions corresponding to (9) are:

$$V_{i1}(\mu_j - t_i\delta_j - \lambda_i) + 2V_{i2}\sum_k x_{ik}\sigma_{jk} = 0, \qquad (j = 1, \ldots, n) \qquad (14)$$

where λ_i is the Lagrange multiplier associated with the constraint that all wealth be invested in risky securities. The vector of asset demands may be written as:

$$\mathbf{x}_1 = \theta_i^{-1}\mathbf{\Omega}^{-1}\mu - (\theta_1^{-1}\lambda_1)\mathbf{\Omega}^{-1}\mathbf{1} - (\theta_1^{-1}\mathbf{t}_1)\mathbf{\Omega}^{-1}\delta. \qquad (15)$$

Note first that if $t_i = 0$ the optimal portfolio for any preferences can be constructed from the two mutual funds $\mathbf{\Omega}^{-1}\mu$ and $\mathbf{\Omega}^{-1}\mathbf{1}$. Heterogeneous taxation of dividends introduces the third mutual fund, which can be interpreted as the solution to the problem of finding the minimum variance portfolio with a given total dividend. Aggregating the demand vectors, and imposing the market clearing conditions, yields an asset pricing equation which contains three utility dependent parameters, λ_m, θ_m and t_m, corresponding to the three funds in (15):

$$\mu = \lambda_m\mathbf{1} = \theta_m V_m\mathbf{\Omega}\mathbf{v_m} + t_m\delta \qquad (16)$$

t_m, the market tax rate, is a weighted average of the personal tax rates, and λ_m, the market shadow interest rate, is referred to for historical reasons as the zero beta return. When $t_m = 0$ (16), it is just the condition for the market portfolio to be the tangency portfolio when the interest rate is λ_m. Thus the Black model, which does not include taxes, differs from the Sharpe–Lintner model only in leaving unspecified the relevant (shadow) riskless interest rate.

97

Non-marketable assets. Mayers (1972) has considered the effect of introducing an extreme form of market imperfection, namely an absolute prohibition on trading certain assets. This is important, for a substantial part of total wealth is not held as part of well diversified portfolios, on account either of prohibitions on trade (human capital), or of market imperfections such as transactions costs and information asymmetries. Thus let $\bar{h}$ denote the expected payoff on the non-marketable wealth (human capital) or investor i, and let σ^i_{jh} denote the covariance between the return on marketable security j and the human capital of investor i. Then the expression for $\bar{W}_i$ must be increased by $\bar{h}$ and the variance of end of period wealth becomes $S^2_i = \Sigma_j \Sigma_k x_{ij} x_{ik} \sigma_{jk} + 2\Sigma_j x_{ij}\sigma^i_{jh} + \sigma^i_{hh}$. The asset demand vector can then be written as

$$\mathbf{x}_i = \theta_i^{-1}\mathbf{\Omega}^{-1}(\boldsymbol{\mu} - r\mathbf{1}) - \mathbf{b}_i \tag{17}$$

where $\mathbf{b}_i = \mathbf{\Omega}^{-1}\sigma^i_n$ is the vector of coefficients from the regression of the return on human wealth on the marketable security returns. Defining $\mathbf{x}^e_i \equiv \mathbf{x}_i + \mathbf{b}_i$ as the vector of effective asset demands, we see from (17) that effective asset demands exhibit the standard separation property. This reflects the fact that, while the returns on human capital are not directly marketable, the component of the return which is linearly related to the returns on the marketable securities is indirectly marketable by appropriate offsetting positions in the marketable securities. The asset holdings of the individual may be represented as the sum of effective asset holdings $\mathbf{x}^e_i$ and an investment in the component of human wealth whose return is orthogonal to the returns on marketable assets. We refer to this as approximate portfolio separation since the first component exhibits portfolio separation, and the second component has no effect on the relative demands for marketable assets.

The Mayers model leads to an asset pricing equation which is identical to that of the Sharpe–Lintner model if the market portfolio is defined as the sum of the effective investment vectors $\mathbf{x}^e_i$.

Inflation and international asset pricing. Stochastic inflation has no effect on the foregoing results, provided that a common inflation rate can be defined for all investors and returns are restated in real terms. However, the international asset pricing models of Solnik (1974) and Stulz (1981) distinguish between nationalities precisely on the basis of their price indices, which may differ on account of either a violation of commodity price parity or differences in tastes and consumption baskets (see Adler and Dumas, 1983).

Define $\tilde{\pi}_i$ as the inflation rate in the numeraire currency for investor i. Then, to a high order of approximation, which becomes exact as the time interval approaches zero, the mean and variance of real wealth can be written as

$$\bar{W}_i = \sum_j x_{ij}(\mu_j - r) + W_{0i}(1 + r - \tilde{\pi}_i + \sigma^i_{\pi\pi}) - \sum_j x_{ij}\sigma^i_{j\pi} \tag{18}$$

$$S^2_i = \sum_j \sum_k x_{ij} x_{ik}\sigma_{jk} - 2W_{0i}\sum_j x_{ij}\sigma^i_{k\pi} + W^2_{0i}\sigma^i_{\pi\pi} \tag{19}$$

where W_{0i} is the investor's initial wealth.

The asset demand vector is then

$$x_i = \theta_i^{-1}\Omega^{-1}(\mu - r\mathbf{1}) + \mathbf{b_i} \qquad (20)$$

where $\mathbf{b_i} \equiv W_{0i}\Omega^{-1}\sigma_x^i$ is the vector of coefficients from the regression at the individual's aggregate inflation risk, $W_{0i}\tilde{\pi}_i$, on security returns. Comparing (20) with (17), it is apparent that this international asset pricing model is isomorphic to the Mayers' non-marketable wealth model with individual inflation risks playing the same role as human capital.

Black (1974) has modeled segmentation in international capital markets by introducing a tax on foreign security holdings for residents of one country. This model is isomorphic to Brennan's (1970) tax model, if the foreign securities are thought of as paying dividends on which only domestic residents are taxable. Stulz (1981) extends Black's model by prohibiting negative taxes on short sales: as one might expect, this causes some indeterminacy in the pricing relations since the marginal conditions of portfolio optimality are no longer always satisfied.

Intertemporal models. Merton (1973) has shown that the classical one period CAPM may be extended to an intertemporal setting in which investors maximize the expected utility of lifetime consumption. With continuous trading and suitable restrictions on the stochastic process of asset prices, the essential mean-variance analysis is retained, the major innovation being that at each instant the individual may be represented as maximising the expected utility of a derived utility function, defined over wealth and a set of S state variables describing the future investment and consumption opportunity sets. The state dependent derived utility function induces $(S + 1)$ fund separation in the risky asset portfolio, and the vector of risky asset demands may be written

$$\mathbf{x_1} = \theta_1^{-1}\Omega^{-1}(\mu - r\mathbf{1}) - \sum_{s=1}^{s} \gamma_{is}\Omega^{-1}\zeta_s \qquad (21)$$

where ζ_s is the vector of covariances of asset returns with the change in state variable S and γ_{is} depends on the utility function. Aggregation of asset demands and the imposition of the market clearing condition leads to an asset pricing equation in which asset risk premia are a linear function of covariances with aggregate wealth *and* covariances with the state variables. In the absence of prior information about the relevant state variables this model is empirically indistinguishable from the Arbitrage Pricing Theory. Breeden (1979) has shown that this 'multi-beta' pricing model may be collapsed to a single beta measured with respect to changes in aggregate consumption if consumption preferences are time separable. Cornell (1981) has shown that unfortunately the relevant betas will be stochastic and Bergman (1985) has shown that the Breeden result does not generalize to non time-separable preferences.

Merton (1973) has employed the interest rate as a possible example of a relevant state variable. Since this obviously does vary stochastically over time it is of interest to enquire under what conditions the classic CAPM will hold even with a stochastic interest rate. Constantinides (1980, 1982) has identified two sets of sufficient conditions. In his models the social investment opportunity set is stationary and consists only of risky investments: stochastic variation in the interest rate then does not affect the CAPM relation if either there is demand aggregation or full Pareto efficiency of asset markets. The intuition behind the result is that either condition is sufficient for prices to be determined as though there existed a single representative individual; for such an individual stochastic variation in the interest rate is irrelevant since the interest rate only represents a shadow price and not a real investment opportunity.

Finally, the single period nature of the CAPM is retained if individuals behave myopically, ignoring stochastic variation in the investment opportunity set in their portfolio choices: this occurs if and only if the utility function is logarithmic.

The foregoing models place restrictions on the joint distribution of security terms. As already mentioned, Cox, Ingersoll and Ross (1985) combine the Merton intertemporal model of returns with production and the assumption of rational expectations to yield a partial differential equation for asset prices. Stapleton and Subrahmanyam (1978) derive the only pure exchange discrete time intertemporal asset pricing model which is consistent with mean-variance analysis. Their model assumes that investors have exponential utility functions and that asset cash flows follow a joint normal distribution; it is implicitly assumed that aggregate consumption follows a random walk.

Distributional assumptions. Comparatively little effort has been expended in relaxing the assumption of homogeneity of investor beliefs underlying the CAPM. However, progress has been made in generalizing the version of the model which is based on the normal distribution. As we have mentioned, Merton (1973) has shown that the model obtains as the decision making horizon shrinks to zero if asset returns belong to the family of *compact distributions*.

In a discrete time setting Ross (1978) has shown that the assumption of normality can be relaxed slightly to that of a two fund separating distribution. Dybvig and Ingersoll (1982) emphasize the critical nature of the distributional assumption since the CAPM result for all securities is vulnerable to the introduction of even a single security whose returns do not satisfy it. This would significantly reduce the usefulness of the model in capital markets which contain securities like options with truncated returns, except that if the market is fully Pareto efficient and return on the market portfolio is normally distributed, then those assets whose returns are jointly normal with the market portfolio will satisfy the CAPM. The reason for this is that Pareto efficiency permits the fiction of the representative investor who holds the market portfolio.

Sharpe (1977), in positing a factor model of returns, derived a multibeta version of the CAPM which is close in spirit to the equilibrium factor models developed more recently from antecedents in the Arbitrage Pricing Theory by Connor (1984) and others.

BIBLIOGRAPHY

Adler, M. and Dumas, B. 1983. International portfolio choice and corporation finance: a synthesis. *Journal of Finance* 38(3), June, 925–84.

Bergman, Y. 1985. Time preference and capital asset pricing models. *Journal of Financial Economics* 14(1), March, 145–59.

Black, F. 1972. Capital market equilibrium with restricted borrowing. *Journal of Business* 45(3), July, 444–55.

Black, F. 1974. International capital market equilibrium with investment barriers. *Journal of Financial Economics* 1(4), December, 337–52.

Breeden, D. 1979. An intertemporal asset pricing model with stochastic consumption and investment opportunities. *Journal of Financial Economics* 7(3), September, 265–96.

Brennan, M. 1970. Taxes, market valuation and corporate financial policy. *National Tax Journal* 23(4), December, 417–27.

Cass, D. and Stiglitz, J. 1970. The structure of investor preferences and asset returns, and separability in portfolio allocation: a contribution to the pure theory of mutual funds. *Journal of Economic Theory* 2(2), June, 122–60.

Connor, G. 1984. A unified beta pricing theory. *Journal of Economic Theory* 34(1), 13–31.

Constantinides, G. 1980. Admissible uncertainty in the intertemporal asset pricing model. *Journal of Financial Economics* 8(1), March, 71–86.

Constantinides, G. 1982. Intertemporal asset pricing with heterogeneous consumers and without demand aggregation. *Journal of Business* 55(2), April, 253–67.

Cornell, B. 1981. The consumption based asset pricing model: a note on potential tests and applications. *Journal of Financial Economics* 9(1), March, 103–8.

Cox, J., Ingersoll, J. and Ross, S. 1985. An intertemporal general equilibrium model of asset prices. *Econometrica* 53(2), March, 363–84.

Dybvig, P. and Ingersoll, J. 1982. Mean-variance theory in complete markets. *Journal of Business* 55(2), April, 233–51.

Fisher, I. 1906. *The Nature of Capital and Income.* New York: Macmillan.

Hicks, J.R. 1934a. A note on the elasticity of supply. *Review of Economic Studies* 2, October, 31–7.

Hicks, J.R. 1934b. Application of mathematical methods to the theory of risk. *Econometrica* 2, April, 194–5.

Lintner, J. 1965. The valuation of risk assets and the selection of risky investments in stock portfolios and capital budgets. *Review of Economics and Statistics* 47, February, 13–37.

Markowitz, H. 1952. Portfolio selection. *Journal of Finance* 7, March, 77–91.

Markowitz, H. 1958. *Portfolio Selection: Efficient Diversification of Investments.* New York: Wiley.

Marschak, J. 1938. Money and the theory of assets. *Econometrica* 6, October, 311–25.

Mayers, D. 1972. Non-marketable assets and capital market equilibrium under uncertainty. In *Studies in the Theory of Capital Markets*, ed. M. Jensen, New York: Praeger.

Merton, R. 1969. Lifetime portfolio selection under uncertainty: the continuous-time case. *Review of Economics and Statistics* 51(3), August, 247–57.

Merton, R. 1972. An analytic derivation of the efficient portfolio frontier. *Journal of Financial and Quantitative Analysis* 7(4), September, 1851–72.

Merton, R. 1973. An intertemporal capital asset pricing model. *Econometrica* 41, September, 867–87.

Roll, R. 1977. A critique of the asset pricing theory's test; Part I: On past and potential testability of the theory. *Journal of Financial Economics* 4(2), March, 129–76.

Ross, S. 1976. The arbitrage theory of capital asset pricing. *Journal of Economic Theory* 13(3), December, 341–60.

Ross, S. 1978. Mutual fund separation in financial theory: The separating distributions. *Journal of Economic Theory* 17(2), April, 254–86.

Rubinstein, M. 1976. The valuation of uncertain income streams and the pricing of options. *Bell Journal of Economics* 7(2), Autumn, 407–25.

Samuelson, P. 1970. The fundamental approximation of theorem of portfolio analysis in terms of means, variances, and higher moments. *Review of Economic Studies* 37(4), October, 537–42.

Sharpe, W.F. 1964. Capital asset prices: a theory of market equilibrium under conditions of risk. *Journal of Finance* 19, September, 425–42.

Sharpe, W.F. 1977. The capital asset pricing model: a 'multi-beta' interpretation. In *Financial Decision Making under Uncertainty*, ed. H. Levy and M. Sarnat, New York: Harcourt Brace Jovanovich, Academic Press.

Solnik, B. 1974. An equilibrium model of international capital markets. *Journal of Economic Theory* 8(4), August, 500–24.

Stapleton, R. and Subrahmanyam, M. 1978. A multiperiod equilibrium asset pricing model. *Econometrica* 46(5), September, 1077–95.

Stulz, R. 1981. A model of international asset pricing. *Journal of Financial Economics* 9(4), December, 383–406.

Tobin, J. 1958. Liquidity preference as behavior towards risk. *Review of Economic Studies* 25, February, 65–86.

Von Neumann, J. and Morgensten, O. 1947. *Theory of Games and Economic Behavior.* 2nd edn, Princeton: Princeton University Press.

Continuous-time Stochastic Models

ROBERT C. MERTON

Models in which agents can revise their decisions continuously in time have proved fruitful in the analysis of economic problems involving intertemporal choice under uncertainty (cf. Malliaris and Brock, 1982). These models frequently produce significantly sharper results than can be derived from their discrete-time counterparts. In the majority of such cases, the dynamics of the underlying system are described by diffusion processes, whose continuous sample paths can be represented by Itô integrals. However, in selected applications, this assumption can be relaxed to include both non-Markov path-dependent processes and Poisson-directed jump processes.

An early application of this mode of analysis was the lifetime consumption-portfolio selection problem (Merton, 1969, 1971). Under the assumptions of continuous trading and asset returns generated by diffusion processes, the derived structure of optimal portfolio demands produce portfolio-separation or mutual fund theorems like those derived in the static Markowitz–Tobin mean-variance model, but without the objectionable assumption of either quadratic preferences or Gaussian-distributed asset prices. Indeed, in the special, but prototypical, case of lognormally-distributed asset prices, the intertemporal optimal rules are identical to those of the mean-variance model. The continuous-time analysis thus provides a reconciliation of this classic model with models of general expected utility maximization in an environment where asset ownership has limited liability.

Using these same assumptions of continuous trading and lognormality of security prices. Black and Scholes (1973) derived a formula for pricing options that provided the foundation for subsequent development of a unified theory of corporation liability evaluation and general contingent-claim pricing. Cox, Ingersoll and Ross (1985a) use the continuous-trading methodology with diffusion processes to derive a general theory for the term structure of interest rates.

Building on the continuous-time model of individual choice, Merton (1973), Breeden (1979) and Cox, Ingersoll and Ross (1985b) develop intertemporal models of equilibrium asset prices. Huang (1985) provides a stronger foundation for these models by showing that if information in an economy with continuous-trading opportunities evolves according to diffusion processes, then equilibrium security prices will also evolve according to diffusion processes.

In the intertemporal version of the Arrow–Debreu general equilibrium model with complete markets, the markets need only to be open 'once' because agents will have no need for further trade. The continuous-trading model is in this respect at the opposite extreme. Economies in which the dynamics of the system are described by diffusion processes will have a continuum of possible states over any finite interval of time. Thus, in the strict sense, to have complete markets in the continuous-time diffusion model requires an uncountable number of pure Arrow–Debreu securities. The continuous-trading model with diffusions, nevertheless, appears to have many of the important properties of the Arrow–Debreu model, but without nearly so many securities.

As is well known, in the absence of complete Arrow–Debreu markets, a competitive equilibrium does not in general produce Pareto optimal allocations. However, Radner (1972) has shown that an Arrow–Debreu equilibrium allocation can be achieved without a full set of pure time-state contingent securities if agents can use the available securities to implement dynamic trading strategies which replicate the payoff structure of the missing pure securities. There is much analysis to suggest that continuous-trading opportunities together with diffusion representations for the evolution of the economy provide a particularly fertile environment for fulfilling the Radner conditions.

Under reasonably general assumptions about agents' preferences and endowments, Breeden (1979) among others has shown that the intertemporal equilibrium allocations generated in economies with continuous trading in a finite number of securities can be Pareto efficient. In the analysis of the individual portfolio selection problem underlying these equilibrium models, the derived portfolio-separation theorems show that the set of individually-optimal portfolios can be generated by combinations of relatively few composite securities or mutual funds.

The extensive literature on options and contingent-claims pricing provides further evidence that continuous-trading opportunities make possible a large reduction in the number of securities markets without loss of efficiency. Although typically partial equilibrium in nature, these analyses show that continuous-trading dynamic portfolio strategies using as few as two securities can replicate a wide range of state and time-dependent payoff structures.

In perhaps the most general analysis to date, Duffie and Huang (1985) study the role continuous trading plays in successfully implementing Arrow–Debreu equilibria with infinite-dimensional commodity spaces, using only a finite number of securities. In particular, they derive necessary and sufficient conditions for continuous-trading portfolio strategies with a finite number of securities to complete markets effectively in a Radner economy. By working with martingale representation theorems, Duffie and Huang show that the class of dynamics for which these results obtain extends beyond vector diffusion processes to include some non-Markov path-dependent processes. They also show that having heterogeneous probability assessments among agents provides no important difficulties with the results, provided all agents' subjective probability measures are uniformly absolutely continuous. Although there remain further technical issues to be resolved, it is evident that the continuous-trading models provide a strong foundation for the belief that a good substitute for having many markets and securities is to have fewer markets which are open for trade more frequently.

A sketch of the derivation of the portfolio separation theorem along the lines of Merton (1971, 1973, 1982a) and Breeden (1979) is as follows:

At each time t, each consumer-investor acts so as to

$$\text{Max } E_t \left\{ \int_t^T U[c(\tau), S(\tau), \tau] \, d\tau + B[W(T), S(T), T] \right\} \tag{1}$$

where E_t is the conditional expectation operator, conditional on information available at time t. $S(t) = [S_1(t), \ldots, S_m(t)]$ is a finite-m vector set of state variables which together with the consumer's current wealth $W(t)$ is sufficient to describe the state of the economy at time t. $c(t)$ denotes the instantaneous consumption flow selected at time t. U is a strictly concave, state-dependent utility function for consumption and B represents utility from bequests at date T.

The evolution of the state variables S is described by a Markov system of Itô stochastic differential equations

$$dS_i(t) = G_i(S, t) \, dt + H_i(S, t) \, dq_i, \qquad i = 1, 2, \ldots, m \tag{2}$$

where $G_i(S, t)$ is the instantaneous expected change in $S_i(t)$ per unit time at time t; H_i^2 is the instantaneous variance of the change in $S_i(t)$, where it is understood that these statistics are conditional on $S(t) = S$. The dq_i are Wiener processes with the instantaneous correlation coefficient per unit time between dq_i and dq_j given by the function $\eta_{ij}(S, t)$, $i, j = 1, \ldots, m$.

At each point in time, the consumer chooses a consumption flow and allocates his wealth among n risky securities and a riskless security whose instantaneous rate of return per unit time is the interest rate $r(t)$. The rate of return dynamics on risky security j can be written as

$$dP_j / P_j = \alpha_j(S, t) \, dt + \sigma_j(S, t) \, dz_j, \qquad j = 1, 2, \ldots, n \tag{3}$$

where α_j is the instantaneous conditional expected rate of return per unit time; σ_j^2 is the conditional variance per unit time; and dz_j is a Wiener process. Denote by $\rho_{jk}(S, t)$ the instantaneous correlation coefficient per unit time between dz_j and dz_k, $j, k = 1, 2, \ldots, n$, and denote by $\mu_{ij}(S, t)$ the instantaneous correlation coefficient between dq_i and dz_j, $i = 1, 2, \ldots, m$ and $j = 1, 2, \ldots, n$.

The accumulation equation for the consumer's wealth can be written as

$$dW = [rW + y - c] \, dt + \sum_{j=1}^n w_j W[dP_j / P_j - r \, dt] \tag{4}$$

where $y = y(S, t)$ is the consumer's wage income; w_j is the fraction of his wealth allocated to risky security j at time t, and $[1 - \Sigma_j^n w_j]$ is the fraction allocated to the riskless asset.

The optimal consumption and portfolio rules, $c^*(W, S, t)$ and $w^*(W, S, t)$, are derived by the technique of stochastic dynamic programming. Among the first-order conditions to be satisfied by these optimal rules are the n conditions for the optimal portfolio holdings at time t, which can be expressed as $j = 1, 2, \ldots, n$

$$0 = \left\{ \alpha_j - r - \left(\sum_1^n w_i^* \sigma_i \sigma_j \rho_{ij} W + \sum_1^m A_i \sigma_j H_i \mu_{ij} \right) \middle/ K \right\} \frac{\partial U}{\partial c} \frac{\partial c^*}{\partial W} W \qquad (5)$$

where

$$K \equiv - \partial U / \partial c / [\partial^2 U / \partial c^2 \cdot \partial c^* / \partial W]$$

and

$$A_i \equiv - [\partial c^* / \partial S_i + (\partial^2 U / \partial c \partial S_i) / (\partial^2 U / \partial c^2)] / (\partial c^* / \partial W), \qquad i = 1, 2, \ldots, m.$$

By inspection, the manifest characteristic of the system of equations (5) is that it is linear in the optimal demands for risky assets. Therefore, if none of the risky assets is redundant, then standard matrix inversion can be used to solve (5) explicitly for these demands. That is,

$$w_j^*(t) W(t) = K \sum_1^n v_{kj}(\alpha_k - r) + \sum_1^m A_i \zeta_{ij}, \qquad j = 1, 2, \ldots, n \qquad (6)$$

where v_{kj} is the $k - j$th element of the inverse of the variance–covariance matrix of returns

$$[\sigma_i \sigma_j \rho_{ij}] \quad \text{and} \quad \zeta_{ij} \equiv \sum_1^n v_{kj} \sigma_k H_i \mu_{ik}.$$

By inspection, $K, A_i, \ldots, A_m$ are the only elements in (6) that depend on the individual investor's preferences or endowment. As an immediate consequence, it follows that there exist $(m + 2)$ portfolios ('mutual funds') constructed from linear combinations of the available securities such that, independent of preferences, wealth distribution, or planning horizon, all investors will be indifferent between choosing their portfolios from combinations of just these $(m + 2)$ funds or combinations of all n risky securities and the riskless security. This portfolio-separation theorem is, of course, vacuous if $m \geqslant n + 1$. If, however, $m \ll n$, then it implies a nontrivial reduction in the number of securities required to generate the set of optimal portfolios.

Although not unique, a set of funds which meets the criterion of the theorem is: fund no. 1 holds the riskless asset; fund no. 2 holds fraction $\Sigma_1^n v_{kj}(\alpha_k - r)$ in security j, $j = 1, \ldots, n$ and the balance in the riskless asset; for $i = 1, 2, \ldots, m$, fund no. $(2 + i)$ holds fraction ζ_{ij} in security j, $j = 1, 2, \ldots, n$ and the balance in the riskless asset. Funds nos. 1 and 2, together generate the set of portfolios with maximum expected return for a given variance of the return (i.e. the mean-variance efficient set). Fund no. $(2 + i)$ provides the maximum feasible correlation between its return and the stochastic component of the instantaneous change in state variable $S_i(t)$, $i = 1, \ldots, m$. As discussed in detail in the cited Breeden and Merton papers, these latter portfolios serve the function of providing the best feasible hedges against utility losses caused by unanticipated changes in the state variables of the economy.

In the important case where the set of available securities is such that the return on fund no. $(2 + i)$ is perfectly correlated with the change in state variable $S_i(t)$ for each i, $i = 1, \ldots, m$, Breeden (1979) shows that the resulting intertemporal equilibrium allocations are Pareto-efficient. This is also the condition under which it is possible to replicate the payoff structure for the complete set of pure. Arrow–Debreu securities using continuous-trading dynamic portfolio strategies with a finite number of securities.

The dynamic strategies for replicating the payoffs to pure Arrow–Debreu securities can be derived in a similar fashion to the derivation of contingent-claim prices in Merton (1977). Suppose that among the available traded securities, portfolios can be constructed whose returns are instantaneously perfectly correlated with changes in each of the state variables, $[S_1(t), \ldots, S_m(t)]$. Without loss of generality, assume that these portfolios are the first m risky securities (i.e. $dz_i = dq_i$, $i = 1, 2, \ldots, m$).

Let $F(S, t)$ satisfy the linear partial differential equation

$$0 = \frac{1}{2}\sum_1^m\sum_1^m H_i H_j \eta_{ij} \frac{\partial^2 F}{\partial S_i \partial S_j} + \sum_1^m [G_j - H_j(\alpha_j - r)/\sigma_j]\frac{\partial F}{\partial S_j} + \frac{\partial F}{\partial t} - rF \quad (7)$$

subject to the boundary conditions: $0 \leqslant F(S, t) < \infty$ for all S and $t < \tau$; $F(S, \tau) = \delta[\bar{S}_1 - S_1(\tau)] \ldots \delta[\bar{S}_m - S_m(\tau)]$ where $\delta[\ ]$ is the Dirac delta function and $\bar{S}_k$ are given parameters, $k = 1, \ldots, m$. Under mild regularity conditions on the functions H, η, G, α, σ and r, a solution to (7) exists and is unique.

Consider the continuous-trading portfolio strategy which allocates fraction $x_j(t) = (\partial F/\partial S_j)H_j/[\sigma_j V(t)]$ to security j, $j = 1, \ldots, m$ and $[1 - \Sigma_1^m x_j(t)]$ to the riskless security at time t, where $V(t)$ denotes the value of the portfolio. It follows from (3) and the prescribed allocation that the dynamics of the portfolio value can be written as

$$dV = V\left\{\left[\sum_t^m x_j(\alpha_j - r) + r\right]dt + \sum_1^m x_j\sigma_j\,dz_j\right\}$$

$$= \left[\sum_1^m \frac{\partial F}{\partial S_j}H_j(\alpha_j - r)/\sigma_j + rV\right]dt + \sum_1^m \frac{\partial F}{\partial S_j}H_j\,dq_j \quad (8)$$

because $dz_j = dq_j$; $j = 1, 2, \ldots, m$.

As a solution to (7), F is twice-continuously differentiable. Thus, Itô's Lemma can be used to describe the stochastic process for F as

$$dF = \left(\frac{1}{2}\sum_1^m\sum_1^m H_i H_j \eta_{ij}\frac{\partial^2 F}{\partial S_i \partial S_j} + \sum_1^m\left[G_j\frac{\partial F}{\partial S_j}\right] + \frac{\partial F}{\partial t}\right)dt + \sum_1^m \frac{\partial F}{\partial S_j}H_j\,dq_j \quad (9)$$

where F is evaluated at $S = S(t)$ at each time t. Because F satisfies (7), (9) can be rewritten as

$$dF = \left[\sum_1^m \frac{\partial F}{\partial S_j} H_j(\alpha_j - r)/\sigma_j + rF \right] dt + \sum_1^m \frac{\partial F}{\partial S_j} H_j \, dq_j. \tag{10}$$

From (8) and (10), $dF - dV = r(F - V) \, dt$, which is an ordinary differential equation with solution $F[S(t), t] - V(t) = [F(S(0), 0) - V(0)] \exp[\int_0^t r(u) du]$. If, therefore, the initial investment in the portfolio is chosen so that $V(0) = F[S(0), 0]$, then $V(t) = F[S(t), t]$ for $0 \leqslant t \leqslant \tau$.

Thus, a dynamic portfolio strategy using $(m + 1)$ available securities has been constructed that has a payoff at $t = \tau$ of $\delta[\bar{S}_1 - S_1(\tau)] \dots \delta[\bar{S}_m - S_m(\tau)]$. By inspection of this payoff structure, it is evident that this security is the natural generalization of Arrow–Debreu pure state securities to an environment where there is a continuum of states defined by $\bar{S}_k$ and τ. By changing the time and state parameters τ and $\bar{S}_k$, one can generate all of the uncountable number of pure securities. Moreover, F, the solution to (7) used to implement each strategy, will also be the equilibrium price for the corresponding pure Arrow–Debreu security.

Continuous trading, like any other continuous-revision process, is of course an abstraction from physical reality. If, however, the length of time between revisions is very short, then the continuous-trading optimal solutions will be a reasonable approximation to their discrete-time counterparts (see Samuelson, 1970 and Merton, 1975b; 1982b). From the work of Magill and Constantinides (1976), this conclusion appears to be robust even in the presence of transactions costs, which cause trading to be discrete almost certainly.

Whether the length of time between revisions is short enough for the continuous solution to provide a good approximation must be decided on a case-by-case basis by making a relative comparison with other time scales in the problem. The continuous-trading assumption appears to be especially appropriate for the analysis of security markets where the aggregate trading volume is large, the minimum unit-size for a transaction is relatively small, and the length of calendar time between successive transactions is quite short.

The continuous analysis may also provide a valid approximation in problems where the calendar length of time between revisions is not short. For example, Bourguignon (1974), Bismut (1975) and Merton (1975a) use this mode of analysis to extend the Solow model of economic growth to an uncertain environment and to analyse the stochastic Ramsey problem. It is the practice in such models to neglect 'short-run' business cycle fluctuations and to assume full employment. Moreover, the exogenous factors usually assumed to affect the time path of the economy in these models are either demographic or technological changes. Since major changes in either factor typically take rather long periods of time, the length of time between revisions in the capital stock, although hardly instantaneous, may well be quite short, relative to the time scale of the exogenous processes.

BIBLIOGRAPHY

Bismut, J.M. 1975. Growth and optimal intertemporal allocation of risks. *Journal of Economic Theory* 10, 239–57.

Black, F. and Scholes, M. 1973. The pricing of options and corporate liabilities. *Journal of Political Economy* 81, 637–54.

Bourguignon, F. 1974. A particular class of continuous-time stochastic growth models. *Journal of Economic Theory* 9, 141–58.

Breeden, D.T. 1979. An intertemporal asset pricing model with stochastic consumption and investment opportunities. *Journal of Financial Economics* 7, 265–96.

Cox, J.C., Ingersoll, J.E., Jr. and Ross, S.A. 1985a. A theory of the term structure of interest rates. *Econometrica* 53, 385–408.

Cox, J.C., Ingersoll, J.E., Jr. and Ross, S.A. 1985b. An intertemporal general equilibrium model of asset prices. *Econometrica* 53, 363–84.

Duffie, D. and Huang, C. 1985. Implementing Arrow–Debreu equilibria by continuous trading of a few long-lived securities. *Econometrica* 35, 1337–56.

Huang, C. 1985. Information structure and equilibrium asset prices. *Journal of Economic Theory* 35, 33–71.

Magill, M.J.P. and Constantinides, G.M. 1976. Portfolio selection with transaction costs. *Journal of Economic Theory* 13, 245–63.

Malliaris, A.G. and Brock, W.A. 1982. *Stochastic Methods in Economics and Finance.* Amsterdam: North-Holland.

Merton, R.C. 1969. Lifetime portfolio selection under uncertainty: the continuous-time case. *Review of Economics and Statistics* 51, 247–57.

Merton, R.C. 1971. Optimum consumption and portfolio rules in a continuous-time model. *Journal of Economic Theory* 3, 373–413.

Merton, R.C. 1973. An intertemporal capital asset pricing model. *Econometrica* 41, 867–87.

Merton, R.C. 1975a. An asymptotic theory of growth under uncertainty. *Review of Economic Studies* 42, 375–93.

Merton, R.C. 1975b. Theory of finance from the perspective of continuous time. *Journal of Financial and Quantitative Analysis* 10, 659–74.

Merton, R.C. 1977. On the pricing of contingent claims and the Modigliani-Miller theorem. *Journal of Financial Economics* 5, 241–9.

Merton, R.C. 1982a. On the microeconomic theory of investment under certainty. In *Handbook of Mathematical Economics*, ed. K.J. Arrow and M.D. Intriligator, Vol. 2, Amsterdam: North-Holland,

Merton, R.C. 1982b. On the mathematics and economics assumptions of continuous-time models. In *Financial Economics: Essays in Honor of Paul Cootner*, ed. W.F. Sharpe and C.M. Cootner, Englewood Cliffs, New Jersey: Prentice-Hall.

Radner, R. 1972. Existence of plans, prices, and price expectations in a sequence of markets. *Econometrica* 40, 289–303.

Samuelson, P.A. 1970. The fundamental approximation theorem of portfolio analysis in terms of means, variances, and higher moments. *Review of Economic Studies* 37, 537–42.

Continuous-time Stochastic Processes

CHI-FU HUANG

Applications of continuous-time stochastic processes to economic modelling are largely focused on the areas of capital theory and financial markets: In these applications as in mathematics generally, the most widely studied continuous time process is a Brownian motion – so named for its early application as a model of the seemingly random movements of particles which were first observed by the English botanist Robert Brown in the 19th century. Einstein (1905), in the context of statistical mechanics, is generally given credit for the first mathematical formulation of a Brownian motion process. However, an earlier development of an equivalent continuous-time process is provided by Louis Bachelier (1900) in theory of stock option pricing. Framed as an abstract mathematical process, a Brownian motion $\{B(t); t \in \mathscr{R}_+\}$ is described by the following properties: (1) for $0 \leqslant s < t < \infty$, $B(t) - B(s)$ is a normally distributed random variable with mean zero and variance $t - s$; (2) for $0 \leqslant t_0 < t_1 < \cdots < t_1 < \infty$,

$$\{B(t_0); B(t_k) - B(t_{k-1}), k = 1, \ldots, l\}$$

is a set of independent random variables.

From this construction, Doob, Feller, Itô, Wiener, among others, went on to develop the general theory of continuous-time stochastic processes.

During the half century of this development of the theory, its application in economics was confined primarily to the formulation and testing of hypotheses concerning time series properties of economic variables. It was not until the 1950s and early 1960s that the theory of continuous-time stochastic processes found its way into economic theory. Motivated by the rediscovery of Bachelier's work on options by L.J. Savage, Samuelson (1965) presents a theory of rational warrant pricing. Unlike Bachelier's assumption of a Brownian motion for a stock price process, Samuelson posits that the *logarithm* of a stock price follows a Brownian motion, and thereby, ensures that model stock prices exhibit non-negativity as required by limited liability. This process, called a *geometric Brownian motion* by Samuelson, remains to this day the prototypical process used by economists to describe stock price behaviour. Working with Samuelson, McKean (1965) uses the theory of optimal stopping to provide a rigorous derivation of the warrant price in Samuelson's theory.

Although it is the standard mode of analysis for warrant and opinion pricing theory today, the celebrated work on stochastic integration by K. Itô (1944, 1951) was not introduced into economic analysis until the late 1960s. Merton (1969, 1971) was the first to use Itô's stochastic calculus in economics. He analysed an agent's optimal consumption and portfolio policies in a continuous-time economy where asset prices are Itô processes.

Itô's contribution to the theory of stochastic processes lies in a definition of an integral with desired properties when the integrator is a Brownian motion. A pathwise definition in the Stieltjes sense may fail since a Brownian motion has sample paths that are nowhere differentiable with probability one. For a classical treatment of the Itô integral, see also Itô and McKean (1965) and McKean (1969). A good reference for modern treatments can be found in Chung and Williams (1983).

Itô's definition of a stochastic integral, in contrast to that of Stratonovich (1966), is much better suited for analysing intertemporal economic decision making. The *non-anticipating* integrand in Itô's definition captures the economic constraint that agents canot anticipate future speculative price movements.

The most useful result of Itô's stochastic calculus is the so-called Itô's lemma: any twice continuously-differentiable function of an Itô process is itself an Itô process. This implies that the agent's wealth process is an Itô process and therefore the Bellman equation in the stochastic dynamic programming problem becomes a second-order partial differential equation. The latter allows one to analyse the portfolio problem by looking at just the first two moments of price processes and to achieve sharp characterizations. Merton (1973a) applied this technique further to study equilibrium relations among risky asset prices and arrived at the *Intertemporal Capital Asset Pricing Model.*

The introduction of Itô's stochastic calculus opened a whole new world for economists. With it, most of the static utility maximization models are readily extended to a dynamic setting with uncertainty. The continuous time set-up allows one to work with differential equations rather than with difference equations. For applications to capital theory and economic growth, see Bismut (1975), Brock and Magill (1979) and Merton (1975); to asset pricing models, see Cox, Ingersoll and Ross (1985a, 1985b).

Itô's work was later extended by Kunita and Watanabe (1967) to the case where integrators are square-integrable martingales. They also proved a *martingale representation theorem* for a Brownian motion: any square-integrable martingale adapted to a Brownian motion filtration (see below) is representable as an Itô integral.

The most general notions of a stochastic process and a stochastic integral to date are in the terrain of the so-called *French School Probability Theory*, or the *General Theory of Processes*. Very abstract, and surely developed for intrinsic intellectual reasons, it nevertheless seems to have been invented for the study of financial markets; for references, see Dellacherie and Meyer (1978, 1982), Jacod (1979) and Meyer (1966, 1976).

Although making no explicit use of French probability theory, the seminal paper of Black and Scholes (1973) in the pricing of stock options nevertheless opens up the possibility of its application in financial economics. This work was subsequently generalized and formalized by Merton (1973b, 1977). The idea is that the payoff of a stock option can be *replicated* by continuous trading in its underlying stock and a riskless asset. The replicating strategy is *self-financing* in that after the beginning of this strategy there are neither additional funds invested into it nor funds withdrawn out of it. Thus, to rule out arbitrage opportunities, the stock option must sell for the exact value of the replicating portfolio at any point in time.

Black and Scholes's theory provided a strong incentive for financial economists to study continuous time stochastic processes. The key observation in this literature was made by Cox and Ross (1976). They noted that since the expected rate of return of the stock does not enter the Black and Scholes pricing formula for a stock option, the price of an option must be determined as if investors were risk neutral and had probability beliefs such that the stock earns an expected rate of return equal to the riskless rate. Harrison and Kreps (1979) formalized this observation in showing that *any* arbitrage-free price system can be converted into a martingale through a change of an equivalent probability after a suitable normalization. Note that this martingale connection of an arbitrage-free price system was vaguely foreshadowed in Samuelson and Merton (1969).

Harrison and Kreps (1979) and Harrison and Pliska (1981) make clear that the answer to whether a contingent claim can be replicated by dynamic trading is intimately related to the martingale representation theorem. A sketch of their arguments will be given.

Taken as primitive is a complete separable probability space $(\Omega, \mathcal{F}, P)$ and a *filtration* $\mathbf{F} = \{\mathcal{F}_t; t \in [0, 1]\}$. A filtration is an increasing family of sub-sigma-algebras of $\mathcal{F}$ representing information revelation over time. For simplicity, we take the time span of the economy to be $[0, 1]$. We assume that agents are endowed with the same information structure $\mathbf{F}$. Readers can think of a filtration to be like an event tree in a discrete time finite state setting. We also assume that agents at time zero know that the true state of the nature is an element $\omega \in \Omega$, which they will learn at time one.

Agents can only consume at time one. For simplicity again, we take the commodity space to be the space of square-integrable random variables defined on $(\Omega, \mathcal{F}, P)$, denoted by $L^2(P)$.

There are $N + 1$ long-lived securities traded indexed by $n = 0, 1, \ldots, N$. A long-lived security is a security available for trading all the time in $[0, 1]$ and is represented by a price process $\{S_n(t)\}$. It pays a dividend only at time one and is equal to $S_n(1)$ almost surely. Price processes are semimartingales (adapted to

F) and $S_n(1) \in L^2(P)$. In modelling a dynamic asset trading economy, before anything interesting can be said, one has to formulate a budget constraint. That naturally involves stochastic integrals. Jacod (1979) has shown that for stochastic integrals to have desired properties, it is necessary that integrators be semimartingales. Thus, semimartingale price processes can be assumed without loss of generality.

In a Walrasian economy, only relative prices are determined. Thus we can assume that the price system has been normalized such that $S_0(t) = 1 \forall t \in [0, 1]$. We will call the 0th security the riskless security and the rest risky securities.

A trading strategy is an $(N + 1)$-dimensional predictable process $\theta = \{\theta_n(t); n = 0, 1, \ldots, N\}$, where we interpret $\theta_n(t)$ to be the number of shares of security n held from $t -$ to t before trading at time t. A process is predictable if its values at time t depend only upon the information available strictly before time t. Given the interpretation of θ, predictability is a natural information constraint.

A trading strategy is said to be *simple* if it is bounded and changes its value at most at a finite number of time points in $[0, 1]$.

A trading strategy θ is said to be *self-financing* if the stochastic integral

$$\int_0^t \theta(s)^{\mathrm{T}} \, \mathrm{d}S(s)$$

is well-defined and if

$$\theta(t)^{\mathrm{T}} S(t) = \theta(0)^{\mathrm{T}} S(0) + \int_0^t \theta(s)^{\mathrm{T}} \, \mathrm{d}S(s) \qquad \forall t \in [0, 1] \ a.s., \tag{1}$$

where ^{T} denotes transpose. That is, the value of the portfolio θ at time t is equal to its initial value plus accumulated capital gains or losses from time zero to time t. There are neither new investments into nor withdrawals of funds out of the portfolio. This is just a natural budget constraint.

Harrison and Kreps (1979) and Kreps (1981) show that if all the simple self-financing trading strategies are allowed and if arbitrage opportunities are absent, then there exists a probability measure Q equivalent to P such that the Radon–Nikodym derivative $\xi \equiv \mathrm{d}Q/\mathrm{d}P$ is an element of $L^2(P)$ and that S is a martingale under Q, or a Q-martingale. Fix Q and note that since P and Q are equivalent, all the *a.s.* statements to follow apply to both.

Now we can specify the space of admissible strategies $\Theta[S]$. A self-financing trading strategy θ is admissible if

$$\int_0^t \theta(s)^{\mathrm{T}} \, \mathrm{d}S(s), \qquad t \in [0, 1]$$

is a Q-martingale and $\theta(1)^{\mathrm{T}} S(1) \in L^2(P)$. [See Jacod (1979) for sufficient conditions for this to be true.] Then one can show that given $\Theta[S]$ there are indeed no arbitrage opportunities.

A contingent claim is an element of $L^2(P)$. A contingent claim x is said to be *marketed* if it can be dynamically manufactured by an admissible trading strategy.

Formally, x is marketed if there exists $\theta \in \Theta[S]$ such that

$$x = \theta(0)^{\mathrm{T}} S(0) + \int_0^1 \theta(t)^{\mathrm{T}} \, dS(t) \qquad a.s.$$

The value of x at time t is $\theta(t)^{\mathrm{T}} S(t)$. By the definition of admissibility, we have

$$\theta(t)^{\mathrm{T}} S(t) = \theta(0)^{\mathrm{T}} S(0) + \int_0^t \theta(s)^{\mathrm{T}} \, dS(s) \qquad a.s.$$

$$= E^*[x \mid \mathscr{F}_t] \qquad a.s., \tag{2}$$

where $E^*[\cdot]$ is the expectation under Q. That is, the value of a marketed contingent claim is also a Q-martingale.

Before proceeding, we shall make one remark. Since $S_0(t) = 1$, the stochastic integral on the right-hand side of the first line of (2) is determined by S_n, $n = 1$, $2, \ldots, N$. That is,

$$\int_0^t \theta(s)^{\mathrm{T}} \, dS(s) = \sum_{n=1}^N \int_0^t \theta_n(s) \, dS_n(s).$$

Now here is the key observation. Let x be a contingent claim. We know from relation (2) that if it is marketed, its value over time is equal to its initial value at time zero plus a stochastic integral with respect to N Q-martingales. Conversely, a contingent claim x is marketed if the conditional expectation $E^*[x \mid \mathscr{F}_t]$, which is a Q-martingale, can be represented by a stochastic integral with respect to the N Q-martingales $\{S_n(t); n = 1, 2, \ldots, N\}$. [Here we should remark that any $x \in L^2(P)$ has a finite expectation under Q by the Cauchy–Schwarz inequality.] This observation turns on the machinery of the martingale representation theorem in the study of market completeness.

The security markets are said to be *dynamically complete* if all contingent claims are marketed. From the above discussion, it follows that markets are dynamically complete if all Q-martingales are representable as stochastic integrals with respect to the N risky Q-martingale prices. In such event, the N Q-martingales are said to have the *martingale representation property*. Readers might be curious by now to know why the riskless asset seems to disappear from the story. Indeed, whether a contingent claim is generated by a (not necessarily self-financing) trading strategy does not depend upon the riskless asset after time zero. The riskless asset, however, is a vehicle through which the budget is balanced over time.

The contribution made by Harrison, Kreps, and Pliska is methodological. They make available a powerful machinery for the study of financial/capital markets: the theory of martingales. Now we shall present some consequences of their work.

Since Merton's (1969, 1971, 1973a) analyses of optimal intertemporal consumption-portfolio policies and their implications on equilibrium asset prices, the conditions under which a price system is representable as an Itô process has been an open question for more than a decade. A short answer found in Huang

(1985a) is as follows: Take the set-up of the economy as above and assume henceforth that there are no arbitrage opportunities. Moreover, assume that the information structure $\mathbf{F}$ is a Brownian motion filtration. We know S is a Q-martingale, so we can write

$$S_n(t) = E^*[S_n(1)|\mathscr{F}_t] \quad a.s.$$

$$= \frac{E[S_n(1)\xi|\mathscr{F}_t]}{E[\xi|\mathscr{F}_t]} \quad a.s.,$$

where the second equality follows from the Bayes' rule, and where we recall that $\xi = dQ/dP$, which is strictly positive by the fact that Q and P are equivalent. The numerator and the denominator of the above relation are both P-square integrable martingales. By the martingale representation theorem of Kunita and Watanabe (1967), we know that any P-square integrable martingale is representable as an Itô integral. Then S_n is an Itô process by Itô's lemma. Hence any arbitrage-free price system is an Itô process when the information structure is a Brownian filtration.

We can also study the sample path properties of a price system, which relates to examining empirically the so-called *efficient market hypothesis*. Much of the empirical work in financial economics and accounting concerns the response of capital/financial asset prices to information. The null hypothesis in this work is typically that the capital/financial markets are *efficient* in the sense that prices rapidly adjust to *new* information. But is it true that prices only make large adjustments at surprises and what exactly is a *surprise*, mathematically? Here we turn to the classification of stopping times in the general theory of processes. In this context, a surprise is a non-predictable stopping time. We also know that a martingale must be continuous at predictable stopping times (provided that a minor technical condition is satisfied). Thus, S can make discrete changes only at nonpredictable stopping times or at surprises. This and other related issues can be found in Huang (1985a, b). A reference for the classification of stopping times is Dellacherie and Meyer (1978).

So we discover that a price system must be an Itô process when the information is a Brownian motion filtration and when there are no arbitrage opportunities. There still remain further questions: does there exist an equilibrium where equilibrium price processes are Itô processes? More importantly, does there exist an equilibrium where although there are only a finite numer of long-lived securities traded, the markets are dynamically complete and thus the equilibrium allocation is Pareto optimal? Note that in the Arrow–Debreu equilibrium theory, markets for all contingent claims are available at time zero. Agents trade to a Pareto optimal allocation. There is no need and no incentive for the markets to reopen after time zero. Of course, this does not conform with actual market structures. We do not have a complete set of contingent markets. What we do have are constantly-open financial markets where a finite number of long-lived assets are traded. Thus it is important to know whether there exists an equilibrium in such a world and to know the efficiency of the resulting allocation.

It follows from the earlier discussion on the martingale representation property of risky price processes that what is needed for an affirmative answer to the above questions is that there be a riskless security with unit price throughout and a finite number of risky long-lived securities that have the martingale representation property. What complicates the story, however, is that the demand and supply of the long-lived securities must be equal in equilibrium. Thus those securities must be picked carefully. Moreover, it is not true that a finite number of martingales having the martingale representation property can always be found. Duffie and Huang (1985, 1986b) and Duffie (1986a), in exchange as well as production economies, demonstrated a procedure to select long-lived securities having the desired properties and conditions under which the number is finite.

The martingale connection of an arbitrage-free system has been generalized to economies where securities can pay dividends and agents can consume at any time in [0, 1]. After a suitable normalization, a price system plus the accumulated dividends form a martingale under an equivalent probability measure. This is done in Huang (1985b). Similar theory is also valid in economies where agents have differential information. Interested readers are referred to Duffie and Huang (1986b) for details.

Although the focus of research has been on capital theory and financial markets, applications of the theory of continuous time stochastic processes to economic problems outside these areas can be found. For example, Duffie (1986b) applies classical potential theory as in the context of Markov processes to valuation of securities, and Li (1984) examines the stochastic theory of the firm in continuous time. He uses point processes to model stochastic demands for commodities and endogenizes a firm's demand for inventories, among other things. For applications of the theory of optimal stopping to game theory, see Hugues (1974) for zero-sum stopping games, and Huang and Li (1986) for nonzero-sum stopping games.

BIBLIOGRAPHY

Bachelier, L. 1900. *Théorie de la speculation*. Paris: Gauthier-Villars.

Bismut, J. 1975. Growth and optimal intertemporal allocation of risks. *Journal of Economic Theory* 10, 239–7.

Black, F. and Scholes, M. 1973. The pricing of options and corporate liabilities. *Journal of Political Economy* 81, 637–54.

Brock, W. and Magill, M. 1979. Dynamics under uncertainty. *Econometrica* 47, 843–68.

Chung, K. and Williams, R. 1983. *An Introduction to Stochastic Integration*. Boston: Birkhauser.

Cox, J. and Ross, S. 1976. The valuation of options for alternative stochastic processes. *Journal of Financial Economics* 3, 145–66.

Cox, J., Ingersoll, J. and Ross, S. 1985a. An intertemporal general equilibrium model of asset prices. *Econometrica* 53, 363–84.

Cox, J., Ingersoll, J. and Ross, S. 1985b. A theory of the term structure of interest rates. *Econometrica* 53, 385–408.

Dellacherie, C. and Meyer, P. 1978. *Probabilities and Potential A: General Theory of Process*. New York: North-Holland Publishing Company.

Dellacherie, C. and Meyer, P. 1982. *Probabilities and Potential B: Theory of Martingales.* New York: North-Holland Publishing Company.

Duffie, D. 1986a. Stochastic equilibria: existence, spanning number and the 'no expected gains for trade' hypothesis. *Econometrica* 54(5), September, 1161–83.

Duffie, D. 1986b. Price operators: extensions, potentials, and the Markov valuation of securities. Research Paper No. 813. Graduate School of Business, Stanford University.

Duffie, D. and Huang, C. 1985. Implementing Arrow–Debreu equilibria by continuous trading of few long-lived securities. *Econometrica* 53(6), 1337–56.

Duffie, D. and Huang, C. 1986a. Multiperiod securities markets with differential information: martingales and resolution times. *Journal of Mathematical Economics* 15(3), 283–303.

Duffie, D. and Huang, C. 1986b. Stochastic production-exchange equilibria. Graduate School of Business, Stanford University.

Einstein, A. 1905. On the movement of small particles suspended in a stationary liquid demanded by the molecular kinetic theory of heat. *Annals of Physics* 17(4), 891–921.

Harrison, M. and Kreps, D. 1979. Martingales and arbitrage in multiperiod securities markets. *Journal of Economic Theory* 20, 381–408.

Harrison, M. and Pliska, S. 1981. Martingales and stochastic integrals in the theory of continuous trading. *Stochastic Processes and their Applications* 11, 215–60.

Huang, C. 1985a. Information structure and equilibrium asset prices. *Journal of Economic Theory* 35, 33–71.

Huang, C. 1985b. Information structure and viable price systems. *Journal of Mathematical Economics* 14, 215–40.

Huang, C. and Li, L. 1986. Continuous time stopping games, Working Paper No. 1796–86, Sloan School of Management, MIT.

Hugues, C. 1974. Markov games. Technical Report No. 33, Department of Operations Research, Stanford University.

Itô, K. 1944. Stochastic integrals. *Proceedings of the Imperial Academy* 22, 519–24, Tokyo.

Itô, K. 1951. On stochastic differential equations. *Memoirs of the American Mathematical Society.* Rhode Island: The American Mathematical Society.

Itô, K. and McKean, H. 1965. *Diffusion Processes and Their Sample Paths.* New York: Springer-Verlag.

Jacod, J. 1979. *Calcul stochastique et problèmes de martingales.* Lecture Notes in Mathematics 714, New York: Springer-Verlag.

Kreps, D. 1981. Arbitrage and equilibrium in economies with infinitely many commodities. *Journal of Mathematical Economics* 8, 15–35.

Kunita, H. and Watanabe, S. 1967. On square-integrable martingales. *Nagoya Mathematics Journal* 30, 209–245.

Li, L. 1984. A stochastic theory of the firm. Unpublished PhD thesis, Northwestern University.

McKean, H. 1965. Appendix: A free boundary problem for the heat equation arising from a problem in mathematical economics. *Industrial Management Review* 6, 32–9.

McKean, H. 1969. *Stochastic Integrals.* New York: Academic Press.

Merton, R. 1969. Lifetime portfolio selection under uncertainty: the continuous case. *Review of Economics and Statistics* 51, 247–57.

Merton, R. 1971. Optimum consumption and portfolio rules in a continuous time model. *Journal of Economic Theory* 3, 373–413.

Merton, R. 1973a. An intertemporal capital asset pricing model. *Econometrica* 41, 867–88.

Merton, R. 1973b. Theory of rational option pricing. *Bell Journal of Economics and Management Science* 4, 141–83.

Merton, R. 1973b. Theory of rational option pricing. *Bell Journal of Economics and Management Science* 4, 141–83.

Merton, R. 1975. An asymptotic theory of growth under uncertainty. *Review of Economic Studies* 42, 375–93.

Merton, R. 1977. On the pricing of contingent claims and the Modigliani-Miller theorem. *Journal of Financial Economics* 5, 241–9.

Meyer, P. 1966. *Probability and Potentials.* Blaisdell Publishing Company.

Meyer, P. 1976. Un cours sur les integrales stochastiques. In *Seminaires de Probabilité X*, Lecture Notes in Mathematics 511, New York: Springer-Verlag.

Samuelson, P. 1965. Rational theory of warrant pricing. *Industrial Management Review* 6, 13–32.

Samuelson, P. and Merton, R. 1969. A complete model of warrant pricing that maximizes utility. *Industrial Management Review* 10, 17–46.

Stratonovich, R. 1966. A new representation for stochastic integrals and equations. *SIAM Journal of Control* 4, 362–71.

Dividend Policy

JAMES A. BRICKLEY AND JOHN J. McCONNELL

There are two major ways in which a firm can distribute cash to its common stockholders. The firm can either declare a cash dividend which it pays to all its common stockholders or it can repurchase stock. Stock repurchases may take the form of registered tender offers, open market purchases, or negotiated repurchases from a large shareholder. By far the most common method of distributing cash to shareholders is through the payment of cash dividends. For example, in 1985, US corporations paid over $83 billion in cash dividends.

Most firms pay cash dividends on a quarterly basis. The dividend is declared by the firm's board of directors on a date known as the 'announcement date'. The board's announcement states that a cash payment will be made to stockholders who are registered owners on a given 'record date'. The dividend checks are mailed to stockholders on the 'payment date' which is usually about two weeks after the record date. Stock exchange rules generally dictate that the stock is bought or sold with the dividend until the 'ex dividend date' which is a few business days before the record date. After the ex-dividend date, the stock is bought and sold without the dividend.

Dividends may be either labelled or unlabelled. Most dividends are not given labels by management. Unlabelled dividends are commonly referred to as 'regular dividends'. At times, managers will give a special label to the dividend. The most common label is the word, 'extra'. About 30 percent of the *increases* in the dividend from the previous quarter are given some special label by management.

AN HISTORICAL PERSPECTIVE

Prior to 1961, academic treatments of dividends were primarily descriptive in nature, as, for example, in Dewing (1953). To the extent that economists considered corporate dividend policy, the commonly held view was that investors preferred high dividend payouts to low payouts (see, for example, Graham and Dodd, 1951). The only question was how much value was attached to dividends

119

relative to capital gains in valuing a security (Gordon, 1959). This view was concisely summarized with the saying that a dividend in the hand is worth two (or some multiple) of those in the bush. The only question was – what is the multiple?

In 1961, scientific inquiry into the motives and consequences of corporate dividend policy shifted dramatically with the publication of a classic paper by Miller and Modigliani. Perhaps the most significant contribution of the Modigliani–Miller paper was to spell out in careful detail the assumptions under which their analysis was to be conducted. The most important of these include the assumption that the firm's investment policy is fixed and known by investors, that there are no taxes on dividends or capital gains, that individuals can costlessly buy and sell securities, that all investors have the same information and that investors have the same information as the managers of the firm, and, finally, that there are no contracting or agency costs associated with stock ownership. With this set of assumptions, Modigliani and Miller demonstrated that a firm's dividend policy is a matter of indifference to stockholders. That is, the value of the firm is independent of the dividend policy adopted by management.

The essence of the Modigliani–Miller proof is that investors can create their own dividends by selling shares of stock. If earnings are retained by the firm and invested in new projects, existing shareholders can sell stock and consume the proceeds, leaving themselves in the same position as if the firm had paid a dividend. Alternatively, if management elects to pay a dividend, new stock must be issued to undertake new projects. If shareholders prefer to reinvest rather than consume, they can do so by buying a pro rata share of the new stock issue with the dividends paid. In this instance, shareholders would be in the same position that they would have been had no dividend been paid. Thus, regardless of corporate dividend policy, investors can costlessly create their own dividend position. For this reason, stockholders are indifferent to corporate dividend policy, and, as a consequence, the value of the firm is independent of its dividend policy.

The conclusion that the market value of the firm is independent of its dividend policy means that corporate investment decisions can be made without regard to dividend policy. It is the case, though, that total cash inflows to and outflows from the firm do depend upon its investment decision. If the level of funds required for investment purposes exceeds internally generated funds, then new shares must be issued (or dividends retained) in order for firm value to be maximized. If internally generated funds exceed investment requirements, then shares must be repurchased or a cash dividend must be paid. Under the Modigliani–Miller assumptions though, the value of the firm is independent of the method used to distribute the cash.

After a brief flurry of debate, the Modigliani–Miller irrelevance proposition was essentially universally accepted as correct under their set of assumptions. There nevertheless remained an underlying notion that dividend policy must 'matter' given that managers and security analysis spend time worrying about it. If so, and if the Modigliani–Miller proposition is accepted, it must be due to violation of one or more of the Modigliani–Miller assumptions in the real world.

Since the early 1960s, the dividend debate has been lively and interesting as economists have analysed the effect on the value of the firm of relaxing the various Modigliani–Miller assumptions and have explored the data for evidence that dividend policy affects security prices and investor behaviour. Economists have focused on three related questions. First, does the *level* of dividends paid by the firm affect the value of the firm? That is, are high dividend-paying firms valued differently by the market than low dividend-paying firms, holding other factors constant? Second, do *changes* in an established dividend level affect the value of the firm? Third, does the method of cash payout affect the value of the firm? For example, are cash dividends valued differently than share repurchases and are labelled dividends valued differently than unlabelled dividends? We organize our discussion around these three questions.

FIRM VALUE AND THE LEVEL OF DIVIDEND PAYOUT

Taxes. Perhaps the obvious starting point for an investigation into the effect of relaxing the Modigliani–Miller assumptions is to introduce taxes. In the US, dividend payments by a corporation do not affect that firm's taxes. However, at least historically, dividends have been taxed at a higher rate than capital gains at the personal level. Thus, superficially, the US tax code appears to favour a low dividend payout policy.

Under the assumption that dividends and capital gains are taxed differentially, Brennan (1970) derived a model of stock valuation in which stocks with high payouts have higher required before-tax returns than stocks with low payouts. However, empirical tests of Brennan's model by Black and Scholes (1974), Litzenberger and Ramaswamy (1979) and Miller and Scholes (1982) have yielded ambiguous results, in which support for a dividend tax effect in stock returns appears to depend heavily upon the definition of dividend yield employed. In a provocative case study, Long (1978) has examined the prices of two classes of stock of Citizens Utility, which differ only in terms of dividends and tax treatments, and finds support for the notion that investors favour a high dividend payout.

As a counterpoint to Brennan (1970), Miller and Scholes (1978) argue that the assumption that dividends are taxed disadvantageously relative to capital gains is inaccurate. They argue that, at least historically, under the US tax code there exist sufficient loopholes so that investors may shelter dividend income so as to drive the effective tax rate on dividends to zero. However, Feenberg (1971) and Peterson, Peterson and Ang (1985) examine data from actual tax returns which indicate the various methods of avoiding taxes described by Miller and Scholes are not used by investors who receive dividends.

Empirical investigation into the effects of taxes on the level of stock prices has not been limited to US data. For example, Poterba and Summers (1984) examine British stocks returns and Morgan (1980) examines Canadian stock returns with no more definitive conclusion than has been reached with US data.

Suffice it to say that, at this point, empirical studies on the relation among dividends, taxes and firm value are inconclusive. Interestingly, the most recent

US tax legislation taxes dividends and capital gains at the same rate. The introduction of this legislation holds forth the prospect of providing an opportunity for a before-and-after examination of the data.

Agency costs. A second potentially important real world violation in the Modigliani–Miller assumptions is the existence of agency costs associated with stock ownership. In particular, managers of firms maximize their own utility, which is not necessarily the same as maximizing the market value of common stock. The costs associated with this potential conflict of interest include expenditures for structuring, monitoring and bonding contracts between shareholders and managers, and residual losses due to imperfectly constructed contracts (Jensen and Meckling, 1976).

Several authors have argued that dividends may be important in helping to resolve manager/shareholder conflicts. If dividend payments reduce agency costs, firms may pay dividends even though these payments are taxed disadvantageously.

Easterbrook (1984) and Rozeff (1982) argue that establishing a policy of paying dividends enables managers to be evaluated periodically by the capital market. By paying dividends, the managers are required to tap the capital market more frequently to obtain funds for investment projects. Periodic review by the market is one way in which agency costs are reduced, which, in turn, raises the value of the firm. If so, the value of the firm is no longer independent of dividend policy. It is still the case, however, that even in these models an 'optimal' dividend payout level is far from obvious.

At this point, no direct (or, even, indirect) tests of the agency cost explanations of corporate dividend policy have been reported. The dearth of empirical tests of these models is due, in part, to their recent development and, in part, to the relative lack of specificity of the theories.

FIRM VALUE AND CHANGES IN THE PAYOUT

While the evidence on whether the level of dividend payouts affects firm value is mixed, studies have consistently documented that stock returns around the announcement of a dividend change are positively correlated with the change in the dividend (Aharony and Swary, 1980; Asquith and Mullins, 1983; Brickley, 1983; Pettit, 1972). The leading explanation of this phenomenon is that dividend changes convey information about current or future earnings of the firm.

Contrary to the Modigliani–Miller assumption that investors have the same information as managers, the information content of dividends hypothesis is based on the assumption that managers possess more information about the prospects of the firm than individuals outside the firm. The hypothesis asserts that dividend changes convey managers' inside information to outsiders. This ideas was suggested by Miller and Modigliani (1961) and has roots in Lintner's (1956) classic study on dividend policy. Lintner interviewed a sample of corporate managers. One of the primary findings of the interviews is that a high proportion of managers attempt to maintain a stable regular dividend. In Lintner's words, managers demonstrate a 'reluctance (common to all companies) to reduce regular rates once established and a consequent conservatism in raising regular rates' (p. 84). Lintner's argument is provided additional empirical support by Fama and Babiak (1968). If managers change regular dividends only when the earnings potential of the firm has changed, changes in regular dividend changes are likely to provide some information to the market about the firm's prospects.

More recently, formal models of dividends and information signalling have been developed. Models in which dividends convey information to outsiders include Bhattacharya (1979, 1980), John and Williams (1985) and Miller and Rock (1985). The assumptions under which these models are developed differ across the models. The major commonality is that managers are presumed to have information not available to outside investors. Typically, the information has to do with the current or future earnings of the firm.

The accumulated empirical evidence indicates that dividend announcements provide information to the market. As such, the evidence is consistent with the asymmetric information models of dividend changes. Whether these models actually capture the information to which the market is responding when dividend changes are announced is still an open question and which of the models best characterizes the process of information dissemination is still open to debate.

FIRM VALUE AND THE FORM OF THE PAYOUT

As with increases in regular cash dividends, specially labelled cash dividends and shares repurchases have been shown to be accompanied by permanent increases in stock prices (Brickley, 1983; Dann, 1981; Vermaelen, 1981). However, the factors that lead managers to choose one method over another are not well understood.

Given the Modigliani–Miller assumptions, the choice of the payout mechanism, like the choice of dividend policy itself, does not affect the value of the firm. Therefore, if the form of the payout is to matter, it must be due to violation of one or more of the Modigliani–Miller assumptions.

Economists have just begun to explore possible explanations as to why a particular form of payout is chosen. To develop a theory to explain the choice of payout mechanism, it must be that there are differential costs and/or benefits associated with the alternative payout methods. Given the preponderance of regular cash dividends relative to stock repurchases and specially-labelled dividends, a convincing explanation must credit regular cash dividends with substantial benefits or debit the alternatives with substantial costs. Furthermore, the relative benefits and/or costs must be especially significant because, at least historically, dividends have been tax-disfavoured (at the personal level) relative to share repurchases.

Two recently developed theories that attempt to explain the choice between cash dividends and share repurchases assume that managers have information not available to outside stockholders. Barclay and Smith (1986) and Offer and Thakor (1985) assume that managers can use this inside information to benefit themselves by means of share repurchases In both cases, however, there are costs associated with the opportunistic use of the information. When the costs to the managers outweigh the benefits, dividends will be used to distribute cash instead of share repurchases.

As with various other hypotheses regarding corporate dividend policy, those explaining the choice between cash dividends and share repurchases have been developed only recently. As a consequence, they also have not yet undergone rigorous empirical testing. As regards the choice between regular cash dividends and specially labelled cash dividends reasonable explanations are even more scarce. However, Brickley (1983) does provide evidence that specially-labelled dividends convey a less positive message about firm value than do increases in regular cash dividends.

CONCLUSION

After twenty-five years of rigorous consideration, what is known about dividend policy is far outweighed by what is not known. We know that firms pay out to stockholders substantial amounts of cash annually and that the vast majority of this payout is in the form of regular cash dividends. Intermittently, firms also make specially labelled cash dividend payments and large-scale share repurchases. We also know that stock prices increase permanently when regular dividends are increased, when special dividends are declared, and when shares are repurchased and that stock prices decline when regular dividends are reduced. There is a growing consensus that the stock price changes come about because the dividend changes reflect information available to managers that is not otherwise available to outside investors. There is, however, little agreement as to what information management is providing to the market through the dividend payment and there is little agreement as to the linkage between the information released and the value of the firm. There also is little agreement as to whether the level of cash payout affects the value of the firm and there is little agreement as to whether the choice of the payout method matters and, if it matters, what factors favour one method relative to another.

It is tempting to conclude this essay on a disappointing note of frustration. But twenty-five years is a very short period of investigation for most economic phenomena. While what we do know about dividend policy is far less than we would like to know, we clearly know more about dividend policy now than we did twenty-five years ago. Undoubtedly, the next twenty-five years will witness further significant progress in understanding the determinants of corporate dividend policy.

BIBLIOGRAPHY

Aharony, J. and Swary, I. 1980. Quarterly dividends, earnings announcements, and stockholder returns. *Journal of Finance* 35(1), March, 1–12.

Asquith, P. and Mullins, D. 1983. The impact of initiating dividend payments on shareholders' wealth. *Journal of Business* 56, January, 77–96.

Barclay, M. and Smith, C.W. 1986. Corporate payment policy. Cash dividends vs. share repurchases: Unpublished ms., August.

Bhattacharya, S. 1979. Imperfect information, dividend policy, and the 'Bird in the hand' fallacy. *Bell Journal of Economics* 10(1), Spring, 259–70.

Bhattacharya, S. 1980. Nondissipative signalling structures and dividend policy. *Quarterly Journal of Economics*, December 95, August, 1–24.

Black, F. and Scholes, M.S. 1974. The effects of dividend yield and dividend policy on common stock prices and returns. *Journal of Financial Economics* 1(1), May, 1–22.

Brennan, M.J. 1970. Taxes, market valuation, and corporate financial policy. *National Tax Journal* 23(4), December, 417–27.

Brickley, J.A. 1983. Shareholder wealth, information signalling, and the specially designated dividend: an empirical study. *Journal of Financial Economics* 12, August, 187–209.

Dann, L.Y. 1981. Common stock repurchases: an analysis of the returns to bondholders and stockholders. *Journal of Financial Economics* 9(2), June, 113–38.

Dewing, A.S. 1953. *The Financial Policy of Corporations.* 5th edn, New York: Ronald Press.

Easterbrook, F.H. 1984. Two agency-cost explanations of dividends. *American Economic Review* 74(4), September, 650–59.

Fama, E.F. and Babiak, H. 1968. Dividend policy: an empirical analysis. *American Statistical Association Journal* 63, December, 1132–61.

Feenberg, D. 1971. Does the investment interest limitation explain the existence of dividends? *Journal of Financial Economics* 9, September, 265–9.

Gordon, M.J. 1959. Dividends, earnings, and stock prices. *Review of Economics and Statistics* 41, May, 99–105.

Graham, B. and Dodd, D. 1951. *Security Analysis: Principles and Techniques.* New York: McGraw-Hill.

Jensen, M.C. and Meckling, W. 1976. Theory of the firm: managerial behavior, agency costs, and capital structure. *Journal of Financial Economics* 3(4), October, 305–60.

John, K. and Williams, J. 1985. Dividends, dilution and taxes: a signalling equilibrium. *Journal of Finance* 40(4), September, 1053–70.

Lintner, J. 1956. The distribution of incomes of corporations among dividends, retained earnings, and taxes. *American Economic Review, Papers and Proceedings* 46, May, 97–113.

Litzenberger, R.H. and Ramaswamy, K. 1979. The effect of personal taxes and dividends on capital asset prices: theory and empirical evidence. *Journal of Financial Economics* 7(2), June, 163–95.

Long, J.B. 1978. The market valuation of cash dividends: a case to consider. *Journal of Financial Economics* 6(2/3), June/September, 235–64.

Miller, M.H. and Modigliani, F. 1961. Dividend policy, growth, and the valuation of shares. *Journal of Business* 34, October, 235–64.

Miller, M.H. and Rock, K. 1985. Dividend policy under asymmetric information. *Journal of Finance* 40(4), September, 1031–51.

Miller, M.H. and Scholes, M.S. 1978. Dividends and taxes. *Journal of Financial Economics* 6(4), December, 333–64.

Miller, M.H. and Scholes, M.S. 1982. Dividends and taxes: some empirical evidence. *Journal of Political Economy* 90(6), December, 1118–41.

Morgan, I. 1980. Dividends and stock price behavior in Canada. *Journal of Business Administration*, Fall.

Offer, A. and Thakor, A. 1985. A theory of stock price response to alternative corporate cash disbursement methods: stock repurchases and dividends. Unpublished ms., December.

Peterson, P.P., Peterson, D.R. and Ang, J.S. 1985. Direct evidence on the marginal rate of taxation on dividend income. *Journal of Financial Economics* 14(2), June, 267–82.

Pettit, R.R. 1972. Dividend announcements, security performance, and capital market efficiency. *Journal of Finance* 27(5), December, 993–1007.

Poterba, J.M. and Summers, L.H. 1984. New evidence that taxes affect the valuation of dividends. *Journal of Finance* 39(5), December, 1397–1415.

Rozeff, M.S. 1982. Growth, beta and agency costs as determinants of dividend payout ratios. *Journal of Financial Research* 2, Fall, 249–59.

Schleifer, A. and Vishny, R.W. 1986. Large stockholders and corporate control. *Journal of Political Economy* 94(3) Part 1, June, 461–88.

Vermaelen, T. 1981. Common stock repurchases and market signalling: an empirical study. *Journal of Financial Economics* 9(2), June, 139–83.

Efficient Market Hypothesis

BURTON G. MALKIEL

A capital market is said to be efficient if it fully and correctly reflects all relevant information in determining security prices. Formally, the market is said to be efficient with respect to some information set, ϕ, if security prices would be unaffected by revealing that information to all participants. Moreover, efficiency with respect to an information set, ϕ, implies that it is impossible to make economic profits by trading on the basis of ϕ.

It has been customary since Roberts (1967) to distinguish three levels of market efficiency by considering three different types of information sets:

(1) The weak form of the Efficient Market Hypothesis (EMH) asserts that prices fully reflect the information contained in the historical sequence of prices. Thus, investors cannot devise an investment strategy to yield abnormal profits on the basis of an analysis of past price patterns (a technique known as technical analysis). It is this form of efficiency that is associated with the term 'Random Walk Hypothesis'.

(2) The semi-strong form of EMH asserts that current stock prices reflect not only historical price information but also all publicly available information relevant to a company's securities. If markets are efficient in this sense, then an analysis of balance sheets, income statements, announcements of dividend changes or stock splits or any other public information about a company (the technique of fundamental analysis) will not yield abnormal economic profits.

(3) The strong form of EMH asserts that all information that is *known* to any market participant about a company is fully reflected in market prices. Hence, not even those with privileged information can make use of it to secure superior investment results. There is perfect revelation of all private information in market prices.

WEAK FORM MARKET EFFICIENCY AND THE RANDOM WALK HYPOTHESIS. If markets are efficient, the (technical) analysis of past price patterns to predict the future

127

will be useless because any information from such an analysis will already have been impounded in current market prices. Suppose market participants were confident that a commodity price would double next week. The price will not gradually approach its new equilibrium value. Indeed, unless the price adjusted immediately, a profitable arbitrage opportunity would exist and could be expected to be exploited immediately in an efficient market. Similarly, if a reliable and profitable seasonal pattern for equity prices exists (e.g. a substantial Christmas rally) speculators will bid up prices sufficiently prior to Christmas so as to eliminate any unexploited arbitrage possibility. Samuelson (1965) and Mandelbrot (1966) have proved rigorously that if the flow of information is unimpeded and if there are no transactions costs, then tomorrow's price change in speculative markets will reflect only tomorrow's 'news' and will be independent of the price change today. But 'news' by definition is unpredictable and thus the resulting price changes must also be unpredictable and random.

The term 'random walk' is usually used loosely in the finance literature to characterize a price series where all subsequent price changes represent random departures from previous prices. Thus, changes in price will be unrelated to past price changes. (More formally, the random walk model states that investment returns are serially independent, and that their probability distributions are constant through time.) It is believed that the term was first used in an exchange of correspondence appearing in *Nature* in 1905 (see Pearson and Rayleigh, 1905). The problem considered in the correspondence was the optimal search procedure for finding a drunk who had been left in the middle of a field. The answer was to start exactly where the drunk had been placed. That point is an unbiased estimate of the drunk's future position since he will presumably stagger along in an unpredictable and random fashion.

The earliest empirical work on the random walk hypothesis was performed by Bachelier (1900). He concluded that commodities prices followed a random walk, although he did not use that term. Corroborating evidence from other time series was provided by Working (1934 – various time series), Cowles and Jones (1937 – US stock prices) and Kendall (1953 – UK stock and commodities prices). These studies generally found that the serial correlation between successive price changes was essentially zero. Roberts (1959) found that a time series generated from a sequence of random numbers had the same appearane as a time series of US stock prices. Osborne (1959) found that stock price movements were very similar to the random Brownian motion of physical particles. He found that the logarithms of price changes were independent of each other.

More recent empirical work has used alternative techniques and data sets and has searched for more complicated patterns in the sequence of prices in speculative markets. Granger and Morgenstern (1963) used the powerful technique of spectral analysis but were unable to find any dependably repeatable patterns in stock price movements. Fama (1965) not only looked at serial correlation coefficients (which were close to zero) but also corroborated his investigation by examining a series of lagged price changes as well as by performing a number of nonparametric 'runs' tests. Fama and Blume (1966) examined a variety of filter techniques –

trading techniques where buy (sell) signals are generated by some upward (downward) price movements from recent troughs (peaks) – and found they could not produce abnormal profits. Other investigators have done computer simulations of more complicated techniques of technical analysis of stock price patterns and found that profitable trading strategies could not be employed on the basis of these techniques. Solnik (1973) measured serial correlation coefficients for daily, weekly and monthly price changes in nine countries and also concluded that profitable investment strategies could not be formulated on the basis of the extremely small dependencies found.

While the empirical data are remarkably consistent in their general finding of randomness, equity markets do not perfectly conform to the statistician's ideal of a random walk. As noted above, while serial correlation coefficients are always found to be small, there are some small dependencies that have been isolated. While 'runs' tests found only slight departures from randomness, there is a slight tendency for runs in daily price changes to persist. Merton (1980) has shown that changes in the variance of a stock's return (price) can be predicted from its variance in the recent past. Such departures from a pure random walk do not violate the weak form of EMH, which states only that unexploited trading opportunities should not exist in an efficient market. Still, the formal random walk model does not strictly hold. The probability distributions of stock prices may be a submartingale rather than a random walk.

In addition, some disturbing seasonal patterns have recently been found in stock price series. Keim (1983) and others have documented a January effect, where stock returns are abnormally high during the first few days of January (especially for small firms) and French (1980) and others have also documented a so-called 'weekend effect' where average returns to stocks are negative from the close of trading on Friday to the close of trading on Monday. Seasonals appear to exist in several international markets as documented by the Gultekins (1983) and by Jaffé and Westerfield (1984). But departures from randomness are generally remarkably small and an investor who pays transaction costs cannot choose a profitable investment strategy on the basis of these anomalies. Thus, while the random-walk hypothesis is not strictly upheld, the departures from randomness that do exist are not large enough to leave unexploited investment opportunities. Consequently, the empirical evidence presents strong evidence in favour of the weak form of the efficient market hypothesis. The history of stock price movements does not offer investors any information that permits them to outperform a simple buy-and-hold investment strategy.

SEMI-STRONG FORM EFFICIENCY. The weak form of EMH has found general acceptance in the financial community, where technical analysts have never been held in high repute. The stronger assertion that all publicly available information has already been impounded into current market prices has proved far more controversial among investment professionals, who practise 'fundamental' analysis of publicly available information as a widely accepted mode of security analysis. In general, however, the empirical evidence suggests that public information is so rapidly impounded into current market prices that fundamental analysis is not likely to be fruitful.

A variety of tests have been performed to ascertain the speed of adjustment of market prices to new information. Fama, Fisher, Jensen and Roll (1969) looked at the effect of stock splits on equity prices. While splits themselves provide no economic benefit, splits are usually accompanied or followed by dividend increases that do convey to the market information about management's confidence about the future progress of the enterprise. Thus, while splits usually do result in higher share prices, the market appers to adjust to the announcement fully and immediately. Substantial returns can be earned prior to the split announcement, but there is no evidence of abnormal returns after the public announcement. Indeed, in cases where dividends were not raised following the split, firms suffered a loss in price, presumably because of the unexpected failure of the firm to increase its dividend. Similarly, while merger announcements, especially where premiums are being paid to the shareholders of the acquired firm, can raise market prices substantially, it appears that the market adjusts fully to the public announcements. Dodd (1981) finds no evidence of abnormal price changes following the public release of the merger information.

Scholes (1972) studied the price effects of large secondary offerings. The general belief among market professionals is that such offerings will depress prices temporarily so as to facilitate a large distribution relative to normal trading volume. Such a *temporary* decline would be inconsistent with market efficiency. Scholes hypothesized that the decline would be permanent, however, reflecting release of privilaged information (since block traders are usually insiders) of an expected decline in the company's performance. Scholes found that the declines were permanent, especially when sales were by insiders, and thus inconsistent with the temporary price-pressure hypothesis. However, Kraus and Stoll (1972) used intraday prices and did find some evidence of a price reversal and an arbitrage opportunity. But these reversals took place within a 15-minute period – a speed of adjustment that suggests the market is remarkably efficient.

While the vast majority of studies support the semi-strong version of EMH, there have been some that do not. Ball (1978) found that stock-price reactions to earnings announcements are not complete. Abnormal risk-adjusted returns are systematically non-zero in the period following the announcement. Ball attributed this to inadequacies in the capital asset pricing model (CAPM) used to adjust for risk differentials and suggested several steps to reduce the estimation bias. Watts (1978), however, performed the steps suggested by Ball and still found systematic abnormal returns. Rendleman, Jones and Latané (1982) also find a relationship between unexpected quarterly earnings and excess returns for common shares subsequent to the announcement date. Roll (1984) found that orange-juice futures prices were made informationally inefficient over short periods by the existence of exchange-imposed maximum daily price moves. Apart from this constraint, however, prices did fully reflect all known information. Moreover, the other abnormalities have not been shown to exist *consistently* over time, and when they did occur, they have usually been small enough that only a professional broker-dealer could have earned economic profits. Thus, it remains to be seen how robust these anomalies are as compared with the vast body of evidence supporting the semi-strong EMH. The evidence in favour of the market's rapid adjustment to new information is sufficiently pervasive that it is now a generally, if not universally, accepted tenet of financial econometric research.

THE STRONG FORM OF THE EFFICIENT MARKET HYPOTHESIS. As the previous studies indicated, stock splits, dividend increases and merger announcements can have substantial impacts on share prices. Consequently insiders trading on such information can clearly profit prior to making the announcement, as has been documented by Jaffe (1974). While such trading is generally illegal, the fact that the market often at least partially anticipates the announcements suggests that it is certainly possible to profit on the basis of privileged information. Thus, the strongest form of the EMH is clearly refuted. Nevertheless, there is considerable evidence that the market comes reasonably close to strong-form efficiency.

Several studies have been performed on the records of professional investment managers. In general they show that randomly selected portfolios or unmanaged indices do as well or better than professionally managed portfolios after expenses. Cowles (1933) examined the records of selected financial services and professional investors. He failed to find any evidence of performance superior to that which could be achieved by investing in the market as a whole. Friend et al. (1962) concluded that the performance of the average mutual fund was insignificantly different from the performance of an unmanaged portfolio with similar asset composition. Jensen (1969) measured the risk-adjusted performance of mutual funds utilizing the capital asset pricing model to measure the appropriate risk return trade-off. Jensen found that while the funds tended to earn *gross* positive abnormal returns, any relative advantage of the professional managers was lost in management fees. Note that the EMH would not rule out small gross abnormal returns as an incentive to acquire information. Grossman and Stiglitz (1980) and Cornell and Roll (1981) have shown that a sensible market equilibrium should leave some incentive for analysis. Those who acquire costly information would have superior gross returns but only average net returns. And the overwhelming evidence on the performance of professional investors is that net returns are only average or below average. For example, during the 20 years to 1984, two-thirds of US professional pension fund managers were out-performed by the unmanaged Standard and Poor's 500 stock index. Moreover, there seems to be little consistency to whatever exceptional performance one finds. It appears that a professional manager who has achieved exceptional performance in one period is just as likely to underperform the market in the next period. It is clear that while superior investment managers may well exist, they are extremely rare.

SOME FURTHER ANOMALIES. In general, the empirical evidence in favour of EMH is extremely strong. Probably no other hypothesis in either economics or finance has been more extensively tested. Thus, it is not surprising that along with general

131

support for EMH there have been scattered pieces of anomalous evidence inconsistent with the hypothesis in its strongest forms. Basu (1977, 1983) found that stocks with low price-earnings (P/E) multiples have higher average risk-adjusted returns than stocks with high P/E's. Banz (1981) found that substantial abnormal (risk-adjusted) long-run rates of return could be earned by investing in portfolios of smaller firms. As was noted above, a large part of this higher return occurs early in January. We know that transactions costs are higher for smaller firms but this factor does not seem to explain the size effect. The size effect appears to persist in varying degrees over time and is related to the evidence regarding higher returns for stocks with low P/E multiples. Of course, we must always keep in mind that these findings of abnormal returns are always joint tests of market efficiency and the particular form of the asset pricing model involved. Thus it is impossible to distinguish if the abnormal returns are truly due to inefficiencies or result instead because of inadequacies of the capital asset pricing model as a method of measuring risk.

In another empirical study rejecting the concept of market efficiency, Shiller (1981) argued that variations in aggregate stock market prices are much too large to be justified by the variation in subsequent dividend payments. This apparent rejection of the Efficient Market Hypothesis for the entire stock market goes far beyond the narrow issue of whether or not some investors or some trading schemes can beat the market. Shiller's tests, however, are joint tests of market efficiency and the correctness of this model of the dividend process. Marsh and Merton (1983) derive an alternative model for dividend and stock price behaviour. They conclude that Shillers findings that stock prices are 'too volatile' is a result of his misspecification of the dividend process rather than a result of market inefficiency. A similar conclusion was reached by Kleidon (1986). Nevertheless, the history of fads and excesses in speculative markets I have reviewed (Malkiel, 1985), from tulip bulbs to blue-chip growth stocks, gives me some doubts that we should always consider the current tableau of market prices represents the best estimates available of appropriate discounted present value.

There have been other scattered instances of inefficiencies as summarized by Jensen (1978) and Ball (1978). I have argued (Malkiel, 1980), that closed-end funds (even those holding essentially 'market' portfolios) were inefficiently priced over many years so that they would provide investors with abnormal returns over and above those involved in buying and holding directly the well-diversified portfolios owned by the funds.

But this last illustration, rather than convincing me of substantial areas of market inefficiency, actually drives me to the opposite conclusion. If there is *truly* some area of pricing inefficiency that can be discovered by the market and dependably exploited, then profit-maximizing traders and investors will eventually through their purchases and sales bring market prices in line so as to eliminate the possibility of extraordinary return. In time investors recognized that closed-end funds at discounts represented extraordinary value and the discounts on these funds were eventually large eliminated.

So we are again driven back to the position of the EMH. Pricing irregularities may well exist and even persist for periods of time, and markets can at times be dominated by fads and fashions. Eventually, however, any excesses in market valuations will be corrected. Undoubtedly with the passage of time and with the increasing sophistication of our data bases and empirical techniques, we will document further departures from efficiency and understand their causes more fully. But I suspect that the end result will not be an abandonment of the profession's belief that the stock market is remarkably efficient in its utilization of information.

BIBLIOGRAPHY

Bachelier, L. 1900. *Théorie de la speculation. Annales de l'Ecole normale Supérieure*, 3rd series, 17, 21–86. Trans. by A.J. Boness in *The Random Character of Stock Market Prices*, ed. P.H. Cootner, Cambridge, Mass.: MIT Press, 1967.

Ball, R. 1978. Anomalies in relationships between securities' yields and yield-surrogates. *Journal of Financial Economics* 6(2–3), 103–26, June/September, 1981

Banz, R. 1981. The relationship between return and market value of common stocks. *Journal of Financial Economics* 9(1), March 3–18.

Basu, S. 1977. Investment performance of common stocks in relation to their price earnings ratios: a test of the efficient markets hypothesis. *Journal of Finance* 32(3), June, 663–82.

Basu, S. 1983. The relationship between earnings' yield, market value and the return of NYSE common stocks: further evidence. *Journal of Financial Economics* 12(1), June, 129–56.

Cornell, B. and Roll, R. 1981. Strategies for pairwise competitions in markets and organizations. *Bell Journal of Economics* 12(1), Spring, 201–13.

Cowles, A. 1933. Can stock market forecasters forecast? *Econometrica* 1(3), July, 309–24.

Cowles, A. and Jones, H. 1937. Some posteriori probabilities in stock market action. *Econometrica* 5(3), July, 280–94.

Dodd, P. 1981. The effect on market value of transactions in the market for corporate control, *Proceedings of Seminar on the Analysis of Security Prices*, CRSP. Chicago: University of Chicago, May.

Fama, E. 1965. The behavior of stock market prices. *Journal of Business* 38(1), January, 34–105.

Fama, E. and Blume, M. 1966. Filter rules and stock market trading. *Security Prices: A Supplement, Journal of Business* 39(1), January, 226–41.

Fama, E., Fisher, L., Jensen, M. and Roll, R. 1969. The adjustment of stock prices to new information. *International Economic Review* 10(1), February, 1–21.

French, K. 1980. Stock returns and the weekend effect. *Journal of Financial Economics* 8(1), March, 55–69.

Friend, I., Brown, F., Herman, E. and Vickers, D. 1962. *A Study of Mutual Funds*. Washington, DC: US Government Printing Office.

Granger, D. and Morgenstern, O. 1963. Spectral analysis of New York Stock Market prices. *Kyklos* 16, January, 1–27.

Grossman, S. and Stiglitz, J. 1980. On the impossibility of informationally efficient markets. *American Economic Review* 70(3), June, 393–408.

Gultekin, M. and Gultekin, N. 1983. Stock market seasonality, international evidence. *Journal of Financial Economics* 12(4), December, 469–81.

Jaffé, J. 1974. The effect of regulation changes on insider trading. *Bell Journal of Economics and Management Science* 5(1), Spring, 93–121.

Jaffé, J. and Westerfield, R. 1984. The week-end effect in common stock returns: the international evidence. Unpublished manuscript, University of Pennsylvania, December.

Jensen, M. 1969. Risk, the pricing of capital assets, and the evaluation of investment portfolios. *Journal of Business* 42(2), April, 167–247.

Jensen, M. 1978. Some anomalous evidence regarding market efficiency. *Journal of Financial Economics* 6(2–3), June–September, 95–101.

Keim, D. 1983. Size related anomalies and stock return seasonality: further empirical evidence. *Journal of Financial Economics* 12(1), June, 13–32.

Kendall, M. 1953. The analysis of economic time series. Part I: Prices. *Journal of the Royal Statistical Society* 96(1), 11–25.

Kleidon, A. 1986. Variance bounds, tests and stock price valuation models. *Journal of Political Economy* 94(5), October, 953–1001.

Kraus, A. and Stoll, H. 1972. Price impacts of block trading on the New York Stock Exchange. *Journal of Finance* 27(3), June, 569–58.

Malkiel, B. 1980. *The Inflation-Beater's Investment Guide.* New York: Norton.

Malkiel, B. 1985. *A Random Walk Down Wall Street.* 4th edn, New York: Norton.

Mandelbrot, B. 1966. Forecasts of future prices, unbiased markets, and martingale models. *Security Prices: A Supplement, Journal of Business* 39(1), January, 242–55.

Marsh, T. and Merton, R. 1983. Aggregate dividend behavior and its implications for tests of stock market rationality. Working Paper, Sloan School of Management, September.

Merton, R. 1980. On estimating the expected return on the market: an exploratory investigation. *Journal of Financial Economics* 8(4), December, 323–61.

Osborne, M. 1959. Brownian motions in the stock market. *Operations Research* 7(2), March/April, 145–73.

Pearson, K. and Rayleigh, Lord. 1905. The problem of the random walk. *Nature* 72, 294, 318, 342.

Rendelman, R., Jones, C. and Latané, H. 1982. Empirical anomalies based on unexpected earnings and the importance of risk adjustments. *Journal of Financial Economics* 10(3), November, 269–87.

Roberts, H. 1959. Stock market 'patterns' and financial analysis: methodological suggestions. *Journal of Finance* 14(1), March, 1–10.

Roberts, H. 1967. Statistical versus clinical prediction of the stock market. Unpublished manuscript, CRSP, Chicago: University of Chicago. May.

Roll, R. 1984. Orange juice and weather. *American Economic Review* 74(5), December, 861–80.

Samuelson, P. 1965. Proof that properly anticipated prices fluctuate randomly. *Industrial Management Review* 6(2), Spring, 41–9.

Scholes, M. 1972. The market for securities: substitution versus price pressure and the effects of information on share prices. *Journal of Business* 45(2), April, 179–211.

Shiller, R.J. 1981. Do stock prices move too much to be justified by subsequent changes in dividends? *American Economic Review* 71(3), June, 421–36.

Solnik, B. 1973. Note on the validity of the random wak for European stock prices. *Journal of Finance* 28(5), December, 1151–9.

Thompson, R. 1978. The information content of discounts and premiums on closed-end fund shares. *Journal of Financial Economics* 6(2–3), June–September, 151–86.

Watts, R. 1978. Systematic 'abnormal' returns after quarterly earnings announcements. *Journal of Financial Economics* 6(2–3), June–September, 127–50.

Working, H. 1934. A random difference series for use in the analysis of time series. *Journal of the American Statistical Association* 29, March, 11–24.

Financial Markets

NILS H. HAKANSSON

One of the more noteworthy developments in economics over the last twenty years or so is the emergence of equilibrium models of the financial market. Included in this term is the market for financial securities such as stocks, bonds, options and insurance contracts. The chief building block and spur in this evolution has been the economics of uncertainty, which itself is of rather recent origin. The results of this new focus and the activities and synergies it has generated is often broadly referred to as financial economics. It is within this new subfield that various models of the financial market occupy the centre stage.

After a brief summary of models based on analysis in return space in section I, this essay will focus on the two-period, pure-exchange model of the financial market beginning in section II. Conditions under which full efficiency is attained in incomplete markets will be identified in section III. Finally, section IV will trace the welfare and price effects resulting from changes in the financial market.

I. RETURN SPACE ANALYSIS

Much of the earlier work in financial equilibrium focused on pay-off returns rather than total pay-offs or consumption levels. While return space is both a natural and intuitive object of concern, and in fact continues to draw much attention, it faces certain shortcomings in addressing many questions of interest where prices, endowments and consumption pay-offs play a central role. I shall therefore provide only a brief review of the main results in return space before moving on to the consumption- and wealth-oriented models.

The so-called capital asset pricing model (CAPM) was more or less independently developed by Sharpe (1964), Lintner (1965) and Mossin (1966). It studies a single-period, frictionless, competitive market of financial securities. Assuming that (a) investors' preferences are a function of only the mean and the variance of the portfolio's anticipated return (with the mean favoured and the variance disfavoured), (b) investors have homogeneous probability assessments

135

of returns and (c) there is a risk-free asset and that unlimited borrowing is available at the lending rate, three principal results are obtained in equilibrium:

1. The expected return on an optimal portfolio is a positive linear function of its standard deviation of return.
2. The expected return on every security (and portfolio) is a positive, linear function of its (return) covariance with the market portfolio of risky assets (the portfolio which includes x per cent of the oustanding shares of all securities in the market).
3. All optimal portfolios are comprised of the market portfolio of risky assets in conjunction with either risk-free borrowing or lending.

Since the CAPM model is consistent with the von Neumann–Morgenstern (1944) theory of rational choice only under quadratic preferences and/or normally distributed returns, it has left many economists uncomfortable. Nevertheless, it has been the basis of a very large number of empirical studies, which on balance show that the CAPM model provides a rather good first approximation of observed return structures in the financial markets of various countries.

A more recent development is the so-called arbitrage pricing theory (APT) developed by Ross (1976b). It posits that security returns are generated by a linear K-factor mode (with K small) in which securities' residual risks are sufficiently independent across securities for the law of large numbers to apply. APT can therefore be viewed as an extension of the single-index model introduced by Markowitz (1952) and developed and extended by Sharpe (1963, 1967), which in turn, of course, is closely related to the CAPM. Not surprisingly, the APT appears to offer a somewhat better fit than the CAPM or single-index model.

In studying the economics of financial markets, however, the CAPM and the APT frameworks do not offer fertile ground. In the CAPM framework, for example, the capital structures of firms are a matter of indifference. To study these and other questions, we must therefore turn to more comprehensive formulations.

II. THE BASIC MODEL

The earliest models systematically incorporating uncertainty in analysing markets were those of Allais (1953), Arrow (1953), Debreu (1959, ch. 7) and Borch (1962). They may therefore be viewed as the forerunners of more comprehensive models of the financial market, including the two-period model developed below.

Assumptions. We consider a pure-exchange economy with a single commodity which lasts for two periods under the standard assumptions. That is, at the end of period 1 the economy will be in some state s where $s = 1, \ldots, n$. There are I consumer-investors indexed by i, whose probability beliefs over the states are given by the vectors $\pi_i = (\pi_{i1}, \ldots, \pi_{in})$, where, for simplicity, $\pi_{is} > 0$, all i, s. The preferences of consumer-investor i are represented by the (conditional) functions $U_{is}(c_i, w_{is})$, where c_i is the consumption level in period 1 and w_{is} is the consumption level in period 2 if the economy is in state s at the beginning of that period. These functions are defined for

$$(c_i, w_{is}) \geq 0 \qquad \text{all } i, s \qquad (1)$$

and are assumed to be increasing and strictly concave.

At the beginning of period 1 (time 0), consumer-investors allocate their resources among current consumption c_i and a portfolio chosen from a set J of securities indexed by j. Security j pays $a_{js} \geq 0$ per share at the end of period 1 and the total number of outstanding shares is Z_j. Let z_{ij} denote the number of shares of security j purchased by investor i at time 0; his portfolio $z_i = (z_{i1}, \ldots, z_{iJ})$ then yields the pay-off

$$w_{is} = \sum_{j \in J} z_{ij} a_{js}$$

available for consumption in period 2 if state s occurs at the end of period 1. Investor endowments are denoted $(\bar{c}_i, \bar{z}_i)$ and aggregate wealth or consumption in state s is given by

$$W_s \equiv \sum_{j \in J} Z_j a_{js}, \qquad \text{all } s.$$

The financial markets, as is usual, are assumed to be competitive and perfect; that is, consumer-investors perceive prices as beyond their influence, there are no transaction costs or taxes, securities and commodities are perfectly divisible, and the full proceeds from short sales (negative holdings) can be invested. The number of securities, however, need not be large (although this is not ruled out). Since our focus is on the structure of the financial market, and changes therein, production decisions (and hence the vector of aggregate consumption (C, W)) are viewed as fixed.

If the rank of matrix $A = [a_{js}]$ is full (equals n), the financial market will be called *complete*; if not, it will be called *incomplete*. The significance of a complete market is that *any* pay-off pattern $w \geq 0$ can be obtained via some portfolio z since the system $zA = w$ will always have a solution. (In incomplete markets, in contrast, some pay-offs patterns $w \geq 0$ are infeasible.) The simplest form of a complete market is that in which $A = I$ (the identity matrix); the financial market is now said to be composed of *Arrow–Debreu* or *primitive* securities (as opposed to *complex* securities.) The main 'advantage' of an Arrow–Debreu market is that it never requires the consumer-investor to take short positions, which is generally necessary in a complete market composed of complex securities. Finally, a financial market which contains a risk-free asset, or makes it possible to construct a risk-free portfolio, is called *zero-risk compatible*.

Under our assumptions, each consumer-investor i maximizes

$$u_i \equiv \sum_s \pi_{is} U_{is}\left(c_i, \sum_{j \in J} z_{ij} a_{js}\right) \qquad (2)$$

with respect to the decision vector (c_i, z_i), subject to (1) and to the budget constraint

$$c_i P_0 + \sum_{j \in J} z_{ij} P_j = \bar{c}_i P_0 + \sum_{j \in J} \bar{z}_{ij} P_j$$

as a price-taker, where P_0 is the price of a unit of period 1 consumption and P_j is the price of security j.

Equilibria and their properties. In view of our assumptions, an equilibrium will exist but need not be unique (see e.g. Hart, 1974; note also that uniqueness is with reference to the consumption allocation (c, w), not allocation (c, z)). The equilibrium conditions for any market structure A, assuming for simplicity that the non-negativity constraints on consumption are not binding may be written

$$\sum_s \pi_{is} \frac{\partial U_{is}\left(c_i, \sum_{j \in J} z_{ij} a_{js}\right)}{\partial c_i} = \lambda_i \qquad \text{all } i \tag{3}$$

$$\sum_s \pi_{is} \frac{\partial U_{is}\left(c_i, \sum_{j \in J} z_{ij} a_{js}\right) a_{js}}{\partial w_{is}} = \lambda_i P_j \qquad \text{all } i, j \tag{4}$$

$$(c_i, z_i A) \geqslant 0 \qquad \text{all } i \tag{5}$$

$$c_i + z_i P = \bar{c}_i + \bar{z}_i P \qquad \text{all } i \tag{6}$$

$$\sum_i (c_i, z_i) = (C, Z) \tag{7}$$

where the λ_i are Lagrange multipliers, (7) represents the market clearing equations, and P_0 has been chosen as numeraire, i.e. $P_0 \equiv 1$.

Any allocation (c, z) which constitutes a solution to the system (3)–(7) (along with a price vector P and a vector λ) is *allocationally efficient with respect to the market structure A* – since the marginal rates of substitution for any two *securities* are the same across individuals. When (c, z) is allocationally efficient with respect to *all* conceivable allocations, whether achieved outside the existing market or not, (c, z) will be said to be *fully allocationally efficient* (FAE).

To be more precise, define the *shadow* prices R'_{is} by

$$R'_{is} \equiv \frac{1}{\lambda_i} \left(\pi_{is} \frac{\partial U_{is}\left(c_i, \sum_{j \in J} z_{ij} a_{js}\right)}{\partial w_{is}} \right).$$

It is well known that (3)–(7) plus

$$R'_{is} = R'_{1s} \qquad \text{all } i \geqslant 2, \qquad \text{all } s \tag{8}$$

is a necessary and sufficient condition for the market allocation (c, z) to be FAE because (8) insures that the marginal rates of substitution of wealth between any two *states* are the same for all investors i. (4) may now be written

$$AR'_1 = P, \qquad \text{all } i. \tag{4'}$$

Implicit Prices. The equilibrium value of a feasible second-period pay-off vector w will be denoted $V(w)$; thus if w is obtainable via portfolio z, we get $w = zA$ and hence

$$V(w) = V(zA) = zP = wR = zAR.$$

In the above expression, $R = (R_1, \ldots, R_n)$ represents the not necessarily unique set of *implicit prices* of (second-period) consumption in the various states implied by P since

$$AR = P. \tag{9}$$

By Farkas' Lemma, a positive implicit price vector is always present in the absence of arbitrage and hence in equilibrium. (Arbitrage is the opportunity to obtain either a pay-off $w \geq 0$, $w \neq 0$, at a cost $zP \leq 0$, or a pay-off $w = 0$ at a cost $zP < 0$.) In view of (4') and (9), shadow prices are always implicit prices, but a set of implicit prices need not be anyone's shadow prices.

III. FULL ALLOCATIONAL EFFICIENCY IN INCOMPLETE MARKETS

When the financial market A is complete, systems (4') and (9) have only one solution, which insures that

$$R'_i = R, \qquad \text{all } i.$$

This condition, as noted, is necessary and sufficient to attain FAE. Complete financial markets, while a useful abstraction, are not an everyday occurrence, however. Securities number at most a few thousand, while the relevant set of states is no doubt much larger. This leads us to the question: under what circumstances is FAE attained in incomplete markets? One such case is trivial and will be dismissed quickly: the case when individuals are identical in their preferences, beliefs and (the value of their) endowments. We now turn to three other sets of conditions when this occurs.

Diverse Endowments. Are there any conditions under which individuals with *diverse* endowments are as well served by a single security in the market as by many? The answer is yes; beliefs must be homogeneous and preferences e.g. of the form

$$U_{is}(c_i, w_{is}) = \begin{cases} U_i^1(c_i) + \rho_s U_i^2(w_{is}) \\ \quad\quad\text{or} \\ U_i^1(c_i)\rho_s U_i^2(w_{is}) \end{cases} \qquad \text{all } i, s \tag{10}$$

(with $\rho_s > 0$), where

$$U_i^2(w_{is}) = (1/\gamma)w_{is}^\gamma, \qquad \gamma < 1, \qquad \text{all } i.$$

That is, preferences for second-period consumption must be separable, isoelastic and homogeneous. Everyone's optimal portfolio is now of the form

$$z_i = k_i Z, \qquad \text{all } i,$$

where the k_i are fractions. In addition, the equilibrium implicit prices R are now unique and completely independent of the market structure A.

Linear Risk Tolerance. To attain FAE with heterogeneous second-period preferences, we need at least two securities in the market. Two-fund separation occurs in every zero-risk compatible market A under homogeneous beliefs (but arbitrary return structures) when preferences are of the form (10) if and only if

$$U_i^2(w_{is}) = \begin{cases} (1/\gamma)(\phi_i + w_{is})^\gamma & \gamma < 1, & \text{all } i \\ \quad\text{or} \\ -(\phi_i - w_{is})^\gamma & \gamma > 1, & \phi_i \text{ large}, & \text{all } i \\ \quad\text{or} \\ -\exp\{\phi_i w_{is}\} & \phi_i < 0, & \text{all } i \end{cases}$$

provided none of the non-negativity constraints on consumption are binding. The optimal policies are now of the form

$$z_i = k_{i1} z' + k_{i2} z'', \qquad \text{all } i,$$

where the portfolio (fund) z' is risk-free and portfolio z'' is risky (see e.g. Rubinstein, 1974). It is evident that with diverse endowments, preferences must belong to a very narrow family, even when beliefs are homogeneous, in order for FAE to be attained.

Supershares. Two states s and s' such that $W_s = W_{s'}$, i.e., with equal aggregate pay-offs, are said to belong to the same superstate t (Hakansson, 1977). If the financial market is complete with respect to the superstate partition T, FAE is attained for arbitrary endowments if and only if

$$\pi_{is}/\pi_{it} = \pi_{1s}/\pi_{1t}, \qquad \text{all } s \in t, \qquad \text{all } i \text{ and } t \tag{11}$$

and

$$U_{is} = U_{is'}, \qquad \text{all } s \text{ and } s' \in t, \qquad \text{all } i \text{ and } t. \tag{12}$$

Note that (11) and (12) require only conditionally homogeneous beliefs and that preferences are insensitive to states *within* a superstate – beliefs and preferences with respect to superstates are unrestricted.

To complete the market with respect to superstates, three simple alternatives are available (Hakansson, 1978). The first is a full set of 'supershares', each share paying \$1 if and only if a given superstate occurs (superstates are readily denominated in either nominal or real terms). The second and third alternatives are a full set of (European) call options or a full set of (European) put options on the market portfolio αZ or αW, where $0 < \alpha \leqslant 1$.

It may be noted that a market in puts and calls on a crude approximation to the United States market portfolio, namely the Standard & Poors 100 Index, was opened in 1983. These options are now the most actively traded of all option instruments.

IV. CHANGES IN THE FINANCIAL MARKET

Changes in the set of securities available in the financial market are everyday occurrences. Early studies on this subject include those of Borch (1968, Ch. 8), Ross (1976a) and Litzenberger and Sosin (1977). To trace fully the effects of such changes involves comparing equilibria, which is a matter of some complexity. However, using the two-period framework of this essay, it is possible to reach some general conclusions on how changes in the market structure from A' to A'', say, affect welfare, prices and other dimensions of interest in a pure exchange setting.

The Feasible Allocations. One of the critical determinants, not surprisingly, is the change in feasible allocations. Recall that a market structure A is any 'full' set of instruments; that is, any set of instruments capable of allocating, in some fashion, aggregate wealth $W = (W_1, \ldots, W_n)$. The set of feasible second-period consumption allocations $w = (w_1, \ldots, w_l)$ obtainable via market structure A will be denoted $F(A)$, i.e.

$$F(A) \equiv \left\{ w \,|\, w_i \geqq 0, w_i = z_i A, \sum_i z_{ij} = Z_j, \quad \text{all } j \right\}.$$

In comparing two market structures A' and A'' with respect to feasible allocations, there are (since holding the market portfolio αZ is always feasible) three possibilities; either

$$F(A') = F(A'') \tag{Type I}$$

or

$$F(A') \subset F(A'') \text{ (or the converse)} \tag{Type II}$$

or

$$\{F(A') \cap F(A'')\} \subset F(A')$$
$$\{F(A') \cap F(A'')\} \subset F(A''). \tag{Type III}$$

These three types of changes will be referred to as feasibility preserving, feasibility expanding (or reducing) and feasibility altering.

A sure way to obtain a feasibility expanding change is to make a finer and finer breakdown of *existing* instruments into an ever larger set of linearly independent (or unique) securities.

Endowment Effects. Since changes in the financial market structure are generally implemented by firms or exchanges and take place when the market is closed, such changes frequently alter investors' endowments. An example would be a

141

merger, which results in the substitution of new securities for old. It is useful to distinguish between three cases:

1. *Strong endowment neutrality.* This occurs if the endowed consumption patterns in the two markets are unaltered, i.e. if

$$(\bar{c}_i', \bar{w}_i') = (\bar{c}_i'', \bar{w}_i''), \qquad \text{all } i.$$

2. *Weak endowment neutrality.* This occurs if the values of the endowments (provided there is a common implicit equilibrium price structure R) are identical in the two markets, i.e. if

$$\bar{c}_i' + \bar{z}_i' P' = \bar{c}_i' + \bar{w}_i' R = \bar{c}_i'' + \bar{w}_i'' R = \bar{c}_i'' + \bar{z}_i'' P'', \qquad \text{all } i$$

where $R > 0$ satisfies $A'R = P'$ and $A''R = P''$.

3. *Non-neutral endowment changes.* While the first two cases are rather rare, strong endowment neutrality typically accompanies non-synergistic (*pro rata*) corporate spin-offs when applicable bonds remain risk-free, as well as the opening of option markets, for example.

The Welfare Dimension. As noted, in comparing different market structures, the comparison which is ultimately relevant is that which compares allocations actually attained; that is, equilibrium allocations. Using (2), we denote investor i's equilibrium expected utility in market structure A'' by u_i'' and his equilibrium expected utility in market structure A' by u_i'. A comparison of any given equilibrium in market A'' with some equilibrium in some other market A' must then yield one of four cases:

$$u_i'' \geqslant u_i', \text{ all } i, \qquad u_i'' > u_i', \text{ some } i \text{ (Pareto dominance)} \tag{i}$$

or

$$u_i'' = u_i', \text{ all } i \qquad \qquad \text{(Pareto equivalence)} \tag{ii}$$

or

$$u_i'' > u_i', \text{ some } i, u_i'' < u_i', \text{ some } i \text{ (Pareto redistribution)} \tag{iii}$$

or

$$u_i'' \leqslant u_i', \text{ all } i, \qquad u_i'' < u_i', \text{ some } i \text{ (Pareto inferiority).} \tag{iv}$$

The task at hand, then, is to identify the conditions under which each of these cases, as well as combinations of these cases, will occur. All comparisons are contemporaneous in the sense that they compare welfare under market structure A'' to what it would be if A' were in use instead.

Principal results. The principal results (Hakansson, 1982) may be summarized as follows:

(1) Feasibility preserving market structure changes yield either Pareto

equivalence or redistributions. To preclude Pareto redistributions we must either have efficient endowments in the first market and strong endowment neutrality, or weak endowment neutrality coupled with unique equilibria. Pareto equivalence is always accompanied by value conservation.

(2) Feasibility expanding market structure changes imply either Pareto dominance, Pareto equivalence or Pareto redistributions. To preclude redistributions we must have efficient endowments in the first market and strong endowment neutrality, or weak endowment neutrality coupled with unique equilibria. Value conservation is highly unlikely.

(3) Feasibility altering changes in the market structure have unpredictable value and welfare effects.

(4) Value and welfare effects are relatively independent.

As noted by Hart (1975), the introduction of multiple commodities or more than two periods is a non-trivial step which may bring about additional complications, such as Pareto-dominated equilibria when feasibility is expanded.

Within the limits of the single-good, two-period model under pure exchange, certain tentative general conclusions concerning common market structure changes can be stated. Even under mild heterogeneity of preferences and/or beliefs, 100 per cent non-synergistic mergers tend to be welfare reducing while (non-synergistic) spin-offs and the opening of option markets tend to be beneficial. The use of risky bonds and preferred stock tends to be virtuous as well, at least apart from bankruptcy costs. Finally, value conservation is a much rarer phenomenon than suggested by Modigliani and Miller (1958) and Nielsen (1978) among others.

BIBLIOGRAPHY

Allais, M. 1953. L'extension des théories de l'équilibre économique général et du rendement social au cas du risque. *Econometrica* 21, April, 269–90.

Arrow, K. 1953. The role of securities in the optimal allocation of risk-bearing. *Review of Economic Studies* 31, April 1964, 91–6.

Borch, K. 1962. Equilibrium in a reinsurance market. *Econometrica* 30, July, 424–44.

Borch, K. 1968. *The Economics of Uncertainty*. Princeton, NJ: Princeton University Press.

Debreu, G. 1959. *Theory of Value*. New York: Wiley.

Hakansson, N. 1977. The superfund: efficient paths toward efficient capital markets in large and small countries. *Financial Decision Making Under Uncertainty*, ed. H. Levy and M. Sarnat, New York: Academic Press.

Hakansson, N. 1978. Welfare aspects of options and supershares. *Journal of Finance* 33(3), June, 759–76.

Hakansson, N. 1982. Changes in the financial market: welfare and price effects and the basic theorems of value conservation. *Journal of Finance* 37(4), September, 977–1004.

Hart, O. 1974. On the existence of equilibrium in a securities model. *Journal of Economic Theory* 9(3), November, 293–311.

Hart, O. 1975. On the optimality of equilibrium when the market structure is incomplete. *Journal of Economic Theory* 11(3), December, 418–43.

Lintner, J. 1965. The valuation of risk assets and the selection of risky investments in stock portfolios and capital budgets. *Review of Economics and Statistics* 47, February, 13–37.

Litzenberger, R. and Sosin, H. 1977. The theory of recapitalizations and the evidence of dual purpose funds. *Journal of Finance* 32(5), December, 1433–55.

Markowitz, H. 1952. Portfolio selection. *Journal of Finance* 7, March, 77–91.

Modigliani, F. and Miller, M. 1958. The cost of capital, corporation finance, and the theory of investment. *American Economic Review* 48, June, 261–97.

Mossin, J. 1966. Equilibrium in a capital asset market. *Econometrica* 34(4), October, 768–83.

Neumann, J. von and Morgenstern, O. 1944. *Theory of Games and Economic Behavior*. Princeton, NJ: Princeton University Press.

Nielsen, N. 1978. On the financing and investment decisions of the firm. *Journal of Banking and Finance* 2(1), March, 79–101.

Ross, S. 1976a. Options and efficiency. *Quarterly Journal of Economics* 90(1), February, 75–89.

Ross, S. 1976b. The arbitrage theory of capital asset pricing. *Journal of Economics Theory* 13(3), December, 341–60.

Rubinstein, M. 1974. An aggregation theorem for securities markets. *Journal of Financial Economics* 1(3), September, 225–44.

Sharpe, W. 1963. A simplified model for portfolio analysis, *Management Science* 9, January, 277–93.

Sharpe, W. 1964. Capital asset prices: a theory of market equilibrium under conditions of risk. *Journal of Finance* 19, September, 425–42.

Sharpe, W. 1967. Linear programming algorithm for mutual fund portfolio selection. *Management Science*, Series A 13, March, 499–510.

Futures Markets, Hedging and Speculation

DAVID M. NEWBERY

Futures markets for grain emerged in Chicago in the middle of the 19th century and spread rapidly to other commodities and centres. Forward contracts, in which two agents agree on the details of a transaction for delivery at a specified future date, must date back to the beginnings of commerce itself, but the distinctive feature of a futures market is that the contracts are standardized, transactions costs minimized, and liquidity is high, so that contracts can be, and typically are, bought and sold many times during their lifetime, in contrast to most forward contracts. The standard explanation for the role of futures markets is that they help to spread and hence reduce risks, and to motivate the collection and dissemination of relevant information. Forward markets provide the same risk-sharing opportunities, but the greater transparency and liquidity of futures markets makes the latter far more potent institutions for 'price discovery'.

The question of how well futures markets (and securities markets more generally) perform this role of collecting, aggregating and disseminating information is a large and important topic, best handled under the wider heading of Information. If we assume agents have rational expectations and share common information, then the price-discovery role of futures markets can be ignored and remaining issues of risk-sharing studied in isolation. In this case there is little conceptual difference between futures and forward markets, and we can concentrate attention on the two characteristic modes of behaviour exhibited by these markets – speculation and hedging.

Speculation is the purchase (or temporary sale) of goods for later resale (repurchase), rather than use, in the hope of profiting from the intervening price changes. In principle, any durable good could be the subject of speculative purchase, but if carrying costs are high, or the good is illiquid, then the margin between the buying and selling price will be large, and speculation in that good will normally be unattractive. Liquidity in this context means that there exists a perfect, or near-perfect, market in which the good can be sold immediately for a well-defined price, and this requirement severely limits the range of assets available for large-scale speculation. There are two types of assets – commodities traded on organized futures markets, and financial assets (bonds, shares) whose properties lend themselves particularly to speculation. Hedging, on the other hand, typically refers to a transaction on a futures market undertaken to reduce the risks arising from some other risky activity, either producing the commodity, storing it or processing it for final sale.

Thus a risk-averse wheat farmer may hedge his future harvest by selling October wheat futures in January, in which case he is 'long' in actuals and 'short' in futures. A risk-averse miller who anticipates being short of wheat may hedge by buying futures now, in which case he will be a 'long' hedger. Speculators may be on the long or short end of any transaction, but in aggregate their position must offset any net imbalance in the long and short hedgers' positions.

It might appear from this that hedging consists in shifting the price risk onto the speculators in return for a risk premium. This view of speculation, advanced by Keynes (1923) and Hicks (1946), has been challenged by Working (1953, 1962), who denies any fundamental difference between the motivation of hedgers and speculators. One danger with looking exclusively at the price risk is that it ignores the more fundamental quantity risks that give rise to the price risks. Once this is appreciated, it is possible to formulate a simple theoretical model in which all agents are alike in attempting to maximize their expected utility but differ in the risks to which they are exposed, and these differences motivate trade on futures markets. Whilst the activities of speculators are quite well defined, those of 'hedgers' are in general a mixture of insurance and speculation, as we shall see.

The simplest model of speculation and hedging has just two time periods. In the first period farmers plant their wheat, and the futures market opens. In the second period the wheat is harvested, sold, and the futures contracts expire. There are only three types of agents – farmers, who produce wheat but do not consume it; speculators, who neither produce nor consume wheat; and consumers, who neither produce wheat nor trade on futures markets. All agents are assumed to have beliefs about the relevant variables, which can be described by (subjective) probability distributions, and their behaviour is described by the theory of expected utility maximization. There are n farmers, and for the moment suppose that they have no choice over the amount of wheat to plant, but only over the size of their sales on the futures market. In the first period farmer i believes that his second period output will be $\tilde{q}_i$ (a random variable), and that the market clearing price will be $\tilde{p}^i$, also a random variable. In particular, he believes that $\tilde{q}_i$ and $\tilde{p}^i$ are jointly normally distributed. The price of futures is f, observable now, and he sells z_i futures, so that he believes his second period income will be

$$\tilde{y}_i = \tilde{p}^i \tilde{q}_i + z_i(f - \tilde{p}^i), \tag{1}$$

a random variable. The farmer's utility function exhibits constant absolute risk aversion, A_i, and takes the form $U^i(y) = -k_i \exp(-A_i \tilde{y})$, where $\tilde{y}$ is the random component of his income. (Any non-random components can be absorbed into the constant, k_i). This particular form has the property that maximizing expected utility is equivalent to maximizing

$$W = Ey - \tfrac{1}{2}A \operatorname{Var} y, \tag{2}$$

where Ey is the expected value of income, $\operatorname{Var} y$ is its variance, provided, as in the case here, that y is normally distributed. (These are the standard assumptions of the capital asset pricing model for portfolio choice, and can be viewed as second-order approximations to more general utility functions; see Newbery and Stiglitz, 1981.) If equation (1) is substituted in (2), and if z_i can be positive (futures sales) or negative (purchases) then the value of z_i that maximizes W is

$$z_i = \frac{\operatorname{Cov}(\tilde{p}^i, \tilde{p}^i \tilde{q}_i)}{\operatorname{Var} \tilde{p}^i} - \frac{E\tilde{p}^i - f}{A_i \operatorname{Var} \tilde{p}^i}. \tag{3}$$

Speculator j has no risky production, so for him $\tilde{q}_j$ is zero, and the first terms in (1) and (3) vanish. Thus the second term in (3) can be identified as the speculative term, and is readily interpreted. The perceived riskiness of the futures contract is measured by $\operatorname{Var} \tilde{p}^i$, and the cost of this risk as $A_i \operatorname{Var} \tilde{p}^i$. The expected return to selling a futures contract is $f - Ep^i$. In order to persuade a risk-averse speculator to *buy* futures and accept the risk, the return to *selling* must be negative, hence f must be below the expected spot price, $E\tilde{p}^i$ – a situation of *normal backwardation*. The first term in (3) is the pure hedging term, for if the futures market appears *unbiased* (i.e. $f = E\tilde{p}^i$) then there is no expected speculative profit, and the only motive for trade is the income insurance offered by the price insurance. The quality of income insurance depends on how well income pq and price risks are correlated; that is, on the ratio of the covariance to the variance. If output is perfectly certain, then income and price are perfectly correlated, the first term will be equal to q_i, and the farmer would sell his entire crop on the futures market if he believed it to be unbiased. In general, though, he will not believe it to be unbiased, and he will wish to speculate in addition to hedging. His net futures trade will reflect the balance of the desire to insure and the returns to speculating.

The futures market clears, so that the sum of z_i across all participants must be zero, and this condition will yield a value for the futures price. What this implies for the value of f and its relation for the subsequent spot price, p, depends on beliefs, as well as preferences. If agents hold *rational expectations*, and have full information about the nature of all production and demand risks, then they will agree on the common values of the expected spot price, Ep, and its variance, $\operatorname{Var} p$. In such a case the only motive for trading on the futures market is to share risk, and speculators will be willing to absorb some of the risk in return, on average, for some profit. If all farmers face perfectly correlated production risk, and if the coefficient of variation of output is σ_q, of price is σ_p, and the correlation coefficient between price and output is r, then market clearing on the futures market gives the bias as

$$\frac{Ep - f}{Ep} = \frac{\bar{Q} \cdot Ep\sigma_p^2 (1 + r\sigma_q/\sigma_p)}{\sum 1/A_i}, \tag{4}$$

147

and a farmer's futures sales will be

$$\frac{z_i}{Eq_i} = \beta_i(1 + r\sigma_q/\sigma_p), \qquad \beta_i \equiv 1 - \frac{\bar{Q}}{Eq_i A_i \sum_j 1/A_j}, \qquad (5)$$

where $\bar{Q} = \Sigma Eq_i$ is average total output (see Newbery and Stiglitz, 1981, p. 186). Thus β_i is a measure of the extent to which the farmer is more risk-averse than the average (the term in A_i) and more exposed to risk ($\bar{q}_i/\bar{Q}$). If there are n identical farmers and m identical speculators, all with the same coefficient of absolute risk aversion, A, then $\beta = m/(n+m)$. If there is no output risk, so $\sigma_q = 0$, then whilst a farmer would sell his entire crop forward on an unbiased futures market, here he would only sell a fraction β, representing the fraction of the total risk which the speculators are willing to bear. If the only source of risk is supply variability, then $r = -1$, $\sigma_q/\sigma_p = \varepsilon$, the elasticity of demand, and the farmer will sell a fraction of his crop $\beta(1 - \varepsilon)$ on the futures market, possibly negative.

What lessons can be drawn from this very simplified model? First, futures markets allow speculators to bear some of the farmer's risks. The more highly correlated income and price risks, the better the market is at insuring farmers, but in general it will only provide partial insurance. It is, however, much better suited to providing insurance to stockholders who store the commodity after the harvest until needed for consumption or processing, and it is not surprising that most hedging is done by stockholders rather than farmers. Second, the greater the agreement over the expected spot price, and the less risk-averse are the speculators, the smaller will be the average perceived bias, and the larger will be the fraction of hedging to speculative sales by producers (or stockholders). Third, the greater the degree of agreement on the expected spot price, the more will speculation be a response to the demand for hedging services. The greater the disagreement on the expected spot price, the more likely it is that speculation, in the form of gambling over the expected spot price, will dominate the market. In a masterly series of studies, Holbrook Working showed that most commodity futures markets depend primarily on hedging for their existence, that the size of the open interest follows the demand for hedging of seasonal storage closely, with speculators standing ready to assume the risks offered by the hedgers (Working, 1962). The cost of these hedging services (i.e. the return to the speculators) was quite remarkably small. Thus for cotton traders, the *gross* profit per dollar of sales over a sample of some 3000 trades was 0.023 of 1 per cent with the traders making losses on 15 out of 43 trading days. (Net profits after paying commissions and expenses were substantially less; Working, 1953). The issue of bias turns out to be more complex than the simple Keynes–Hicks risk-premium view, for even in a bilateral market of farmers and speculators, the bias can go either way. Once stockholders and processors are brought into the picture, the relative demands for long and short hedges will change yet again, and in turn influence the direction of speculation (long or short) and hence of the risk premium, or bias.

Several important questions can be asked about the role of speculators. Do they tend to destabilize the spot market and/or the futures market? Do they improve efficiency? Do they have adverse macroeconomic effects? To the layman the association of speculative activity with volatile markets is often taken as proof that speculators are the cause of the instability, though the body of informed opinion is that the volatility creates a demand for hedging or insurance, which is met by the willingness of speculators to bear the risk. It is hard to test the proposition that speculation is stabilizing, for speculative activity (notably, stockholding) can take place without futures markets. In practice, the usual question is, do futures markets, which, by lowering transaction costs, greatly facilitate speculative behaviour, improve the stability of the spot market? Even this question is not straightforward. Futures markets provide an incentive to collect information about the future market-clearing spot price, though, as often with information gathering, there are public good problems associated with its use. Much theoretical effort has been devoted to the question of whether futures prices perfectly reveal the relevant information available to participants, and if so, what incentives would remain for its collection. It now appears that, except in special cases, the information is only partially revealed in the market, leaving incentives for its collection, but nevertheless improving the forecasts of otherwise uninformed traders. If so, and if the spot market is intrinsically volatile (because of variations in supply caused by weather, or demand caused by the trade cycle) then better forecasts of future spot prices will tend to elicit compensating supply responses – if prices are expected to be high tomorrow, then it will pay to produce more, and to carry more stocks forward, tending to reduce, or stabilize, price fluctuations. To the extent that futures markets reduce storage risks, storage becomes cheaper, and this will tend to stabilize supplies and prices directly. On the other hand, anticipated disturbances will have a more immediate effect on current prices, and will tend to make them more responsive to news. A frost in Brazil expected to affect next year's coffee production is likely to have a more rapid effect on current coffee prices in the presence of a futures market than in its absence. Nevertheless, it improves the efficiency of the current market if it does respond to this relevant information.

The clearest example of the stabilizing effect of futures market is provided by cobweb models, in which producers base current production decisions on last year's realized price, with consequent self-sustaining fluctuations in output without any exogenous shocks. If a futures market is set up, then producers initially planning to expand production in response to last year's high price, and selling futures, would cause the futures price to fall to the predicted spot price, and would lead them to revise their incorrect production plans, hence eliminating the cobweb and stabilizing the market.

Two other factors bear on the question of market stability. It is clear that much hinges on the nature of expectations. Speculation without hedging is a zero-sum game, and if two speculators, each holding different views of the future price, $E\tilde{p}^i$, trade with each other, one will gain whilst the other will lose. If they are rational, and risk-averse, they should not be willing to engage in such swaps.

On this view, speculators who are more successful at forecasting the future price will make money, and those who are less successful will lose, and be forced to leave the market, until only the good forecasters are left, and they only make money in the course of moving futures prices towards the forecast spot price. However, it is possible that a steady supply of less good speculators, who add noise to the system, lose money and exit to be replaced by others. Their presence may worsen the predictive power of the futures price or, by increasing the returns to information gathering by the informed speculators, may actually improve the predictive power of the futures prices (Anderson, 1984a, Kyle, 1984). Depending on the direction of the net effect of uninformed speculators, the presence of a futures market (which provides them with the opportunity to gamble) may improve or worsen the efficiency of the spot market.

The other possibility is that futures markets will provide opportunities for market manipulation, either by the better informed at the expense of the less well-informed (corners, squeezes) or of the larger at the expense of the smaller. It is easy to show that the futures price has an effect on production decisions by extending the model of equation (1) to allow producers to choose inputs. In the case of pure demand risk (no output uncertainty) it can be shown that the producer will base his production decisions solely on the future price. Large producers (Brazil for coffee, OPEC for oil, etc.) may then find it profitable to intervene in the futures market to influence the production decisions of their competitors in the spot market, and in extreme cases may find it profitable to increase price instability, though the extent to which this is feasible will be limited by the supply of and risk tolerance of other speculators in the futures market (Newbery, 1984). This is true even if all agents hold rational expectations, and share full information (except about the actions of the large producers). If some agents use naive forecasting rules to guide their futures trading, and if these rules are known to other agents who possess market power, then it may pay the large rational agents to destabilize the price and exploit the irrationalities in the forecasting behaviour of the naive agents (Hart, 1977).

Although speculation may stabilize prices, it is quite possible for it to make prices more unstable, even if all agents have equal information and hold rational expectations. Compare two possible arrangements. In the first, futures markets are prohibited, the commodity is perishable, so there is no scope for speculative storage or speculation on the futures market. The commodity can be produced by two methods, one perfectly safe, the other risky, but on average more profitable (e.g. two varieties of irrigated rice, one higher yielding, but susceptible to rust in certain weather conditions). Farmers allocate their land between the two production techniques but, in the absence of the futures market, find the risky technique relatively unattractive and so produce little. In the second arrangement, futures markets are permitted and speculators are willing to trade for a very low risk-premium. Farmers are now able to sell the crop forward, and are therefore more willing to produce the risky crop, whose supply is very variable. Total supply variability increases, and hence the spot price becomes more variable.

It is quite possible that destabilizing speculation of this type yields higher potential social welfare, for yields are higher, if riskier, and the risks are borne at relatively low cost. It is also perfectly possible for speculation on a futures market to be stabilizing (by reducing the costs of storage and therefore improving arbitrage between crop years) and yet make everyone worse off (e.g. see Newbery and Stiglitz, 1981). We now know that if the market structure is incomplete, creating additional markets can make matters worse. Speculation, which creates a market in price risks, does not thereby complete the market structure because quantity risks may remain imperfectly insured. The reason is that the market in price risks causes changes in the market equilibrium which affects the degree to which the other risks (income and quantity risks) are effectively insured. In particular, if prices are stabilized, but quantities remain unstable, incomes may be less stable than if prices were free to move in response to the quantity changes.

Finally, there remains the old Keynesian question of whether speculation which succeeds in stabilizing prices will exacerbate income fluctuations. The argument, due to Kaldor (1939), is straightforward. Speculators undertake or assume the risks for storage, which then responds to mismatches in supply and demand. These stocks, or inventories of goods, will fluctuate markedly and will have the same macroeconomic effect as fluctuations in investment, tending, through the multiplier, to have a magnified effect on national income. Whether these speculative stock movements are stabilizing or destabilizing then turns on whether they offset or amplify the fluctuations in income associated with the mismatch in demand and supply that caused the stock change. Kaldor's view was that stock changes caused by supply shocks would tend to stabilize total income, whilst those caused by demand stocks would be destabilizing, but much will depend on the commodity price elasticities of demand and the nature of the various transmission mechanisms, particularly the lag structure. Nevertheless, the OPEC oil shocks have demonstrated that commodity supply shocks can cause significant macroeconomic disturbances, whilst the increasing ease of currency speculation as restrictions are removed and transaction costs lowered, has reawakened the fear that speculation may, in some cases, destabilize income and impose needless costs.

BIBLIOGRAPHY

Anderson, R.W. 1984a. The industrial organization of futures markets: a survey. Ch. 1 of Anderson (1984b).

Anderson, R.W. (ed.) 1984b. *The Industrial Organization of Futures Markets*. Lexington, Mass.: Lexington Books.

Hart, O.D. 1977. On the profitability of speculation. *Quarterly Journal of Economics* 91(4), November, 579–97.

Hicks, J.R. 1946. *Value and Capital*. 2nd edn, Oxford: Oxford University Press.

Kaldor, N. 1939. Speculation and economic stability. *Review of Economic Studies* 7, October, 1–27. Reprinted in N. Kaldor, *Essays on Economic Stability and Growth*, London: Duckworth, 1960.

Keynes, J.M. 1923. Some aspects of commodity markets. *Manchester Guardian Commercial, Reconstruction Supplement* 29, March. Reprinted in *The Collected Writings of John Maynard Keynes*, London: Macmillan; New York: St. Martin's Press, 1971.

151

Kyle, A.S. 1984. A theory of futures market manipulation. Ch. 5 of Anderson (1984b).

Newbery, D.M.G. 1984. The manipulation of futures markets by a dominant producer. Ch. 2 of Anderson (1984b).

Newbery, D.M.G. and Stiglitz, J.E. 1981. *The Theory of Commodity Price Stabilization.* Oxford: Clarendon Press.

Working, H. 1953. Futures trading and hedging. *American Economic Review* 43, June, 314–43.

Working, H. 1962. New concepts concerning futures markets and prices. *American Economic Review* 52, June, 432–59.

Futures Trading

H.S. HOUTHAKKER

The object of futures trading is the *futures contract*, which may be defined as a highly standardized forward contract. Although the terms 'forward' and 'futures' are often used interchangeably in the older literature, the distinction is essential to the understanding of futures trading. Forward contracts are widely used; thus an agreement in which an automobile dealer undertakes to deliver a car of a specified make, type and colour to a customer at some later date is a forward contract; so is an employment contract, in which the employee promises to perform specified services during a certain period of time. Because forward contracts are typically quite specific, the employee in the last example cannot substitute another worker for himself without the employer's consent. Futures contracts, by contrast, exist only for a limited number of commodities and financial instruments, and are used only by a relatively small number of firms and individuals.

Futures contracts are of two types. The traditional contract provides for actual delivery of the underlying merchandise or financial instruments. In the early 1980s contracts with 'cash settlement' were introduced; they are settled not by delivery but by calculating traders' gains and losses from a known price, for instance an index of equity prices. Cash settlement is inherently simpler than delivery, but it is of limited application because in most markets there is no single price that could be used for this calculation. The following discussion focuses on futures contracts with delivery, though most of it also applies to cash-settlement contracts.

The standardization characteristic of futures contracts generally involves five elements: (1) *Quantity*: buyers and sellers can deal only in lots of fixed size, for instance 5000 bushels of wheat or bonds with a face value of $100,000; of course they can buy or sell any number of such lots. (2) *Quality*: the commodity or instrument is usually not completely specified but can be anywhere in a range (e.g. all wheat of certain grades, or all government bonds maturing within a certain interval). (3) *Delivery time*: the lot can be delivered at any time within a specified period say a month. In most markets only contracts for selected delivery months are traded; thus the bond futures market has contracts for March, June, September and December. (4) *Location*: the lot must be delivered in specified places (e.g. warehouses or banks) in one or more specified cities. (5) *Identity of contractors*: after the initial contract is established, the buyer and seller normally have no further dealings with each other, thus eliminating credit risk. The execution is guaranteed by a clearing house, which acts as seller to all buyers and as buyer to all sellers. The clearing house can offer this guarantee by virtue of the security deposits, known as 'margin', it collects from its members.

The immediate purpose of this standardization is to minimize transaction costs and thereby to endow the futures contract with the ready negotiability that forward contracts, heterogeneous as they are, normally lack. Futures contracts are intended to be traded by 'open outcry' on the floor of an organized exchange. Such exchanges are found in a number of commercial centres, especially in Chicago, New York and London.

The overall market for a commodity or financial instrument can be divided into the futures market, which is centralized and trades only standardized contracts, and the cash market, which is dispersed and deals in actual parcels of the commodity or instrument. The cash market can be further divided into the spot market and the forward market.

Traders may have long or short positions in any or all of these three markets; thus a merchant who holds a physical inventory is considered to be long in the spot market. A trader whose net position in the case market is offset by his position in the futures market is called a *hedger*; more particularly he is a 'short hedger' if he is long in the cash market and short in the futures market, and a 'long hedger' if these positions are reversed. Traders who are net long or net short in the overall market (and hence in at least one of its submarkets) are known as *speculators*. In the futures market there are also 'spreaders' or 'straddlers', whose long position in one or more futures contracts exactly matches their short position in other futures contracts.

In both the futures and the forward markets the net position of all traders combined must be zero, since there is a sale for every purchase. This is not true in the spot market, where the aggregate net position is positive to the extent of the existing inventories. The total of all long (or short) positions in the futures market is called the 'open interest'.

The prices prevailing in the cash and futures markets at any time are not necessarily equal. However, there are two main links between these markets; one is provided by the delivery mechanism and the other by hedging. As to delivery, when a futures contract reaches maturity (as the May contract does in the month of May) the remaining shorts have to deliver what they have sold, and the remaining longs have to accept and pay for what they have bought. Clearly the shorts will not deliver anything that could be sold at a higher price in the spot market, nor will the longs take delivery of anything that they could buy more cheaply elsewhere. At delivery time, therefore, the futures price must be equal to the spot price of the items that are actually delivered. Since this ultimate equality is widely anticipated, it will also influence futures and spot prices prior to delivery time.

Hedging also serves to relate futures prices and spot prices. As Working (1953) pointed out, it is essentially a form of arbitrage between the two markets. If a futures price is high compared to a spot price, hedgers will buy in the spot market and sell futures. They can do so without risk if the futures price exceeds the spot price by more than the *carrying charge*, which is the cost of holding physical inventories between the present and the maturity of the futures contract. The futures price therefore cannot exceed the current spot price by more than the prevailing carrying charge.

It does not follow, however, that a futures price must always exceed the spot price by the relevant carrying charge. Positive inventories may be held even if the spot price is above the futures price. This is because inventories have what Kaldor (1939) called a 'convenience yield', derived from their availability when buyers need them. The profits of merchants, in fact, depend in large part on their ability to assess and realize the convenience yield. Its size depends primarily on the size of total inventories; if they are small, the marginal convenience yield will be high, but if they are large, it may be zero. Working (1953) described the relationship between the size of inventories and the return of them as the *supply curve of storage*.

The view of hedging expressed above is not necessarily inconsistent with the older interpretation of hedging as an effort to shift the price risk inherent in holding inventories to those (namely the speculators) willing to assume this risk in the hope of profiting from favourable price movements. It should be noted, however, that hedging need not reduce the total risk to which a hedger is exposed. Bankers are generally willing to finance a larger proportion of the value of hedged inventories than of unhedged inventories. By hedging, consequently, a merchant can support a larger inventory with his own capital, thereby giving more scope to the exercise of his merchandising skills. The connection between hedging and risk aversion is not as clear-cut as the older view would suggest.

Regardless of the economic interpretation of hedging, its existence has another important implication discovered by Keynes (1923, 1930) and elaborated by Hicks (1939) and Houthakker (1968). If merchants can increase their profits by hedging, they must be willing to pay a *risk premium* for the opportunity to do so. It is conceivable that short hedging (defined above) exactly offsets long hedging, in which case any premiums paid by hedgers would cancel out. There is considerable evidence, however, that in most markets short hedging exceeds long hedging at most times. The basic reason for this asymmetry is that, as pointed out earlier, the net position in the spot market (and hence in the overall market) is positive. In seasonal commodities an excess of long hedging over short hedging is usually found only towards the end of the crop year, when inventories are small.

Now if the hedgers are net short in futures, the speculators in futures must be net long. Keynes and his followers argued that speculators will only be net long

155

if they expect futures prices to rise. At any particular moment the speculators may of course be wrong, but on the average they are right, and each futures price will tend to rise until, at the maturity of the contract, it equals the relevant spot price. The speculators' gain is the hedgers' loss; thus the speculators receive a risk premium proportionate to the amount of hedging they make possible. This risk premium is implicit in the hedgers' willingness to sell futures contracts that have a tendency to appreciate.

This, in brief, is Keynes's theory of *normal backwardation*. ('Backwardation' designates a situation where the futures price is below the spot price; strictly speaking the term 'normal backwardation' applies only to the nonseasonal markets that Keynes had in mind, but the fundamental idea carries over to markets with seasonality.) The theory anticipated the positive relation between risk and return that is the main result of the Capital Asset Pricing Model developed in the 1960s. Consistency with the CAPM also requires, however, that the risk of buying futures cannot be eliminated by diversification, and that has not yet been demonstrated. The theory of normal backwardation can also be summarized as saying that futures prices, when viewed as predictors of the spot price in the future, have a downward bias.

The empirical validity of the theory of normal backwardation remains in dispute. Favourable evidence has been presented by Houthakker (1957, 1961, 1968), Cootner (1960) and Bodie and Rozansky (1980). For adverse evidence see Telser (1958, 1981), Gray (1961), Rockwell (1967) and Dusak (1973). According to the latter group of authors, futures prices are unbiased predictors of spot prices, and no risk premium is paid. The most telling argument of the critics of normal backwardation is that as a body, small speculators appear to lose money rather consistently.

If true, the theory of normal backwardation would also shed light on an observation made earlier, namely the fairly limited scope of futures trading. To be viable, the theory implies, a futures market has to be nourished by the risk premium transferred from the hedgers to the speculators; in its absence the latter would be gradually driven out by the transaction costs they incur. The futures contract must therefore be primarily designed to attract hedging.

It is not a simple matter to design futures contracts that will attract enough hedging to ensure their continued viability. Hedgers need a high correlation between the futures prices and the particular spot prices in which they are interested; consequently the contract should be neither too broad (i.e. include too many deliverable grades) nor too narrow. There must also be enough variability in prices to make hedging and speculation worthwhile.

This is why futures trading was for many years confined to grains, oilseeds, sugar, cotton, non-ferrous metals and a few other staples that can be easily graded and have volatile prices. There is no futures trading in such important commodities as steel, paper and synthetic fibres. In the 1970s, when exchange rates and interest rates became more variable, futures trading was successfully introduced in various financial instruments – first in foreign exchange, then in government securities and similar claims, and most recently in indexes of share prices. Financial futures now account for most of the activity in futures markets. The most important recent addition in the non-financial sector has been futures trading in crude oil and some of its derivatives.

Despite the controversy over normal backwardation it is widely agreed that one of the economic functions of futures trading is risk transfer. Another such function is sometimes called *price discovery*. It consists in the establishment of a competitive reference price for a commodity or financial instrument. Since the cash market is typically heterogeneous, it is convenient to have a single price from which spot and forward prices can be derived as differences. Thus the forward price for a specific transaction may be quoted as a number of cents over or under the May futures price.

Futures trading also facilitates the *allocation of production and consumption over time*, particularly by providing market guidance in the holding of inventories through the supply curve of storage (see above). More generally futures prices provide information relevant to the planning of production and consumption; if the futures prices for distant deliveries are well below those for early delivery, for instance, postponing consumption is more attractive.

The economic functions of futures markets will be performed most effectively when they are highly competitive. If one or more traders are large enough to assert their market power, futures prices (and quite possibly cash prices) may not reflect the underlying supply and demand conditions. The prevention of such distortions – particularly of 'corners', where one or more longs manipulate both the cash and the futures market – is a major concern of futures exchanges and their regulators. In the United States the Commodity Futures Trading Commission supervises the markets with a view to preventing and penalizing these and other abuses, though it has not always succeeded. In Britain the Bank of England has somewhat similar responsibilities.

BIBLIOGRAPHY

Bodie, Z. and Rozansky, V.J. 1980. Rise and return in commodity futures. *Financial Analysts' Journal* 36, May–June, 27–31, 33–39.

Cootner, P. 1960. Returns to speculators: Telser *vs.* Keynes. *Journal of Political Economy* (with reply by Telser and rejoinder by Cootner) 68, August, 396–418.

Dusak, K. 1973. Futures trading and investor returns: an investigation of commodity market risk premiums. *Journal of Political Economy* 81(6), November–December, 1387–1406.

Gray, R. 1961. The search for a risk premium. *Journal of Political Economy* 69, June, 250–60.

Hicks, J.R. 1939. *Value and Capital*. Oxford: Clarendon Press.

Houthakker, H.S. 1957. Can speculators forecast prices? *Review of Economics and Statistics* 39, May, 143–52.

Houthakker, H.S. 1961. Systematic and random elements in short-term price movements. *American Economic Review, Papers and Proceedings* 51, May, 164–72.

Houthakker, H.S. 1968. Normal backwardation. In *Value, Capital and Growth*, ed. J.N. Wolfe, Edinburgh: Edinburgh University Press; Chicago: Aldine Publishing Co.

Kaldor, N. 1939. Speculation and economic stability. *Review of Economic Studies* 7, October, 1–27.

Keynes, J.M. 1923. Some aspects of commodity markets. *Manchester Guardian Commercial, Reconstruction Supplement* 29, March. Reprinted in *The Collected Writings of John Maynard Keynes*, Vol. VII, London: Macmillan, 1973; New York: St. Martin's Press, 1973.

Keynes, J.M. 1930. *A Treatise on Money*, Vol. II. London: Macmillan.

Rockwell, C.S. 1967. Normal backwardation, forecasting and the return to commodity futures traders. *Food Research Institute Studies* 7, Supplement, 107–30.

Telser, L.G. 1958. Futures trading and the storage of cotton and wheat. *Journal of Political Economy* 66, June, 233–55.

Telser, L.G. 1981. Why there are organized futures markets. *Journal of Law and Economics* 24(1), April, 1–22.

Working, H. 1953. Hedging reconsidered. *Journal of Farm Economics* 35, November, 544–61.

Gearing

J.S.S. EDWARDS

The question whether a company's choice of the proportion of debt to equity finance in its capital structure matters has involved a great deal of controversy. This choice, known as the gearing decision in the UK and the leverage decision in the USA, is widely regarded by corporate finance directors, investors, stock market participants and many others as an issue of considerable importance, yet the basic result of conventional economic theory applied to this question is that the gearing decision is irrelevant; there is no advantage to a firm in choosing one debt–equity ratio rather than another. This striking contrast between theory and practice has, of course, led to much critical examination of the assumptions of the theory, and some progress has been made in identifying ways in which gearing may matter. However it remains true that the determinants of a firm's gearing decision, and its importance, are not yet fully understood.

The argument that the gearing decision is a matter of irrelevance, affecting neither the firm's value nor its cost of capital (and hence its investment decision), is due to Modigliani and Miller in a celebrated article (Modigliani and Miller, 1958). Their fundamental insight was that, in a world of perfect and complete capital markets in which taxation and asymmetric information are absent, individual investors can create any particular pattern of returns from holdings of securities by borrowing on their own account. This ability of investors to engage in 'home-made leverage' means that there is no reason for firms to concern themselves about the amount of debt in their capital structure: investors can create for themselves any pattern of returns which would be given by a share in a firm with a particular gearing ratio, so firms cannot gain by offering one such pattern rather than another.

To see this, consider the following simple illustration of the Modigliani–Miller argument (based on Nickell, 1978). Suppose that a firm possesses assets which yield $1000\,\tilde{\theta}$ per annum in perpetuity, where $\tilde{\theta}$ is a random variable, and that this firm has 1000 equity shares outstanding, but no debt in its capital structure. The price of a claim to an income stream yielding $\tilde{\theta}$ in perpetuity is determined

159

by a perfect capital market to be 1, so the value of the firm's equity is 1000. If the firm borrows, say, 200 at a rate of 10% per annum with no risk of default, each share will now yield $\tilde{\theta}-0.02$ per annum in perpetuity, because there is a certain interest payment to be made from the returns on the firm's assets in each year before shareholders receive anything. If individual investors can borrow at the same interest rate as the firm the price of a share will now be 0.8, since an investor could have created a $\tilde{\theta}-0.02$ income stream in the original situation by borrowing 0.2 (on which the annual interest payment is 0.02) and using 0.8 of his own to buy one share for 1. Thus if the firm does borrow 200 the value of its equity will fall to 800, and its overall value (the sum of the values of outstanding debt and equity) remains constant at 1000. Home-made leverage enables an individual investor to create any combination of $\tilde{\theta}$ and a certain return whatever combination of $\tilde{\theta}$ and a certain return the firm offers, so that there is no reason for the firm to concern itself with the choice of a particular combination of the two.

Modigliani–Miller's original argument rested on a number of restrictive assumptions, such as the existence of risk classes within which firm's operating earnings were perfectly correlated, which were relaxed in subsequent work. One of the most general proofs of the Modigliani–Miller theorem was that by Stiglitz (1974), which did not need to make any assumptions about the existence of risk classes, the source of uncertainty, individuals having the same expectations, or the interest rate paid by a firm being unaffected by the amount of capital it raises. Stiglitz noted three critical limitations to his proof however, and it is these which begin to suggest ways in which gearing may be a relevant decision for firms. One is that individuals' expectations about future prices and firm valuations must not be affected by changes in companies' financial policy: this in effect rules out the possibility of financial policy acting as a signal in a world of asymmetric information. The second limitation is that individual borrowing must be a perfect substitute for firm borrowing, while the third is that there must be no bankruptcy.

At first sight these last two limitations would appear to indicate clearly why gearing is important in practice. But matters are not so straightforward. Companies may be able to borrow on better terms than individuals, but this may be because they are better risks: the Modigliani–Miller theorem only requires that individuals and firms borrow on the same terms for debt of equivalent risk. It is certainly not true that companies can always borrow on better terms than individuals: mortgages for house purchase, for example, are sometimes available at rates below those charged on corporate borrowing. Even if it is true that firms can borrow on better terms than individuals for equivalent risk loans, so that they can gain in value by offering this service to individuals, firms can compete by so doing and this may eliminate the gain in value: the supply of corporate debt expands until the Modigliani–Miller proposition is re-established.

A similar argument applies in the case of bankruptcy. When a firm issues risky debt it creates a security which individuals, lacking limited liability, cannot replicate by borrowing on their own account. This expands the range of portfolio opportunities open to investors, which they should in principle be willing to pay for, thus enabling the firm to increase its value by use of some debt finance.

However the extent to which a particular firm can gain by issuing risky debt depends on whether it can offer something special to investors that is not already available; it is difficult to believe that one more firm's risky debt significantly expands the set of portfolio opportunities available to investors.

A more promising approach to understanding the importance attached to the gearing decision in practice would appear to be the relaxation of the assumption that there is no taxation. Most corporation tax systems allow interest payments on debt finance to be deductible against corporation tax, and this has been widely argued to provide the obvious explanation for the use of some debt in a firm's capital structure (by Modigliani–Miller among many others). Tax advantages to debt might imply that firms should use all-debt finance, but this unsatisfactory conclusion has been avoided by introducing costs of bankruptcy and financial distress, which reduce the size of the total payout to investors in certain contingencies that are more likely the larger the firm's gearing ratio. These include costs of reorganization and liquidation associated with bankruptcy, together with costs of financial distress, such as the foregoing of profitable investment opportunities which may be necessitated by bankruptcy, and the making of suboptimal investment decisions in an attempt to forestall bankruptcy. These costs will result in the firm's market value beginning to decline beyond some level of gearing, so that together with the corporation tax advantage of debt a theory of optimal gearing ratios seems to result.

This theory is perhaps the most commonly accepted one for explaining the importance of gearing, but it is by no means uncontroversial. One reason for its lack of universal acceptance is that evidence on the size of the costs of bankruptcy and financial distress is limited and, where available (Warner, 1977), it does not suggest that they are large. Another reason is that this theory only takes account of corporate taxes in arguing that there is a tax advantage to the use of debt finance. Investors are subject to personal taxes on interest and dividend income and capital gains, and these tax rates differ usually between income and capital gains, and certainly between different investors. This causes a number of problems. If personal tax is higher on debt interest than on equity income (taking account of both dividends and capital gains) the use of debt finance may reduce the firm's value. The variation of personal tax rates across investors means that it is likely that some would prefer debt on tax grounds while others would prefer equity. Indeed differences in personal tax rates were used by Miller (1977) to reintroduce an irrelevance result (in which bankruptcy costs were ignored): he argued that investors would specialize their holdings in debt or equity according to whether their after-all-tax income from a unit of pre-tax debt cash flow (1 − personal tax rate on debt income) was greater or less than their after-tax income from a unit of pre-tax equity cash flow ((1 − personal tax rate on equity income) times (1 − corporation tax rate)). There would be a determinate aggregate debt–equity ratio, at which point marginal investors would be indifferent between holding debt or equity on tax grounds, but the gearing decision would be irrelevant for individual firms.

Miller's argument shows that when heterogeneous personal tax rates are considered, as they must be, it is not obvious that there is a tax advantage to corporate borrowing. But there are problems with this argument too. Auerbach and King (1983) show that the Miller equilibrium requires the existence of certain constraints on investors: without such constraints (on, for example, borrowing and short-selling) questions arise concerning the existence of an equilibrium, for with perfect capital markets realistic tax systems provide opportunities for unlimited arbitrage at government expense between investors and firms in different tax positions. Auerbach and King also show that the combined effect of taxation and risk is to produce a situation in which gearing is relevant. With individual investors facing different tax rates and wishing to hold diversified portfolios the Miller equilibrium can no longer be sustained: investors who on tax grounds alone would hold only equity may nevertheless hold some debt because an equity-only portfolio would be too risky. Miller's argument also does not take account of the implications of uncertainty and the asymmetric treatment of profits and losses which is a feature of most corporation tax systems. De Angelo and Masulis (1980) argued that the probability of interest tax shields being lost or deferred precluded the Miller equilibrium, and suggested that an optimal gearing ratio existed for a firm where the cost of debt finance, taking account of the probability of being unable to offset interest fully against corporation tax, equalled the cost of equity.

Miller's argument should thus be seen as one which raises important questions about whether taxation really does give incentives for individual firms to use debt finance, but does not clearly establish that there are no such incentives. It therefore weakens the theory based on trading off tax advantages of debt against costs of bankruptcy and financial distress, but does not destroy it. Another way in which this theory has been weakened is as a result of work on capital structure and financial policy which drops the assumption that the probability distribution of a firm's profits is common knowledge and independent of the firm's financial structure (this is essentially the first of the three critical limitations to Stiglitz's proof of the Modigliani–Miller theorem discussed above). There are a number of models based on asymmetric information of one sort or another in which a firm's gearing decision is not irrelevant. One type of model is where the firm's managers know more about the firm's possible returns than do outside investors. Ross (1977) assumes that managerial rewards depend on the current value of the firm and its future returns, and managers know the distribution of future returns while outside investors do not. The amount of debt chosen acts as a signal: managers of firms with higher expected future returns choose larger amounts of debt because only the managers of the better firms are willing to incur the increased risk of bankruptcy and its related costs associated with higher debt. Another type of model is based on principal–agent considerations: firms are run by managers (agents) on the behalf of shareholders (principals), but managers have some scope for pursuing their own interests at shareholders' expense because of asymmetric information. This is, however, recognized by the shareholders. The general form of models of this type is that managers choose a financial structure of the firm which determines managerial incentives: the capital market understands the incentives implied by a particular financial structure, and values the firm accordingly: this evaluation is taken into account by the managers in choosing financial structure. It is clear how a determinate capital structure can emerge from this framework, and Jensen and Meckling (1976) and Grossman and Hart (1982) are two examples of papers where gearing is important because of these reasons.

This work on asymmetric information and capital structure is highly suggestive of factors which may make gearing important, but as yet all we have in this area are insights rather than a complete and coherent theory. In particular there has been little integration of the traditional taxation arguments into the asymmetric information approach. Hence economists' understanding of firms' gearing decisions is still imperfect.

BIBLIOGRAPHY

Auerbach, A.J. and King, M.A. 1983. Taxation, portfolio choice and debt-equity ratios: a general equilibrium model. *Quarterly Journal of Economics* 98(4), November, 587–609.

De Angelo, H. and Masulis, R.W. 1980. Optimal capital structure under corporate and personal taxation. *Journal of Financial Economics* 8(1), March, 3–29.

Grossman, S.J. and Hart, O.D. 1982. Corporate financial structure and managerial incentives. In *Economics of Information and Uncertainty*, ed. J. McCall, Chicago: University of Chicago Press.

Jensen, M.C. and Meckling, W.H. 1976. Theory of the firm: managerial behavior, agency costs and ownership structure. *Journal of Financial Economics* 3(4), October, 305–60.

Miller, M.H. 1977. Debt and taxes. *Journal of Finance* 32(2), May, 261–75.

Modigliani, F. and Miller, M.H. 1958. The cost of capital, corporation finance, and the theory of investment. *American Economic Review* 48, June, 261–97.

Nickell, S.J. 1978. *The Investment Decisions of Firms*. Cambridge and New York: Cambridge University Press.

Ross, S.A. 1977. The determination of financial structure: the incentive-signalling approach. *Bell Journal of Economics and Management Science* 8(1), Spring, 23–40.

Stiglitz, J.E. 1974. On the irrelevance of corporate financial policy. *American Economic Review* 64(6), December, 851–66.

Warner, J.B. 1977. Bankruptcy costs: some evidence. *Journal of Finance* 32(2), May, 337–47.

Hedging

GREGORY CONNOR

Hedging is the purchasing of an asset or portfolio of assets in order to insure against wealth fluctuations from other sources. A hedge portfolio is any asset or collection of assets purchased by one or more agents for hedging. A grain dealer may hedge against losses on an inventory of grain by selling grain futures; a Middle Eastern businessman may hedge against political turmoil (and the resulting losses) by buying gold; a pension fund may hedge against capital losses on its equity portfolio by buying stock index put options.

1. A COMPETITIVE EQUILIBRIUM MODEL OF HEDGING. The fundamental concepts of hedging can best be described in a state space model. Consider a one period economy with M agents and one end-of-period consumption good. For simplicity, assume that there is no consumption at the beginning of the period. Each agent possesses a real asset which produces a random amount of the consumption good at the end of the period. Agents have homogeneous beliefs. There are N possible states of nature, with probabilities $\Pr(1), \ldots, \Pr(N)$. Agents have concave, possibly state-dependent utility functions and wish to maximize the expected utility of end-of-period consumption. Let $U_j(C_j, \theta_i)$ denote the end-of-period utility of agent j given that his consumption is C_j and the state is θ_i.

A *financial asset* is a claim to a random amount of end-of-period output, which is traded between agents at the beginning of the period. A *hedge portfolio* is a particular type of financial asset or collection of financial assets which protects an agent against some particular risky outcome(s).

The analysis is simplest if we assume that the hedge portfolio consists of a mixed asset/liability with positive payoffs in some states and negative payoffs in other states, balanced so as to give a competitive equilibrium price of zero. Under this formulation, a hedge portfolio is a portfolio which pays off positively in states where the agent would otherwise have a high marginal utility of consumption (i.e. in 'bad' states) and negatively in states where he would otherwise have a low marginal utility of consumption. If the agent's 'expected' marginal utility (marginal utility times the probability of the state) is equalized across the relevant states after purchasing the hedge portfolio, then he is fully hedged; if the hedge position lowers but does not eliminate the disparity, then he is partially hedged.

Who takes the other side of the hedging transaction? There are three possibilities. First, if there exist two agents who have real asset cash flows which vary inversely, then they can trade in a way which allows both to hedge simultaneously. For example, a grain dealer who holds an inventory of grain may be able to sell a futures contract to a bread producer who has committed himself to using grain at a later stage of his production process. Both parties consider themselves as hedging. Second, one agent may be less risk-averse toward certain states of nature than another. The less risk-averse may be willing to sell the hedge asset to the more risk-averse at a price which produces mutual gains in expected utility. Third, the hedging agent may be able to trade small quantities of the hedge asset with many agents, who can then eliminate all or most of the risk of the trade by combining the asset with many others (i.e. by diversifying away the risk). For example, insurance companies can sell fire insurance policies to many individuals and leave very little risk to be absorbed by the company's shareholders.

Let the number of distinct types of assets be K and let Y denote the $N \times K$ matrix of their payoffs in the N possible states of nature. The set of available trades is span (Y) where span $(.)$ denotes the subspace spanned by the matrix. In an economy without frictions, agents will create new financial assets until all mutually beneficial trade opportunities are in span (Y). All mutually beneficial trades have been consummated if there exist positive scalars $\lambda_1, \ldots, \lambda_M$ such that

$$\lambda_j U'_j(C_j, \theta_i) = \lambda_h U'_h(C_h, \theta_i) \qquad i = 1, \ldots, N; \qquad j, h = 1, \ldots, M. \quad (1)$$

The invisible hand drives agents toward creating all the types of financial assets which can lead to mutually beneficial trades. However, there are many external factors which can offset this tendency. If agents have some control over outcomes, then moral hazard problems may limit hedging opportunities. For example, agents may not be able to hedge against changes in labour income if work requires imperfectly observable effort. If agents have special knowledge, then adverse selection can similarly limit trade. If a car owner knows more about its quality than a prospective buyer, then an agent cannot sell his car at a reasonable price when he experiences financial distress. The administrative costs of trade can also limit hedging before the full efficiency condition (1) is fulfilled.

The model described above is static. In an intertemporal model, dynamic strategies increase the set of hedging opportunities beyond the linear span of the matrix of asset payoffs. Agents can create a rich set of payoff claims by dynamically varying the proportions invested in the individual assets. With continuous trading, this process reaches its natural limit: if an asset price follows Brownian Motion, then a continuously adjusted portfolio consisting of only this risky asset and a

165

riskless asset can be constructed which replicates the payoff to any put or call option on the risky asset.

The proliferation of complex financial assets, such as options on futures and interest rate and currency options, and the increased sophistication of traders, has led to a bewildering array of dynamic hedging strategies, especially by large institutional investors. *Portfolio insurance* provides a good example of the kind of sophisticated new hedging instrument which can be created with a dynamic trading strategy. Consider a pension fund with a large equity portfolio and an aversion to large capital losses on this portfolio. A portfolio insurance strategy can put a floor on the random rate of return to the pension fund's portfolio. The return floor can be any rate lower than the available riskless rate (it can be a negative net return, so that the fund bounds its losses rather than assuring itself of a small gain). The strategy works as follows. At the starting date of the insurance strategy, the fund has most of its money invested in equities and a small proportion in a riskless asset (i.e. government notes). If the equities fall in price, the fund sells some of the equities and places the cash in the riskless asset. If equity prices continue to fall, the fund increases the proportion of investment in the riskless asset. If there is a sustained fall in equity prices, the fund will end the insurance programme invested entirely in the riskless asset. It will have earned a rate equal to the pre-chosen minimally acceptable return. The fund makes a 'soft landing' at this minimal value: the proportion of money invested in the riskless asset approaches one as the value of the portfolio approaches the minimally acceptable level.

Portfolio insurance is not a free lunch. In exchange for the return floor, the pension fund sacrifices some of the upside potential of pure equity investment. For example, if the equity market declines sharply and then rises, the fund will miss the upturn, since it will have defensively decreased its position in equities before the upturn.

There are numerous other dynamic hedging strategies, not only in equity markets but in fixed income, currency and options markets. In terms of the volume of trade, hedging in financial markets now greatly outpaces the activity in commodities futures markets, which is the original and classic example of a market often used for hedging.

2. RISK PREMIA AND HEDGING. An economically interesting question is whether agents 'pay a premium' to hedge. Assume again that the current price of the hedge portfolio is set to zero by appropriate balancing of the asset and liability sides of the hedge (a futures contract is a natural example). If the expected cash flow is negative (positive) next period, then the hedge portfolio carries a positive (negative) implicit risk premium. If the expected cash flow is zero, then the implicit risk premium is zero.

Much of the early literature on hedging was centred on hedging in commodity futures contracts. One of the key questions was whether agents who sold futures pay a positive risk premium. Keynes (1930) considers this problem for the case of commodity futures contracts. He argues that the natural supply of short hedgers (sellers of futures contracts) outnumbers long hedgers (buyers) in this market. Therefore, the implicit risk premia for holding a futures contract should be negative, in order to induce other agents (henceforth called 'speculators') to absorb the excess hedging demand of short hedgers. This will be true if the futures price increases on average over the life of the contract, so that the expected cash flow from holding the contract is positive. The empirical evidence for this positive drift (sometimes called *normal backwardation*) in commodity futures prices is weak at best.

Keynes's analysis implicitly assumes that the commodity futures market is isolated from other asset markets so that hedgers must pay the speculator a premium to induce them to take a position in the market. In an integrated set of asset markets, hedgers need not pay any premium to induce other agents to trade. Rather, the existence of a risk premium depends upon the covariance between the payoffs to the hedge asset and the economy-wide risks faced by all the agents. If the hedge asset is uncorrelated with market-wide risks, then it will carry no risk premium, even though it may have a high value to a particular hedger due to his specific income stream. A hedge asset which protects against market risk will carry a risk premium.

There is another source of return to speculators, which is not captured in the competitive pricing model. Speculators may charge an explicit or implicit bid–ask spread when trading with hedgers. If hedgers buy and hold for a long period, then this is equivalent to the return premium described above. However, if hedgers trade frequently then a bid–ask spread can lower their realized returns, and raise the realized returns to speculators, without affecting the observed long-run return premium of the hedge asset as reflected in transactions prices. This may explain the lack of empirical evidence for normal backwardation in commodities futures markets. This effect of a bid–ask spread was not recognized in most of the early literature on commodity futures markets.

The bid–ask spread need not be explicit. Even open-floor markets will contain a set of implicit bid–ask spreads, to the extent that trader strategies reflect a greater willingness to sell at higher prices and to buy at lower ones. One can view the feverish activity which is common in floor trading as speculators searching for transactions at the outer edges of an implicit bid–ask spread. Hedgers, who are off the floor and are more anxious to complete a particular trade, take the losing side of the implicit spread.

3. THE ROLE OF HEDGERS IN A MARKET WITH HETEROGENEOUS INFORMATION. The model in sections 1 and 2 assumes homogeneous information across agents. If agents have differential information about the payoffs to assets then the trading strategies of rational agents cannot have the simple competitive form. Agents must treat trade opportunities as signals of the information of other agents about the value of the trade.

The presence of differential information can lead to fewer hedging opportunities and/or raise the expected cost of hedging. Milgrom and Stokey (1982) show that rational agents will not trade solely because they have different beliefs about the

167

value of an asset. If agents are distinguished merely by their differential information, then they will refuse all trades, since the willingness of the other agent to trade signals that the terms are unfavourable. This means that a financial asset market will fail to open in the absence of other motives for trade. This is a market failure due to adverse selection.

The needs of some agents for hedging can provide an additional reason for trade which overcomes the adverse selection problem and eliminates the market failure. Hedgers will be willing to trade even if they suspect that the other party to the transaction has superior information. Informed agents will be gaining at the expense of hedgers, but they will also be providing an insurance/liquidity service to hedgers, and so hedgers may be willing to trade with them despite their informational disadvantage. This in turn has the side-effect of permitting superior information to be reflected in market prices.

I will follow Glosten and Milgrom (1985) and assume that there exist costless, competitive, risk-neutral market makers who intervene in all trades. This is for analytical convenience and is not necessary to the basic model. Suppose that certain agents ('hedgers') have a strong preference for a given hedge asset, i.e., their preference is such that they will buy (and sell) some non-zero amount at a price higher (lower) than the market-clearing equilibrium price. This implies that they are willing to trade even if they must pay a bid–ask spread around the equilibrium price. Informed agents (henceforth 'speculators') will also trade despite a bid–ask spread as long as the expected profit from their superior information is larger than the bid–ask spread. The market makers can set an equilibrium bid–ask spread which allows the hedgers to trade at an expected loss and the speculators at an expected gain, leaving the market makers with an expected profit of zero (their equilibrium condition). The market makers will respond to the net demands of all traders (which partially reveals the net demand of speculators) to adjust the bid and ask prices, and so (partially) capture in market price the superior information of speculators.

One intriguing feature of this model is the symbiotic roles of speculators and hedgers. Without speculators (informed traders), the hedgers would lose liquidity; without hedgers, speculators would lose the opportunities to gain on their superior information. Without both speculators and hedgers, the price in the market would no longer provide a useful signal for agents making production and consumption decisions. Kyle (1984) develops a model in which this symbiotic relationship is made clear and describes the effects of more or fewer speculators or hedgers on the informational efficiency and liquidity of the market. Some of the results are counter-intuitive: for instance, increasing the number of hedgers, who are uninformed, can *increase* the informational efficiency of prices.

4. RISK PREMIA ON HEDGE PORTFOLIOS AND GENERAL EQUILIBRIUM PRICING. In section 2, I described two types of hedge portfolios – those with and without risk premia – and how the distinction between them depends on the covariance between the hedge portfolio's returns and the market-wide risks in the economy.

In this section, I will describe a relationship between hedge portfolios which protect against market-wide risks and the general equilibrium pricing of assets.

Let Q_t denote the discounted expected utility of lifetime consumption for some agent at time t:

$$Q_t = E_t \left[\sum_{\tau=t+1}^{\infty} \rho^\tau U(C_\tau, \theta_\tau) \right],$$

where ρ is the agent's discounted factor and $U(,)$ is his utility function. Let J_t denote the change in discounted expected utility given a change in the agent's time t wealth:

$$J_t = \partial Q_t / \partial W_t,$$

where W_t is his wealth at time t. Note that at time $t-1$, J_t is a random variable. Let r_u denote the return from time $t-1$ to t of the ith financial asset. If the agent holds an equilibrium amount of this asset then the following first order condition is satisfied:

$$E_{t-1}[r_{it} J_t] = \partial U(C_{t-1}, \theta) / \partial C,$$

which can be re-written (using $E[ab] = E[a]E(b) + \text{cov}[a, b]$) as:

$$E_{t-1}[r_{it}] = r_{0t} + (1/\gamma)\text{cov}_{t-1}[r_{it}, J_t], \tag{2}$$

where $\gamma = \partial U(C_{t-1}, \theta) / \partial C$ and r_{0t} is the expected return on an asset with a riskless payoff at time t. Suppose that, at time $t-1$, J_t equals a sum of a set of K uncorrelated random variables $Z_{1t}, Z_{2t}, \ldots, Z_{Kt}$:

$$J_t = Z_{1t} + \cdots + Z_{Kt}. \tag{3}$$

The variables $Z_1, \ldots, Z_K$ describe the K random shocks which affect the agent's marginal utility. They could be interest rate movements, output shocks, inflation shocks, etc. Assume that there exists a set of K portfolios with returns $r_{1t}^*, \ldots, r_{Kt}^*$ such that the jth portfolio has perfect negative correlation with Z_{jt}:

$$\text{cov}_{t-1}[r_{jt}^*, z_{jt}] = (\text{var}_{t-1}[r_{jt}^*] \text{var}_{t-1}[Z_{jt}])^{1/2}. \tag{4}$$

These portfolios are potential hedges against the K types of risk which affect the investor. (The agent would short-sell the portfolio to hedge since the portfolio return varies inversely with marginal utility.) I will call $r_{1t}^*, \ldots, r_{Kt}^*$ an *indexing set of hedge portfolios* since the portfolios index the random shocks to the agent's marginal utility. Using (3) and (4) we can re-write (2) as:

$$E_{t-1}[R_{it}] = r_{0t} + \beta_{i1t} \pi_{1t} + \cdots + \beta_{iKt} \pi_{Kt}, \tag{5}$$

where

$$\beta_{ijt} = \text{cov}_{t-1}[r_{it}, r_{jt}^*] / \text{var}_{t-1}[r_{jt-1}^*]$$

and

$$\pi_{jt} = E_{t-1}[r_{jt}^* - r_{0t}].$$

169

Equation (5) is an asset pricing relationship: it says that the expected return on any asset equals the riskless return plus a linear combination of the covariances of the asset's return with an indexing set of hedge portfolios.

In general, there will not exist a finite set of portfolios fulfilling (4). Merton (1973) develops a continuous time model in which there does exist an indexing set at each instant of time. Breeden (1984) shows that Merton's model with $K > 1$ can be simplified to a $K = 1$ model without loss of generality.

One limitation of this model is that the beta coefficients (β_{ijt}) and risk-premia (π_{jt}) in (5) are only defined at a single point in time. In empirical applications of the model, one must use time series of asset returns and other variables to estimate these parameters. Time-varying parameters are not estimable from a time series sample unless their time series behaviour is specified. A typical assumption, which is not always consistent with the theoretical model, is that the betas and risk premia are constant through time. Despite the limitations on estimatibility, this model is important and illustrates the role of hedging in asset pricing theory.

BIBLIOGRAPHY

Arrow, K.J. 1964. The role of securities in the optimal allocation of risk-bearing. *Review of Economic Studies* 31, 91–6.

Breeden, D.T. 1979. An intertemporal asset pricing model with stochastic consumption and investment opportunities. *Journal of Financial Economics* 7(3), 265–96.

Breeden, D.T. 1984. Futures markets and commodity options: hedging and optimality in incomplete markets. *Journal of Economic Theory* 32, 275–300.

Brennan, M.J. 1958. The supply of storage. *American Economic Review* 48, 50–72.

Cootner, P.H. 1967. Speculation and hedging. *Food Research Institute Studies*, Supplement to Volume 7, 65–105.

Duffie, D. and Huang, C. 1985. Implementing Arrow–Debreu equilibria by continuous trading of a few long-lived securities. *Econometrica* 53, 1337–56.

Glosten, L. and Milgrom, P.R. 1985. Bid, ask, and transaction prices in a specialist market with heterogeneously informed traders. *Journal of Financial Economics* 14, 71–100.

Grauer, F.L. and Litzenberger, R.H. 1979. The pricing of nominal bonds and commodity futures contracts under uncertainty. *Journal of Finance* 34, 69–84.

Gray, R.W. 1961. The search for a risk premium. *Journal of Political Economy* 69, 250–60.

Grossman, S. 1976. On the efficiency of competitive stock markets when traders have diverse information. *Journal of Finance* 31, 573–85.

Hoffman, G.W. 1954. Past and present theory regarding futures trading. *Journal of Farm Economics* 19, 1–11.

Houthakker, H.S. 1957. Can speculators forecast prices? *Review of Economics and Statistics* 39, 143–52.

Keynes, J.M. 1930. *A Treatise of Money. Volume II: The Applied Theory of Money.* London: Macmillan. Reprinted in *The Collected Writings of John Maynard Keynes*, London: Macmillan, New York: St. Martin's Press, 1971.

Kyle, A.S. 1984. Market structure, information, futures markets, and price formation. In *International Agricultural Trade: Advanced Readings in Price Formation, Market Structure, and Price Instability*, ed. G. Storey, A. Schmitz and A. Sarris, London: Westview.

Leland, H. 1980. Who should buy portfolio insurance. *Journal of Finance* 35, 581–94.

Malinvaud, E. 1972. The allocation of individual risk in large markets. *Journal of Economic Theory* 4, 312–28.

Merton, R.C. 1973. An intertemporal capital asset pricing model. *Econometrica* 41, 867–87.

Milgrom, P. and Stokey, N. 1982. Information, trade and common knowledge. *Journal of Economic Theory* 26, 17–27.

Working, H. 1953a. Futures trading and hedging. *American Economic Review* 43, 314–43.

Working, H. 1953b. Hedging reconsidered. *Journal of Farm Economics* 35, 544–61.

Working, H. 1967. Tests of a theory concerning floor trading on commodity exchanges. *Food Research Institute Studies*, Supplement to Volume 7, 5–48.

Interest Rates

J.E. INGERSOLL

Interest is payment for use of funds over a period of time, and the amount of interest paid per unit of time as a fraction of the balance is called the interest rate. In some contexts, economists have found it conceptually useful to refer to a single number, the interest rate. In fact, at any point in time there are many prevailing interest rates. The rate actually charged will depend on such factors as the maturity of the loan, the credit-worthiness of the borrower, the amount of collateral, tax treatment of interest payments for both parties and special features such as call provisions or sinking fund requirements.

A complete treatment of interest rates would account for all of these factors, but in fact it is hard enough to handle any one of them adequately. This entry considers one factor, the term to maturity for default-free bonds. This analysis of the *term structure of interest rates* will be approached from the partial equilibrium perspective of finance: the determinants of interest rates and the impact of changing short and long interest rates on the macroeconomy are not discussed.

Merton (1970 and other unpublished work) was the first to formulate the term structure problem using the continuous-time no-arbitrage framework exposited here. Cox, Ingersoll and Ross (1985a, 1985b), Dothan (1978), Richard (1978) and Vasicek (1977) solved term structure problems of this type for different stochastic processes.

INTEREST RATES IN A CERTAIN ENVIRONMENT. Historically, the theory of interest rates has been burdened with cumbersome notation designed to distinguish among spot rates, forward rates and rates of different terms. Notation and terminology will be kept to a minimum here. The instantaneous spot rate of interest at time t for a loan to be repaid an instant later will be denoted by $r(t)$. $R(t, T)$ will denote the continuously compounded interest rate for a zero coupon bond sold at t to be repaid at T, and $P(t, T)$ will be the price or present value per $1 face value of such a bond. The relation between these three quantities is

$$r(t) \equiv \lim_{T \downarrow t} R(t, T) \tag{1a}$$

$$P(t, T) \equiv e^{-R(t,T)(T-t)}. \tag{1b}$$

An investor who has funds to invest until time T could buy a T-period zero coupon bond with a guaranteed annualized return of $R(t, T)$. Alternatively, the investor could roll over a series of shorter bonds or buy a longer bond with the intention of selling it at time T. In the absence of uncertainty, all of these plans would have to realize the same final return to avoid the possibility of arbitrage. In particular

$$\frac{1}{P(t, T)} = \exp\left[\int_t^T r(s)\, ds \right] \tag{2}$$

or the continuously compounded long rate must be the average of the instantaneous rates,

$$R(t, T) = \frac{1}{T-t} \int_t^T r(s)\, ds. \tag{3}$$

(Note that with discrete compounding one plus the long rate is equal to the geometric mean of one plus the single-period rates. See Dybvig, Ingersoll and Ross (1986) for a catalogue of related results in both continuous and discrete time.)

ONE-FACTOR MODELS OF INTEREST RATES IN AN UNCERTAIN ENVIRONMENT. When future interest rates are not known in advance, these relations need not be realized, even on average, but the equilibrium that obtains will still depend on the trade-offs between different bond portfolio strategies. The resulting equilibrium relation among the interest rates will depend primarily on the information structure perceived by investors and, in particular, on the temporal resolution of uncertainty.

In this section we will assume that the information structure is Markov in the currently prevailing short rate, which is assumed to capture all currently available information relevant for pricing default-free bonds. $P(r, t, T)$ denotes the price at t of a zero coupon bond maturing at T with a face value of $1, given that the currently prevailing short rate is r. The evolution of the interest rate is assumed to follow a diffusion process,

$$dr = f(r, t)\, dt + g(r, t)\, d\omega. \tag{4}$$

Here $f(\cdot)$ measures the expected change in the interest rate per unit time, $g(\cdot)$ measures the standard deviation of changes in the interest rate per unit time, and $d\omega$ is the increment to a Wiener process.

The price of a zero coupon bond evolves according to

$$dP(r, t, T)/P(r, t, T) = \alpha(r, t, T)\, dt + \delta(r, t, T)\, d\omega \tag{5}$$

where $\alpha(\cdot)$ is the bond's (endogenous) instantaneous expected rate of return and

$\delta(\cdot)$ is its instantaneous standard deviation. By Itô's lemma

$$\alpha(r, t, T)P(r, t, T) = \tfrac{1}{2}g^2(r, t)P_{rr} + f(r, t)P_r + P_t \tag{6a}$$

$$\delta(r, t, T)P(r, t, T) = g(r, t)P_r \tag{6b}$$

where subscripts denote partial differentiation.

Equation (6a) is a partial differential equation relating the prices of a given bond at different points of time and with different prevailing short rates. Together with the known value of a bond at its maturity [$P(r, T, T) = 1$] and mild regularity conditions, (6a) is equivalent to the integral

$$P(r, t, T) = E\left[\exp\left\{ -\int_t^T \alpha[r(s), s, T]\, ds \right\} \right] \tag{7}$$

(Friedman, 1975, Theorem 5.2). This integral demonstrates that when the source of uncertainty is a stochastically varying discount rate rather than a random cash flow, it is generally improper to discount by using the expected discount rate. Rather, we should use the geometric mean across states of the discount rate.

To price bonds using (6a) or (7), we must know $\alpha(\cdot)$. Intuitively, $\alpha(\cdot)$ will be equal to the risk-free rate plus a risk premium. As there is but a single source of uncertainty, the returns on all bonds will be perfectly correlated; therefore, the risk premium on any bond will be proportional to its exposure to the risk, and knowing $\alpha(\cdot)$ for one bond (for all interest rate levels) is sufficient. We can specify $\alpha(\cdot)$ by fiat, or it can be derived from an equilibrium model.

One equilibrium condition that is often imposed is the 'local' expectations hypothesis, $\alpha(r, t, T) = r$ (Cox, Ingersoll and Ross, 1981). Under the local expectations hypothesis the partial differential equation for bond pricing derived from (6a) and the integral in (7) are fully determined given the distribution of interest rate changes. The local expectations hypothesis is a strong assumption, but for asset pricing purposes it is the only case that needs consideration. It can be shown that the absence of arbitrage implies that we can artificially reassign probabilities so that the local expectations hypothesis holds without changing any asset prices. The artificial probabilities are called the risk neutral probabilities or the equivalent martingale measure. Here is an informal proof in our context.

Consider any two zero coupon bonds. From (6a) their realized returns are perfectly correlated. Therefore, to ensure the absence of arbitrage possibilities, their expected excess returns must be proportional to their standard deviations

$$\alpha(r, t, T) - r = \pi(r, t)\delta(r, t, T)$$

$$= \pi(r, t)(P_r/P)g(r, t). \tag{8}$$

The risk premium term $\pi(\cdot)$ cannot depend on the bond in question, which is why it does not depend on T. We can now write the equivalent diffusion process under the martingale measure. Because we can infer the variance of any diffusion from its sample path and because the martingale measure has the same set of possible events as the original probability measure, the martingale standard deviations must be the same i.e., $g(\cdot)$. The drift under the martingale measure must equate expected returns across assets. Therefore, the drift term under the equivalent martingale measure must be $f^*(r, t) \equiv f(r, t) - \pi(r, t)g(r, t)$. Using the martingale measure, (6a) therefore becomes

$$rP = \tfrac{1}{2}g^2(r, t)P_{rr} + f^*(r, t)P_r + P_t \tag{9}$$

and its solution analogous to (7) is

$$P(r, t, T) = E^*\left\{\exp\left[-\int_t^T r(s)\,\mathrm{d}s\right]\right\} \tag{10}$$

where $E^*[\cdot]$ denotes expectation under the modified process with f^* as the drift term.

To illustrate how these tools are used, consider the simplest model in Cox, Ingersoll and Ross (1985b). The stochastic process for the interest rate is

$$\mathrm{d}r = \kappa(\mu - r)\,\mathrm{d}t + \sigma\sqrt{r}\,\mathrm{d}\omega. \tag{11}$$

For this process, the interest rate is attracted elastically toward its mean value μ and is influenced by a noise term whose variance is proportional to the prevailing level of the interest rate. As a consequence, the interest rate cannot become negative. Assuming logarithmic utility, the drift term for the equivalent process is $f^* = \kappa\mu - (\kappa + \lambda)r$.

With this specification of f^*, (9) or (10) is solved by

$$P(r, t, T) = A(T - t)\mathrm{e}^{-B(T-t)r} \tag{12}$$

where

$$A(\tau) \equiv \left[\frac{2\eta\,\mathrm{e}^{(\kappa + \lambda + \eta)\tau/2}}{b(\tau)}\right]^{2\kappa\mu/\sigma^2}, \qquad B(\tau) \equiv \left[\frac{2(\mathrm{e}^{\eta\tau} - 1)}{b(\tau)}\right]$$

$$b(\tau) \equiv 2\eta + (\kappa + \lambda + \eta)(\mathrm{e}^{\eta\tau} - 1), \qquad \eta \equiv \sqrt{(\kappa + \lambda)^2 + 2\sigma^2}.$$

The resulting zero coupon yield has a limit of

$$R_\infty = 2\kappa\mu/(\eta + \kappa + \lambda)$$

regardless of the current short rate. (The constancy of the long rate may seem like a severe restriction of this model. Actually, it is a property that is to be expected of any recurrent model. See Dybvig, Ingersoll and Ross, 1986.) If the current short rate is below R_∞, then the yield curve is upward sloping. If the current rate is greater than μ, then the yield curve slopes downward. For interest rates between these two levels the yield curve has a single hump.

Brown and Dybvig (1986) have estimated a reduced form of this model, yield curve by yield curve, to obtain a time series of parameter estimates. They found that the implied variance tracks actual interest rate volatility well. They also find some evidence of misspecification, including what appears to be a tax effect.

BOND PRICING WITH MULTIPLE SOURCES OF UNCERTAINTY. One criticism of previous models is that they permit only a single source of uncertainty. As a result of this assumption all bonds are perfectly correlated and all yield curves are characterized by a single parameter. Typically there would be factors that influence long and short rates differently. However, the basic techniques for bond pricing remain the same.

Suppose for simplicity that interest rates are determined by the short rate and one other state variable, x. The assumed dynamics for the two state variables are

$$dr = f(r, x, t)\,dt + g(r, x, t)\,d\omega_1$$
$$dx = \phi(r, x, t)\,dt + \gamma(r, x, t)\,d\omega_2. \tag{13}$$

The resulting partial differential equation for bond pricing is

$$rP = \tfrac{1}{2}g^2 P_{rr} + \rho g\gamma P_{rx} + \tfrac{1}{2}\gamma^2 P_{xx} + f^* P_r + \phi^* P_x + P_t \tag{14}$$

where as before $f^*(\cdot)$ and $\phi^*(\cdot)$ denote the modified (risk adjusted) drift terms under the equivalent martingale measure, and ρ is the correlation between the two Wiener processes. Solving this problem requires a specification of the joint stochastic process and the necessary modification of the equivalent martingale measure.

If the second state variable, x, is the price of some asset, then the risk premium, $-\pi_2(\cdot)\gamma(\cdot)$, associated with ω_2 is $rx - \phi(\cdot)$ giving $\phi^* = rx$ as in the Black–Scholes option pricing model. We can also infer the risk premium if x is functionally related to an asset's value and time. For example suppose that x is the yield-to-maturity on a zero coupon bond maturing at s. The price of this bond, $P(r, x, t, s)$, must itself satisfy the pricing equation. As $P(r, x, t, s) \equiv \exp[-x(s-t)]$, we know all of its required partial derivatives. Substituting them into (14) and solving for $\phi^*(\cdot)$ gives

$$\phi^*(r, x, t) = \frac{r - x - \tfrac{1}{2}\gamma^2(\cdot)(s-t)^2}{t - s} \tag{15}$$

(Ingersoll, 1987). Of course, if x is not known to be related to a marketed asset, we can still specify the second risk premium arbitrarily or by reference to an equilibrium model.

Brennan and Schwartz (1979) used a finite difference numerical approximation to analyse a two factor model. In a test with US Government bonds, they concluded that the two factor model predicted bond prices much better than did a one factor model and on the whole was an adequate description of bond prices.

The traditional forecasting models using geometrically smoothed averages of past short rates as predictors of future rates can also be viewed as two (or more) factor models of this sort. (See Dobson, Sutch and Vanderford (1976) for a survey of the forecasting models.) For example, consider the model of Malkiel (1966) in which the short rate tends to return to a 'normal level', measured by a geometric average of past interest rates

$$x(t) \equiv \beta \int_0^\infty e^{-\beta s} r(t-s) \, ds. \tag{16}$$

The dynamics of this model are

$$dr = \kappa(x - r) \, dt + \sigma(\cdot) \, d\omega \tag{17a}$$

$$dx = \beta(r - x) \, dt. \tag{17b}$$

As changes in the state variable x are locally deterministic, no risk adjustment is required. The modification to the stochastic process for r is handled in the usual fashion.

No closed form solution is known for this model when $\sigma(\cdot) = \sigma \sqrt{r}$ as in the Cox, Ingersoll and Ross (1985b) model. A solution for this and similar problems with other lag structures is given in Cox, Ingersoll and Ross (1981) when the variance is a constant.

Another form of two factor model uses real interest rates and expected inflation as its two state variables (Richard, 1978; Cox, Ingersoll and Ross, 1985b). Besides providing more flexibility for a better empirical fit, this formulation permits an identification of real and nominal effects for separate consideration.

APPLICATIONS OF INTEREST RATE MODELS. This continuous-time no-arbitrage method of pricing bonds is an outgrowth of the option pricing literature which gives it certain advantages over more traditional approaches. One advantage is the provision of a fully specified model of bond prices for empirical work. Another major advantage of term structure models of this type is that they provide a framework for valuation that is consistent with all of our other models based on the absence of arbitrage.

Thus, in addition to pricing zero coupon bonds and determining the term structure, this method can handle any other interest rate valuation problem. For example Cox, Ingersoll and Ross (1985b) value call options on interest rates. Applications to futures contracts, variable rate instruments, mortgages, loan commitments, etc. have also been published. Equation (9) or a multiple factor version such as (14) remains the fundamental relation among interest rate contingent claims. To value a particular claim the appropriate boundary condition is used in place of $P(r, t, T) = 1$.

Another advantage of such models is that they give an explicit measure of the risk characteristics of the priced assets. These risk measures can be used in immunizing bond portfolios or in relative performance measurement. Because they are derived in models based on the absence of arbitrage they are not subject to the same criticisms that have been made of traditional duration measures (see Ingersoll, Skelton and Weil, 1978).

Of theoretical interest is the relation between these models and the risk neutral or equivalent martingale valuation procedure. With a constant interest rate it can be shown that the value of a derivative asset that pays $H(S_T)$ at time T, contingent on the value S_T of its primitive asset and makes no other disbursements, is

$$V(S, t) = e^{-r(T-t)}E^*[H(S_T)].$$ (18)

The expectation $E^*[\cdot]$ is taken with respect to the risk neutral process for the primitive's price under which the actual expected rate of return is replaced by the risk-free interest rate. With a stochastic interest rate, the valuation is

$$V(S, t) = E^*\left\{\exp\left[-\int_t^T r(s)\, ds\right]H(S_T)\right\}.$$ (19)

This equation generalizes both equations (18) and (10). The expectation in (19) is over the joint distribution under the martingale measure of interest rate paths and S_T. That is, the expectation assumes that

$$dS(t) = r(t)S\, dt + \sigma(\cdot)S\, d\omega_S$$ (20a)

$$dr(t) = f^*(\cdot)\, dt + g(\cdot)\, d\omega_r,$$ (20b)

plus the modified processes of any other state variables that determine the term structure.

BIBLIOGRAPHY
Brennan, M.J. and Schwartz, E.S. 1979. A continuous time approach to the pricing of bonds. *Journal of Banking and Finance* 3(2), September, 133–55.
Brown, S.J. and Dybvig, P.H. 1986. The empirical investigation of the Cox, Ingersoll, Ross theory of the term structure of interest rates. *Journal of Finance* 41(3), July, 616–30.
Cox, J.C., Ingersoll, J.E. and Ross, S.A. 1981. A re-examination of traditional hypotheses about the term structure of interest rates. *Journal of Finance* 36(4), September, 769–99.
Cox, J.C., Ingersoll, J.E. and Ross, S.A. 1985a. An intertemporal general equilibrium model of asset prices. *Econometrica* 53(2), March, 363–84.
Cox, J.C., Ingersoll, J.E. and Ross, S.A. 1985b. A theory of the term structure of interest rates. *Econometrica* 53(2), March, 385–407.
Dobson, S., Sutch, R. and Vanderford, D. 1976. An evaluation of alternative empirical models of the term structure of interest rates. *Journal of Finance* 31(4), September, 1035–65.
Dothan, L.U. 1978. On the term structure of interest rates. *Journal of Financial Economics* 6(1), March, 59–69.
Dybvig, P.H., Ingersoll, J.E. and Ross, S.A. 1986. Long forward rates can never fall. Unpublished working paper, Yale University.
Friedman, A. 1975. *Stochastic Differential Equations and Applications*. Vol. 1, New York: Academic Press.
Ingersoll, J.E. 1987. *Theory of Financial Decision Making*. Totowa, NJ: Rowman and Littlefield.
Ingersoll, J.E., Skelton, J. and Weil, R.L. 1978. Duration forty years later. *Journal of Financial and Quantitative Analysis* 13(4), November, 627–50.
Malkiel, B.G. 1966. *The Term Structure of Interest Rates: Expectations and Behavior Patterns*. Princeton: Princeton University Press.

Merton, R.C. 1970. A dynamic general equilibrium model of the asset market and its application to the pricing of the capital structure of the firm. Unpublished working paper, Sloan School of Management, MIT.

Richard, S.F. 1978. An arbitrage model of the term structure of interest rates. *Journal of Financial Economics* 6(1), March, 33–57.

Vasicek, O.A. 1977. An equilibrium characterization of the term structure. *Journal of Financial Economics* 5(2), November, 177–88.

Intertemporal Portfolio Theory and Asset Pricing

DOUGLAS T. BREEDEN

The intent of this entry is to present intertemporal portfolio theory and asset pricing models, to explain their results and to illustrate the differences between multiperiod and single-period models. To appreciate intertemporal portfolio theory and asset pricing, it is necessary to understand the state of finance theory prior to the seminal intertemporal works of Merton (1969, 1971, 1973), Samuelson (1969), Fama (1970), Hakansson (1970) and Rubinstein (1974). Section I presents single-period theory and some general results on portfolio statistics. Section II presents intertemporal portfolio theory. Section III presents the intertemporal asset pricing model, and Section IV presents the consumption-oriented representation of it. Section V gives important extensions (without proof) and concludes the essay.

I. SINGLE-PERIOD PORTFOLIO THEORY AND ASSET PRICING

Portfolio choice in terms of means and variance of alternative portfolios' returns was rigorously modelled first in a single-period world by Markowitz (1952, 1959) and Tobin (1958). This theory was significantly extended by Sharpe (1964) and Lintner (1965). By requiring markets to clear in equilibrium, Sharpe and Lintner developed the well-known theory of equilibrium asset prices known as the capital asset pricing model (CAPM). This model was the premier general theoretical model of asset pricing, prior to Merton's (1973) development of the *intertemporal* capital asset pricing model (ICAPM). In fact, despite the development of the theoretically superior (more general) intertemporal asset pricing models, the single-period CAPM is widely used by investment practitioners today.

I.A. PORTFOLIO STATISTICS. In deriving both the single-period and the intertemporal CAPM, there are a few well-known facts about portfolio statistics that are used repeatedly to expedite the derivations. Those will be presented with the notational definitions that follow. First, let $\mathbf{w}^k$ be individual k's $A \times 1$ vector of portfolio weights for risky assets; the ith element represents the fraction of total wealth that is invested in the ith risky asset. From the investor's budget constraint, the amount placed in the riskless asset must be the residual fraction, i.e.,

$$w_0^k = 1 - \sum_i w_i^k.$$

The riskless asset's return is denoted r_f, and risky assets have normally distributed returns with an $A \times 1$ vector of means, μ, and a variance–covariance matrix $\mathbf{V}$. Two statistical results permit the mean and variance of any portfolio and the covariance between any two portfolios' returns to be found from the weights of the portfolios and from the joint distribution of individual assets' returns. (The reader may verify these results from elementary statistical theory on the mean and variance of a linear combination of random variables.)

$$\text{Mean portfolio return} = \mu_p = w_0 r_f + \mathbf{w}'\mu = r_f + \mathbf{w}'(\mu - r_f\mathbf{1}). \tag{1}$$

$$\text{Covariance of 2 portfolios' returns} = \sum_i \sum_j w_i^x w_j^y \sigma_{ij} = \mathbf{w}'_x \mathbf{V}\mathbf{w}_y = \sigma_{xy}, \tag{2}$$

where $\mathbf{w}'_x$ and $\mathbf{w}_y$ are the risky asset portfolios and $\mathbf{1}$ is an $A \times 1$ vector of ones. A useful special case of (2) is that the variance of any portfolio's return is $\sigma^2 = \mathbf{w}'\mathbf{V}\mathbf{w}$. Another useful special case of (2) is that, for any portfolio $\mathbf{w}$, the matrix product $\mathbf{V}\mathbf{w}$ gives the $A \times 1$ vector of covariance of all assets returns with the specified portfolio's return. To see this, view each row of the $A \times A$ identity matrix $\mathbf{I}$ as a 1-asset portfolio, and then apply fact (2) row by row to the matrix product $\mathbf{IV}\mathbf{w} = \mathbf{V}\mathbf{w}$. For reference, these two special cases of (2) will be denoted (2') and (2''), respectively. Armed with these definitions and facts, we can now expeditiously derive the well-known single-period portfolio theory and CAPM of Sharpe (1964) and Lintner (1965).

I.B. OPTIMAL PORTFOLIO CHOICE. Each individual chooses at time 0 a portfolio that maximizes the expected value of a von Neumann–Morgenstern utility function for wealth at time 1, i.e., $\max E[u^k(\tilde{W}_1^k)]$. Since the return on a portfolio is a linear combination of the returns on individual assets, and since the returns on individual assets are assumed to be normally distributed, wealth at time 1 is normally distributed. Thus, given initial wealth W^k, the entire probability distribution for wealth at time 1 is described by the mean and variance of the individual's portfolio return. Rewriting the individual's expected utility as a function of portfolio mean and variance and omitting superscripts for the individual's preferences and portfolio weights, the portfolio choice problem is:

$$\max_{\{\mathbf{w}\}} U(\mu_W, \sigma_W^2), \tag{3}$$

where $\mu_W = r_f + \mathbf{w}'(\mu - r_f\mathbf{1})$ and $\sigma_W^2 = \mathbf{w}'\mathbf{V}\mathbf{w}$.

Since individuals like higher mean and lower variance, each portfolio that is maximal for (3) will be 'mean-variance efficient'. Efficient portfolios are those with the highest mean for a given variance, or alternatively, are lowest variance for a given mean.

The choices of the portfolio weights for risky assets are unconstrained in the above problem, since the budget constraint is imposed by making the weight in the riskless asset the residual (negative amounts indicating borrowing). Implicitly differentiating (3) with respect to the vector of risky portfolio weights and setting the partials equal to zero gives a set of linear equations. Solving these by matrix inversion gives the following optimal risky asset portfolio:

$$\mathbf{w}^k W^k = T^k [\mathbf{V}^{-1}(\mu - r_f \mathbf{1})], \qquad \text{for all individuals } k, \qquad (4)$$

where $T^k = -(\partial U/\partial \mu) W^k /[2(\partial U/\partial \sigma^2)]$ is individual k's compensating variation in variance for a unit change in mean, holding utility constant. Thus, the higher T^k is, the higher k's risk tolerance. Dividing (4) by the sum of the risky asset weights eliminates the individual's wealth and risk tolerance from the new equation, giving the optimum mix of risky asset holdings relative to the total in risky assets.

Thus, we have a remarkable result (first attributed to Tobin, 1958): the optimal mix of risky assets in the individual's portfolio depends only upon the means, variances and covariances of risky returns (as perceived by that individual). The individual's current wealth and preferences only affect risky assets' demands through a scalar that is the same for all risky assets. This shows that an individual may separate the choice of the optimal risky portfolio mix from the choice of how much to place in that portfolio and how much in the riskless asset. Sharpe (1964) showed that if all individuals have the same probability beliefs $\{\mu, \mathbf{V}\}$, then the optimal mix of risky assets is the same for all individuals. In fact, if there were a mutual fund that held all risky assets in the proportions given by $\mathbf{V}^{-1}(\mu - r_f \mathbf{1})$, all individuals could achieve their optimal portfolios with that fund and a riskless asset holding. This property is known as 'two-fund portfolio separation'.

1.C. MARKET EQUILIBRIUM: CAPITAL ASSET PRICING MODEL. The aggregate values of individuals' asset holdings, divided by the aggregate market value of wealth of the economy (M), gives 'the market's' portfolio weights. Summing (4) over individuals k and dividing by aggregate wealth M gives the market portfolio, $\mathbf{w}^M$:

$$\mathbf{w}^M = T^M [\mathbf{V}^{-1}(\mu - r_f \mathbf{1})], \qquad (5)$$

where

$$T^M = \left(\sum_k T^k \right) / M.$$

Since the market portfolio is a solution to (3) for an appropriate constant, the market portfolio is mean–variance efficient. Pre-multiplying (5) by $\mathbf{V}$ and using the statistical fact (2″), we have that the expected excess returns on assets in equilibrium are proportional to their covariances with the market's return, V_{aM}:

$$\mu - r_f 1 = (1/T^M)V_{aM}. \qquad (6)$$

Pre-multiplying (5) by $w'V$, using formulae for the mean and variance of a portfolio, and rearranging gives the value for the risk tolerance parameter: $(1/T^M) = (\mu_M - r_f)/\sigma_M^2$. The inverse of risk tolerance is termed risk aversion, so higher risk aversion among investors shows up as a higher expected excess return per unit of variance for the market portfolio. Substituting this into (6) gives the well known capital asset pricing model of Sharpe (1964) and Lintner (1965):

CAPM: $$\mu - r_f 1 = \beta_M(\mu_M - r_f), \qquad (7)$$

where $\beta_M = V_{aM}/\sigma_M^2$ is the $A \times 1$ vector of assets' betas relative to the market portfolio. They are analogous to the slope coefficients in regressions of assets' returns on the market portfolio's return.

To this date, this single-period capital asset pricing model has been the most widely tested general model of asset prices under uncertainty. It makes the very strong prediction that the expected excess returns across assets are proportional in equilibrium to their betas relative to the market portfolio. Alternatively, it predicts that the market portfolio is mean–variance efficient, in that it gives the highest expected excess return per unit of standard deviation, considering all possible portfolio combinations. Empirical tests of the single-period CAPM usually reject it. Higher beta assets do have higher returns, but the CAPM of (7) is rejected as a representation of the data. Virtually every assumption used in the derivation of the CAPM has been weakened and empirically examined. What follows is the generalization to *multiperiod* or *intertemporal* consumption and investment decisions – probably the most important and productive generalization.

II. INTERTEMPORAL PORTFOLIO THEORY

Relaxation of the single-period assumption in portfolio theory has proceeded concurrently in two very similar types of models. First, discrete-time multiperiod models consider individuals who make consumption and investment decisions at fixed points in time, where the interval between decisions is a somewhat arbitrary choice. It is unlikely that an individual would choose only to revise at fixed dates in time, regardless of what happens in between, so these models initially cause concern. However, that concern is alleviated somewhat by the fact that the qualitative properties of optimal policies in many models are unaffected by the choice of updating interval. Key works in discrete-time multiperiod frameworks are those of Samuelson (1969), Hakansson (1970), Fama (1970), Rubinstein (1974, 1976), Long (1974), Dieffenbach (1975), Kraus and Litzenberger (1978) and Brennan (1979).

The other model used for intertemporal portfolio theory and asset pricing is the continuous-time model pioneered by Merton (1969, 1971, 1973), and further developed by Cox, Ingersoll and Ross (1985a,b) and Breeden (1979, 1984, 1986).

The continuous-time model assumes that individuals make consumption and portfolio decisions continuously. Although this is not realistic, since individuals do sleep and do things other than make economic decisions, it will not miss important consumption and portfolio adjustments due to the modelling of a fixed time between decisions.

In Merton's continuous-time model, the underlying random processes driving economic uncertainties are assumed to follow continuous-time stochastic processes with normally distributed increments and continuous sample paths. The underlying normality makes the continuous-time model a logical extension for the single-period CAPM and also gives it mathematical tractability that is often not bound in discrete-time models. For example, with discrete-time models, a normally distributed stock return results in non-zero probability of a negative stock price. In the continuous-time model, the variance of the stock's return can approach zero as the stock's price approaches zero in such a way as to prevent negative stock prices, but have normally distributed increments at every instant in time. This essay will utilize the continuous-time model, but any important economic intuition found can also be derived in a discrete-time model.

In the intertemporal model, it is assumed that individuals choose consumption and investment policies that maximize their expected utilities across possible *lifetime* consumption paths. In both continuous-time and discrete-time models, preferences are typically assumed to be time-additive and state-independent, i.e., expected lifetime utility for individual k is: $E[\int u^k(c^k, t) \, dt]$. Although these preferences are not as general as theorists would like, much has been learned with them. It is assumed that the utility of consumption at any instant is monotonically increasing and strictly concave in consumption, in that partial derivatives are: $u_c^k > 0$ and $u_{cc}^k < 0$.

In using the techniques of stochastic dynamic programming to find the best consumption and portfolio policies, it is convenient to break the remaining utility of lifetime consumption into two parts and maximize the sum. At time t the first part is $u^k(c^k, t)$, the utility of the current consumption over the next period (or instant in time). The second part is the expected utility of consumption for all subsequent periods to that, $J^k(W^k, \mathbf{s}, t)$, which will be explained more fully below. Thus, the objective function is:

$$\max_{\{c, w\}} \{ u^k(c^k, t) + E_i[J^k(W^k, \mathbf{s}, t)] \} \qquad (8)$$

The current choice of consumption affects only the first part directly, but affects the budget constraint for investments made for future consumption. Differentiating (8) with respect to current consumption, taking into account that each additional unit of consumption today is a unit less of investible wealth, gives the standard condition that the marginal utility of consumption equals the marginal utility of wealth for an optimal policy:

$$u_c^k[c^k(W^k, \mathbf{s}, t), t] = J_W^k(W^k, \mathbf{s}, t). \qquad (9)$$

The key difference between single-period portfolio theory and its CAPM and the optimal results in an intertemporal equilibrium arises from the nature of the indirect utility function for wealth, $J(W^k, s, t)$. The portfolio mix decision affects only the probability distribution of future wealth and therefore only affects J in (8) – the expected utility of future consumption that wealth will be used to buy. The $S \times 1$ vector s is a set of 'state variables' that describe consumption, investment and employment opportunities. When a person expects to live not just for an instant more, but for a period of time, the investment portfolio and consumption rate should be reviewed and adjusted continually. The utility that one expects to get during one's remaining lifetime depends positively on current wealth (since higher wealth buys more goods), but also depends upon the state of investment opportunities. For example, a current wealth of $100,000 provides a lower real consumption stream if the real riskless interest rate is 2 per cent, than if the real rate is 5 per cent. In this case, the real riskless rate is one of the state variables for investment opportunities. Examples of other economic state variables are the expected inflation rate(s) of goods, the expected productivity of capital or the expected return on the market portfolio, and the level of uncertainty about economic activity or of productivity. Of course, most of these would be considered as endogenous variables; more generally, the underlying exogenous variables could be substituted and the stochastic processes for the endogenous variables derived.

To see the effect of a stochastic investment opportunity set on the investment portfolio, consider a retiree who is relatively averse to risk and holds the single-period optimal portfolio – a little money in the market portfolio and a lot in riskless securities. With that portfolio, the investor has the same wealth if the market is up 10 per cent and the riskless rate is 2 per cent, as when the market is up 10 per cent and the riskless rate is 5 per cent. This may not be optimal, since this retiree has to reinvest his wealth and live off the income. The retiree is financially hurt in the state where the real riskless rate is 2 per cent, and is well off in the 5 per cent state. In addition to the market portfolio, this investor may optimally wish to buy some long-term bonds or interest rate futures contracts that go up in value as rates fall. Then the investor is hedged, by having more wealth to compensate for the poor reinvestment rate. If rates increase, the retiree has a capital loss on the bonds and, therefore, less wealth, but has a better reinvestment rate. Some investors may well prefer this to just holding the market portfolio. Thus, as we shall see, the single-period CAPM's two-fund theorem and the asset pricing model itself will not necessarily hold in a multiperiod economy. These are points all made clear in Merton's (1973) pathbreaking work.

Merton (1973) derived the optimal portfolio rules for an individual in an exchange economy, and Cox, Ingersoll and Ross (1985b) verified those same portfolio rules in a general equilibrium economy with production. Let subscripts of the indirect utility function be partial derivatives, and let V_{aa} now be the $A \times A$ variance–covariance matrix for assets' returns and V_{as} be the $A \times S$ covariance matrix of assets' returns with the various state variables. The optimal portfolio of risky assets in the intertemporal economy is:

185

$$\mathbf{w}^k W^k = T^k [\mathbf{V}_{aa}^{-1}(\boldsymbol{\mu} - r_f \mathbf{1})] + \mathbf{V}_{aa}^{-1} \mathbf{V}_{as} \mathbf{H}_s^k, \qquad \text{for all individuals } k, \quad (10)$$

where $\mathbf{H}_s^k = -\mathbf{J}_{sW}^k / J_{WW}^k$. Notice that the first RHS term of (10) is the mean–variance efficient portfolio as in the single-period equations of (4). As for the other term, Breeden (1979) showed that each column j of the product matrix $\mathbf{V}_{aa}^{-1} \mathbf{V}_{as}$ represents the portfolio of assets that is most highly correlated in return with movements in state variable j. To see this, note that the portfolio that has the maximum correlation with state variable s_j is the one with the highest covariance with s_j, given a fixed portfolio variance. Mathematically:

Objective: $\qquad \max_{\{\mathbf{w}_j\}} L = \mathbf{w}_j' \mathbf{V}_{a,sj} + \lambda [\sigma^2 - \mathbf{w}_j' \mathbf{V}_{aa} \mathbf{w}_j]$

Solution: $\qquad\qquad \mathbf{w}_j = [\mathbf{V}_{aa}^{-1} \mathbf{V}_{a,sj}](1/2\lambda). \qquad\qquad\qquad (11)$

(The scalar does not matter, since all portfolios that are scalar multiples are perfectly correlated and have the same correlations with all other variables.) Thus, those S portfolios are the best hedge portfolios available for individuals to use in hedging opportunity set changes. The coefficient vector in (10), $\mathbf{H}_s^k$, gives individual k's holdings of those hedge portfolios (which may be positive or negative).

Aggregating individual's portfolios gives the market portfolio. Substituting this back into (10) gives:

$$\mathbf{w}^k W^k = (T^k/T^M) \mathbf{w}^M + [\mathbf{V}_{aa}^{-1} \mathbf{V}_{as}][\mathbf{H}_s^k - (T^k/T^M) \mathbf{H}_z^M],$$

$$\text{for all individuals } k, \qquad (12)$$

where

$$T^M = \sum_k T^k \qquad \text{and} \qquad \mathbf{H}_s^M = \sum_k \mathbf{H}_s^k.$$

From this, it is clear that all individuals' portfolios can be obtained with $S + 2$ funds: (1) the market portfolio, (2) the riskless asset, and (3) the S best hedge portfolios for the state variables. No preferences are needed to set up the mutual funds. Breeden (1984) showed that if each of the S hedge portfolios is *perfectly* correlated with the state variable it hedges, then the allocation of contingent claims is an unconstrained Pareto-optimal allocation (ex ante, as in Arrow, 1951). If there is not a perfect hedge for some state variable, then preferences can be chosen so that the allocation is not unconstrained Pareto-optimal.

To complete the analysis, the $\mathbf{H}_s^k$ terms need to be examined, so we know what types of holdings different individuals should have in the hedge portfolios. Without stronger preference assumptions, analysis of the hedging terms is difficult. However, if one assumes that the vector of percentage compensating variations in k's wealth for state variables' changes ($\gamma_s^k = -\mathbf{J}_s^k / W^k J_W^k$) are not a function of k's wealth, then Breeden (1984) has shown that:

$$\mathbf{H}_s^k = W^k (1 - T^{*k}) \gamma_s^k, \qquad\qquad\qquad (13)$$

where T^{*k} is k's Pratt–Arrow measure of relative risk tolerance. Since $\mathbf{H}_s^k$ give individual k's holdings of the hedge portfolios for opportunity set changes, an individual will attempt to hedge if and only if his or her relative risk tolerance is less than unity. Since unity represents the logarithmic utility case, those more risk averse than the log will tend to hedge, whereas those more tolerant than the log will tend to 'reverse hedge'. This type of result has been obtained by Merton (1969), Grauer and Litzenberger (1979), Dieffenbach (1975) and Breeden (1984).

The optimality of reverse hedging if relative risk tolerance is greater than unity is a very interesting result, since one certainly cannot rule out those preferences. To understand this result, consider a stochastic expected return on investments in the stock market. Apart from holding the market portfolio, one might wish to hedge or reverse hedge changes in the expected return on the market. For both hedger and reverse hedger, let us assume that an increase in expected return on the market is a good thing, in that expected lifetime utility is positively related to that opportunity. A hedger would say that when the expected return on the market is high, he needs less wealth; on the other hand, when the expected return is low, he needs more wealth to keep up his planned lifetime consumption level.

The person who would reverse hedge would view things differently, but not irrationally. That person would wish to have a lot of wealth to invest when the expected return on the market is high, in order to take advantage of the good returns. When returns are poor, our relatively risk tolerant person would wish to have little wealth to invest. Clearly, this strategy generates a higher multiperiod mean return and a higher multiperiod variance of return than does the hedging strategy. Neither strategy dominates the other for all risk averse individuals. Which is chosen depends upon the person's marginal rate of substitution function of mean for variance.

III. INTERTEMPORAL CAPITAL ASSET PRICING MODEL (ICAPM)

Given the general portfolio theory of the last section, this section derives the general intertemporal asset pricing model of Merton (1973). The first step shows that equilibrium expected returns on all assets are linear combinations of their covariances with the market portfolio and with the S portfolios that are most highly correlated with the opportunity set variables. To see this, aggregate individuals' asset demands (12) to get the market portfolio, pre-multiply that by $\mathbf{V}_{aa}(M/T^M)$, and rearrange to get:

$$\boldsymbol{\mu} - r_f \mathbf{1} = [\mathbf{V}_{aM}\mathbf{V}_{as}]\begin{pmatrix} M/T_M \\ -\mathbf{H}_s^M/T_M \end{pmatrix}. \tag{14}$$

It is easy to verify that the covariances of assets with the state variables are the same as their covariances with the returns on portfolios that are maximally correlated with the state variables (s^*), which have weights of $\mathbf{w}_{s^*} = \mathbf{V}_{aa}^{-1}\mathbf{V}_{as}$.

The next step is to derive the expected excess returns on the $S + 1$ mutual funds that individuals hold. Pre-multiplying (14) by the matrix of portfolio weights

187

for the $S + 1$ funds, their expected excess returns are:

$$\begin{pmatrix} \mu_M - r_f \\ \mu_{s^*} - r_f 1 \end{pmatrix} = \begin{pmatrix} \sigma_M^2 & V_{Ms^*} \\ V_{s^*M} & V_{s^*s^*} \end{pmatrix} \begin{pmatrix} M/T_M \\ -H_s^M/T^M \end{pmatrix}. \tag{15}$$

To see the implications of this, note that if the S hedging portfolios were uncorrelated with the market portfolio and with each other, their expected excess returns would be zero in the single-period CAPM. However, in the intertemporal model, the expected excess return on a hedge portfolio is negatively related to the aggregate hedging demand (opposite if reverse hedging), and proportional to the variance of the hedging portfolio's return. Thus, if individuals in aggregate wish to hedge investment opportunities with a portfolio, they bid up its price and bid down its expected return in equilibrium. As shown earlier, with normal hedging, those state variables with the largest compensating variations in wealth will have the largest hedging demands and will deviate the most from the single-period CAPM's return predictions, *ceteris paribus*.

The final step in Merton's intertemporal CAPM is to substitute expected excess returns on the $S + 1$ key portfolios from (15) for preference parameters in (14):

$$\mu - r_f 1 = [V_{aM} V_{as}] \begin{pmatrix} \sigma_M^2 & V_{Ms^*} \\ V_{s^*M} & V_{s^*s^*} \end{pmatrix}^{-1} \begin{pmatrix} \mu_M - r_f \\ \mu_{s^*} - r_f 1 \end{pmatrix}$$

$$\text{(ICAPM)} \qquad = \beta_{a,Ms^*} \begin{pmatrix} \mu_M - r_f \\ \mu_{s^*} - r_f 1 \end{pmatrix}. \tag{16}$$

Thus, in the intertemporal economy, betas with respect to the market portfolio are not enough to describe the relevant risk of a security. Its covariances with the investment opportunity set also matter for both pricing and optimal portfolios.

IV. CONSUMPTION-ORIENTED CAPITAL ASSET PRICING MODEL (CCAPM)

Following seminal articles on asset pricing in discrete-time economies by Rubinstein (1976), Lucas (1978) and Breeden and Litzenberger (1978), Breeden (1979) showed that Merton's (1973) multi-beta intertemporal CAPM could be re-expressed with a single risk measure. The result found, which is derived below, is that Merton's multi-beta ICAPM reduces to a market price of risk multiplied by the asset's *consumption-beta*, which is its sensitivity of return to percentage movements in aggregate real consumption. This model is the consumption-based capital asset pricing model (CCAPM).

The optimal rate of current consumption in the continuous-time model is a function of the individual's current wealth and the state vector for investment opportunities, $c^k = c^k(W^k, s, t)$. In the continuous-time model, the first-order Taylor series approximation is correct for the *stochastic* part of consumption movements. (In contrast, a second-order approximation is required to describe the *expected* change in consumption.) Thus, the stochastic movements in consumption, and the co-variances of assets' returns with k's consumption changes $V_{a,ck}$, may be written as follows:

$$d\tilde{c}^k = c_W^k (d\tilde{W}^k) + \mathbf{c}_s^k (d\tilde{\mathbf{s}})$$

$$\mathbf{V}_{a,ck} = \mathbf{V}_{a,Wk} c_W^k + \mathbf{V}_{as} \mathbf{c}_s^k. \tag{17}$$

The risk aversion and hedging preference parameters that determine an individual's asset holdings can be rewritten in terms of an individual's direct utility function for consumption. To see this, implicitly differentiate the envelope condition [eqn (9), superscript k suppressed]:

$$T = -J_W/J_{WW} = -u_c/(u_{cc}c_W) = T_c/c_W \tag{18}$$

$$\mathbf{H}_s = -J_{sW}/J_{WW} = -\mathbf{c}_s/c_W, \qquad \text{for each individual.} \tag{19}$$

Substituting these formulae into Merton's optimal asset demands, (10), pre-multiplying them by $(c_W^k \mathbf{V}_{aa})$ and using (17) to simplify gives:

$$\mathbf{V}_{a,ck} = T_c^k [\boldsymbol{\mu} - r_r \mathbf{1}], \qquad \text{for each individual } k. \tag{20}$$

This shows that each individual holds assets in proportions that result in an optimal consumption rate that covaries with each asset in proportion to its expected excess return. The next step is to aggregate these individual optimality conditions, which shows that each asset's expected excess return is proportional to its covariance with *aggregate* consumption.

Define the 'consumption beta' for any asset or portfolio j, β_j, to be the covariance of j's return with percentage changes in aggregate consumption, divided by the variance of percentage changes in aggregate consumption. Thus, the consumption beta is the slope in the regression of the asset's return on percentage changes in (real, per capita) consumption. The consumption-oriented CAPM (CCAPM) follows easily from the aggregated version of (20), where the risk tolerance parameter is eliminated by using the expected excess return per unit of consumption beta for *any* portfolio M:

$$\boldsymbol{\mu} - r_f \mathbf{1} = [\boldsymbol{\beta}_C/\beta_{MC}](\mu_M - r_f), \tag{21}$$

Thus, Breeden (1979) showed that Merton's intertemporal CAPM, which required $S + 1$ betas to determine an asset's systematic risks and equilibrium return, can be collapsed into a consumption oriented CAPM, with only a single beta with respect to consumption. This helps the intuition in determining which types of assets should have equilibrium returns that are substantially different in multiperiod economies than in the single-period world of the original market-oriented CAPM. How much the CCAPM representation helps in the testing of the intertemporal model is the subject of much current debate.

In the intertemporal economy, the market portfolio is no longer mean–variance efficient. The portfolio that has the highest correlation of returns with aggregate real consumption is now mean–variance efficient. To see this, pre-multiply an aggregate version of (20) by $\mathbf{V}_{aa}^{-1}$: the LHS gives the maximum correlation portfolio for consumption, and the RHS shows that it satisfies the mean–variance efficiency property of eqn (4). The reason is simply that in the intertemporal economy one gets paid to take consumption-related risk, and no other. Any

189

portfolio that has not got the highest correlation with consumption has wasted risk for no additional return.

Our understanding of these results is greatly enhanced by understanding the relation of asset prices to marginal utilities. Hirshleifer's (1970, ch. 9) presentation of the time-state preference model of Arrow (1964) and Debreu (1959) is used extensively by Fama (1970), Rubinstein (1974, 1976), Long (1974), Hakansson (1977), Lucas (1978), Breeden and Litzenberger (1978), Brennan (1979) and Cox, Ingersoll and Ross (1985b) in asset pricing models that were fundamental precursors to the developments here. They showed that the value and fair price of one more share of an asset is the expected marginal utility of its payoffs. The expected marginal utility of its payoffs depends on the expected sizes of the payoffs, the dates they are received and the covariances of their sizes with the marginal utilities at different dates of a unit of consumption or wealth [see (9)]. Assets that have their highest payoffs when consumption is high (positive consumption betas) are paying the most when least needed, i.e., when the marginal utility of consumption is low; they are less valuable and have higher equilibrium required returns than assets that pay most when consumption is down.

The consumption CAPM follows directly from the marginal utility insights, since with time-additive utility functions, consumption at any date t is a sufficient statistic for marginal utility at date t. Wealth is not a sufficient statistic for marginal utility in an intertemporal economy, since the quality of the investment opportunity set also affects the marginal utility of a unit payoff. The reason that covariance with the market (aggregate wealth) determines risk in the single-period CAPM is that with one period, consumption equals wealth. Since marginal utility is one-to-one with consumption, it is also one-to-one with wealth in the single-period model. In that case, consumption betas and market betas are the same and the CCAPM reduces to the CAPM.

V. EXTENSIONS AND CONCLUSIONS

Space prohibits the proof of other important results that have been proven or can be proven. For example, Breeden and Litzenberger (1978) showed that if the capital markets allocation is unconstrained Pareto-optimal in this intertemporal economy, then each individual's consumption is monotonically increasing in aggregate consumption and in every other person's consumption. All individual's consumption rates should go up and down together, though not necessarily proportionally. Each individual's optimal portfolio is the one that results in the highest correlation of the individual's consumption with aggregate consumption. Breeden (1979) showed: (1) All assets have the same covariances with a portfolio that is maximally correlated with aggregate consumption as with consumption itself. As a result, the CCAPM may be stated and tested in terms of assets' betas with respect to that maximally correlated portfolio. (2) With commodity price uncertainty, the CCAPM holds in terms of expected real returns and the betas of real returns with real, per capita consumption. (3) The CCAPM holds without a riskless asset, by just replacing r_f with the expected return on a portfolio that is uncorrelated with real consumption movements. A similar result was shown earlier by Black (1972) for the single-period CAPM. Finally, Bergman (1985) showed that if preferences are time-multiplicative, rather than time-additive, Merton's intertemporal CAPM still holds, but Breeden's (1979) CCAPM extension does not. Thus, the ICAPM is more general than the CCAPM.

In conclusion, the past three decades have seen important developments in the modelling of consumption and portfolio choices under uncertainty. In my opinion, the intertemporal portfolio theory and asset pricing models presented here are the strongest and most useful theoretical models that we currently have. Finally, I must say that there were many more authors that were important to the development of this area than were described in this essay. The bibliography gives a more complete (but still abridged) listing of papers that serious students should read.

BIBLIOGRAPHY

Arrow, K.J. 1951. An extension of the basic theorems of classical welfare economics. In *Proceedings of the Second Berkeley Symposium on Mathematical Statistics and Probability*, ed. J. Neyman, Berkeley: University of California Press, 507–31.

Arrow, K.J. 1964. The role of securities in the optimal allocation of risk-bearing. *Review of Economic Studies* 31, 91–6.

Arrow, K.J. 1964. The theory of risk aversion. In K.J. Arrow, *Aspects of the Theory of Risk-Bearing*, Helsinki: Yrjö Jahnsson Foundation.

Banz, R.W. and Miller, M.H. 1978. Prices for state-contingent claims: some estimates and applications. *Journal of Business* 51, 653–72.

Beja, A. 1971. The structure of the cost of capital under uncertainty. *Review of Economic Studies* 38, 359–76.

Bergman, Y.Z. 1985. Time preference and capital asset pricing models. *Journal of Financial Economics* 14, 145–60.

Bhattacharya, S. 1981. Notes on multiperiod valuation and the pricing of options. *Journal of Finance* 36, 163–80.

Black, F. 1972. Capital market equilibrium with restricted borrowing. *Journal of Business* 45, 444–55.

Black, F. and Scholes, M.S. 1973. The pricing of options and corporate liabilities. *Journal of Political Economy* 81, 637–54.

Breeden, D.T. 1979. An intertemporal asset pricing model with stochastic consumption and investment opportunities. *Journal of Financial Economics* 7, 265–96.

Breeden, D.T. 1984. Futures markets and commodity options: hedging and optimality in incomplete markets. *Journal of Economic Theory* 32, 275–300.

Breeden, D.T. 1986. Consumption, production, inflation, and interest rates: a synthesis. *Journal of Financial Economics* 16, 3–39.

Breeden, D.T. and Litzenberger, R.H. 1978. Prices of state-contingent claims implicit in option prices. *Journal of Business* 51, 621–51.

Brennan, M.J. 1979. The pricing of contingent claims in discrete time models. *Journal of Finance* 34, 53–68.

Constantanides, G.M. 1982. Intertemporal asset pricing with heterogeneous consumers and without demand aggregation. *Journal of Business* 55, 253–67.

Cox, J.C., Ingersoll, J.E. and Ross, S.A. 1985a. A theory of the term structure of interest rates. *Econometrica* 53, 385–407.

Cox, J.C., Ingersoll, J.E. and Ross, S.A. 1985b. An intertemporal general equilibrium model of asset prices. *Econometrica* 53, 385–407.

Debreu, G. 1959. *Theory of Value*. New York: Wiley.

Dieffenbach, B.C. 1975. A quantitative theory of risk premiums on securities with an application to the term structure of interest rates. *Econometrica* 43, 431–54.

Fama, E.F. 1970. Multiperiod consumption-investment decisions. *American Economic Review* 60, 163–74.

Ferson, W.E. 1983. Expected real interest rates and aggregate consumption: empirical tests. *Journal of Financial and Quantitative Analysis* 18, 477–98.

Fischer, S. 1975. The demand for index bonds. *Journal of Political Economy* 83, 509–34.

Garman, M. 1977. A general theory of asset pricing under diffusion state processes. Working Paper No. 50, Research Program in Finance, University of California, Berkeley.

Grauer, F. and Litzenberger, R. 1979. The pricing of commodity futures contracts, nominal bonds and other risky assets under commodity price uncertainty. *Journal of Finance* 34, 69–83.

Grossman, S.J. and Shiller, R.J. 1982. Consumption correlatedness and risk measurement in economies with non-traded assets and heterogeneous information. *Journal of Financial Economics* 10, 195–210.

Hakansson, N.H. 1970. Optimal investment and consumption strategies under risk for a class of utility functions. *Econometrica* 38(5), September, 587–607.

Hakansson, N.H. 1977. Efficient paths toward efficient capital markets in large and small countries. In *Financial Decision Making under Uncertainty*, ed. H. Levy and M. Sarnat, New York: Academic Press.

Hall, R.E. 1978. Stochastic implications of the life cycle-permanent income hypothesis: theory and evidence. *Journal of Political Economy* 86, 971–87.

Hansen, L.P. and Singleton, K.J. 1983. Stochastic consumption, risk aversion, and the temporal behavior of asset returns. *Journal of Political Economy* 91, 249–65.

Hirshleifer, J. 1970. *Investment, Interest and Capital*. Englewood Cliffs: Prentice-Hall.

Huang, C.-F. 1985. Information structure and equilibrium asset prices. *Journal of Economic Theory* 34, 33–71.

Kraus, A. and Litzenberger, R.H. 1975. Market equilibrium in a state preference model with logarithmic utility. *Journal of Finance* 30(5), December, 1213–27.

Kydland, F.E. and Prescott, E.C. 1982. Time to build and aggregate fluctuations. *Econometrica* 50, 1345–70.

Lintner, J. 1965. Valuation of risk assets and the selection of risky investments in stock portfolios and capital budgets. *Review of Economics and Statistics* 47, February, 13–37.

Long, J.B. 1974. Stock prices, inflation, and the term structure of interest rates. *Journal of Financial Economics* 2, 131–70.

Lucas, R.E. 1978. Asset prices in an exchange economy. *Econometrica* 46, 14–45.

Marsh, T.A. and Rosenfeld, E.A. 1982. Stochastic processes for interest rates and equilibrium bond prices. *Journal of Finance* 38, 635–46.

Markowitz, H. 1952. Portfolio selection. *Journal of Finance* 12, 77–91.

Markowitz, H. 1959. *Portfolio Selection: Efficient Diversification of Investment*. New York: John Wiley.

Merton, R.C. 1969. Lifetime portfolio selection under uncertainty: the continuous-time case. *Review of Economics and Statistics* 51, 247–57.

Merton, R.C. 1971. Optimum consumption and portfolio rules in a continuous-time model. *Journal of Economic Theory* 3(4), 373–413.

Merton, R.C. 1973. An intertemporal capital asset pricing model. *Econometrica* 41, 867–87.

Mossin, J. 1966. Equilibrium in a capital asset market. *Econometrica* 34, October, 768–83.

Pratt, J.W. 1964. Risk aversion in the small and in the large. *Econometrica* 32(1–2), January–April, 122–36.

Pye, G. 1972. Lifetime portfolio selection with age dependent risk aversion. In *Mathematical Methods in Investment and Finance*, ed. G. Szego and K. Shell, Amsterdam: North-Holland, 49–64.

Richard, S.F. 1974. Optimal consumption, portfolio and life insurance rules for an uncertain lived individual in a continuous-time model. *Journal of Financial Economics* 2, 187–203.

Roll, R. 1977. A critique of the asset pricing theory's tests. Part I: On past and potential testability of the theory. *Journal of Financial Economics* 4, 129–76.

Ross, S.A. 1976. The arbitrage theory of capital asset pricing. *Journal of Economic Theory* 3, 343–62.

Rubinstein, M. 1974. A discrete-time synthesis of financial theory. In *Research in Finance*, Vol. 3, Greenwich, Conn.: JAI Press, 53–102.

Rubinstein, M. 1976. The valuation of uncertain income streams and the pricing of options. *Bell Journal of Economics and Management Science* 7, 407–25.

Samuelson, P.A. 1969. Lifetime portfolio selection by dynamic stochastic programming. *Review of Economics and Statistics* 57(3), August, 239–46.

Sharpe, W.F. 1964. Capital asset prices: A theory of market equilibrium under conditions of risk. *Journal of Finance* 19, 429–42.

Stulz, R.M. 1981. A model of international asset pricing. *Journal of Financial Economics* 9, 383–406.

Sundaresan, M. 1984. Consumption and equilibrium interest rates in stochastic production economies. *Journal of Finance* 39, 77–92.

Tobin, J. 1958. Liquidity preference as behavior towards risk. *Review of Economic Studies* 25, 65–86.

Mean–Variance Analysis

HARRY M. MARKOWITZ

In a mean–variance portfolio analysis (Markowitz, 1959) an n-component vector (portfolio) X is called feasible if it satisfies

$$AX = b \qquad X \geqslant O$$

where A is an $m \times n$ matrix of constraint coefficients, and b an m-component constant vector. An EV combination is called feasible if

$$E = \mu^{\mathrm{T}} X$$

$$V = X^{\mathrm{T}} CX$$

for some feasible portfolio. Here E is the expected return of the portfolio, V the variance of the portfolio, μ the vector of expected returns on securities, and C a positive semidefinite covariance matrix of returns among securities.

A feasible EV combination is called inefficient if some other feasible combination has either less V and no less E, or else greater E and no greater V. A feasible EV combination is called efficient if it is not inefficient. A feasible portfolio X is efficient or inefficient according to whether its EV combination meets the one definition or the other. As in linear programming, the constraints ($AX = b$, $X \geqslant O$) can represent inequalities by introducing slack variables, and can incorporate variables which are allowed to be negative, by separating the positive and negative parts of such variables.

Markowitz (1956) shows that if V is strictly convex over the set of feasible portfolios – for example when C is positive definite – the set of efficient portfolios is piecewise linear, and the set of efficient EV combinations is piecewise parabolic. There may or may not be a kink in the efficient EV set at a 'corner portfolio', where two pieces of the efficient portfolio set meet. Markowitz (1959, Appendix A) shows for arbitrary semidefinite C that, while there may be more than one efficient portfolio for given efficient EV combination, there is a piecewise linear set of efficient portfolios which contains one and only one efficient portfolio for each efficient EV combination. The piecewise linear nature of the efficient set is illustrated graphically, for small n, in Markowitz (1952, 1959).

The fact that the mean–variance analysis selects a portfolio for only one period does not imply that the investor plans to retire at the end of the period. Rather, it assumes that in the dynamic programming (Bellman, 1957) solution to the many period investment problem, current wealth is the only state variable to enter the implied single period utility function (see Markowitz, 1959, Ch. 13; Samuelson, 1969; Ziemba and Vickson, 1975). Mossin (1968) shows conditions under which the optimum solution to the many period problem is 'myopic' in that the single period utility function is the same as an end-of-game utility function. This is an example of – but not the only example of – a class of games in which wealth is the only state variable.

The Markowitz (1959) justification for the use of mean–variance analysis further assumes that if one knows the E and V of a portfolio one can estimate with acceptable accuracy the expected value of the one-period utility function. Samuelson (1970) and Ohlson (1975) present conditions under which mean and variance are asymptotically sufficient as the length of holding periods – that is, the intervals between portfolio revisions – approaches zero. For 'long' holding periods, for example for time between revisions as long as a year, Markowitz (1959), Young and Trent (1969), Levy and Markowitz (1979), Pulley (1981) and Kroll, Levy and Markowitz (1984) have each found mean–variance approximations to be quite accurate for a variety of utility functions and historical distributions of portfolio return.

This leads to an apparent anomaly: if you know mean and variance you practically know expected utility; the mean–variance approximation to expected utility is based on a quadratic approximation to the single-period utility function; yet Arrow (1965) and Pratt (1964) show that any quadratic utility function has the objectionable property that an investor with such a utility function becomes increasingly averse to risks of a given dollar amount as his wealth increases. Levy and Markowitz (1979) show that the anomaly disappears if you distinguish three types of quadratic approximation:

(1) Assuming that the investor has a utility-of-wealth function that remains constant through time – so that as the investor's wealth changes he moves along the curve to a new position – fit a quadratic to this curve at some instant of time, and continue to use this same approximation subsequently. (Note that the assumption here, that the investor has a constant utility-of-wealth function is sufficient, but not necessary, for the investor to have a single period utility function at each period.)

(2) Fit the quadratic to the investor's current single period utility function. For example, if the investor has an unchanging utility-of-wealth function, choose a quadratic to fit well near current wealth (i.e. near portfolio return equal zero).

(3) Allow the quadratic approximation to vary from one portfolio to another, that is, let the approximation depend on the mean, and perhaps the standard deviation, of the probability distribution whose expected value is to be estimated.

The Pratt–Arrow objections apply to an approximation of type (1). The approximations proposed in Markowitz (1959) are of types (2) and (3). Levy and Markowitz (1979) show that, under quite general assumptions, the type 3 mean–variance maximizer has the same risk aversion in the small (in the sense of Pratt) as does the original expected utility maximizer.

USES OF MEAN–VARIANCE ANALYSIS

Two areas of use deal with: (a) actual portfolio management using mean–variance analysis, and (b) implications for the economy as a whole of the assumption that all investors act according to the mean–variance criteria. We refer to these, respectively, as 'normative' and 'positive' uses of mean–variance analysis.

The positive application of mean–variance analysis is dealt with elsewhere. Seminal works in the field include the Tobin (1958) analysis of liquidity preference; and the Sharpe (1964), Lintner (1965) and Mossin (1966) Capital Asset Pricing Models (CAPMs). As in the Tobin model, these CAPMs assume that the investor can either lend all he has or borrow all he wants at the same 'risk-free' rate of interest. From this assumption (plus assumptions that all investors have the same beliefs and seek mean–variance efficiency subject to the same constraint set) they conclude that the excess return on each security (its expected return minus the risk-free rate) is proportional to its 'beta', where the latter is the regression of the security's return against the return of the market as a whole. Black (1972) drops the assumption that the investor can borrow at a risk-free rate; assumes instead that the investor can sell short and use the proceeds to buy long; and derives a formula for excess return just like that of Sharpe–Lintner–Mossin except that the expected return on a zero-beta portfolio is substituted for the risk-free rate in the formula for excess return. Merton (1969) has developed mean–variance theory in continuous time. This has been used, for example, in the analysis of option prices by Black and Scholes (1973) from which a vast literature of further implications followed.

As compared with the models used in normative analysis, the models of positive analysis tend to use quite simple constraint sets and other special assumptions (e.g. all investors have the same beliefs). The justification for such assumptions is that they give concrete, therefore testable, implications; and indeed have been the subject of extensive empirical testing.

In the use of mean–variance analysis for actual money management, the question immediately arises as to how to estimate the large number of required covariances. Sharpe (1963) concluded, and Cohen and Pogue (1967) confirmed, that a simple one-factor model of covariance was sufficient. King (1966) showed that, in addition to one pervasive factor, there were ample industry sources of covariance. By the mid-1970s it was clear to many practitioners that the one-factor model was not adequate, since, for example, sometimes 'the market', as measured by some broad index, went up while high beta stocks went down, to an extent that could not be explained by chance. Many-factor models such as that of Rosenberg (1974) are now widely used.

Other models of covariance used in practice include scenario and combined scenario and factor models (Markowitz and Perold, 1981), and a model which assumes that all correlation coefficients are the same (Elton and Gruber, 1973). The use of factor, scenario or constant correlation models, in addition to simplifying the parameter estimation problem, can considerably accelerate the computation of efficient sets for analyses containing hundreds of securities. For example, the Perold (1984) code will solve large portfolio selection problems for arbitrary A and C, but is especially efficient in handling upper bounds on variables and sparse (mostly zero) A and C matrices. (The introduction of 'dummy' securities into the analysis allows one to 'sparsify' the C matrix for factor, scenario or constant correlation models.) Even faster solutions are obtained by Elton, Gruber and Padberg (1976 and 1978) for the one-factor and constant correlation models for certain common constraint sets.

BIBLIOGRAPHY

Arrow, K. 1965. *Aspects of the Theory of Risk Bearing.* Helsinki: Yrjö Jahnsson Foundation.

Bellman, R.E. 1957. *Dynamic Programming.* Princeton: Princeton University Press.

Black, F. 1972. Capital market equilibrium with restricted borrowing. *Journal of Business* 45(3), July, 444–55.

Black, F. and Scholes, M. 1973. The pricing of options and corporate liabilities. *Journal of Political Economy* 81(3), May–June, 637–54.

Cohen, J.K. and Pogue, J.A. 1967. An empirical evaluation of alternative portfolio-selection models. *Journal of Business* 40, April, 166–93.

Elton, E.J. and Gruber, M.J. 1973. Estimating the dependence structure of share prices. *Journal of Finance* 28(5), December, 1203–32.

Elton, E.J., Gruber, M.J. and Padberg, M.W. 1976. Simple criteria for optimal portfolio selection. *Journal of Finance* 31(5), December, 1341–57.

Elton, E.J., Gruber, M.J. and Padberg, M.W. 1978. Simple criteria for optimal portfolio selection: tracing out the efficient frontier. *Journal of Finance* 33(1) March, 296–302.

King, B.F. 1966. Market and industry factors in stock price behavior. *Journal of Business* 39, Supplement, January, 139–90.

Kroll, Y., Levy, H. and Markowitz, H.M. 1984. Mean variance versus direct utility maximization. *Journal of Finance* 39(1), March, 47–61.

Levy, H. and Markowitz, H.M. 1979. Approximating expected utility by a function of mean and variance. *American Economic Review* 69(3), June, 308–17.

Lintner, J. 1965. The valuation of risk assets and the selection of risky investments in stock portfolios and capital budgets. *Review of Economics and Statistics* 47, February, 13–37.

Markowitz, H.M. 1952. Portfolio selection. *Journal of Finance* 7(1), March, 77–91.

Markowitz, H.M. 1956. The optimization of a quadratic function subject to linear constraints. *Naval Research Logistics Quarterly* 3, 111–33.

Markowitz, H.M. 1959. *Portfolio Selection: Efficient Diversification of Investments.* New Haven: Yale University Press. Reprinted, New York: John Wiley and Sons, 1970.

Markowitz, H.M. and Perold, A. 1981. Portfolio analysis with factors and scenarios. *Journal of Finance* 36(14) September.

Merton, R.C. 1969. Lifetime portfolio selection under uncertainty: the continuous-time case. *Review of Economics and Statistics* 51(3), August, 247–57.

Mossin, J. 1966. Equilibrium in a capital asset market. *Econometrica* 34, October, 768–83.

Mossin, J. 1968. Optimal multiperiod portfolio policies. *Journal of Business* 41, 215–29.

Ohlson, J.A. 1975. The asymptotic validity of quadratic utility as the trading interval approaches zero. In *Stochastic Optimization Models in Finance*, ed. W.T. Ziemba and R.G. Vickson, New York: Academic Press.

Perold, A.F. 1984. Large-scale portfolio optimization. *Management Science* 30(10), October, 1143–60.

Pratt, J.W. 1964. Risk aversion in the small and in the large. *Econometrica* 32, January–April, 122–36.

Pulley, L.B. 1981. A general mean–variance approximation to expected utility for short holding periods. *Journal of Financial and Quantitative Analysis* 16(3), September, 361–73.

Rosenberg, B. 1974. Extra-market components of covariance in security returns. *Journal of Financial and Quantitative Analysis* 9(2), March, 263–74.

Samuelson, P.A. 1969. Lifetime portfolio selection by dynamic stochastic programming. *Review of Economics and Statistics* 51(3), August, 239–46.

Samuelson, P.A. 1970. The fundamental approximation theorem of portfolio analysis in terms of means, variances and higher moments. *Review of Economic Studies* 37(4), October, 537–42.

Sharpe, W.F. 1963. A simplified model for portfolio analysis. *Management Science* 9(2), January, 277–93.

Sharpe, W.F. 1964. Capital asset prices: a theory of market equilibrium under conditions of risk. *Journal of Finance* 19(3), September, 425–42.

Tobin, J. 1958. Liquidity preference as behavior toward risk. *Review of Economic Studies* 25, February, 65–86.

Young, W.E. and Trent, R.H. 1969. Geometric mean approximations of individual security and portfolio performance. *Journal of Financial and Quantitative Analysis* 4(2) June, 179–99.

Ziemba, W.T. and Vickson, R.G. (eds) 1975. *Stochastic Optimization Models in Finance*. New York: Academic Press.

Option Pricing Theory

JONATHAN E. INGERSOLL, JR.

Financial contracting is as old as human history. Deeds for the sale of land have been discovered that date to before 2800 BC. The Code of Hammurabi (c1800 BC) regulated, among other things, the terms of credit. Contingent contracting was also common. Under the Code crop failure due to storm or drought served to cancel that year's interest on a land loan. The trading of the first options is probably equally ancient.

Although options have certainly been traded for centuries, it is only in recent years that they have reached any degree of importance. In 1973 the Chicago Board of Trade founded The Chicago Board Options Exchange to create a centralized market for trading call options on listed stock. The American, Pacific and Philadelphia Stock Exchanges followed suit within a few years. In 1977 the trading of puts on these exchanges began.

By the early 1980s puts and calls could be traded on over 400 listed stocks, and options were available on many other financial instruments such as Treasury bonds and bills, foreign currencies and futures contracts. The volume of trade had grown as well. In terms of the number of shares controlled, option volume often exceeded that on the New York Stock Exchange.

Curiously the recent revolution in option pricing theory also dates to 1973 with the publication by Fischer Black and Myron Scholes of their classic paper on option valuation. In the past decade and a half, the valuation of options or various other contingent contracts has been one of the primary areas of research among financial economists.

Option contracts are examples of derivative securities; that is securities whose values depend on those of other securities or assets. For example, a call option on a share of stock gives the owner the right to purchase a share of that stock at a set price. The value of this right obviously depends on the price per share of the stock on which the option is based.

199

TERMINOLOGY. Before discussing the academic study of options, it is useful to consider some terminology. The two most common types of option contracts are puts and calls. A *call* is an option to buy, and a *put* is an option to sell. Puts and calls are contracts between two investors. The purchaser of the option is the party to whom the contract gives certain rights or 'options'. The call's owner is said to have a *long* position. The creator or writer of the call has certain financial obligations if the owner chooses to exercise the option. The writer of an option is said to have a *short* position.

The owner of a call has the right, but not the obligation, to buy a fixed amount (usually 100 shares for exchange listed stock options) of a particular asset on or before a given date, the *maturity of expiration date*, upon payment of a stated fee. This fee is called the *exercise price, striking price* or *contract price*. The owner of the call does not receive any dividends paid by the common stock or have any other rights of ownership until the option is exercised. The owner of the put has the right to sell on similar terms.

When purchasing the option, the amount that the long party pays to the short party is called the *premium*. If the stock price is above the striking price then the difference is the call's *intrinsic value*, i.e., for a call with a striking price of X on a stock with price S, the intrinsic value is $\text{Max}(S - X, 0)$. For a put the intrinsic value is the exercise price less the stock price when the former is larger, i.e. $\text{Max}(X - S, 0)$. An option's intrinsic value is sometimes called the *when-exercised* value. An option's intrinsic value does not measure its market value. Typically an option sells for more than its intrinsic value.

When options are first written the striking price is usually set near the currently prevailing stock price. The option is then said to be *at-the-money*. As the stock price changes, the option will become *in-the-money* or *out-of-the-money*. A call option is in-the-money when the stock price is above the striking price and out-of-the-money when the stock price is below the striking price.

The options just described are *American* options. They can be exercised at any time on or before the expiration date. Options that can only be exercised at maturity are called *European* options. Actually this is a misnomer. While American options are traded on exchanges in the United States and Canada (and Europe), European contracts are not traded on that continent.

A *warrant* is similar to a call option. The primary difference is that a warrant is issued by a corporation against its own stock. When a warrant is exercise, the corporation issues new shares to the owner of the warrant. Warrants typically have maturities of several years or longer. There have even been a few perpetual warrants issued. When they are issued, warrants are usually substantially out-of-the-money.

A *rights issue*, like a warrant, is granted by a corporation against new stock. Usually a rights issue expires in a few weeks to a few months after it is issued. When rights are issued, they are typically substantially in-the-money.

Many other financial contracts contain implicit or explicit options. Convertible bonds, for example, give the owner the right to swap the bonds for shares of stock. This option is like a warrant. Instead of paying a cash exercise price, the bondholder relinquishes the right to the future interest and principal payments. A callable bond includes the company's right to 'repurchase' a bond at a set call price. Much of the development in option pricing subsequent to the Black–Scholes option pricing model has been in the application of the model to these and other situations.

PRELIMINARY CONSIDERATIONS. Call options are the most common and one of the simplest types of derivative assets so this discussion will be illustrated primarily with calls. Most of the general principles apply with only minor changes to any derivative asset.

A call option with an exercise price of X on a share of stock with a current price per share of S is worth $S - X$ if exercised, for it enables its owner to purchase for X something worth S. To avoid any possibility of arbitrage a call option must sell for at least this difference. In addition because a call has limited liability (that is the owner cannot be forced to exercise when it is not advantageous to do so), it must be worth at least zero. Thus, $C(S, \tau) \geqslant \text{Max}(S - X, 0)$, where $C(S, \tau)$ is the market price of a call with time to maturity of τ.

As a general rule this inequality will be strict, and the call will be worth more 'alive' than when exercised. One exception is at the time a call matures. Then the owner has only two choices – exercise the option or let it expire. At this point the preceding relation must hold as an equality, $C(S, 0) = \text{Max}(S - X, 0)$. It is this functional relation between the value of the call at maturity and the stock price prevailing at that time that makes the call a derivative asset and allows its price to be determined as a function of the prevailing stock price.

Some general restrictions on option values can be derived with no assumptions beyond the absence of arbitrage opportunities. For example, a call with a low exercise price must be worth at least as much as an otherwise identical call with a high exercise price. The intuition is simple. The owner of the call with the low striking price could exercise whenever the owner of the other call did and would always have a lower cost of doing so. Two important restrictions of this type are Stoll's (1969) put–call parity relation and the proof that a call option on stock which pays no dividend should not be exercised prior to maturity.

The put–call parity relation holds for European puts and calls on stocks not paying dividends. It is

$$P(S, \tau) + S = C(S, \tau) + X/(1 + r)^\tau. \tag{1}$$

To prove this relation consider two portfolios. The first holds one share of stock and a put. The second holds a call and a zero coupon bond with a face value of X maturing on the options' expiration date. If the stock price is S_T at the expiration of the option, then the first portfolio is worth $\text{Max}(X - S_T, 0) + S_T = \text{Max}(S_T, X)$. The second is worth $\text{Max}(S_T - X, 0) + X = \text{Max}(S_T, X)$. These values are the same, and neither portfolio makes any interim disbursements. Therefore, absence of arbitrage implies that the current value of the two portfolios must be equal. Equation (1) expresses the equality of these two portfolios' current values. One importance of this relation is that once either the put or call pricing problem has been solved, the answer to the other is also known.

To prove the optimality of holding a call option until maturity consider the following two portfolios. The first holds just one share of stock. The second holds the call and a zero coupon bond with a face value of X. At expiration, the first portfolio is worth S_T. The second is worth $\text{Max}(S_T, X)$. As the former value is never larger, the current value of the first portfolio cannot be greater than that of the second, or

$$C(S, \tau) \geqslant S - X/(1 + r^\tau) > S - X. \tag{2}$$

This proves that an option is worth more alive than when exercised. An investor who no longer wishes to hold a call could realize more by selling the option than exercising it.

These two relations do not exhaust the general statements that can be made about option prices. Other propositions, also depending only on the absence of arbitrage, have been proved by Merton (1973) and Cox and Ross (1976b). To go beyond general propositions of this type and derive a precise value for an option, further assumptions must be made.

There were many attempts at a consistent and self-contained model of option valuation. All of these models made assumptions about the distribution of the stock's return (a lognormal distribution was the usual choice) and the absence of market frictions such as taxes, transactions costs and short sales constraints. Most of the models included unspecified parameters which had to be measured to use the formulae.

This area of research was revolutionized with the 1973 publication of the Black–Scholes option pricing model deriving a formula depending on only five directly observable variables, the stock's price (S), the exercise price (X), the time to maturity (τ), the risk-free rate of interest (r), and the variance of changes in the logarithm of the stock price (σ^2).

OPTION MODELS PRIOR TO BLACK–SCHOLES. Option pricing theory did not begin with the Black–Scholes model. Many economists had tackled this problem previously. While some of the attempts are flawed by current standards, later developments almost certainly would not have come about without the earlier works. There is room here only to highlight some of the more important steps leading to the Black–Scholes model.

The earliest model of option pricing was probably developed by Louis Bachelier (1900). In examining stock price fluctuations he was led to some aspects of the mathematical theory of Brownian motion five years prior to Einstein's classic paper of 1905. Postulating an absolute Brownian motion without drift and with a variance of σ^2 per unit time for the stock price process, he determined that the expected value of the call option at maturity should be

$$C = S \cdot \Phi\left(\frac{S - X}{\sigma\sqrt{\tau}}\right) - X \cdot \Phi\left(\frac{S - X}{\sigma\sqrt{\tau}}\right) + \sigma\sqrt{\tau} \cdot \phi\left(\frac{S - X}{\sigma\sqrt{\tau}}\right) \tag{3}$$

where $\Phi(\cdot)$ and $\phi(\cdot)$ are the standard cumulative normal and normal density functions. In keeping with an assumption of a zero expected price change for the stock, he did not discount this expectation to find a present value. This model was rediscovered more than fifty years later by Kruizenga (1956).

By contemporary standards this model must have been very advanced. The model is only lacking in two primary areas. The use of absolute Brownian motion allows the stock price to become negative – a condition at odds with the assumption of limited liability. The assumption of a mean expected price change of zero ignores a positive time value for money, the different risk characteristics of options and the underlying stock, and risk aversion. Despite these shortcomings, the formula is actually quite good at predicting the prices of short-term calls. It fails at long maturities, however, by requiring the option price to grow proportionally to the square root of maturity.

Most of the developments in option pricing for the next half century or more were *ad hoc* econometric models. Typical of this type is the model of Kassouf (1969) who estimated call prices with the formula

$$C = X([(S/X)^\gamma + 1]^{1/\gamma} - 1], \qquad 1 \leqslant \gamma < \infty. \tag{4}$$

This formula does bound the call price above by the stock price and below by its intrinsic value, $\text{Max}(S - X, 0)$. It also gives correct maturity values for calls when the parameter γ is set to ∞. Kassouf fit his model by estimating the parameter γ using time to maturity, dividend yield and other variables.

Major new developments in option pricing began in the 1960s. Sprenkle (1961) assumed a lognormal distribution for the stock price with a constant mean and variance (although not specifically a diffusion) and allowed for a positive drift in the stock's price. His equation for a call value can be written as

$$C = e^{\alpha\tau} S \cdot \Phi\left[\frac{\ln(S/X) + (\alpha + \frac{1}{2}\sigma^2)\tau}{\sigma\sqrt{\tau}}\right] - (1 - \pi)X \cdot \Phi\left[\frac{\ln(S/X) + (\alpha - \frac{1}{2}\sigma^2)\tau}{\sigma\sqrt{\tau}}\right].$$

$$\tag{5}$$

The parameter π was an adjustment for the market 'price for leverage'. Sprenkle did not discount this expectation to determine the option value. (Note that if π is set to zero, (5) gives the expected terminal value for the option.)

Boness's (1964) model was very similar. He also assumed a stationary lognormal distribution for stock returns, and recognized the importance of risk premiums. For tractability he assumed that '[i]nvestors are indifferent to risk'. He used this last assumption to justify discounting the expected final option value by α, the expected rate of return on the stock. His final model was

$$C = S \cdot \Phi\left[\frac{\ln(S/X) + (\alpha + \frac{1}{2}\sigma^2)\tau}{\sigma\sqrt{\tau}}\right] - e^{-\alpha\tau}X \cdot \Phi\left[\frac{\ln(S/X) + (\alpha - \frac{1}{2}\sigma^2)\tau}{\sigma\sqrt{\tau}}\right]. \tag{6}$$

This equation is identical in form to the Black–Scholes formula described below. Its only difference is its use of α, the expected rate of return on the stock, rather than the risk-free rate of interest. If Boness had carried his assumption that investors are indifferent to risk to its logical conclusion that $\alpha = r$, he would have derived the Black–Scholes equation. Of course, his derivation would still have been based on the *assumption* of risk neutrality.

Samuelson (1965) recognized that the expected rates of return on the option and stock would generally be different due to their different risk characteristics. He posited a higher (constant) expected rate of return for the option, β, although recognizing that a 'deeper theory would deduce the value of [the expected rate of return]'. He also realized that this assumption would mean that it might be optimal to exercise a call option prior to its maturity but was unable to solve for the optimal exercise policy except in the case of perpetual calls. His model for a European call was

$$ C = e^{(\alpha - \beta)\tau} S \cdot \Phi \left[\frac{\ln(S/X) + (\alpha + \frac{1}{2}\sigma^2)\tau}{\sigma\sqrt{\tau}} \right] - e^{-\beta\tau} X \cdot \Phi \left[\frac{\ln(S/X) + (\alpha - \frac{1}{2}\sigma^2)\tau}{\sigma\sqrt{\tau}} \right]. $$

(7)

Boness's equation above is a special case of this model for $\alpha = \beta$.

Samuelson and Merton (1969) examined option pricing in a simple equilibrium model of portfolio choice that allowed them to determine the stock's and option's expected rates of return endogenously. They verified that the option problem could be stated in 'utili-probability' terms in a function form identical to the problem statement in terms of the true probabilities. When stated in this fashion, the adjusted expected rates of return on the stock and option were the same. This approach anticipated the development of the risk-neutral or preference-free method of valuing options that is now accepted as a matter of course.

THE BLACK–SCHOLES OPTION PRICING MODEL. The Black–Scholes option pricing model is based on the principle that there should be no arbitrage opportunities available in the market. The following simple model, due to Cox, Ross and Rubinstein (1979), can be used to illustrate the principle behind the Black–Scholes model.

Assume that over a single period the stock price can change in only one of two ways. From its current level S, the stock price can increase to hS or fall to kS. Let $C(S, n)$ denote the value of a call option on the stock when the stock price is S and there are n of these 'steps' remaining before the option matures.

Consider a portfolio that is short one call option and long N shares of stock. This portfolio is currently worth $NS - C(S, n)$. After one period this portfolio will be worth either $NhS - C(hS, n-1)$ or $NkS - C(kS, n-1)$. Suppose N is chosen so that these last two quantities are equal; i.e.,

$$ N = \frac{C(hS, n-1) - C(kS, n-1)}{(h-k)S} $$

(8)

then after one period the portfolio will be worth

$$ \frac{kC(hS, n-1) - hC(kS, n-1)}{(h-k)} $$

(9)

with certainty. To avoid an arbitrage opportunity the current value of the portfolio must be equal to this value discounted at $(1 + R)$ where R is the risk-free rate of interest (not annualized) over the time of a single step in the stock price. That is,

$$C(S, n) = \frac{1}{1 + R}\left[\frac{1 + R - k}{h - k}C(hS, n - 1) + \frac{h - 1 - R}{h - k}C(kS, n - 1)\right]. \quad (10)$$

This equation relates the value of a n step call option to the value of a $n - 1$ step call. At the time it matures, the value of a call with an exercise price of X is $C(S, 0) = \text{Max}(S - X, 0)$. As this functional form is known, (10) can be used to derive the value of a one-period call for different stock prices. Given these values, (10) can be used again to derive the value of a two-period call. The value of any call can be computed by using (10) recursively.

The resulting formula for a n step call is

$$C(S, n) = (1 + R)^{-n}\sum_{i=I}^{n}\frac{n!}{i!(n - i)!}q^i(1 - q)^{n-i}(Sh^ik^{n-i} - X) \quad (11)$$

where $q \equiv (1 + R - k)/(h - k)$ and I is the smallest integer for which $Sh^ik^{n-i} \geqslant X$.

The fraction and the next two terms involving q in the summation can be recognized as the probability of i successes in n trials with a success probability of q from a binomial distribution. Thus the formula in (11) can be rewritten as

$$C(S, n) = (1 + R)^{-n}E^*[\text{Max}(S_n - X, 0)] \quad (12)$$

where S_n is the random stock price after n steps and $E^*[\cdot]$ denotes the expectation using the artificial probabilities q and $1 - q$ for the up and down steps. Similarly equation (10) can be expressed as

$$C(S, n) = \frac{1}{1 + R}[qC(hS, n - 1) + (1 - q)C(kS, n - 1)]$$

$$= \frac{1}{1 + R}E^*[C(S, n - 1)]. \quad (13)$$

Again an 'artificial' expectation has been taken. It should be noted that q is not the actual probability that the stock price will change from S to hS – in fact this true probability has not been used here at all.

In deriving their model Black and Scholes did not assume that the stock price followed this binomial step process. They used instead a geometric or lognormal Brownian motion process. Geometric Brownian motion can be constructed as the limit of this type of binomial process as the step sizes $h - 1$ and $k - 1$ shrink to zero while the number of steps per unit time goes to infinity.

Taking these limits in (10) gives the Black–Scholes partial differential equation

$$\tfrac{1}{2}\sigma^2S^2C_{SS} + rSC_S - rC + C_t = 0 \quad (14)$$

where r is the continuously-compounded (annualized) rate of interest on a risk-free asset, σ^2 is the variance of changes in the logarithm of the stock price per unit time and subscripts on C denote partial differentiation. Applying the limits to (11) yields the Black–Scholes call option pricing formula

$$C(S,\tau) = S \cdot \Phi\left[\frac{\ln(S/X) + (r + \frac{1}{2}\sigma^2)\tau}{\sigma\sqrt{\tau}}\right] - e^{-r\tau}X \cdot \Phi\left[\frac{\ln(S/X) - (r + \frac{1}{2}\sigma^2)\tau}{\sigma\sqrt{\tau}}\right]$$

(15)

where $\Phi(\cdot)$ is the standard cumulative normal distribution function and $\tau \equiv T - t$ is the time until maturity. (Black and Scholes derived this differential equation and its solution working directly with the continuous time diffusion and not by taking limits.)

The Black–Scholes formula is identical to Samuelson's with $\alpha = \beta = r$ and to Boness's with $\alpha = r$. In fact the most remarkable feature about the model is that the resulting formula does not depend on the stock's or the option's expected rates of return or any measure of the market's risk aversion. Only five variables determine the option's price: S, τ, r, X and σ^2. Except for the variance, each of these variables is known, and the variance can be measured with a high degree of certainty.

The absence of the expected rates of return or any measure of risk aversion from the Black–Scholes model was at first troubling. This puzzle was explained by Cox and Ross (1976a) and Merton (1976) who introduced the risk neutral or martingale representation. This idea was later developed more formally by Harrison and Kreps (1979) and others.

The fact that a hedging argument can be used to derive (10), which does not include explicitly expected rates of return, investor preferences, or probabilities means that given the stock price and the interest rate, the value of the option can not depend *directly* on these either. To solve for the option price, then, we need only find the equilibrium solution in some world where returns, preferences and probabilities are consistent with the actual stock price process and interest rate. The solution obtained will then be generally applicable.

The most convenient choice of equilibrium is often an economy with risk neutral investors. In such an economy all expected rates of return must be equal to the risk-free rate. If the stock price has a lognormal distribution, then Boness's model applies with $\alpha = r$.

In the risk neutral economy the Black–Scholes formula has an interpretation identical to that in (12). The cumulative normal in the second term in (14) is the risk neutral 'probability' that the option will mature in-the-money. Thus, the second term is the discount factor multiplied by the 'expected' exercise payment. The first term is the discounted value of the expectation of the stock's price at expiration conditional on $S_T > X$.

EXTENSIONS OF THE BLACK–SCHOLES MODEL. The derivation of the Black–Scholes model rests on six assumptions: (i) There are no transactions costs, taxes or restrictions on short sales. (ii) The risk-free rate of interest is constant. (iii) The stock pays no dividends. (iv) The stock price evolution is geometric Brownian motion. (v) The market is open continuously for trading. (vi) The option is European.

Subsequent modifications of the basic model have shown that it is quite robust with respect to relaxations of these assumptions. Thorpe (1973) examined the short sale constraint. Leland (1985) allowed for transactions costs. Ingersoll (1976) and Scholes (1976) considered the effects of differing tax rates on capital gains and dividends. Merton (1973) generalized the model to allow for dividends and a stochastic interest rate. He also proved that assumption (vi) was not necessary if the stock did not pay dividends. Cox and Ross (1976a) and Merton (1973) utilized alternative stochastic processes. Cox and Ross (1976a) and Merton (1976) considered the option problem when the stock's price evolution did not have a continuous sample path. Rubinstein (1976) and Brennan (1979) obtained the Black–Scholes solution with discrete-time trading by imposing conditions on the utility function of the representative investor.

Other types of options have also been valued using the same methods or extensions of them. Some examples are European puts by Black and Scholes (1973), 'down-and-out' options by Merton (1973), commodity options by Black (1976) and interest rate options by Cox, Ingersoll and Ross (1985b). To solve these or similar problems, the Black–Scholes partial differential equation (14) is used.

While (10) and, therefore, (14) were developed to price call options, the characteristics of the call are captured entirely by the condition at maturity $C(S, 0) = \text{Max}(S - X, 0)$. Thus, this equation is a general one that can be used to price calls, puts, or any other derivative asset whose value depends on just the price of the primitive asset.

To solve this equation for other problems the appropriate boundary condition is required

$$C(S, T) = H(S). \tag{16}$$

$H(\cdot)$ specifies a contractual or otherwise known payment at the derivative asset's maturity. If the derivative asset's value arises solely from this payment at maturity, then the formal solution to (14) with boundary condition (16) is

$$C(S, t) = e^{-r(T-t)} E^*[H(S)]. \tag{17}$$

For some contracts a portion or all of the value may be due to payments that are received at random times prior to maturity. In this case (17) does not measure the full value. For example, a down-and-out option is a call contract that is cancelled if and when the stock price falls below the 'knock-out' price. At this point a partial rebate is usually given. Let K and R denote the knock-out price and rebate. Then the conditions imposed to value this option are

$$C(K, u) = R \qquad \forall u < T$$

$$C(S, T) = \text{Max}(S - X, 0) \qquad \text{if} \quad S(u) > K \quad \text{for} \quad t < u < T. \tag{18}$$

The value of the down-and-out option is

$$C(S, t) = R E^*[e^{-r(U-t)} I(U \leqslant T)] + e^{-r(T-t)} E^*[\text{Max}(S_T - X, 0) I(U > T)]. \tag{19}$$

Here U is a random variable that takes on the value u if the first time that the stock price drops to K is u. $I(\cdot)$ is an indicator function with the value one if its argument is true and zero otherwise. The first expectation is taken over the random variable U. This term measures the value contributed by the receipt of the rebate. The second expectation is taken over both random variables U and S_T. This term measures the value contributed by the right to exercise if it was not cancelled.

The pricing of the American put has a similar feature. The payment received upon exercise, $X - S$, is known (conditional on the stock price at that time) but its timing is not. In addition, unlike the timing of the rebate in the previous problem, the timing of the exercise is not contractually stated. It is chosen by the put's owner.

Suppose that the put owner chooses a rule for exercising. This rule will generate a random time U at which the option is exercised. The random variable U must be a Markov time; that is, whether or not exercise occurs at a particular time can depend on information known at that time but cannot in any way anticipate the future. For a given rule U, the put's value is

$$E^*[e^{-r(U-t)}(X - S_U)]. \tag{20}$$

As the owner of the put has the choice, the rule chosen will be that which maximizes the value of the option

$$P(S, t) = \sup_U E^*[e^{-r(U-t)}(X - S_U)]. \tag{21}$$

In principle the American put could be valued by solving (20) for all exercise rules and choosing that one which maximized the value. Samuelson (1965) conjectured and Merton (1973) proved that in such problems the value and the optimal exercise rule could be determined simultaneously by imposing the 'high contact' condition.

The partial differential equation (14) is solved subject to the maturity condition $P(S, T) = \text{Max}(X - S, 0)$ and

$$P[K(t), t] = X - K(t) \tag{22a}$$

$$\left. \frac{\partial P(S, t)}{\partial S} \right|_{S = K(t)} = -1. \tag{22b}$$

$K(t)$ denotes the optimal exercise policy; that is if the stock price falls to $K(t)$ at time t, then the put is exercised. Equation (22a) is the standard condition at exercise. Equation (22b) is the high contact condition.

The high contact requirement assures that for the optimal policy the slope of the pricing function, $P(\cdot)$ is equal to the slope of the payoff function (-1 in the relevant region of exercise). This is just the usual tangency condition at an optimum.

No analytical solution to the American put problem has yet been derived. Brennan and Schwartz (1977), Parkinson (1977) and others have described numerical techniques for these problems and other contracts for which there are no analytical solutions.

APPLICATIONS OF OPTION PRICING TO VALUING CORPORATE SECURITIES. After deriving their call option formula Black and Scholes make an observation that may be one of the most important in the field of finance. They argue that the same methods can be used to value other contingent claims, in particular the components of a firm's capital structure. This observation has led to an enormous amount of research. Option pricing techniques have been applied to a wide variety of financial instruments and contracts including corporate bonds, futures, variable rate mortgages, insurance, investment timing advice and the tax code.

For the simplest problems the call formula can be applied directly. Consider a firm with assets whose value, V, evolves according to a geometric Brownian process. The firm's capital structure consists of common stock and single issue of zero coupon bonds with an aggregate face value of B which mature at time T. At that time the firm will be liquidated.

If $V_T \geqslant B$, then the bondholders can be paid and the equity will be worth $V_T - B$. If $V_T < B$, the assets will be insufficient to pay the bondholders, and there will be nothing left for the shareholders. Thus, the payoff to the common shares is $\text{Max}(V_T - B, 0)$. This is just like a call option, so currently the equity must be worth $C(V, T - t; B)$. By the Modigliani–Miller irrelevancy theorem, the value of the debt and equity must sum to V so the debt is worth

$$D(V, T - t; B) = V - C(V, T - t; B). \tag{23}$$

This same valuation applies even if the firm is not to be liquidated. To repay the bondholders, the firm must raise B dollars. Selling assets to do this is the same as a liquidation. The only other way to raise this money is by a new offering of securities. To raise B dollars the firm will have to offer a security that is worth B. If the firm's assets are not worth at least B, this cannot be done. If they are, then again by the Modigliani–Miller theorem the original equity will be worth $V_T - B$.

A zero coupon convertible bond can be priced similarly. Suppose there are N common shares outstanding and the convertibles can be exchanged for n shares in aggregate. If all the bondholders convert, then they will own the fraction $\gamma \equiv n/(N + n)$ of the equity. Clearly the bondholders will convert if $\gamma V_T > B$. Otherwise they will receive B, unless the firm is insolvent, in which case they will get just V_T. Thus, the bondholders will receive

$$\text{Max}[\gamma V, \text{Min}(V, B)] = \text{Max}(\gamma V - B, 0) + [V - \text{Max}(V - B, 0)]. \tag{24}$$

This is the payoff to an option plus an ordinary zero coupon bond so the convertible's value must be $C(\gamma V, T - t; B) + D(V, T - t; B)$. If the convertible is also callable, as most are, then methods used to determine the optimal exercise policy for and the value of an American put must be used. This problem has been solved by Ingersoll (1977).

Most corporate securities received periodic coupons or dividends. While a

209

default-free coupon bond can be valued as a portfolio of zero coupon bonds, this method will not work when there is default risk because the omission of one coupon puts the whole bond in default. These securities can be priced as a series of options, however.

Consider a company with common stock on which it is not paying dividends and a single issue of coupon bonds with aggregate periodic coupons of c, at times $T_1, \ldots, T_n$, and an aggregate par value of B, repaid at T_n. Once the next to last coupon is paid only a single payment remains, $B + c$. Therefore, just after the next to last payment the bond can be treated like a zero coupon bond. Its value at that time is

$$D_{n-1}(V, T_{n-1}) = D(V, T_n - T_{n-1}; B + c).$$

Between times T_{n-2} and T_{n-1} the company makes no payments to the holders of its securities so the standard Black–Scholes equation (14) applies. The solution for the bond's value at time T_{n-2} is

$$D_{n-2}(V, T_{n-2}) = e^{-r(T_{n-1} - T_{n-2})} E^* [D(V_{T_{n-1}}, T_{n-1})] \tag{25}$$

as given in (17). The price at earlier times can be determined by a recursive application of (25). Geske (1977) addresses this compound option problem.

Another way to price claims with coupons or dividends is to approximate the sequence of payments as continuous flows. The general problem is to value a particular claim, $F(S, t)$, when the price evolution of the firm's value is

$$dV = [\alpha V - \Delta(V, t)] \, dt + \sigma V \, d\omega. \tag{26}$$

$\Delta(V, t)$ is the total flow of all disbursements (dividends, coupons, etc.) paid by the firm and $d\omega$ is the increment to a Wiener process.

The equilibrium price process for the claim is

$$dF(V, t) = [\beta(V, t) F - \delta(V, t)] \, dt + (F_v/F) \sigma V \, d\omega \tag{27}$$

where $\beta(\cdot)$ is the (endogenous) expected rate of return on the derivative asset and $\delta(\cdot)$ is the portion of the total disbursement received by the owners of the derivative asset.

Itô's Lemma is used to determine the expected rate of price appreciation which is equated to the rate of capital gains required in equilibrium to earn β.

$$\tfrac{1}{2}\sigma^2 V^2 F_{VV} + [\alpha V - \Delta(V, t)] F_V + F_t = \beta(V, t) F(V, t) - \delta(V, t). \tag{28}$$

The equivalent risk neutral processes replace α and β by r, the risk-free rate. Thus, the general valuation equation is

$$\tfrac{1}{2}\sigma^2 V^2 F_{VV} + [rV - \Delta(V, t)] F_V - rF + F_t - \delta(V, t) = 0. \tag{29}$$

Equation (29) is the fundamental valuation equation for the financial claims against a firm. It can be used for any situation when the standard Black–Scholes conditions hold and the value of the claim to be priced depends solely on time and the value of assets of the firm. The basic requirement for this second condition is that there be no other sources of uncertainty beyond that affecting the value of the assets. Thus, the interest rate cannot be stochastic, the dividend policy must be a known function of the firm value and time, and the firm cannot alter its investment or financing policies in unanticipated ways.

If this second requirement is not met, then the value of the claim being priced will depend on other variables as well – variables that measure the overall state of the economy. Cox, Ingersoll and Ross (1985a) have developed a theoretical context in which all these pricing problems can be handled. The basic Black–Scholes method is still valid, but the pricing equation will include these additional state variables.

OTHER APPLICATIONS OF OPTION PRICING. In recent years option pricing techniques have been used in a great variety of situations. PBGC insurance and the effects of ERISA on corporate pension plans have been considered as have FDIC insurance and the implicit insurance in government loan guarantees. The asymmetries of the tax code and their effects on corporations and investors have been analysed. Option pricing methods have been used to value market timing advice and to examine the efficiency of dynamic portfolio strategies such as contingent immunization. More on the applications of option pricing and extensive bibliographies can be found in the survey articles by Mason and Merton (1985) and Smith (1976) and in the texts by Cox and Rubinstein (1985) and Ingersoll (1987).

It should be clear that the realm of applications goes far beyond the more obvious corporate securities. A bibliography of the published papers alone would be extensive, and working papers are continually added. Option pricing theory has become an important element in our understanding of financial contracting and a practical tool in widespread applications.

BIBLIOGRAPHY

Bachelier, L. 1900. Théorie de la spéculation. *Annales de l' Ecole Normale Superieure*, Trans. by A.J. Boness in *The Random Character of Stock Market Prices*, ed. P.H. Cootner, Cambridge, Mass.: MIT Press, 1967.

Black, F. 1976. The pricing of commodity contracts. *Journal of Financial Economics* 3(1–2), January–March, 167–79.

Black, F. and Scholes, M.J. 1973. The pricing of options and corporate liabilities. *Journal of Political Economy* 81(3), May, 637–54.

Boness, A.J. 1964. Elements of a theory of stock option value. *Journal of Political Economy* 72(2), April, 163–75.

Brennan, M.J. 1979. The pricing of contingent claims in discrete time models. *Journal of Finance* 34(1), March, 53–68.

Brennan, M.J. and Schwartz, E.S. 1977. The valuation of American put options. *Journal of Finance* 32(2), May, 449–62.

Cox, J.C., Ingersoll, J.E. and Ross, S.A. 1985a. An intertemporal general equilibrium model of asset prices. *Econometrica* 53(2), March, 363–84.

Cox, J.C., Ingersoll, J.E. and Ross, S.A. 1985b. A theory of the term structure of interest rates. *Econometrica* 53(2), March, 385–407.

Cox, J.C. and Ross, S.A. 1976a. The valuation of options for alternative stochastic processes. *Journal of Financial Economics* 3(1–2), January–March, 145–66.

211

Cox, J.C. and Ross, S.A. 1976b. A survey of some new results in financial option pricing policy. *Journal of Finance* 31(2), May, 383–402.

Cox, J.C., Ross, S.A. and Rubinstein, M. 1979. Option pricing: a simplified approach. *Journal of Financial Economics* 7(3), September, 229–63.

Cox, J.C. and Rubinstein, M. 1985. *Options Markets.* Englewood Cliffs, NJ: Prentice-Hall.

Geske, R. 1977. The valuation of corporate liabilities as compound options. *Journal of Financial and Quantitative Analysis* 12(4), November, 541–52.

Harrison, J.M. and Kreps, D. 1979. Martingales and arbitrage in multiperiod securities markets. *Journal of Economic Theory* 20(3), June, 381–408.

Ingersoll, J.E. 1976. A theoretical and empirical investigation of the dual purpose funds: an application of contingent-claims analysis. *Journal of Financial Economics* 3(1–2), January–March, 83–123.

Ingersoll, J.E. 1977. A contingent-claims valuation of convertible securities. *Journal of Financial Economics* 4(3), May, 289–322.

Ingersoll, J.E. 1987. *Theory of Financial Decision Making.* Totowa, NJ: Rowman and Littlefield.

Kassouf, S.T. 1969. An econometric model for option price with implications for investors' expectations and audacity. *Econometrica* 37(4), October, 685–94.

Leland, H.E. 1985. Option pricing and replication with transactions costs. *Journal of Finance* 40(5), December, 1283–301.

Mason, S.P. and Merton, R.C. 1985. The role of contingent claims analysis in corporate finance. In *Recent Advances in Corporate Finance*, ed. E.I. Altman and M.G. Subramanyam, Homewood, Ill.: Richard D. Irwin.

Merton, R.C. 1973. The theory of rational option pricing. *Bell Journal of Economics and Management Science* 4, Spring, 141–83.

Merton, R.C. 1976. Option pricing when underlying stock returns are discontinuous. *Journal of Financial Economics* 3(1–2), January–March, 125–44.

Parkinson, M. 1977. Option pricing: the American put. *Journal of Business* 50(1), January, 21–36.

Rubinstein, M. 1976. The valuation of uncertain income streams and the pricing of options. *Bell Journal of Economics and Management Science* 7(2), Autumn, 407–25.

Samuelson, P.A. 1965. Rational theory of warrant pricing. *Industrial Management Review* 6(2), Spring, 13–32.

Samuelson, P.A. and Merton, R.C. 1969. A complete model of warrant pricing that maximizes utility. *Industrial Management Review* 10, Winter, 17–46.

Scholes, M.J. 1976. Taxes and the pricing of options. *Journal of Finance* 31(2), May, 319–32.

Smith, C.W. 1976. Option pricing: a review. *Journal of Financial Economics* 3(1–2), January–March, 3–51.

Sprenkle, C.M. 1961. Warrant prices as indicators of expectations and preferences. *Yale Economic Essays* 1(2), 178–231. Reprinted in *The Random Character of Stock Market Prices*, ed. P.H. Cootner, Cambridge, Mass.: MIT Press, 1967.

Stoll, H.R. 1969. The relationship between put and call option prices. *Journal of Finance* 24(5), December, 801–24.

Thorpe, E.O. 1973. Extensions of the Black–Scholes option model. *Bulletin of the International Statistical Institute, Proceedings of the 39th Session*, 522–9.

Options

ROBERT C. MERTON

A 'European-type call (put) option' is a security that gives its owner the right to buy (sell) a specified quantity of a financial or real asset at a specified price, the 'exercise price', on a specified date, the 'expiration date'. An American-type option provides that its owner can exercise the option on or before the expiration date. If an option is not exercised on or before the expiration date, it expires and becomes worthless.

Options and forward or futures contracts are fundamentally different securities. Both provide for the purchase (or sale) of the underlying asset at a future date. A long position in a forward contract obliges its holder to make an unconditional purchase of the asset at the forward price. In contrast, the holder of a call option can choose whether or not to purchase the asset at the exercise price. Thus, a forward contract can have a negative value whereas an option contract never can.

The first organized market for trading options was the Chicago Board Options Exchange (CBOE) which began trading options on common stocks in 1973. The initial success of the CBOE was followed by an expansion in markets to include options on fixed-income securities, currencies, stock and bond indices and a variety of commodities. Although these markets represent an increasingly large component of total financial market trading, options are still relatively specialized financial securities. Option pricing theory has, nevertheless, become one of the cornerstones of financial economic theory.

This central role for options analysis derives from the fact that option-like structures pervade virtually every part of the field. Black and Scholes (1973) provide an early example: shares of stock in a firm financed in part by debt have a payoff structure which is equivalent to a call option on the firm's assets where the exercise price is the face value of the debt and the expiration date is the maturity date of the debt. Option pricing theory can thus be used to price levered equity and, therefore, corporate debt with default risk.

Identification of similar isomorphic relations between options and other

213

financial instruments has led to pricing models for seniority, call provisions and sinking fund arrangements on debt; bonds convertible into stock, commodities, or different currencies; floor and ceiling arrangements on interest rates, stock and debt warrants; rights and stand-by agreements. In short, option pricing theory provides a unified theory for the pricing of corporate liabilities.

The option-pricing methodology has been applied to the evaluation of noncorporate financial arrangements including government loan guarantees, pension fund insurance and deposit insurance. It has also been used to evaluate a variety of employee compensation packages including stock options, guaranteed wage floors, and even tenure for university faculty.

Perhaps the most significant among the more recent extensions of option analysis, is its application in the evaluation of operating or 'real' options in the critical budgeting decision problem. For example, a production facility which can use various inputs and produce various outputs provides the firm with operating options that it would not have a specialized facility which uses a fixed set of inputs and produces a single type of output. Option-pricing theory provides the means of valuing these production options for comparison with the larger initial cost or lower operating efficiency of the more flexible facility. Similarly, the choice among technologies with various mixes of fixed and variable costs can be treated as evaluating the various options to change production levels, including abandonment of the project. Research and development projects can be evaluated by viewing them as options to enter new markets, expand market share or reduce production costs.

As these examples suggest, option analysis is especially well suited to the task of evaluating the 'flexibility' components of projects. These, corporate strategists often claim, are precisely the components whose values are not properly measured by traditional capital-budgeting techniques. Hence, the option-pricing theory holds forth the promise of providing quantitative assessments for capital budgeting projects that heretofore were largely evaluated qualitatively. Survey articles by Smith (1976) and Mason and Merton (1985) provide detailed discussions of these developments in option analysis along with extensive bibliographies.

The lineage of modern option pricing theory began in 1900 with the Sorbonne thesis, 'Theory of Speculation', by the French mathematician Louis Bachelier. The work is rather remarkable because, in analysing the problem of option pricing, Bachelier derives much of the mathematics of probability diffusions; this, five years before Einstein's famous discovery of the theory of Brownian motion. Although, from today's perspective, the economics and mathematics of Bachelier's work are flawed, the connection of his research with the subsequent path of attempts to describe an equilibrium theory of option pricing is unmistakable. It was now, however, until nearly 75 years later with the publication of the seminal Black and Scholes article (1973), that the field reached a sense of closure on the subject and the explosion in research on option pricing applications began.

As with Bachelier and later researchers, Black and Scholes assume that the dynamics for the price of the asset underlying the option can be described by a diffusion process with a continuous sample path. The breakthrough nature of the Black–Scholes analysis derives from their fundamental insight that a dynamic trading strategy in the underlying asset and a default-free bond can be used to hedge against the risk of either a long or short position in the option. Having derived such a strategy, Black and Scholes determine the equilibrium option price from the equilibrium condition that portfolios with no risk must have the same return as a default-free bond. Using the mathematics of Itô stochastic integrals, Merton (1973, 1977) formally proves that with the continuous trading, the Black–Scholes dynamic portfolio will hedge all the risk of an option position held until exercise or expiration, and therefore, that the Black–Scholes option price is necessary to rule out arbitrage.

Along the lines of the derivation for general contingent claims pricing in Merton (1977), a sketch of the arbitrage proof for the Black–Scholes price of a European call option on a nondividend-paying stock in a constant interest rate environment is as follows:

Assume that the dynamics of the stock price, $V(t)$, can be described by a diffusion process with a stochastic differential equation representation given by:

$$dV = \alpha V \, dt + \sigma V \, dz \tag{1}$$

where α is the instantaneous expected rate of return on the stock; σ^2 is the instantaneous variance per unit time of the return, which is a function of V and t; and dz is a standard Wiener process. Let $F[V, t]$ satisfy the linear partial differential equation:

$$0 = \tfrac{1}{2}\sigma^2 V^2 F_{11} + rV F_1 - rF + F_2 \tag{2}$$

where subscripts denote the partial derivatives and r is the interest rate. Let F be such that it satisfies the boundary conditions:

$$F/V \leqslant 1; \qquad F(0, t) = 0; \qquad F[V, T] = \max[0, V - E]. \tag{3}$$

Note from (3) that the value of F on these boundaries are identical to the payoff structure on a European call option with exercise price E and expiration date T. From standard mathematics, the solution to (2) and (3) exists and is unique.

Consider the continuous-time portfolio strategy which allocates the fraction $w(t) \equiv F_1[V, t]V(t)/P(t)$ to the stock and $1 - w(t)$ to the bond, where $P(t)$ is the value of the portfolio at time t. Other than the initial investment in the portfolio, $P(0)$, there are no contributions or withdrawals from the portfolio until it is liquidated at $t = T$.

The prescription for the portfolio strategy for each time t depends only on the first derivative of the solution to (2)–(3) and the current values of the stock and the portfolio. It follows from the prescribed allocation $w(t)$ that the dynamics for the value of the portfolio can be written as:

$$dP = w(t)P \, dV/V + [1 - w(t)]rP \, dt = F_1 \, dV + r[P - F_1 V]dt. \tag{4}$$

As a solution to (2), F is twice-continuously differentiable. Hence, we can use Itô's Lemma to express the stochastic process for F as:

$$dF = [\tfrac{1}{2}\sigma^2 V^2 F_{11} + \alpha V F_1 + F_2]dt + F_1 \sigma V \, dz \tag{5}$$

where F is evaluated at $V = V(t)$ at each point in time t. But, F satisfies (2). Hence, we can rewrite (5) as:

$$dF = F_1 \, dV + r[F - F_1 V]dt. \tag{6}$$

Define $Q(t)$ to be the difference between the value of the portfolio and the value of the function $F[V, t]$ evaluated at $V = V(t)$. From (4) to (6), we have that $dQ = rQ \, dt$, which is a nonstochastic differential equation with solution $Q(t) = Q(0)\exp[rt]$ and $Q(0) = P(0) - F[V(0), 0]$. Hence, if the initial investment in the portfolio is chosen so that $P(0) = F[V(0), 0]$, then $Q(t) \equiv 0$, and $P(t) = F[V(t), t]$ for all t.

Thus, we have constructed a dynamic portfolio strategy in the stock and a default-free bond that exactly replicates the payoff structure of a call option on the stock. The solution of (2) and (3) for F and its first derivative F_1 provides the 'blueprint' for that construction. The standard no-arbitrage condition for equilibrium prices holds that two securities with identical payoff structures must have the same price. It follows, therefore, that the equilibrium price of the call option at time t must equal the Black–Scholes price, $F[V(t), t]$.

The extraordinary impact of the Black–Scholes analysis on financial economic research and practice can in large part be explained by three critical elements: (1) the relatively weak assumptions for its valid applications; (2) the variables and parameters required as inputs are either directly observable or relatively easy to estimate, and there is computational ease in solving for the price; (3) the generality of the methodology in adapting it to the pricing of other options and option-like securities.

Although framed in an arbitrage type of analysis, the derivation does not depend on the existence of an option on the stock. Hence, the Black–Scholes trading strategy and price function provide the means and the cost for an investor to create synthetically an option when such an option is not available as a traded security. The findings that the equilibrium option price is a twice continuously-differentiable function of the stock price and that its dynamics follow an Itô process are derived results, not assumptions.

The striking feature of (2) and (3) is not the variables and parameters that are needed for determining the option price but, rather, those not needed. Specifically, determination of the option price and the replicating portfolio strategy does not require estimates of either the expected return on the stock, α, or investor risk preferences and endowments. In contrast to most equilibrium models, the pricing of the option does not depend on price and joint distributional information for all available securities. The only such information required is about the underlying stock and default-free bond. Indeed, the only variable or parameter required in the Black–Scholes pricing function that is not directly observable is the variance rate function, σ^2. This observation has stimulated a considerable research effort on variance-rate estimation in both the academic and practising financial communities.

With some notable exceptions, equations (2) and (3) cannot be solved analytically for a closed-form solution. However, powerful computational methods have been developed to provide high-speed numerical solutions of these equations for both the option price and its first derivative.

As in the original Black and Scholes article, the derivation here focuses on the pricing of a European call option. Their methodology is, however, easily applied to the pricing of other securities with payoff structures contingent on the price of the underlying stock. Consider, for example, the determination of the equilibrium price for a European put option with exercise price E and expiration date T. Suppose that in the original derivation we change the boundary conditions specified for F in (3) so as to match the payoff structure of the put option on these boundaries. That is, we now require that F satisfy $F \leqslant E$; $F[0, t] = E \exp[-r(T - t)]$; $F[V, T] = \max[0, E - V]$. Once F and its derivative are specified, the development of the replicating portfolio proceeds in identical fashion to show that $P(t) = F(V(t), t]$. With the revised boundary conditions, the portfolio payoff structure will match that of the put option at exercise or expiration. Thus, $F[V(t), t]$ is the equilibrium put option price.

As shown in Merton (1977), the same procedure can be used to determine the equilibrium price for a security with a general contingent payoff structure, $G[V(T)]$, by changing the boundary conditions in (3) so that $F[V, T] = G[V]$. A particularly important application of this procedure is in the determination of pure state-contingent prices.

Let $\pi[V, t; E, T]$ denote the solution of (2) subject to the boundary conditions:

$$\pi < \infty; \qquad \pi[0, t; E, T] = 0; \qquad \pi[V, T; E, T] = \delta(E - V)$$

where $\delta(x)$ is the Dirac delta function with the properties that

$$\delta(x) = 0 \text{ for } x \neq 0$$

and $\delta(0)$ is infinite in such a way that

$$\int_a^b \delta(x) dx = 1 \text{ for } a < 0 < b.$$

By inspection of this payoff structure, it is evident that this security is the natural generalization of Arrow–Debreu pure state securities to an environment where there is a continuum of states defined by the price of the stock and time. That is loosely, $\pi[V, t; E, T]dE$ is the price of a security which pays \$1 if $V(T) = E$ at time T and \$0, otherwise.

As is well known from the Green's functions method of solving differential equations, the solution to equation (2) subject to the boundary condition $F[V, T] = G[V]$ can be written as:

$$F[V, t] = \int_0^\infty G[E]\pi[V, t; E, T]dE. \tag{7}$$

Thus, just as with the standard Arrow–Debreu model, once the set of all pure state-contingent prices, $\{\pi\}$, are derived, the equilibrium price of any contingent payoff structure can be determined by mere summation or quadrature.

To underscore the central importance of call option pricing in the general theory of contingent claims pricing, consider a portfolio containing long and short positions in call options with the same expiration date T where each 'unit' contains a long position in an option with exercise price $E - \varepsilon$; a long position in an option with exercise price $E + \varepsilon$; and a short position in two options with exercise price E. If one takes position in $1/\varepsilon^2$ units of this portfolio, the payoff structure at time T with $V(T) = V$ is given by:

$$\{\max[0, V + \varepsilon - E] - 2\max[0, V - E] + \max[0, V - \varepsilon - E]\}/\varepsilon^2. \quad (8)$$

The limit of (8) as $\varepsilon \to 0$ is $\delta(E - V)$ which is the payoff structure to a pure contingent-state security. If $F[V, t; E, T]$ is the solution to (2) and (3), then it follows from (8) that:

$$\pi[V, t; E, T] = \lim_{\varepsilon \to 0} \{F[V, t; E - \varepsilon, T] - 2F[V, t; E, T] + F[V, t; E + \varepsilon, T]\}/\varepsilon^2$$

$$= \frac{\partial^2 F[V, t; E, T]}{\partial E^2} \quad (9)$$

Hence, once the call-option pricing function has been determined, the pure state-contingent prices can be derived from (9).

For further discussion of options, see especially the January/March 1976 issue of the *Journal of Financial Economics*; the October 1978 issue of the *Journal of Business*; and the excellent book by Cox and Rubinstein (1985).

BIBLIOGRAPHY

Bachelier, L. 1900. *Théorie de la speculation*. Paris: Gauthier-Villars, cf. English translation in *The Random Character of Stock Market Prices*, ed. P. Cootner, revised edn, Cambridge, Mass.: MIT Press, 1967. 17–78.

Black, F. and Scholes, M. 1973. The pricing of options and corporate liabilities. *Journal of Political Economy* 81, May–June, 637–59.

Cox, J. and Rubinstein, M. 1985. *Options Markets*. Englewood Cliffs, NJ: Prentice-Hall.

Mason, S. and Merton, R.C. 1985. The role of contingent claims analysis in corporate finance. In *Recent Advances in Corporate Finance*, ed. E.I. Altman and M.G. Subrahmanyan, Homewood, Ill.: Richard D. Irwin, 7–54.

Merton, R.C. 1973. Theory of rational option pricing. *Bell Journal of Economics and Management Science* 4, Spring, 141–83.

Merton, R.C. 1977. On the pricing of contingent claims and the Modigliani–Miller theorem. *Journal of Financial Economics* 5, November, 241–50.

Smith, C.W. 1976. Option pricing: a review. *Journal of Financial Economics* 3(1/2), January–March, 3–51.

Organization Theory

THOMAS MARSCHAK

Since all the social sciences deal with human organizations (families, bureaucracies, tribes, corporations, armies), the term 'organization theory' appears in all of them. What has distinguished the economists' pursuit of organization theory from that of sociologists, of political scientists and of psychologists (say those psychologists working in the field called 'organizational behaviour')? First, the real organizations that have inspired the theorizing of economists are the economy, the market and the firm. Second, economists, with their customary taste for rigour, have sought to define formally and precisely the vague terms used in informal discourse about organizations, in such a way as to capture the users' intent. They have sought to test plausible propositions about organizations – either by proving that they follow from simple, reasonable and precisely stated assumptions, or (rarely) by formulating the propositions as statements about observable variables on which systematic rather than anecdotal data can be collected, and then applying the normal statistical procedures of empirical economics. (Here we shall only consider testing of the first type.) Third, much of the economists' organization theory is not descriptive but normative; it concerns not what is, but what could be. It takes the viewpoint of an organization *designer*. The organization is to respond to a changing and uncertain environment. The designer has to balance the 'benefits' of these responses against the organization's *informational costs*; good responses may be costly to obtain. In addition, the designer may require the responses to be *incentive-compatible*: each member of the organization must *want* to carry out his/her part of the total organizational response in just the way the designer intends.

The design point of view has old and deep roots in economics. Adam Smith's 'invisible hand' proposition is a statement about the achievements of markets as resource-allocating devices. If one reinterprets it as a comparative conjecture about alternative designs for a resource-allocating organization – namely, that a design using prices is superior to other possible designs – then it becomes an ancestor of the organization-design point of view. In any case, that point of view appears very clearly in Barone's 'The Ministry of Production in the Collectivist State' (1908), and in the debates about 'the possibility of socialism' (i.e. of a centrally directed economy) in the 1930s and 1940s (Hayek, 1935; Lange, 1938; Dobb, 1940; Lerner, 1944).

Nearly all the debtors agreed that if the designer of resource-allocating schemes for an economy has a clean slate and can construct any scheme at all, then he must end up choosing some form of the price mechanism; for example, a scheme of the Lange–Lerner sort. Here a Centre announces successive trial prices; in response to each announcement, profit-maximizing demands are anonymously sent to the Centre by managers, and utility-maximizing demands are sent by consumers; in response to the totals of intended demands, the Centre announces new prices; the final announced prices are those which evoke zero excess demands, and the corresponding intended productions and consumptions are then carried out. The debate dealt largely with the informational virtues of such a price scheme as compared to an extreme centralized alternative scheme. The alternative scheme (never made very explicit) appears to be one wherein managers and consumers report technologies, tastes and endowments to the Centre, which thereupon computes the economy's consumptions and productions; those become commands to be followed.

In retrospect, the extreme centralized alternative seems an unimaginative straw man, since one can imagine a whole spectrum of designs lying between extreme centralization, on the one hand, and the price scheme, on the other; namely, designs in which some of the agents' private information is centrally collected (or pooled), but not all of it. In any case, the debaters agreed that the price scheme is informationally superior to the centralized alternative because (1) in the former, small computations are performed simultaneously by very many agents (though possibly many times), whereas in the latter an immense central computation is required (though required only once), and (2) the messages required in the former (prices and excess demands) are small (though sent many times) while in the latter a monstrously large information transmission is required (though only once).

Persuasive as this claim may appear, a moment's thought reveals how very many gaps need to be filled before the claim becomes provable or disprovable. If a proposed scheme is to be operated afresh at regular intervals (in response, say, to new and randomly changing tastes, technologies and endowments), then what is the designer's measure of a proposed allocation scheme's gross performance (against which a scheme's cost must be balanced)? Is it, for example, the expected value of the gross national product in the period which follows each operation of the scheme? Or is it perhaps a two-valued measure which takes the value one when the scheme's final allocation is Pareto-optimal and individually rational (i.e. every consumer ends up with a bundle at least as good as his/her endowment) and takes the value zero otherwise? When is the scheme to be determined if it comprises a sequence (possibly infinite) of steps? What interim action (resource allocation) is in force while the proposed scheme is in operation and before it yields a final action? For alternative investments in information-processing facilities, how long does the sequence's typical step take? (The longer a step takes, the longer one waits until a given terminal step is reached and the longer an unsatisfactory interim action is in force.)

Once such gaps are filled in, the claim becomes, in principle, a verifiable conjecture. Without venturing to fill them in, economists were nevertheless sufficiently intrigued by the intuitive (but quite unverified) informational appeal of the Lange–Lerner scheme so that they proceeded to construct many more schemes of a similar kind in a variety of settings, including multidivisional firms, for example, as well as planned economies with technologies less well behaved than the classic (convex) ones (see Heal, 1986). These efforts were partly stimulated by (and, in turn, stimulated) the development of algorithms for general constrained optimization, which often had a natural interpretation as schemes wherein a 'Centre' makes announcements and other 'persons' respond without directly revealing their private information. (One can so interpret, for example, certain gradient methods for constrained optimization, as well as the 'decomposed' version of the simplex algorithm for linear programming.)

If the informational appeal of schemes of the Lange–Lerner type was powerful but unverified, what of the incentive side? Here the 'possibility-of-socialism' writers were divided. A sceptic like Hayek (1935, pp. 219–20) asked why a manager would want to follow the Lange–Lerner rules. One (unsupported) reply – hinted at in various places in the debate – is that to induce a manager to follow the rules we need only pay him a reward which is some non-decreasing function of his enterprise's profit. The incentive question becomes acute when one turns to the scheme that is the analogue of the Lange–Lerner scheme if there are public goods; namely, the Lindahl scheme (Lindahl, 1919), when that is given a central-price-announcer interpretation. (The scheme was developed before the possibility-of-socialism debates but appears to have been unknown to the debaters.) For here, as Samuelson (1954) was the first to note, the prospective consumer of a public good may perceive an advantage in falsifying his demand for it; that is, in disobeying the designer's rules. (In fact, it turned out later (Hurwicz, 1972) that the same difficulty can arise without public goods; that is, in the original Lange–Lerner scheme itself.) It took about three decades after the possibility-of-socialism debate until one had the framework to study with precision the question of when incentive-compatible schemes of the price-announcer type – or indeed of any type – can be constructed for economies or for organizations in general.

On the informational side of the design question, a 1959 paper by Hurwicz (Hurwicz, 1960) proved to be a major step towards precise conjectures (as opposed to broadly appealing but unverifiable claims) about the informational merits of alternative resource-allocating schemes for economies, or indeed alternative designs for organizations in general. The key notion is that of an *adjustment process*, to be used by an n-person organization confronting a changing environment $e = (e_1, \ldots, e_n)$, lying always in some set E of possible environments. Here e_i is that aspect of the environment e observed by person i. Assume that the possible values of e_i comprise a set E_i and that $E = E_1 \times \ldots \times E_n$. If, for example, the organization is an exchange economy, then e_i is composed of i's endowment and i's preference ordering on alternative resource allocations; if $n = 2$, then E might be the set of classic Edgeworth-box economies. An adjustment process is a quadruple $\pi = (M, m_0, f, h)$, where M is a set called a *language* and is the cartesian product of n *individual languages* M_i; f is an n-tuple $(f_1, \ldots, f_n)$; f_i is a function from $M \times E_i$ to M_i; $m_0 = (m_{01}, \ldots, m_{0n})$ is an *initial* message n-tuple in M; h is a function, called the *outcome function*, from $M \times E$ to A; and A is a set of organization *actions* or *outcomes* (e.g. resource allocations). Imagine the environment to change at regular intervals. Following each environment, person i emits the initial message m_{0i} in M_i. At step 1, person i emits the message $m_{1i} = f_i(m_0, e_i)$ in M_i, and at the typical subsequent step t, person i emits $m_{ti} = f_i(m_{t-1}, e_i)$, where $m_{ti} \in M_i$ and m_{t-1} denotes an element of M; namely, $(m_{t-1,1}, \ldots, m_{m-1,n})$. At a terminal step T, the organization takes the action (or puts into effect the outcome $h(m_T, e)$ in A which is its final response to the environment e. The process is *privacy-preserving* in the sense that e enters i's function f_i only through e_i, which is i's private knowledge. One might require a similar property for h, that is, that h be an n-tuple $(h_1, \ldots, h_n)$, where h_i is a function from $M \times E_i$ to a set A_i of possible values of i's *individual action* (thus A is the cartesian product $A_1 \times \ldots \times A_n$). In the useful special case of a 'non-parametric' outcome function, where h does not depend on e at all, such privacy-preservation for action selection holds trivially.

Note that we can endow person i with a memory. To do so, let every element m_i of the set M_i be a *pair* (m_i^*, m_i^{**}), where m_i^* denotes memory and m_i^{**} denotes a message sent to (noticed by) others; specify that for $k \neq i$, f_k is insensitive to (its value does not depend on) m_i^*. By making the set in which m_i^* lies sufficiently large, we can let i remember, at every step, all that he has observed of the organization's messages thus far. We can, moreover, let i send messages always to j and to no one else by specifying that for $k \neq i$, $k \neq j$, f_k is insensitive to the ith component of m. We can let i send a message to j and to no one else *at some specific step* t^* by specifying that when all persons' memories tell them that t^* has been reached, then for $k \neq i$, $k \neq j$, f_k is insensitive to the ith component of m.

The adjustment process, as the object to be chosen by the designer, is a concept sufficiently broad and flexible to accommodate all the economists' iterative resource allocation schemes for economies as well as a rich variety of designs for other organizations. All organizations, after all, respond to a changing environment of which each member observes only some aspect in which he/she is the specialist, and the environment's successive values are unknown to the designer when a design is to be chosen. If those values *were* known (e.g. if the environment were constant), then there would be no need for message exchanges at all: each member could simply be programmed once and for all to take a correct (a best) action or sequence of actions. In all organizations, moreover, members engage in dialogue that eventually yields an organizational response to the current environment (an action).

With regard to the classic claim that price schemes are informationally superior designs when the organization is an economy, the adjustment-process concept has permitted a first rigorous test. The test takes the view that we can (as a reasonable starting place) ignore the pre-equilibrium performance of a price scheme (formulated as an adjustment process), and can focus entirely on its *equilibrium* achievements. For any e in E let M^e denote the set of *equilibrium messages*; that is, every $m^e = (m_1^e, \ldots, m_n^e)$ in M^e satisfies $f_i(m^e, e_i) = m_i^e$ for all i. Confine attention to processes with non-parametric outcome functions h (i.e. h depends only on m, not on e) and, for the case where E is a set of exchange economies, formulate the competitive (the Walrasian) mechanism as a non-parametric process, say $\pi^* = (M^*, m_0^*, f^*, h^*)$. The typical element m of M^* comprises a vector of proposed prices and an $(n-1)$-tuple of proposed trade vectors; f_i yields i's intended trade vector – or, in an alternative version, a *set* of acceptable trade vectors – at the just-announced prices; and h is a projection function yielding the 'trade' portion of m. For the process π^* and for every e in classical set E, all the *equilibrium outcomes for e* – that is, all those allocations (trade $(n-1)$-tuples) a satisfying $a = h^*(m)$ for all m in M^{*e} – are Pareto-optimal and individually rational. One now asks the following question: does there exist any other process $\pi = (M, m_0, f, h)$ such that (i) for all e in the same set E every equilibrium outcome is again Pareto-optimal and individually rational, and (ii) the process π is informationally 'cheaper' than π^*? A natural starting place for the assessment of informational cost is size of the language. If one confines oneself to processes π in which M is in a finite Euclidean space, then a natural measure of language size is dimension. But then the question just posed has a trivial Yes as its answer, since one can always code a message of arbitrary dimension as a one-dimensional message. To rule out such coding, one imposes 'smoothness' on the process π. For example, one considers the mapping t from A (the set of outcomes), to the subsets of E, such that for ever e in $t(a)$, a is an equilibrium outcome for e, and one requires that t contain a Lipschitzian selection. It turns out that for classic sets E and for language dimension as the cost measure, no smooth process satisfying (i) and (ii) exists (Hurwicz, 1972). The result extends (for more general sorts of smoothness requirements) to processes with non-Euclidean languages and language-size measures more general than dimension (Mount and Reiter, 1974; Walker, 1977; Jordan, 1982).

These results are clearly a first step towards vindicating the classic claim that the price process is informationally superior. To go further, one would like to consider pre-equilibrium outcomes – so that the final allocation is the one attained at a fixed, but well-chosen, terminal step – and to take account of the change in the time required to reach that terminal step as one varies the investment in the information-processing facilities available for carrying out the typical step. It seems plausible that a version of the competitive process that converges rapidly to its equilibrium messages will rank high relative to other processes once this complication is added. One would like the 'smoothness' requirement to arise naturally from a model of a well-behaved information technology rather than being introduced (as at present) in an ad-hoc manner. One would like to leave the setting just sketched, wherein messages and outcomes are points of a

223

continuum, to see whether analogous results hold when both messages and outcomes (allocations) have to be rounded off to a chosen precision. A limited analogue to the dimensional-minimality result just sketched has in fact been obtained in such a discrete setting (Hurwicz and Marschak, 1985).

For organizations in general, the requirements of Pareto-optimality and individual rationality are replaced by some given set of desired (and equally acceptable) responses to every possible given environment. The problem facing a designer who is unconcerned about incentive aspects can then be put as follows. Given a set E and a *desired-performance correspondence* ϕ from E to the subsets of an outcome (action) set A, find an adjustment process $\pi = (M, m_0, f, h)$ which *realizes* ϕ – that is, which satisfies $a \in \phi(e)$ if $a = h(m, e)$ and $m \in M^e$ – and whose informational costs (suitably measured) are no less than those of any other process which realizes ϕ.

Note that a far more ambitious task could be given the designer instead. Let the designer have preferences over alternative environment/outcome/cost triples and let the preferences be represented by a utility function. The ambitious task is then to find a process π, and an accompanying selection function, which chooses a unique equilibrium outcome in the set M^e for every e, so as to maximize the designer's expected utility (expectation being taken with respect to the random variable e). It seems clear that such unbounded designer's rationality is too ambitious a standard; organization theory would freeze in its tracks if it adopted such a standard. The realization of a given performance correspondence at minimum informational cost is a reasonable step towards bounded rationality, especially if the performance correspondence is not stringent. (Thus ϕ might assign to e all outcomes which are within a certain specified distance of an outcome that is 'ideal' for e – say an outcome that maximizes some pay-off function.)

The preceding bounded-rationality version of the designer's task can again be modified by allowing some 'dynamics'; that is, permitting choice of terminal step rather than focusing on equilibrium outcomes. Whether we do so or not, we now have a precise version of the general performance-versus-cost problem which we claimed at the start to be a distinctively 'economists' contribution to organization theory. (The problem is surveyed in more detail in Marschak, 1986.)

When one turns to incentive issues, a certain 'contraction' of the adjustment-process concept has proven useful. The object chosen by the designer now becomes a *game form* (S, g), where $S = S_1 \times \ldots \times S_n$; S_i is the set of person i's possible *strategies* s_i; and g is an outcome function from S to A (the set of organizational actions or outcomes). Person i's local environment e_i specifies (among other things) i's preferences over the alternative organizational outcomes. The set of Nash-equilibrium strategy n-tuples associated with the triple (S, g, e), denoted $N_{sg}(e)$, is the set of n-tuples $s = (s_1, \ldots, s_n)$ such that given $e = (e_1, \ldots, e_n)$, each person i regards the outcome $g(s)$ to be at least as good as the outcome $g(s_1, \ldots, s_{i-1}, \bar{s}_i, s_{i+1}, \ldots, s_n)$ for all $\bar{s}_i$ in S_i. Suppose the designer is again given a desired-performance correspondence ϕ from E to the subsets of A. Then the incentive problem may be put this way: find a game form (S, g) such that for every e in E and every s in $N_{sg}(e)$, the outcome $g(s)$ is contained in the set $\phi(e)$. Such a game form *Nash-implements* ϕ. We can trivially find an adjustment process (M, m_0, f, h) whose equilibrium outcomes for every e comprise exactly the set $\{a: a = g(s); s \in N_{sg}(e)\}$. (To do so, let $M = M_1 \times \ldots \times M_n = S_1 \times \ldots \times S_n$; let f_i satisfy $f_i((s_1, \ldots, s_n), e_i) = s_i$ if and only if, given e_i, i regards the outcome $g(s)$ to be at least as good as the outcome $g(s_1, \ldots, s_{i-1}, \bar{s}_i, s_{i+1}, \ldots, s_n)$ for all $\bar{s}_i$ in S_i; and let $h(s) = g(s)$.) Much has now been learned about what sorts of performance functions ϕ (including economically interesting ones) can be implemented and what sorts cannot (for a survey, see Hurwicz, 1986). We again have the 'dynamic' shortcoming noted before: if, for every e, an outcome in the set $\{a \in N_{gs}(e): s \in S\}$ is indeed to be reached by operating an adjustment process (as in the economists' allocation mechanisms), then the behaviour of the process prior to equilibrium must be studied. Doing so may, moreover, introduce quite new strategic considerations, since a fresh incentive problem may arise at each step of the process: at each step a member may ask whether carrying out the designer's instructions (applying f_i) is what he/she really wants to do.

Thus both on the informational and the incentive sides, a very large research agenda stretches before the economic organization theorist. Moreover, the abstract theorizing we have sketched is very far indeed from making good contact with the institutional facts about real organizations. One may take the design point of view, but even a designer is constrained by those facts.

In particular, the notion of *hierarchy* (the 'organization chart'), which appears so often in popular discourse, is very hard indeed to pin down in the adjustment-process framework. To define 'hierarchy', we first have to define 'authority'. When does an adjustment process have the property that person 1 is in authority over person 2? Probably the best one can hope for (Hurwicz, 1971) is this: person 1 is in authority over person 2 if (1) at the terminal step T, m_{T2} depends only on $m_{T-1,1}$; and (2) $m_{T-1,1}$ is sensitive to e_1. If we did not add requirement (2), then person 1's apparent terminal instruction to person 2 (embodied in the pre-terminal message $m_{t-1,1}$) might in fact be a robot-like repetition (perhaps in recoded form) of a 'command' that 2 gave to 1 at step $T - 2$. On the other hand, we might satisfy the sensitivity required by (2) in such a trivial way that we have not really succeeded in ruling out person 2 as the 'true' (though somewhat disguised) commander. Authority is, in short, a very fragile concept from a formal point of view.

Yet it is a central concept in influential writings like those of Williamson (1975). His book is a rich source of institutionally motivated conjectures about how organizations work, but it teems with terms, concepts and conjectures that the formal theorist must struggle mightily to make precise. The task of precise pinning down is so daunting that the stage of testing the conjectures (trying to prove them) seems likely to be reached. The book argues for these conjectures nevertheless, and many of them appear, at some level, to be plausible. Here is one example: 'it is elementary that the advantages of centralization vary with the degree of independence among the members, being ... almost certainly great in an integrated task group' (p. 51). To the formal theorist, that is not 'elementary' at all. One requires five or six definitions before one even knows what is being claimed.

Nevertheless, such informal but insightful institution-based essays are an essential challenge to formal theory. The economists' organization theory of the future will grow out of the tension between highly imprecise but widely believed and institutionally grounded claims and the harsh demands of formal argument.

BIBLIOGRAPHY

Barone, E. 1908. The Ministry of Production in the collectivist state. In *Collectivist Economic Planning*, ed. F.A. von Hayek, London: Routledge, 1935, 245–90; New York: A.M. Kelley, 1967.

Dobb, M.H. 1940. *Political Economy and Capitalism*. New York: Macmillan.

Hayek, F. von. (ed.) 1935. *Collectivist Economic Planning*. London: Routledge; New York: A.M. Kelley, 1967.

Heal, G. 1986. Planning. In *Handbook of Mathematical Economics*, Vol. III, ed. K.J. Arrow and M.D. Intriligator, Amsterdam: North-Holland.

Hurwicz, L. 1960. Optimality and informational efficiency in resource allocation processes. In *Mathematical Methods in the Social Sciences*, ed. K.J. Arrow, S. Karlin and P. Suppes, Stanford: Stanford University Press.

Hurwicz, L. 1971. Centralization and decentralization in economic processes. In *Comparison of Economic Systems*, ed. A. Eckstein, Berkeley: University of California Press.

Hurwicz, L. 1972. On informationally decentralized systems. In *Decision and Organization*, ed. C.B. McGuire and R. Radner, Amsterdam: North-Holland.

Hurwicz, L. 1972. On the dimensional requirements of informationally decentralized Pareto-satisfactory processes. In *Studies in Resource Allocation Processes*, ed. K.J. Arrow and L. Hurwicz, Cambridge: Cambridge University Press, 1977.

Hurwicz, L. 1986. Incentive aspects of decentralization. In *Handbook of Mathematical Economics*, Vol. III, ed. K.J. Arrow and M.D. Intriligator, Amsterdam: North-Holland.

Hurwicz, L. and Marschak, T. 1985. Discrete allocation mechanisms: dimensional requirements for resource-allocation mechanisms when desired outcomes are unbounded. *Journal of Complexity*, December.

Jordan, S.J. 1982. The competitive allocation process is informationally efficient uniquely. *Journal of Economic Theory* 28, January, 1–18.

Lange, O. 1936–7. On the economic theory of socialism. In *On the Economic Theory of Socialism*, ed. B. Lipincott, Minneapolis: University of Minnesota Press, 1938.

Lerner, A.P. 1944. *The Economics of Control*. New York: Macmillan.

Lindahl, E. 1919. Just taxation: a positive solution. In *Classics in the Theory of Public Finance*, ed. R. Musgrave and A. Peacock, London, New York: Macmillan, 1958.

Marschak, T. 1986. Organization design. In *Handbook of Mathematical Economics*, Vol. III, ed. K.J. Arrow and M.D. Intriligator, Amsterdam: North-Holland.

Mount, K. and Reiter, S. 1974. The informational size of message spaces. *Journal of Economic Theory* 8(2), 161–92.

Samuelson, P.A. 1954. The pure theory of public expenditure. *Review of Economics and Statistics* 36, November, 387–9.

Walker, M. 1977. On the informational size of message spaces. *Journal of Economic Theory* 15(2), August, 366–75.

Williamson, O.E. 1975. *Markets and Hierarchies, Analysis and Antitrust Implications: a Study in the Economics of Internal Organizations*. New York: Free Press.

Portfolio Analysis

NILS H. HAKANSSON

Many observers trace the beginnings of modern financial investment theory to the pioneering article of Markowitz (1952), published only a third of a century ago. This is not surprising in view of the dominant position that the mean–variance approach to portfolio choice analysed by Markowitz has attained in the last two decades, particularly in empirical studies. Financial investment theory under uncertainty goes well beyond this particular model, however, and somewhat further back in time as well. This essay will first examine the pure portfolio model, both the single period and the intertemporal varieties. It will then turn to consumption-investment formulations.

1. PURE PORTFOLIO ANALYSIS

A. SINGLE-PERIOD MODELS. Even though the mean–variance model 'dominates' single-period analysis, it will be expedient to begin with the approach which is a direct application of the theory of rational choice, also known as expected utility portfolio models.

The experienced utility approach. The investor, starting the period with initial capital $w_0 > 0$, is assumed to have preferences that are rational (in the von Neumann–Morgenstern (1944) sense) with respect to end-of-period distributions of wealth and therefore representable by a utility function, u, defined on end-of-period wealth w. Thus, the investor's problem is to maximize $E[u(w)]$, where E denotes the expectation operator. Letting r_i denote the (generally random) return per unit of investment in opportunity i and z_i the amount (to be) invested in opportunity (asset, security) i, $i = 1, \ldots, m$, we obtain

$$w = \sum_i z_i (1 + r_i), \qquad \sum_i z_i = w_0,$$

where the second expression is the budget constraint. Solving the second

227

expression for z_1 and inserting the result in the first equality, the investor's problem becomes

$$\text{P1:} \quad \max_{z_2,\dots,z_m} E\left\{u\left[\sum_{i=2}^{m}(r_i-r_1)z_i+w_0(1+r_1)\right]\right\} \tag{1}$$

subject to

$$\text{miscellaneous constraints.} \tag{2}$$

At this point, several remarks are in order. First, in our expression for w we have implicitly assumed a perfect market, that is an absence of transaction costs and taxes, perfect divisibility, a competitive securities market, constant returns to scale, and that the investor has full use of the proceeds from short sales (negative holdings). These assumptions are standard and will be maintained throughout. Second, when some security is risk-free over the holding period, it carries the subscript $i=1$ above; in this case, the first $m-1$ terms in (1) represents the excess earned (over and above what an entirely risk-free portfolio would have provided) on the risky holdings (this excess may of course be negative). Third, it is usually assumed (quite innocuously from an empirical viewpoint) that the investor prefers more to less and is averse to risk, that is that

$$u' < 0, u'' < 0. \tag{3}$$

Finally, the constraints (2) usually represent institutional and/or self-imposed barriers on borrowing (e.g. margin requirements), on short positions and on solvency (such as $\Pr\{w>0\}=1$).

The solution to P1 is usually denoted $z^*(w_0)=z_2^*(w_0),\dots,z_m^*(w_0)$. It exists under various innocent conditions: one set imposes bounded returns on the available securities, 'no-easy-money' and a solvency constraint. The no-arbitrage or no-easy-money condition precludes both a payoff $w\geqslant 0$, where $\Pr\{w>0\}>0$, from a nonpositive net investment, as well as a payoff $w=0$ from a negative net investment. Given existence, the second part of (3) (strict concavity of u) implies that the optimal payoff distribution w^* (though not necessarily the optimal portfolio z^*) will be unique.

Define $a(w)$ (the absolute risk aversion function) and $r(w)$ (the relative risk aversion function) by

$$a(w) \equiv -u''(w)/u'(w), \qquad r(w) \equiv wa(w).$$

Arrow (1965) demonstrated that if $E[r_2] >$,

$$a'(w) \gtreqless 0 \Rightarrow \frac{dz_2^*}{dw_0} \lesseqgtr 0$$

when there are only two assets available, one risky and one risk-free. While the result does not extend in general to the case of many risky assets (Cass and Stiglitz, 1972), the empirical observation that a given portfolio of risky assets is overwhelmingly treated as a normal (as opposed to inferior) good lends strong support to the notion that the preferences of the great majority of investors have the property

$$a'(w) < 0 \tag{4}$$

in addition to those given in (3). Beyond this, however, we have little to say about investors' preference functions with respect to wealth.

Since properties (3) and (4) leave much room for individuality, there is rather little one can say in general about the solution to P1 – except that the optimal portfolio will be well diversified. This observation was probably first made in a scholarly context by Bernoulli (1738) in his advocacy of the logarithmic measure of welfare.

There are, however, two cases of special interest. One is the case in which the optimal investment policy is *proportional* to initial capital. This occurs if and only if utility is a member of the family of power functions (the isoelastic family), that is

$$u(w) = \begin{cases} -w^{\gamma}, & \gamma < 0 \\ \ln w, & (\gamma = 0), \\ w^{\gamma}, & 0 < \gamma < 1 \end{cases} \tag{5}$$

which in turn implies, and is implied by, constant relative risk aversion. [For the family above, $r(w) = 1 - \gamma$.] The optimal policy is now of the form

$$z_i^*(w_0) = x_{i\gamma}^* w_0, \quad \text{all } i, \gamma, \tag{6}$$

where the $x_{i\gamma}^*$'s are constants corresponding to the proportions to be invested in the various assets.

A second special case is that of *linear* optimal investment policies (of which (6) is obviously a special case). This occurs, *assuming a risk-free asset or portfolio is available*, if and only if preferences exhibit linear risk tolerance [$a(w)^{-1}$ is linear] or, equivalently, hyperbolic absolute risk aversion, that is

$$u(w) = \begin{cases} \gamma^{-1}(w + \phi)^{\gamma} & \gamma < 1 & a' < 0 \quad (7a) \\ -(\phi - w)^{\gamma} & \gamma > 1, \phi \text{ large} & a' > 0 \quad (7b) \\ -\exp\{\phi w\} & \phi < 0 & a' = 0. \quad (7c) \end{cases}$$

The optimal policies are given, in the three cases, by

$$z_i^*(w_0) = \begin{cases} x_{i\gamma}^* \left(w_0 + \dfrac{\phi}{1 + r_1} \right) & (8a) \\ x_{i\gamma}^* \left(\dfrac{\phi}{1 + r_1} - w_0 \right) & i = 2, \ldots, m \quad (8b) \\ \text{a constant } (\phi) & (8c) \end{cases}$$

and are said to exhibit the *separation* property. This name derives from the fact that the *mix* of risky assets (the ratio of $z_i^*(w_0)/z_j^*(w_0)$, any $i, j \geq 2$) is independent of initial wealth w_0 (it is also independent of the preference parameter ϕ). *In the absence of a risk-free asset or portfolio*, separation obtains only for quadratic utility, or when $\gamma = 2$ in (7b). Thus we have the remarkable observation that, for arbitrary return distributions, two individuals of differing initial wealth levels would be willing to delegate the choice of risky asset proportions to the same mutual fund only if they share probability beliefs *and either* a risk-free portfolio is available and both individuals' preference functions being to either (7a) or (7b) with a common γ or to (7c), *or* both investors have quadratic utility. When it comes to risky investments, individuality runs strong indeed!

Separation based on return distributions rather than preferences can also occur but only under highly restrictive assumptions (Ross, 1978). The most noteworthy case is when returns are normally distributed, which is discussed in the next section.

The mean–variance approach. The essence of the mean–variance model is that more expected return is preferred to less and that less variance of return is preferred to more, *ceterius paribus*. In addition, it is usually assumed that indifference curves in standard deviation–mean space are convex. Since the return r on a portfolio is $w/w_0 - 1$, we obtain, defining x_i as the fraction of w_0 invested in opportunity i or $x_i \equiv z_i/w_0$ and using (1),

$$r(x) = \sum_{i=2}^{m} (r_i - r_1)x_i + 1 + r_1.$$

More formally, the mean–variance approach can thus be viewed as postulating a preference function $f(E[r], V[r])$, where $V[r]$ is the variance of r, such that

$$\frac{\partial f}{\partial E} > 0, \quad \frac{\partial f}{\partial V} < 0, \quad \frac{d^2 E}{d(\sqrt{V})^2}\bigg|_{f=f_0} > 0. \tag{9}$$

The first two properties of (9) provide the basis for the central notion of mean–variance (MV) dominance: return distribution r_i is said to MV-dominate distribution r_k if and only if

$$E_i \geqslant E_k, \quad V_i \geqslant V_k$$

and at least one inequality is strict. Given the set of feasible portfolios, dominated portfolios are referred to as *inefficient* and nondominated portfolios as *efficient*. The first two properties of (9) thus generate a partial ordering of payoff distributions in a manner similar to that of the various stochastic dominance criteria.

In the absence of a risk-free asset or portfolio, $E[r]$ is (except in pathological cases) a strictly concave function of $\sigma[r](= \sqrt{V[r]})$ for the set of efficient portfolios. In the presence of a risk-free asset, the expected return of any efficient portfolios p is given by the linear equation

$$E[r_p] = r_1 + \frac{E[A] - r_1}{\sigma[A]}\sigma[r_p],$$

where A is the one portfolio composed solely of risky assets that is efficient. In other words, all efficient portfolios are combinations of the risk-free asset and portfolio A, that is the separation property holds.

As noted, Markowitz is viewed as the originator of mean–variance portfolio theory, although Tobin (1958) also made important early contributions. However, the mean–variance approach itself has three other independent and rather interesting origins. Marschak (1951), using a Taylor series expansion as an approximation to the expected utility of return, obtained, on the basis of the first three terms, the expression

$$E[r] - b(E[r])^2 - bV[r], \qquad b > 0,$$

which is an eligible form of the mean–variance function $f(E, V)$. Roy (1952) argued for maximizing the probability of exceeding some disaster level d, or the criterion

$$\max \Pr\{r > d\}.$$

Applying Chebychev's inequality, he obtained the operational expression

$$\max_x \frac{E[r(x)] - d}{\sigma[r(x)]},$$

which clearly captures the essence of the mean–variance framework. Finally, Freund (1956), assuming negative exponential utility [see 7(c)] and normally distributed returns, obtained

$$E[u(w)] = -\exp\left\{ k\left(E[w] + \frac{k}{2} V[w] \right) \right\}, \qquad k < 0,$$

where, upon optimization, each permissible value of k implies a mean–variance efficient solution.

The mean–variance model is consistent with the expected utility criterion in two principal cases. First, under arbitrary return distributions, utility must be quadratic $[u(w) = w - bw^2, b > 0]$, which unfortunately implies $u' \leqslant 0$ for $w \geqslant b/2$ and that risky assets are inferior goods (see 8b). Second, when returns are normally distributed, consistency occurs for that subset of preferences for which the expected utility integral exists (a necessary condition for this is that $u(w)$ is defined on the whole real line – this excludes the family (7a), for example).

Although normally distributed returns are a poor approximation of actual returns in a world of limited liability, and quadratic utility leaves much to be desired, the mean–variance model is by far the most widely used. This appears to be attributable to three principal properties. First, MV-efficient portfolios are (like the portfolios of risk averse expected utility maximizers) well diversified. Second, the MV-model makes more modest input demands and is computationally much simpler than the (non-quadratic) expected utility models. (What business person would appreciate the advice that (s)he maximize expected utility?) Finally, the normality assumption appears to provide a reasonable approximation of the returns for well diversified portfolios in many cases, and the quadratic function, over a limited range, is often a satisfactory approximation to an arbitrary utility function.

B. MULTI-PERIOD MODELS. This section addresses the type of models in which a large number of sequential portfolio choices is of the essence. We shall therefore employ the subscript i to denote period t; w_t represents wealth at the end of period t. The returns r_{it} will be assumed to be independent with respect to t (but not i).

The long-run growth model. Let $R_t(x_t) \equiv 1 + r_t(x_t)$; R_t is now called the relative wealth for period t. Thus, under full re-investment of the previous period's payoffs.

$$w_t = w_0 R_1(x_1) \dots R_t(x_t) = w_0 \exp \left\{ \sum_{n=1}^{t} \ln R_n(x_n) \right\},$$

where we assume that $R_t(x_t) \geqslant 0$, all t. Letting

$$G_t(\langle w_t \rangle) \equiv \sum_{n=1}^{t} \ln R_n(x_n)/t \tag{10}$$

and observing that the variates $\ln R_1$, $\ln R_2, \dots$ (under mild restrictions) obey the law of large numbers, we obtain

$$[w_t \rightarrow \begin{cases} 0 & \text{if } E[G_t] \leqslant \delta < 0 \\ \infty & \text{if } E[G_t] \geqslant \delta > 0 \end{cases} \quad t \geqslant T, T \text{ large.} \tag{11}$$

Thus, it is the expectations of the logs of the wealth relatives which are the principal determinants of what happens to your capital over the long haul.

In view of (11), it is natural to think of maximizing the expectation of G since this almost surely leads to more capital in the long run than any other (significantly different) strategy. To do this, it is necessary and sufficient to

$$\max_{x_t} E[\ln R_t(x_t)], \qquad \text{each } t, \tag{12}$$

that is to solve (12) one period at a time. Note that (12) is equivalent to maximizing the geometric mean of R_t in each period. This model appears to have been independently discovered by Williams (1936), Kelly (1956), Latané (1959), and Breiman (1960).

The long-run growth model has several noteworthy properties. First, the decision rule (12) implies, and is implied by, logarithmic utility of wealth in each period. Thus, it is inconsistent with all (significantly) different preferences (including the mean–variance model). In other words, almost surely having more capital does not imply higher expected utility (or conversely). Various writers have on occasion been confused on this point.

Second, the 'growth-optimal' investment policy is not only proportional to initial wealth but (12) implies that it is *myopic*, that is independent of the return

232

distributions beyond the current period (this is true even under returns that are weakly dependent over time). Finally, with relative risk aversion equal to 1, the model tells us that to do well in the long run in terms of capital accumulation, one must be averse to risk; furthermore, both greater and smaller risk aversion almost surely leave one with less capital than logarithmic risk aversion.

Terminal utility models. Now consider the case in which the investor's preferences for wealth w at some (distant) terminal point in time h are represented by the utility function $U_h(w_h)$. Letting w_n be the investor's wealth with n periods to go, we obtain, under full reinvestment for each period's proceeds,

$$w_{n-1}(z_n) = \sum_{i=2}^{m} (r_{in} - r_{1n})z_{in} + w_n(1 + r_{1n}), \qquad n = 1, 2, \ldots$$

where, for convenience, we set $j = 0$. Defining $U_n(w_n)$ as the maximum expected utility obtainable with w_n, we obtain the recursive equation

$$U_n(w_n) \equiv \max_{z_n} E[U_{n-1}[w_{n-1}(z_n)]\}, \qquad n = 1, 2, \ldots \tag{13}$$

Consequently, $U_n(w_n)$ is the derived or induced utility of wealth with n periods to go.

The conditions for the existence of a solution to system (13) are the same as for the single-period model; when U_0 has properties (3), so do the induced functions $U_1, \ldots, U_n$. In general, $U_n(w_n)$ depends on all of the inputs: U_0, the joint distribution functions $F_1(r_1), \ldots, F_n(r_n)$ and the interest rates $r_{11}, \ldots, r_{1n}$. There are, however, two special cases. First, when $U_0(w_0)$ belongs to class (5), U_n becomes a positive linear transformation of U_0 so that in effect

$$U_n(w) = U_0(w), \qquad n = 1, 2, \ldots$$

Consequently, the optimal investment policy $z_n^*(w_n)$ depends in this case only on the current period's inputs, $F_n(r_n)$ and r_{1n}, and is thus *myopic*. This was first shown by Mossin (1968).

The second special case occurs when interest rates follow a deterministic process. Then, when U_0 belongs to class (7a) with $\phi \leqslant 0$. U_n depends only on U_0 and $r_{11}, \ldots, r_{1n}$, which is called *partial myopia*. U_n and z_n^* are now given by

$$U_n(w_n) = \gamma^{-1}(w_n + A_n)^{\gamma}, \qquad \gamma < 1$$

$$z_{in}^*(w_n) = x_{in\gamma}^*(w_n + A_n), \qquad i = 2, \ldots, m,$$

where $A_n = \phi[(1 + r_{11}) \ldots (1 + r_{1n})]^{-1}$. In the other cases of family (7), partial myopia occurs locally, that is for w_n greater than or equal to a (positive) lower bound.

The most interesting aspect of the terminal utility model, however, is a strong set of convergence results (see e.g. Hakansson, 1974). Under very general conditions, we obtain from (13) that U_n converges to a member of the isoelastic family (5) that is,

$$U_n(w_n) \to \frac{1}{\gamma} w_n^{\gamma}, \qquad \text{some } \gamma < 1.$$

In addition,

$$z_n^*(w_n) \to x_{n\gamma}^* w_n.$$

Thus, we have the remarkable result that reinvesting individuals with distant horizons should follow an isoelastic investment policy independently of their terminal preferences as long as their horizon remains distant.

The continuous-time model. Since transaction costs are zero under the perfect market assumption, it is natural to consider shorter and shorter periods between reinvestment decisions. In the limit, reinvestment takes place continuously. Assuming that the returns on risky assets can be described by diffusion processes, we obtain that optimal portfolios are mean–variance efficient in that the instantaneous variance is minimized for a given instantaneous expected return. The intuitive reason for this is that as the trading interval is shortened, the first two moments of the change in a security's price become more and more dominant (see also Samuelson, 1970). The optimal portfolios also exhibit the separation property – as if returns over very short periods were normally distributed. Over any fixed interval, however, payoff distributions are, due to the compound effect, usually lognormal.

II CONSUMPTION–INVESTMENT ANALYSIS

In consumption–investment models, investment is merely a means to an end – future consumption and bequests. Thus, preferences are defined on consumption and bequest programmes, $c_1, c_2, \ldots, c_n, b_n$, where c_t is the *level* of consumption in period t and b_n the bequest at the end of the last period, assuming death occurs in period n. The utility of wealth is therefore not a primitive but must be induced or derived. Preferences may of course be conditional on n and depend on the environment s, in which case they may be written

$$U_{ns}(c_1, \ldots, c_n, b_n), \tag{14}$$

where it is usually assumed that the functions U_{ns} reflect a preference for more to less and are strictly concave. Commonly studied forms of (14) are those in which (14) is additive or multiplicative. When additive and state-independent, (14) may be written

$$u_1(c_1) + u_2(c_2) + \cdots + u_n(c_n) + g_n(b_n).$$

Wealth is now governed by the difference equation

$$w_{t+1} = \sum_{i=2}^{m} (r_{its} - r_{1ts}) z_{it} + (w_t - c_t)(1 + r_{1ts}) + t_{ts},$$

where y_{ts} is employment income.

The simplest consumption–investment model is based on just two periods and can profitably be used to study such questions as, 'How does the investor respond to increasing investment risk?' Answer: any which way – see e.g. Rothschild and Stiglitz (1971). In multi-period formulations, additional issues that must be addressed are the probabilistic nature of the investor's lifespan and the stochastic process obeyed by returns. Dynamic programming formulations of this problem become rather lengthy (see e.g. Hakansson 1970, 1971). The most general models posit a state-contingent opportunity set where the states obey a Markov process.

When preferences are either additive or multiplicative and $u_t(c_t)$ belongs to the family (7a) with $\phi \leqslant 0$, the separation property is preserved; when $\phi < 0$, $-\phi$ assumes the role of subsistence level. For the family (7b) and (7c), on the other hand, the non-negative constraint on consumption is generally binding and poses insurmountable problems for the mean–variance model. However, as in the pure reinvestment model, mean–variance efficiency is restored by moving to a continuous-time formulation (Merton, 1971).

BIBLIOGRAPHY

Arrow, K. 1965. *Aspects of the Theory of Risk-bearing*. Helsinki: Yrjö Jahnssonin Sätiö.

Bernoulli, D. 1738. Exposition of a new theory on the measurement of risk. Trans. by L. Sommer, *Econometrica* 22, January, 1954, 23–36.

Breiman, L. 1960. Investment policies for expanding business optimal in a long-run sense. *Naval Logistics Quarterly, December.*

Cass, D. and Stiglitz, J. 1972. Risk aversion and wealth effects on portfolios with many assets. *Review of Economic Studies* 39(3), July, 331–54.

Freund, R. 1956. The introduction of risk into a programming model. *Econometrica* 24, July, 253–63.

Hakansson, N. 1970. Optimal investment and consumption strategies under risk for a class of utility functions. *Econometrica* 38(5), September, 587–607.

Hakansson, N. 1971. Optimal entrepreneurial decision in a completely stochastic environment. *Management Science: Theory* 17(7), March, 427–49.

Hakansson, N. 1974. Convergence to isoelastic utility and policy in multiperiod portfolio choice. *Journal of Financial Economics* 1(3), September, 20–24.

Kelly, J.L., Jr. 1956. A new interpretation of information rate. *Bell System Technical Journal* 35, August, 917–25.

Latané, H. 1959. Criteria for choice among risky ventures. *Journal of Political Economy* 67, April, 144–55.

Markowitz, H. 1952. Portfolio selection. *Journal of Finance* 7(1), March, 77–91.

Marschak, J. 1951. Why 'should' statisticians and businessmen maximize 'moral expectation'? In *Proceedings of the Second Berkeley Symposium on Mathematical Statistics and Probability*, ed. J. Neyman, Berkeley: University of California Press.

Merton, R. 1971. Optimum consumption and portfolio rules in a continuous time model. *Journal of Economic Theory* 3(4), August, 373–413.

Mossin, J. 1968. Optimal multiperiod portfolio policies. *Journal of Business* 41, April, 215–29.

Ross, S. 1978. Mutual fund separation in financial theory: the separating distributions. *Journal of Economic Theory* 17(2), April, 254–86.

Rothschild, M. and Stiglitz, J. 1971. Increasing risk II: its economic consequences. *Journal of Economic Theory* 3(1), March, 66–84.

Roy, A. 1952. Safety first and the holding of assets. *Econometrica* 20, July, 431–49.

Samuelson, P.A. 1970. The fundamental approximation theorem of portfolio analysis in terms of means, variances, and higher moments. *Review of Economic Studies* 37(4), October, 537–42.

Tobin, J. 1958. Liquidity preference as behavior towards risk. *Review of Economic Studies* 25, February, 65–86.

von Neumann, J. and Morgenstern, O. 1944. *Theory of Games and Economic Behavior.* Princeton: Princeton University Press.

Williams, J. 1936. Speculation and the carryover. *Quarterly Journal of Economics* 50, May, 436–55.

Present Value

STEPHEN F. LEROY

The present-value relation says that, under certainty, the value of a capital good or financial asset equals the summed discounted value of the stream of revenues which that asset generates. The discount factor will be that determined by the interest rate over the relevant period. The justification for the present-value relation lies in the fact that (in perfect capital markets) an asset must earn a rate of return exactly equal to the interest rate; otherwise arbitrage opportunities emerge, which is inconsistent with equilibrium. Thus if r_t is the one-period interest rate at t, p_t is the (ex-dividend) price of an asset and d_t is its dividend, it must be true that

$$r_t = (d_{t+1} + p_{t+1})/p_t - 1 \tag{1}$$

since the right-hand side equals the rate of return on the asset. Solving for p_t,

$$p_t = (d_{t+1} + p_{t+1})/(1 + r_t) \tag{2}$$

Replacing t by $t+1$, (2) becomes an equation expressing p_{t+1} as a function of r_{t+1}, d_{t+2} and p_{t+2}. Substituting this in (2) and proceeding similarly n times, it follows that

$$p_t = \sum_{i=1}^{n} d_{t+i} \Big/ \prod_{j=0}^{i-1} (1 + r_{t+j}) + p_{t+n} \Big/ \prod_{j=0}^{n-1} (1 + r_{t+j}). \tag{3}$$

Assuming that speculative price bubbles do not occur (see below), the right-most term in (3) converges to zero as n goes to infinity, so there results the present value equation

$$p_t = \sum_{i=1}^{\infty} d_{t+1} \Big/ \sum_{j=0}^{i-1} (1 + r_{t+j}). \tag{4}$$

If in addition the interest rate is constant $r_t = \rho$, the present-value relation may be written as

237

$$p_t = \sum_{i=1}^{\infty} (1+\rho)^{-i} d_{t+i}. \qquad (5)$$

In the special cases in which d_{t+i} is constant at d, or grows from d_t at rate g, (5) simplifies to

$$p_t = d/\rho \qquad (6)$$

or

$$p_t = (1+g)d_t/(\rho - g) \qquad (7)$$

respectively.

In introductory finance courses, the present-value relation makes an early appearance in the chapter on capital budgeting, where it is taught that corporations should accept any investment project that promises a positive present value (net of costs), and only these. This wealth-maximization decision rule – Fisher's separation principle – is the correct one independent of agents' preferences because the consumption set that it generates dominates that generated by any other capital budgeting criterion. Other criteria, such as accepting that project with the shortest payback period, or that with the highest internal rate of return, are either equivalent to present-value maximization, ambiguous (sometimes, for example, a single project may have no real internal rate of return, or more than one) or wrong, depending on the characteristics of the project's returns.

Under uncertainty, but assuming complete markets, the present value maximization rule for capital budgeting carries over without modification (except that the discount factors are no longer necessarily interpretable as interest rates). This is not surprising since, as Arrow and Debreu showed, under complete markets uncertainty can be handled by the simple device of defining new commodities to represent consumptions of a given commodity in different states. Hence the analysis under certainty is formally identical to that under certainty – the only difference is that more commodities are involved. If markets are incomplete, however, there will generally be many different sets of contingent-claims prices consistent with equilibrium in those goods and securities which are traded. Hence even if all agents agree about the probability distribution of the returns on a project, unanimity may break down: some agents may assign a given project a positive present value and others will assign the same project a negative present value.

A recent series of papers has attempted to determine sufficient conditions for unanimity in incomplete markets. One such condition has to do with 'spanning': unanimity will obtain if the return on a new project lies in the subspace spanned by existing securities, so that the present value calculation can be made without ambiguity. This spanning condition, while sufficient for unanimity, is not necessary, however. It is possible to construct examples in which the spanning requirement is not satisfied, so that new projects create new trading opportunities by widening the set of markets, but in which agents' appraisals of new projects always agree. Unanimity obtains in these examples because of special assumptions which ensure that agents attach no value to these new trading opportunities (see Krouse, 1985 and the papers cited there).

Under uncertainty the present-value relation may be written as

$$p_t = \sum_{i=1}^{\infty} (1 + \rho_t)^{-i} E_t(d_{t+i}), \tag{8}$$

which differs from (4) only in that the level of future dividends is replaced by their conditional expectation, and ρ_t is not restricted to equal the interest rate. But (8) is nearly empty – it says only that there is some sequence of discount factors ρ_t that will reconcile future expected dividends to current asset price. A natural specialization is to assume constancy of the discount factor:

$$p_t = \sum_{i=1}^{\infty} (1 + \rho)^{-i} E_t(d_{t+i}). \tag{9}$$

This version of the present-value relation has received extensive study, especially in the early finance literature. It is easily shown to imply

$$E_t(r_t) = \rho, \tag{10}$$

saying that the conditional expectation of the rate of return on the asset equals a constant independent of the conditioning set (Samuelson, 1965, 1973). This strong restriction provides the basis for most empirical tests of what has been called 'capital market efficiency' (Fama, 1970, 1976; LeRoy, 1976, 1982): if (10) is true, no information publicly available at t should be correlated with the rate of return on the asset from t to $t + 1$. In this sense prices 'fully reflect' all publicly available information.

The present-value relation may also be interpreted from the vantage point of its martingale implication: if the asset is priced according to (9), the value x_t of a mutual fund which holds the asset and reinvests all of its dividend income will follow a martingale with drift ρ, defined by

$$E_t(x_{t+1}) = (1 + \rho)x_t. \tag{11}$$

To see this, assume that the mutual fund holds h_t shares of the asset so that

$$x_t = h_t p_t \quad \text{and} \quad |x_{t+1} = h_{t+1} p_{t+1}.$$

When dividend income as reinvested, h_{t+1} is given by

$$h_{t+1} p_{t+1} = h_t(p_{t+1} + d_{t+1}).$$

Then

$$E_t(x_{t+1}) = E_t(h_{t+1} p_{t+1}) = h_t E_t(d_{t+1} + p_{t+1}) = x_t(1 + \rho), \tag{12}$$

using (1) and (10). To see that the correction for dividends payout is needed, observe that (10) implies that

$$\rho = E_t(d_{t+1})/p_t + E_t(p_{t+1})/p_t - 1, \tag{13}$$

239

so that changes in the expected dividend yield are always offset one-for-one by changes in the expected rate of capital gain. If p_t by itself were a martingale the expected rate of capital gain would be a constant, implying that p_t is a constant multiple of expected dividends. But this is not an implication of the present-value relation (take dividends as given by a first-order autoregressive process, for example). Hence p_t by itself does not follow a martingale.

The present-value-martingale model appears in many contexts in finance. If a futures price is assumed equal to the conditional expectation of the relevant spot price, then the futures price will follow a martingale (Samuelson, 1965). If the term structure of interest rate follows (a version of) the expectations hypothesis, then future interest rates implied by the term structure follow a martingale. If owners of an exhaustible resource like petroleum extract it at optimal rates, then in some settings the price of reserves will appreciate according to a martingale with drift equal to the interest rate. These applications are surveyed in LeRoy (1982). Finally, the expected present-value relation has implications for the volatility of asset prices. Informally, the expected present-value relation implies that stock prices are like a moving average of the dividend stream to which they give title. Since a moving average is smoother than its components, it follows that stock prices should show less volatility than dividends. Volatility tests along these lines were originally reported by Shiller (1979) for bond interest rates and LeRoy and Porter (1981) for stock prices. A number of subsequent papers extended and criticized the finding of excess volatility; see LeRoy (1984) for a brief survey.

Equation (10), which requires that the conditional expectation of the rate of return does not depend on the value taken on by the conditioning variables, is very restrictive. Unlike its certainty analogue (1), kwhich reflects only the assumption of zero transactions costs, (10) constitutes a restriction on the equilibrium probability distribution of the endogenously determined stock prices much stronger than anything implied by the idea of capital market efficiency alone. The question becomes: what restrictions on preferences and the production technology are needed to derive (10)? LeRoy (1973) showed that if agents are risk-neutral, then in an exchange economy (10) will be satisfied (see also LeRoy (1982) for discussion in a more general setting). The result is a consequence of the obvious fact that if agents are risk neutral they will ignore moments in the distribution of rates of return higher than the first. Under nonzero risk aversion, however, the conditional expected rate of return will contain a risk premium which generally depends on the realizations of the conditioning variables. Hence (10) will generally not be true. LeRoy (1973) and Lucas (1978) discussed a class of models in which the expected present-value property fails except as a special case.

If restrictions on dividend distributions are adopted, however, the expected present-value relation may be satisfied under restrictions on preferences weaker than risk neutrality. For example, Ohlson (1977) showed that if agents have constant (but not necessarily zero) relative risk-aversion and dividend growth rates are serially independent, then (10) will obtain. These sets of requirements are very restrictive theoretically, but the considerable evidence in favour of 'capital market efficiency' suggests that they may not be too unrealistic empirically (since the alternative of risk-neutrality is completely implausible.

If under certainty the rate of return on an asset is constant at ρ, but the convergence condition

$$\lim_{n \to \infty} (1 + \rho)^{-n} p_{t+n} = 0 \tag{14}$$

is not satisfied, then asset prices are characterized by a speculative bubble. The asset's price is higher than the present value of the stream of dividends the asset is title to, but nonetheless investors are willing to hold the asset because its price is expected to rise in the future. The definition of speculative bubbles under uncertainty is analogous (whether speculative bubbles exist or not has nothing to do with uncertainty). If speculative bubbles can occur, the present value equation must be generalized to

$$p_t = \sum_{i=1}^{\infty} (1 + \rho)^{-i} d_{t+i} + \gamma (1 + \rho)^t, \tag{15}$$

where γ is an arbitrary non-negative constant capturing the magnitude of the speculative bubble. Equation (15) is the class of solutions to the difference equation

$$\rho = (d_{t+1} + p_{t+1})/p_t - 1, \tag{16}$$

where γ is the constant of integration ($\gamma \geqslant 0$ results from the requirement that asset prices be always non-negative). In the special case $\gamma = 0$, speculative bubbles are absent and the present value relation results. Since even in the presence of speculative bubbles the rate of return on all assets equals ρ, there is no way that investors can simultaneously borrow (lend) money and buy (sell) the asset and earn a one-period arbitrage profit. By induction, the same is true for an investment plan covering any finite number of periods.

When investors can conduct an infinite arbitrage on an asset, then a speculative bubble cannot exist for that asset. Specifically, if investors can go short on the asset and long on its stream of dividends, they could earn an arbitrage profit equal to the magnitude of the bubble, if one existed. Effectively investors are then issuing their own stock. But the existence of such arbitrage opportunities is inconsistent with equilibrium, so it follows that if the outlined arbitrage is possible a speculative bubble cannot exist. However, on assets for which no such arbitrage opportunity exists, there is no inconsistency between equilibrium and the existence of speculative bubbles. The most recent major theoretical paper on speculative bubbles is Tirole (1985).

BIBLIOGRAPHY

Fama, E.F. 1970. Efficient capital markets: a review of theory and empirical work. *Journal of Finance* 25, May, 383–417.

Fama, E.F. 1976. Reply. *Journal of Finance* 31, March, 143–5.

Krouse, C.G. 1985. Competition and unanimity revisited, again. *American Economic Review* 75, December, 109–14.

LeRoy, S.F. 1973. Risk aversion and the martingale property of stock prices. *International Economic Review* 14, June, 436–46.

LeRoy, S.F. 1976. Efficient capital markets: comment. *Journal of Finance* 3, March, 139–41.

LeRoy, S.F. 1982. Expectations models of asset prices: a survey of theory. *Journal of Finance* 37, March, 185–217.

LeRoy, S.F. 1984. Efficiency and the variability of asset prices. *American Economic Review* 74, May, 183–7.

LeRoy, S.F. and Porter, R.D. 1981. The present-value relation: tests based on implied variance bounds. *Econometrica* 49, May, 555–74.

Lucas, R.E., Jr. 1978. Asset prices in an exchange economy. *Econometrica* 46, November, 1429–45.

Ohlson, J. 1977. Risk aversion and the martingale property of stock prices: comment. *International Economic Review* 18, February, 229–34.

Samuelson, P.A. 1965. Proof that properly anticipated prices fluctuate randomly. In *Collected Scientific Papers of Paul A. Samuelson*, ed. R.C. Merton, Vol. 3, Cambridge, Mass.: MIT Press, 1972, 782–90.

Samuelson, P.A. 1973. Proof that properly discounted present values of assets vibrate randomly. *Bell Journal of Economics and Management Service* 2, Autumn, 894–6.

Shiller, R.J. 1979. The volatility of long-term interest rates and expectations models of the term structure. *Journal of Political Economy* 87, December, 1190–219.

Tirole, J. 1985. Asset bubbles and overlapping generations. *Econometrica* 53, September, 1071–100.

Retention Ratio

A. COSH

The retention ratio of a corporation in any period may be defined as the ratio of retained earnings to the sum of retained earnings and dividend payments. The retention ratio is one factor in the decision concerning the optimal level of investment and the manner in which this investment is financed. The related variable, the dividend payout ratio, is defined as the proportion of available earnings paid out as dividends. In principle the sum of the retention ratio and time payout ratio should be unity. A major part of the economic debate concerning the retention ratio has mirrored the debate surrounding the debt-to-equity ratio chosen by a firm.

The subject of debate has been whether the market valuation of a firm is dependent upon its retention ratio. Miller and Modigliani (1961) conclude that, given the production and investment strategy of a firm, which determine its future earnings, the financing decision has no impact on its market value. First assume a world of perfect certainty and perfect capital markets in which all participants are price takers with costless access to all relevant information and in which there are no taxes or transactions costs. Under these conditions the choice of retention ratio will affect only the division of the return to the shareholder between dividend and capital gain and not the market valuation. When uncertainty is introduced, Lintner (1962) argues, different subjective assessments of a firm's prospects by investors will undermine the view that dividend policy is irrelevant. Furthermore, Gordon (1963) proposes that the discount rate will rise (and market value fall) with increases in the retention ratio due to the greater uncertainty of future returns. These attacks do not successfully undermine the argument in favour of the irrelevancy of dividend policy given the assumptions of perfect capital markets and the independence of the investment and financing decisions. However, the issue becomes more difficult to resolve when it is recognized that neither of these assumptions is likely to be true in reality.

Sources of capital market imperfections include transactions costs, taxes, lack of information and constraints on the supply of finance. Transactions costs include all charges concerned with the sale and purchase of shares and flotation of new shares. The existence of transactions costs limits the ability of the investor to create a 'home-made' payout ratio through dealing in shares. Taxation may influence retention ratios in a number of ways. In general, taxation of dividends is higher than that of capital gains. This will generally result in higher retentions being favoured, due to the lower rate of tax and tax deferral advantages of capital gains over dividends. However, different types of shareholders are affected in different ways, ranging from the charity or pension fund which is tax exempt to the wealthy private investor who may face a high marginal taxation of dividend income. This suggests that different types of shareholders will be attracted to different retention ratios. In equilibrium the range of retention ratios will reflect the range of shareholders, and no price advantage will be achieved by the firm through the choice of any particular retention ratio. Corporate taxation might itself be dependent upon the retention ratio and a system which taxes dividends differentially will tend to reduce the payout ratio. Lack of information and risk aversion will tend to bias shareholders in favour of dividends. If there is a limited supply of finance, either in general or to specific companies, a higher retention ratio might result.

The residual theory of dividends suggests that the investment decision and the financing decision should be taken jointly. Providing the debt-to-equity ratio is optimal and given that taxes and transactions costs exist, the retention ratio will be determined by the availability and potential profitability of investment opportunities. Investment is taken to the point at which its prospective return is equal to the perceived opportunity cost to shareholders of dividends foregone. There are other equally important reasons for suggesting that the investment and financing decisions are not independent, which together imply that the market value may be influenced by the choice of retention ratio. Managerial models of the firm assume that management has discretion over the choice of business objectives and do not accord shareholder welfare-maximization a primary role in these objectives. In such models management may take investment beyond its optimal level financed by a higher retention ratio. This would generate a lower market valuation associated with a higher retention ratio. Less scrutiny by shareholders of investment financed by retentions would reinforce this effect. If cost-plus pricing is being employed and the margin is related to the firm's financial requirements, the retention ratio and the profitability (and market valuation) may be inversely related.

It might be hoped that empirical analysis would resolve the question of whether these multiple, and often conflicting, influences of dividend policy on market valuation yield a definite conclusion in practice. This is not the case. The evidence demonstrates that dividends are more stable than earnings and that efforts are made to avoid reductions in dividends. Dividends adapt to earnings changes over a period of time. This phenomenon means that there is an information content of dividends. Changes in dividends may provide the best guide to investors in a world of uncertainty to the future path of earnings. This results in considerable difficulty in distinguishing between the impact on share prices of changes in retention ratios themselves from the impact of the associated implications for future earnings and investment.

Therefore, the empirical evidence has not proved conclusive, but the observed dispersion of retention ratios across firms, even within the same industry, suggests that the market value is fairly insensitive to the choice of retention ratio. On the other hand, since different groups of shareholders may not be indifferent to the choice of retention ratio, and since changes in target retention ratios may be misinterpreted by shareholders, the analysis suggests that firms will not wish to change their target retention ratio.

BIBLIOGRAPHY

Gordon, M. 1963. Optimal investment and financing policy. *Journal of Finance* 18, May, 264–72.

Lintner, J. 1962. Dividends, earnings, leverage, stock prices and the supply of capital to corporations. *Review of Economics and Statistics* 44, August, 243–69.

Miller, M.H. and Modigliani, F. 1961. Dividend policy, growth and the valuation of shares. *Journal of Business* 34, October, 411–33.

Stochastic Optimal Control

A.G. MALLIARIS

In the long history of mathematics, stochastic optimal control is a rather recent development. Using Bellman's Principle of Optimality along with measure-theoretic and functional-analytic methods, several mathematicians such as H. Kushner, W. Fleming, R. Rishel. W.M. Wonham and J.M. Bismut, among many others, made important contributions to this new area of mathematical research during the 1960s and early 1970s. For a complete mathematical exposition of the continuous time case see Fleming and Rishel (1975) and for the discrete time case see Bertsekas and Shreve (1978).

The assimilation of the mathematical methods of stochastic optimal control by economists was very rapid. Several economic papers started to appear in the early 1970s among which we mention Merton (1971) on consumption and portfolio rules using continuous time methodology and Brock and Mirman (1972) on optimal economic growth under uncertainty using discrete time techniques. Since then, stochastic optimal control methods have been applied in most major areas of economics such as price theory, macroeconomics, monetary economics and financial economics.

In this essay we (1) state the stochastic optimal control problem, (2) explain how it differs from deterministic optimal control and why that difference is crucial in economic problems, (3) present intuitively the methodology of optimal stochastic control and, finally, (4) give an illustration from optimal stochastic economic growth.

Consider the problem:

$$J[k(t), t, \infty] = \max E_t \int_t^\infty e^{-\rho s} u[k(s), v(s)] \, ds \qquad (1)$$

subject to the conditions

$$dk(t) = T[k(t), v(t)] \, dt + \sigma[k(t), v(t)] \, dZ(t), \qquad k(t) \text{ given.} \qquad (2)$$

246

Here $v = v(t) = v(t, \omega)$ is the control random variable, $k = k(t) = k(t, \omega)$ is the state random variable, $\rho \geqslant 0$ is the discount on future utility, u denotes a utility function, T is the drift component of technology, σ is the diffusion component, dZ is a Wiener process and E_t denotes expectation conditioned on $k(t)$ and $v(t)$.

We note immediately that (1) and (2) generalize the deterministic optimal control by incorporating *uncertainty*. The modelling of economic uncertainty is achieved by allowing both the control and state variables to be random and, more importantly, by postulating that condition (2) is described by a stochastic differential equation of the Itô type.

In the problem described by (1) and (2), if $\sigma(k, v) = 0$ and if k and v are assumed to be real variables instead of random then (1) and (2) reduce to the special case of deterministic optimal control. Thus, the stochastic optimal control problem differs from the deterministic optimal control in the sense that the former generalizes the latter, or equivalently, in the sense that the latter is a special case of the former. This is a crucial mathematical difference.

For the economist, the generalization achieved from stochastic optimal control means that the analysis of dynamic economic models becomes more realistic. The economic theorist who uses stochastic optimal control in positive or in welfare economics, in free market or centrally planned economies allows for randomness. Measurement errors, omission of important variables, non-exact relationships, incomplete theories and other methodological complexities are modelled in stochastic optimal control by allowing the control and state variables to be random, and also, by incorporating *pure randomness* through the white noise factor $dZ(t)$. The random variable $dZ(t)$ describes increments in the Wiener process $\{Z(t), t \geqslant 0\}$ that are independent and normally distributed with mean, $E[dZ(t)] = 0$ and variance $\mathrm{Var}[dZ(t)] = dt$.

In particular, equation (2) is a significant economic generalization of the analogous equation in deterministic control. The reader may recall that in deterministic control the constraint is given by $\dot{k} \equiv dk(t)/dt = T[k(t), v(t)]$. Because $dk(t)$ in (2) is a random variable we can compute its mean and variance. They are given by

$$E[dk(t)] = T[k(t), v(t)]; \qquad \mathrm{Var}[dk(t)] = \sigma^2[k(t), v(t)]\, dt.$$

Thus (2) is a meaningful generalization of its counterpart in deterministic control because it involves means, standard deviations and pure randomness in capturing the complexities of economic reality. A comprehensive analysis of Itô equations, such as (2), is given in Malliaris and Brock (1982).

The problem in (1) and (2) is a stochastic analogue of the deterministic one studied in Arrow and Kurz (1970, pp. 27–51). A standard technique for our problem, as in the case of Arrow and Kurz, is Bellman's (1957, p. 83) *Principle of Optimality* according to which 'an optimal policy has the property that, whatever the initial state and control are, the remaining decisions must constitute an optimal policy with regard to the state resulting from the first decision'. The problem in equations (1) and (2) is studied here for the undiscounted, finite horizon case, i.e. for $\rho = 0$ and $N < \infty$.

Using Bellman's technique for dynamic programming, equations (1) and (2) can be analysed as follows:

$$J[k(t), t, N] = \max E_t \int_t^N u(k, v)\, ds$$

$$= \max E_t \int_t^{t+\Delta t} u(k, v)\, ds + \max E_{t+\Delta t} \int_{t+\Delta t}^N u(k, v)\, ds$$

$$= \max E_t \left\{ \int_t^{t+\Delta t} u(k, v)\, ds + J[k(t+\Delta t), t+\Delta t, N] \right\}$$

$$= \max E_t \{ u[k(t), v(t)]\Delta t + J[k(t), t, N]$$

$$+ J_k \Delta k + J_t \Delta t + \tfrac{1}{2} J_{kk}(\Delta k)^2$$

$$+ J_{kt}(\Delta k)(\Delta t) + \tfrac{1}{2} J_n(\Delta t)^2 + o(\Delta t)\}. \tag{3}$$

Observe that Taylor's theorem is used to obtain (3) and therefore it is assumed that J has continuous partial derivatives of all orders less than 3 in some open set containing the line segment connecting the two points $[k(t), t]$ and $[k(t+\Delta t), t+\Delta t]$. Let (2) be approximated and write

$$\Delta k = T(k, v)\Delta t + \sigma(k, v)\Delta Z + o(\Delta t). \tag{4}$$

Insert (4) into (3) and use the multiplication rules

$$(\Delta Z) \times (\Delta t) = 0, \quad (\Delta t) \times (\Delta t) = 0 \quad \text{and} \quad (\Delta Z) \times (\Delta Z) = \Delta t$$

to get

$$0 = \max E_t[u(k, v)\Delta t + (J_k T + J_t + \tfrac{1}{2} J_{kk}\sigma^2)\Delta t + J_k \sigma \Delta Z + o(\Delta t)]. \tag{5}$$

For notational convenience let

$$\Delta J = [J_t + J_k T + \tfrac{1}{2} J_{kk}\sigma^2]\Delta t + J_k \sigma \Delta Z. \tag{6}$$

Using (6), equation (5) becomes

$$0 = \max E_t[u(k, v)\Delta t + \Delta J + o(\Delta t)]. \tag{7}$$

This is a partial differential equation with boundary condition $[(\partial J)/\partial k][k(N), N, N] = 0$. Pass E_t through the parentheses of (7) and after dividing both sides by Δt, let $\Delta t \to 0$ to conclude

$$0 = \max[u(k, v) + J_t + J_k T(k, v) + \tfrac{1}{2} J_{kk}\sigma^2(k, v,)]. \tag{8}$$

This last equation is usually written as

$$-J_t = \max[u(k, v) + J_k T(k, v) + \tfrac{1}{2} J_{kk}\sigma^2(k, v)] \tag{9}$$

and is known as the *Hamilton–Jacobi–Bellman equation* of stochastic control theory.

Next, we define the costate variable $p(t)$ as

$$p(t) = J_k[k(t), t, N]$$

from which it follows that its partial derivative with respect to k is

$$p_k = \partial p / \partial k = J_{kk}. \tag{10}$$

Therefore, we may rewrite (9) as

$$-J_t = \max H(k, v, p, \partial p / \partial k), \tag{11}$$

where H is the functional notation of the expression inside the brackets of (9). Assume next that a function v exists that solves the maximization problem of (11) and denote such a function by

$$v^0 = v^0(k, p, \partial p / \partial k). \tag{12}$$

Note that v^0 is a function of $k(t)$ and t alone, along the optimum path, because J_k is a function of $k(t)$ and t alone, In the applied control literature, and more specifically in economic applications, v^0 is called a *policy function*. Assuming then that a policy function v^0 exists, (11) may be rewritten as

$$-J_t = \max H(k, v, p, \partial p / \partial k) = H[k, v^0(k, p, \partial p / \partial k), p, \partial p / \partial k]$$
$$= H^0(k, p, \partial p / \partial k). \tag{13}$$

This last equation is again a functional notation of the right-hand side expression of (9) under the assumption of the existence of an optimum control v^0, that is,

$$H^0(k, p, \partial p / \partial k) = u(k, v^0) + pT(k, v^0) + \frac{1}{2} \frac{\partial p}{\partial k} \sigma^2(k, v^0). \tag{14}$$

Equipped with the above analysis we can now state:

Proposition 1 (Pontryagin Stochastic Maximum Principle). Suppose that $k(t)$ and $v^0(t)$ solve for $t \in [0, N]$ the problem:

$$\max E_0 \int_0^N u(k, v) \, dt$$

subject to the conditions

$$dk = T(k, v) \, dt + \sigma(k, v) \, dZ, \qquad k(t) \text{ given.}$$

Then, there exists a costate variable $p(t)$ such that for each t, $t \in [0, N]$:

(1) v^0 maximizes $H(k, v, p, \partial p / \partial k)$ where

$$H(k, v, p, \partial p / \partial k) = u(k, v) + pT(k, v) + \frac{1}{2} \frac{\partial p}{\partial k} \sigma^2;$$

(2) the costate function $p(t)$ satisfies the stochastic differential equation $dp = -H_k^0 \, dt + \sigma(k, v^0) J_{kk} \, dZ$; and

249

(3) the transversality condition holds

$$p[k(N), N] = \frac{\partial J}{\partial k} [k(N), N, N] = 0,$$

$$p(N)k(N) = 0.$$

Finally, we briefly illustrate the stochastic optimal control techniques as applied to the stochastic Ramsey problem studied in Merton (1975). The problem is to find an optimal saving policy s^0 to

$$\text{maximize } E_0 \int_0^T u(c)\, dt \tag{15}$$

subject to

$$dk = [sf(k) - (n - \sigma^2)k]\, dt - \sigma k\, dZ \tag{16}$$

and $k(t) \geqslant 0$ for each t. Here, u is a strictly concave, von Neumann–Morgenstern utility function of per capita consumption c for the representative consumer and $f(k)$ is a well-behaved production function. Note that $c = (1 - s)f(k)$ and that equation (16) generalizes Solow's equation of neoclassical economic growth. Uncertainty enters (16) via randomness in the rate of growth of the labour force. Let

$$J[k(t), t, T] = \max_s E_t \int_t^T u[(1 - s)f(k)]\, dt.$$

The Hamilton–Jacobi–Bellman equation is given by

$$0 = \max \{ u[(1 - s)f(k)] + J_t + J_k[sf(k) - (n - \sigma^2)k] + \tfrac{1}{2}J_{kk}\sigma^2 k^2 \} \tag{17}$$

which yields

$$\frac{du}{dc} [(1 - s^0)f(k)] = J_k. \tag{18}$$

To solve for s^0, in principle, one solves (18) for s^0 as a function of k, $T - t$ and J_K, and then substitutes this solution into (17) which becomes a *partial differential equation for J*. Once (17) is solved, then its solution is substituted back into (18) to determine s^0 as a function of k and $T - t$. The nonlinearity of the Hamilton–Jacobi–Bellman equation causes difficulties in finding a closed form solution for the optimal saving function. However, if we let $\sigma = 0$ in (17) one obtains the classical Ramsey rule of the certainty case.

From the fact that numerous economic questions involve uncertainty and can be formulated as stochastic optimal control problems, one may conclude that economic interest is likely to be lively in this area for some time to come.

BIBLIOGRAPHY

Arrow, K.J. and Kurz, M. 1970. *Public Investment, the Rate of Return, and Optimal Fiscal Policy.* Baltimore: Johns Hopkins Press.

Bellman, R. 1957. *Dynamic Programming*. Princeton: Princeton University Press.

Bertsekas, D.P. and Shreve, S.E. 1978. *Stochastic Optimal Control: the Discrete Time Case*. New York: Academic Press.

Brock, W.A. and Mirman, L. 1972. Optimal economic growth and uncertainty: the discounted case. *Journal of Economic Theory* 4, 479–513.

Fleming, W.H. and Rishel, R.W. 1975. *Deterministic and Stochastic Optimal Control*. New York: Springer-Verlag.

Malliaris, A.G. and Brock, W.A. 1982. *Stochastic Methods in Economics and Finance*. Amsterdam: North-Holland.

Merton, R.C. 1971. Optimal consumption and portfolio rules in a continuous-time model. *Journal of Economic Theory* 3, 373–413.

Merton, R.C. 1975. An asymptotic theory of growth under uncertainty. *Review of Economic Studies* 42, 375–93.

Takeovers and The Stock Market

ALAN HUGHES AND AJIT SINGH

In a market economy the stock exchange has a triple role, first to pool together society's savings dispersed among individual savers; second to channel selectively these savings to companies with the best investment prospects, and third to encourage the efficient use of assets embodying past savings. Two interrelated mechanisms are involved. A primary market mechanism, whereby new issues of shares are made by companies wishing to raise funds, and a secondary market mechanism whereby trade in the existing shares of companies is carried out. A company whose equities are traded at a relatively low price will find it relatively expensive or impossible to raise new funds in the primary market. It may also be subject to the threat of a takeover in which a majority ownership stake in its equity is acquired by another company whose objective is to change policies to improve the stock price. Management teams may thus compete in a market for corporate control, and takeovers may then be interpreted as a central part of the stock market selection process.

Ever since the emergence of the joint stock company and the subsequent growth in the UK and US of equity capital markets at the end of the 19th century takeovers have been a pervasive feature of industrial life, and periodic waves of takeover activity have transformed the corporate structure of these and other industrial economies. The post World War II period, in particular, has been characterized by massive merger waves. These have been accompanied in the US and the UK by a growth in the importance of takeovers in the form of direct bids or tender offers to the shareholders of target companies, rather than takeover through some form of merger negotiation between the respective boards of directors, followed by referral to an agreed deal to shareholders for their approval. There are a number of reasons for these latest developments. In the US and the UK for instance an increased dispersion of shareownership created a more volatile structure of ownership and control, whilst regulatory and legal changes enforced a greater public disclosure of corporate information and made bids a relatively

252

cheap form of takeover (Davies, 1976; Hannah, 1976; Dodd, 1986). Thus takeover for whatever purpose, and the takeover bid or tender offer form were facilitated.

Whereas in the UK in successive periods prior to 1950 takeovers as a whole never accounted for more than a third of the 'deaths' of quoted companies, in the period 1948 to 1958 they accounted for over two-thirds, and in the periods 1959 to 1965, and 1966 to 1972, for four-fifths. The upshot was an unprecedently high death rate, both overall and from takeover (Hart and Prais, 1956; Singh, 1971; and authors' own calculations). In 1954 there were a little over 2000 manufacturing firms quoted on the UK stock market; of these 400 were acquired by 1960. The chances of dying by takeover were twice as high again in the takeover boom years of 1967–70. In the decade 1972–82 one in three of the largest 730 quoted companies were acquired, whilst in the mid-1980s' boom 137 of the largest 1000 non-financial companies died through takeover in the four years from 1982 to 1986 (Singh, 1971, 1975; Hughes and Kumar, 1985; Hughes, 1987).

In the United States a similar picture emerges. A company ranked in the top 1000 largest manufacturing firms in 1950 had a one in three chance of dying by 1972, with takeovers (which occurred primarily in the 1960s) accounting for 95% of deaths (Mueller, 1986). In the merger peak years 1967–69 the annual average percentage of the assets of the largest 2000 manufacturing and mining companies disappearing through takeover fluctuated between 2.5% and 3.3%, compared with around 1% in the years 1961–66, and less than 0.5% in the years 1971–72 (Steiner, 1975). In the two decades 1963–82, one in seven of the companies quoted on the New York and American stock exchanges disappeared through acquisition (Dodd, 1986), whilst, as in the UK, a resurgence of giant company mergers in the mid-1980s meant that, in the single year 1985 alone, 21 of the *Fortune* 500 Industrials were taken over, accounting for around 2% of that population's total assets, sales and employment (*Fortune*, 1986a, 1986b).

Similar surges of takeovers have occurred elsewhere in the industrial economies making the post-war period an unprecedently significant period of activity out-stripping the earlier waves of the turn of the century and the inter-war years in scale and persistence (Hughes and Singh, 1980). There is therefore no doubt that an extremely active market in corporate control exists. However, as we shall see below, the selection process that it embodies is not so easily characterized.

I. In view of the sheer size of takeover activity and the fact that takeovers are now the main cause of 'death' of large firms, their significance cannot be exaggerated either for economic theory (the theory of the stockmarket, the theory of economic 'natural' selection, the theory of the firm) or for economic policy.

Traditionally, an extremely important line of defence of the neoclassical theory of the firm and its central assumption of profit-maximization has been the concept of economic 'natural' selection. It is argued that despite the separation of ownership from control in large corporations and their complex and varied internal organizations, the forces of competition compel them to maximize profits whatever the wishes of the management or other groups in the corporation; for, if they do not, they will not long surve in the marketplace (Friedman, 1953; Alchian, 1950; Johnson, 1968; for a much earlier assertion of this 'natural selection' or the competitive survival theory, see Marx, volume 1 of *Capital*). However, Winter (1964, 1971) has shown that profit-maximizers are not the only survivors in a competitive selection process in all states of the world. Specifically, in a world of uncertainty, barriers to entry, oligopolistic markets and cost advantages to scale, it may easily be the growth-maximizing or 'satisficing' (those who seek satisfactory rather than maximum profits) firms who survive rather than the profit-maximizers.

Moreover, in an environment of imperfect product markets, Leibenstein's important paper (1966) focused attention on the phenomenon of X-efficiency, i.e. that many firms do not operate on the bounds of their production possibility frontiers and minimize costs (as envisaged by orthodox theory). The degree of X-efficiency (the distance between the production possibility surface and the actual level of firm's operations), it is suggested, is positively related to the market power the firm enjoys in the product market. Similarly, it has been recognized that in large corporations where there is a separation of ownership from control, there is a so-called 'agency problem'. This problem arises from the fact that, typically, the owners, i.e. the shareholders of large corporations, are dispersed and, therefore, find it difficult to act in concert. Consequently, it may be too costly for them to monitor the firm's management and to ensure that it acts as the owners' 'agents' and thus maximizes profits and the stockmarket valuation of the firm rather than pursue its own goals, e.g. growth, or large administrative expenditures (Jensen and Meckling, 1976).

Notwithstanding imperfect product markets and the agency problem, the profit-maximization hypothesis and the neoclassical theory of the firm can be rescued by the functioning of an efficient takeover mechanism on the stockmarket. For, if all firms for which there is a discrepancy between their existing stockmarket valuation and what it could be under an alternative management were bid for and taken over by the latter, no non-profit maximizers will survive (Alchian and Kessel, 1962; Meade, 1968). Moreover, as far as the internal organization of large corporations is concerned, the takeover mechanism of this type will ensure that only those firms with the optimal organizational structure are able to survive (Alchian and Demsetz, 1972).

The validity of this line of reasoning depends on the following crucial conditions. First, that the share prices generated by the stockmarket are 'efficient' in the specific sense that they reflect the relative expected profitability of firms. For, if this were not the case, the takeover mechanism could easily produce perverse results, e.g. if the share prices were unrelated to firm profitability, many unprofitable rather than just profitable firms may be selected for survival. Second, there should be sufficient knowledge about the internal operations of firms so that any discrepancy between the actual and the potential profitability of their resource use can be detected by the market and by other corporate managements. Third, there should be sufficient supply of corporate raiders to eliminate rapidly any discrepancies between actual and potential profitability which may exist.

II. Many economists argue that for both theoretical and practical reasons, the conditions necessary for an efficient takeover mechanism of the kind characterized above do not exist in actual stockmarkets. First, consider share prices. There are many studies purporting to show that stock-market prices are 'efficient' in the sense, for instance, of rapidly incorporating new information (Keane, 1983). There is not much, however, to suggest that share price movements are systematically related to the current, past, or subsequent underlying performance variables of companies, or to longer run equilibrium considerations, rather than for those of short run disequilibrium (Nerlove, 1968; Little and Rayner, 1966; Shiller, 1979; Summers, 1986). This leaves considerable scope for takeovers based on speculative and other motives where corporate control changes hands because of differences of information or opinion about the accuracy of stock-market valuations between sellers and purchasers of control, rather than because of proposed changes in management objectives or operating efficiency (Gort, 1969; Hughes, Mueller and Singh, 1980; Grossman and Hart, 1981). It also leaves plenty of scope for promoters and arbitrageurs to attempt to manipulate, and benefit from, changes in stock prices associated with takeovers, or the threat of them, in a way unconnected with underlying performance variables (Boesky, 1985; Markham, 1955). As one early stock-market observer noted:

> Since property here exists in the form of stock, its movement and transfer become purely a result of gambling on the stock exchange, where the little fish are swallowed by the sharks and the lambs by the stock exchange wolves (Marx, 1971).

Equally, mature managerially controlled corporations whose preference for growth may be characterized by the use of a lower discount rate than the market as a whole, will be faced with a sea of undervalued takeover opportunities (Mueller, 1969). They may then initiate takeovers not to benefit shareholders but to satisfy their own empire building ambitions (Rhoades, 1985; Marris, 1964). Moreover, it has been argued that

> [this] pursuit of growth may be self-reinforcing; the more managers pursue this objective, the more other managers feel they must conform; thus rather than deviant managerial behaviour being driven out by stockholder welfare-maximising behaviour, the so-called 'deviant' behaviour has more likely driven out the other (Marris and Mueller, 1980, p. 42).

Even where takeovers are stockholder welfare-maximizing in intent, and stock prices are an efficient guide to such action, failures in the market for corporate control may still occur because of transactions cost considerations and because acquiring companies may not be able to capture for themselves all the benefit of the raid.

Disciplinary raids are not costless; the price of identifying mismanagement and the transaction costs of correcting it through takeover can be high so that there will always be some margin of management discretion. Indeed, since

255

contested takeovers with higher associated legal and advisory costs are more likely to occur in the case of large than small bids (Newbould, 1970), these costs may be greater for larger 'managerial' companies giving more discretion just where it needs to be most curbed. In more general terms, the greater the discretionary benefit of control, the more rivalrous the market for control may be, and the more raided management may resist, and thus the higher these transaction costs may become. To the extent that the costs of identifying mismanagement are lower for raids within the same industry and the likelihood of contests therefore greater (Halpern, 1983), then where monopolistic structures exist the costs of imposing discipline will be relatively high since either the companies involved will be within the same industry but typically large, or the bid will involve an outsider with higher costs of information gathering. The sums involved are not negligible. In the US just the fees paid to deal-makers to effect the largest 10 takeovers in 1985 amounted to around $200 million. On one estimate, the three leading dealing firms together made around $600 million in 1985 from takeover bids, not counting commissions or the costs of raising funds for the deals. Whilst in the UK a failed diversifying contested bid for a major company in 1986 is said to have cost the raider £54 million in advisers' and other bid fees (Jay, 1986; *Fortune*, 1986b, 1986c). These transaction costs are in part a function of defensive takeover tactics which are designed to raise either the pre- or post-acquisition costs of gaining control; such methods are well developed in the US and are spreading to the UK. 'Shark repellent' constitutional arrangements to protect existing directors by staggered elections to the board, or particular voting schemes for bid approvals; 'golden parachutes' to raise the costs of firing incumbent management; and either counterbidding against the raider, seeking a 'white knight' to contest the unwanted bid, or raiding a third party (Greer, 1986) all throw cost-increasing sand into the works. Whether this is a virtue or vice depends upon how genuine disciplinary raids are, and upon the reasons for, and terms which shareholders extract from, top executives in return for offering them this sort of protection from job loss through takeover. In principle, many of these devices could be used as part of an overall remuneration and conditions package for the managers which emphasized whatever incentive structure the active shareholders desired. This, however, may be expecting rather a lot given the current structure of governance in the modern corporation in which managers play a leading role in determining their own remuneration and in selecting outside directors to serve on corporate boards (Herman, 1981).

At the other end of the corporate size scale the presence of stronger owner-controlling interests in small companies may also clog up the takeover mechanism. If the valuation placed by owner managers upon their shares exceeds the marginal valuation ruling in the market, there will be a premium to be paid to effect control which may vary from company to company without any necessary connection with the extent of deviations from value-maximizing policies. As far as small companies are concerned it means that it may be (e.g. in the case of majority ownership) impossible to obtain control, or very costly in the face of a hostile board with large holdings (Davies and Kuehn, 1977). The upshot of these arguments is that the costs of disciplinary action might restrict its exercise to the medium size ranges of companies.

In addition to market failure problems due to transaction costs, it has also been argued that the incentive structure in bids may lead to too few bids from the point of view of disciplining management (Grossman and Hart, 1980). If each of the shareholders in the target firm in a raid believes that an individual decision to sell out will not prevent the bidder from gaining effective control then there is for each of them an incentive to hang on to their equity as minority shareholders in the post-bid situation and 'free ride' on the stock price gains following the new management's efficiency improvements. This prevents the raider from reaping all the benefits, and, in the limit, could prevent successful raids altogether if sufficient shareholders hang on for the free ride.

The implication of this argument is that *ceteris paribus*, the level of merger activity will be less than is warranted since the private return to the raider is less than the overall return which is split between the raiders and the free riders. On the other hand it may be argued that if minority rights of sellers are not protected then partial bids (e.g. for 51%) will occur followed by exploitation of control at the expense of the remaining minority shareholders. This may occur whether the incumbent management are value-maximizers or not since in effect the buyer gains complete control whilst paying only half the full purchase price. This could lead to too many 'undesirable' bids, in the sense that they incur transaction costs but merely redistribute wealth between the raider and the oppressed minority rather than create net social value (Yarrow, 1985).

The force of each of these arguments depends upon the institutional and legal constraints within which bidders and potential free riders must operate during and after the bid process. In general, the problem in principle is how to ensure that there are costs imposed on free riding minority interests whilst ensuring that there is no undue oppression of minority shareholders after partial bids, or unequal treatment of shareholders in the process of the bid itself. In the institutional context of the UK at least there are grounds for thinking that the free rider problem is not a serious deterrent inhibiting the level of merger activity, whilst there is some attempt to deter partial oppressive bids (Yarrow, 1985; Hughes, 1987; Johnston, 1980). In any event the idea that free riding has seriously restricted the overall level of takeover activity does not seem very convincing in the face of the huge takeover booms in the post-war period.

III. In view of these competing theories about the nature of the takeover selection mechanism on the stockmarket and its significance for economic theory, the subject clearly needs to be investigated empirically. Using the experience of takeovers in the UK during the period 1954–60, Singh (1971) was the first study explicitly to explore this phenomenon. By comparing the characteristics of the 'living' (non-taken-over firms) and the 'dead' (the taken-over firms), he attempted to find out what kind of firms are selected for survival on the stockmarket. This research also involved a comparative analysis of the economic and financial characteristics of the 'predators' (the taking-over firms) and their 'victims' (the firms they took over). In a subsequent study (Singh, 1975), he examined these questions in relation to the takeover boom of 1967–70 to discover to what extent, if any, the nature of the selection process changes during a period of high takeover activity.

The main results which emerge from these studies may be summarized as follows. There is a very large degree of overlap between the characteristics of taken over and non-taken over firms so that it is not very easy to distinguish between the two groups, the degree of overlap being somewhat greater during the takeover booms. Thus, on a univariate basis, although profitability (which performed slightly better than other performance indicators such as growth and Marris's 'valuation ratio') was a statistically significant discriminator, it achieved very poor discrimination between the two groups. For example, during 1967–70, 46% of the firms would have been misclassified (as against 50% on random allocation) if this variable alone had been used to distinguish between the taken over and non-taken over companies. Strikingly, only a slightly greater distinction between the 'living' and the 'dead' could be achieved if all the variables were combined together to distinguish between the two groups on a multivariate basis: the degree of misclassification on the basis of all the relevant variables was 43%, compared with 46% on the basis of profitability and 50% on random allocation.

Overall, the two most important discriminators between the taken over and non-taken over companies were found to be size and profitability. However, there was an important (but different) non-linear relationship between each of these variables and probability of acquisition. The probability of takeover was much the same for all size class of firms except the largest ones for which it declined sharply with an increase in firm size. With respect to profitability, the probability of acquisition was appreciably higher than average for extremely unprofitable firms; it was, however, more or less constant for firms ranked from the third to the highest decile in the profitability league.

The two studies found that there were sharper differences (a smaller degree of overlap) between the 'predators' (the acquiring firms) and their 'victims' (the firms they took over) than between the taken over and the surviving firms. The acquiring firms were, on average, bigger and more profitable, faster-growing, more liquid and more highly geared than those they acquired; the former also showed greater improvements in profits and retained more of them. However, the most important discriminator by far was size: 75% of the firms would have been correctly classified (as against 50% on random allocation) if size alone had been used to distinguish between the acquiring and the acquired firm. Other variables (e.g. profitability, change in profitability and growth) were also statistically significant discriminators but they did not help achieve much *additional* discrimination between the two groups than that attained on the basis of size alone. Singh's research also found that there were statistically significant differences between the acquiring and non-acquiring firms but they were not as important as those between the acquiring and the acquired firms.

The above results have been broadly confirmed in most other empirical studies of takeovers in the UK (Hughes, 1987, provides a comprehensive reivew for the

UK; for the US see e.g. Schwartz, 1982; Harris et al., 1982; Mueller, 1980). Kuehn (1975) arrived at somewhat different conclusions; but, if allowance is made for the different methodology used by him, his results can be reconciled with those reported above. In view of the acquisition of very large corporations in the current takeover boom of the mid-1980s in the UK and the US, Hughes' (1987) results are interesting. He found that the probability of acquisitions for the largest firms (say the 100 largest) is still very low and declines with an increase in firm size. However, the middle-sized giants (e.g. those ranked between 100 to 200 in the size rankings) have become more vulnerable to raids by those among the top 100. Comparisons of pre- and post-takeover performance (as opposed to studies of pre-merger characteristics alone) suggest that at best the impact of takeover on 'efficiency' or profitability is neutral. If stockholders and/or managers anticipate gains in these areas, on average they will be disappointed. They may be less disenchanted, however, if their objective is higher investment or growth, both of which appear to be less likely to be negatively affected than other performance measures (see e.g. Meeks, 1977; Cosh, Hughes and Singh, 1980; Cowling et al., 1980; Ravenscraft and Scherer, 1986; Kumar, 1984; Hughes 1987).

IV. The above studies would seem to lend scant support to the view that the takeover mechanism on the stockmarket selects only the efficient firms for survival or that it leads overall to a more profitable allocation of society's assets (Reddaway, 1972). There is, however, another group of studies, based exclusively on stockmarket data, which purports to arrive at a rather different conclusion on the effectiveness of the market for corporate control. This evidence, suggesting that takeover on the capital market leads to a systematic transfer of control away from inefficient towards shareholder welfare-maximizing management, comes from studies of share price effects before, during, and after takeover announcements. With one or two exceptions the studies involved use an 'event study' methodology to isolate the impact of takeover. A model of stock price returns (price change plus dividends) is estimated for both acquiring and target firms, excluding data for a period before and after the takeover event, and then actual returns prior to, and at the announcement of the takeover, and subsequent to it, are compared with the counterfactual returns based on the estimated equation. The counterfactual estimating equations vary from study to study but are most often based on some version of the capital asset pricing model, in which the historical relationship between the return on a stock and that on the market as a whole is used to predict the 'normal' return from which the 'abnormal' deviations due to the takeover event are measured. The precise results obtained vary with: the periods over which abnormal returns are measured; the form of the takeover; the way it is financed; whether or not it is consummated; and the historical period examined. The broad picture given by these studies is, however, reasonably clear. For longer term periods prior to takeover the acquiring companies are doing somewhat better than 'normal' and the targets somewhat worse. In the shorter run, prior to and upon announcement of the takeover, there are abnormal benefits for the targets' shareholders and abnormal losses or neutral effects for those of the acquiring company. After takeover, negative or neutral effects on the acquiring companies' stock are the norm. Depending upon the period over which returns are measured the joint net effects of the combined acquiring and target company share price movements are positive or neutral. The longer the post-merger period the worse the net effect appears to be (Jensen and Ruback, 1983; Firth, 1979 and 1980; Hughes, 1987).

There are, however, problems with evidence based on this sort of approach. Even if it were accepted that in the short run the joint effects of merger on abnormal returns may be positive, several problems of interpretation remain. Takeovers may change the risks associated with holding the shares of the companies involved and hence the underlying relation between those stocks and the market, thus biasing the estimated abnormal returns. Moreover, takeovers themselves are related to variation in stock-market activity which in turn may affect the underlying counterfactual equations which the event study method assumes to represent equilibrium values (Conn, 1985). At a more fundamental level the underlying methodology of the event studies assumes that demand curves for stocks are horizontal so that normally trading investors may buy or sell any amount of stock without systematically affecting the price. The marginal price reflects average opinion; when sharp movements in price occur in association with an event (e.g. a takeover) they are then interpreted as a response to the 'new information' imparted by it. Positive abnormal returns associated with bids may therefore be interpreted to suggest that the market expects improved performance to follow from merger, and shareholders benefit accordingly. The distribution of these gains between the stockholders of the acquired and acquiring companies is then determined by the competitiveness of the bid market, the presence or absence of rival bids, contests by incumbent management, and so on. If, however, there are for instance, divergences of expectations and opinion over security values so that the marginal trading valuation reflects marginal opinion only, then the market demand curve may slope downwards to the right, and some investors will require a price above that at the margin before selling (Hughes, Mueller and Singh, 1980; Cragg and Malkiel, 1982; Miller, 1977; Black, 1986; Schleifer, 1986; Mayshar, 1983). Premia will therefore be necessary simply to effect the ownership transfer in a takeover, and they may vary, for instance, with the dispersion of stock holdings and the dispersion of divergent opinion across the various blocks of shares. They are also subject to fraudulent insider trading manipulations. These premia will therefore be highly ambiguous guides to relative expected efficiency gains either when taken on average or in relation to particular mergers. They tell us merely what the short term windfall wealth effects of merger are relative to a particular counterfactual, for those individuals directly involved as shareholders (or the larger number indirectly involved via changes in pensions and insurance policy premia following financial institutions' portfolio responses to bids). There is no necessary connection between the direction and magnitude of these premia and underlying real changes in the management and performance of the assets over which the property rights embodied in the stock give control. Thus Kuehn (1976) could not find any systematic relationship for the UK between the financial and performance variables of acquiring and acquired firms and the size of the bid premiums paid to effect takeovers. All that may be deduced is that for *some* reasons the bidders felt it worth while to offer the premia and the sellers felt it worth while to accept. These reasons, as mentioned earlier, may be as much related to the pursuit of monopoly power, and empire building, as to enhanced management techniques, scale and scope economies, or other profit enhancing objectives.

V. Overall, to the extent that the empirical studies show that the takeover selection process operates both on size and profitability and that the selection on the basis of profitability is very weak, it supports the postulates of the managerial and behavioural theories of the firm rather than those of the neoclassical theory and its associated doctrine of economic natural selection.

It has been argued nonetheless that, if the market for corporate control was working well, then the threat of discipline for poor profitability would in fact produce the sort of results reported for pre-merger profitability levels and post-merger effects. Thus, with a perfectly effective disciplinary threat, all firms would be making maximum potential profits and the remaining takeovers would be occurring for other non-disciplinary reasons. Therefore the data cannot, it is argued, distinguish between the view, on the one hand that the deterrent is ineffective because the threat is unreal, and on the other that the deterrent is very effective and so is the threat (Hannah and Kay, 1977, pp. 123–5). This is not particularly convincing. In so far as a deterent is perceived it must be based on learning from the nature of takeover activity, so that punishment and crime can be connected. If the thousands of mergers which have occurred have been essentially random then there is no evidence from which to learn anything systematic.

Moreover, this argument ignores altogether the role of size in the selection process which is consistently emphasized by all the available empirical studies. Size rather than profitability or market valuation emerges clearly as the most consistently successful discriminator between acquiring and acquired companies. Thus, if large size is associated with 'managerialism' and market power, then discipline on the stock market may be most restricted in just those cases where the size of the companies involved suggests that product market constraints on managers will be weakest.

Direct evidence on large company managers' perceptions of discipline is also inconsistent with the view that they link poor profit performance with the threat of takeover. Minimising the threat of takeover was chosen as the least significant of 10 possible long run objectives offered to senior executives of 18 large UK quoted companies in an interview and questionnaire study carried out in the period 1974–76. Moreover, minimizing the risk of takeover was also thought to be the least important of nine possible reasons for pursuing profits as a long term objective (Francis, 1980). Even if profitability and increases in size were both seen by managers as significantly positively related to a reduced probability of takeover then it is possible to argue that, where they have some degree of

261

internal discretion, managers will prefer increases in size to the extent that their remuneration status and power are more closely related to it than to profitability. Since size and the variability of profitability over time are also inversely related, increasing size would also help reduce the threat of takeover due to short term swings in profits. Making an acquisition to increase size might then itself become a tactic to avoid acquisition (Greer, 1986; Singh, 1971).

The results based on accounting and other non-stockmarket data may thus be used to provide a managerialist interpretation of the stock price effect studies, by emphasising the lack of stock price gains to the acquiring companies' stockholders, compared to the positive impacts of takeover on corporate growth, and by attributing the premia paid to effect takeovers more to the kind of non-profit factors discussed earlier in our comments of the event study methodology, rather than to anticipated but apparently unrealised long term efficiency gains. They are also, however, consistent with the view that at the margin we should not expect takeovers to be any more or less profitable than other forms of corporate investment. However, if we then take the event study results at face value it appears that the stock market has been systematically wrong and over-optimistic in anticipating that things could be otherwise.

Neither interpretation is very comfortable for those who would argue that the stock market takeover selection process and the pricing signals on which it is based are likely to be effective guardians of economic efficiency, even in the severely narrow sense reflected by changes in private profitability and stockholder welfare.

REFERENCES

Alchian, A.A. 1950. Uncertainty, evolution, and economic theory. *Journal of Political Economy* 58, June, 211–22.

Alchian, A.A. and Kessel, R.A. 1962. Competition monopoly and the pursuit of pecuniary gain. In *Aspects of Labour Economics*, N.B.E.R. Princeton, pp 157–75.

Alchian, A.A. and Demsetz, H. 1972. Production, information costs and economic organization. *American Economic Review* 62, 777–95.

Black, F. 1986. Noise. *Journal of Finance*, July, 549–543.

Boesky, I.F. 1985. *Merger Mania*. New York: Holt Rinehart & Winston.

Conn, R.L. 1985. A re-examination of merger studies that use the capital asset pricing methodology. *Cambridge Journal of Economics*, March, 43–57.

Cowling, K. et al. 1980. *Mergers and Economic Performance*. Cambridge: Cambridge University Press.

Cragg, J. and Malkiel, B. 1982. *Expectations and the Structure of Share Prices*. Chicago: University of Chicago Press.

Davies, J.R. and Kuehn, D.A. 1977. An investigation into the effectiveness of a capital market sanction on poor performance. In *Welfare Aspects of Industrial Markets*, A.P. Jacquemin and H.W. de Jong, ed. Leiden: Martinus Nijhoff.

Davies, P.L. 1976. *The Regulation of Take-Overs and Merger*. London: Sweet & Maxwell.

Dodd, P. 1986. The market for corporate control: a review of the evidence. In *The Revolution in Corporate Finance*, ed. J.M. Stern and D.H. Chew, Jr. Oxford: Oxford University Press.

Firth, M. 1979. The profitability of takeovers and mergers. *Economic Journal* 89, June,

316–28.

Firth, M. 1980. Takeovers, shareholder returns and the theory of the firm. *Quarterly Journal of Economics* 94, March, 235–60.

Fortune 1986a. The *Fortune* 500, 28 April.

Fortune 1986b. Deals of the year, 20 January.

Fortune 1986c. Merger fees that bend the mind, 20 January.

Francis, A. 1980. Company objectives, managerial motivations and the behaviour of large firms: an empirical test of the theory of managerial capitalism. *Cambridge Journal of Economics*, December, 349–61.

Friedman, M. 1953. *Essays in Positive Economics*. Chicago: Chicago University Press.

Gort, M. 1969. An economic disturbance theory of mergers. *Quarterly Journal of Economics* 83, November, 624–42.

Greer, D.F. 1986. Acquiring in order to avoid acquisition. *The Anti-Trust Bulletin*, Spring.

Grossman, S.J. and Hart, O.D. 1980. Takeover bids, the free rider problem and the theory of the corporation. *The Bell Journal of Economics* 11(1), Spring, 42–64.

Grossman, S.J. and Hart, O.D. 1981. The allocation role of takeover bids in conditions of assymetric information. *Journal of Finance* 36, 297–319.

Halpern, P. 1983. Corporate acquisitions: a theory of special cases? A review of event studies applied to acquisitions. *Journal of Finance*, May.

Hannah, L. 1976. *The Rise of the Corporate Economy*. London: Methuen.

Hannah, L. and Kay, J.A. 1977. *Concentration in Modern Industry*. London: Macmillan.

Harris, R.S., Stewart, J.F., Guilkey, D.K. and Carleton, W.T. 1982. Characteristics of acquired firms: fixed and random coefficients probit analysis. *Southern Economic Journal*, July.

Hart, P.E. and Prais, S.J. 1956. The analysis of business concentration. *Journal of the Royal Statistical Society*, Series A, 119 (Part 2), 150–91.

Herman, E.S. 1981. *Corporate Control Corporate Power*. Cambridge: Cambridge University Press.

Hughes, A., Mueller, D.C. and Singh, A. 1980. Hypotheses about mergers. In Mueller (1980).

Hughes, A. and Singh, A. 1980. Merger concentration and competition in advanced capitalist economies: an international perspective. In Mueller (1980).

Hughes, A. and Kumar, M.S. 1985. Merger concentration and mobility amongst the largest UK non-financial corporations 1972–82. A Report to the Office of Fair Trading, Department of Applied Economics, Cambridge (mimeo).

Hughes, A. 1987. The impact of merger: a survey of empirical evidence for the UK. In *Mergers and Merger Policy*, ed. J.A. Kay and J. Fairburn, London (forthcoming).

Jay, J. 1986. Argyll recounts the cost. *Sunday Times*, 21 December, p. 27.

Jensen, M.C. and Meckling, W.H. 1976. Theory of the firm: managerial behaviour, agency costs and ownership structure. *Journal of Financial Economics* 3, 305–60.

Jensen, M.C. and Ruback, R.S. 1983. The market for corporate control; the scientific evidence. *Journal of Financial Economics* 11(1–4), 5–50.

Johnson, H.G. 1968. The economic approach to social questions. London School of Economic and Political Science.

Johnston, Sir A.J. 1980. *The City Take-Over Code*. Oxford: Oxford University Press.

Keane, S.M. 1983. *Stock Market Efficiency*. Oxford: Philip Allan.

Kuehn, D.A. 1975. *Takeovers and the Theory of the Firm*. London: Macmillan.

Kumar, M.S. 1984. *Growth Acquisition and Investment*. Cambridge: Cambridge University Press.

Leibenstein, H. 1966. Allocative efficiency v. X-efficiency. *American Economic Review* 56, 392–415.

Little, I.M.D. and Rayner, A.G. 1966. *Higgledy Piggledy Growth Again.* Oxford: Oxford University Press.

Markham, J.W. 1955. Survey of the evidence and findings on mergers, in *Business Concentration and Price Policy.* New York: National Bureau of Economic Research.

Marris, R.L. 1964. *The Economic Theory of Managerial Capitalism.* London.

Marris, R.L. and Mueller, D.C. 1980. The corporation, competition and the invisible hand. *Journal of Economic Literature,* March, 32–64.

Marx, K. 1971. *Capital. A Critique of Political Economy,* Vol. III. London: Lawrence & Wishart.

Mayshar, J. 1983. On divergence of opinion and imperfections in the capital market. *American Economic Review* 73, March, 114–28.

Meade, J.S. 1968. Is the 'New Industrial Estate' inevitable? *Economic Journal,* June.

Meeks, G. 1977. Disappointing Marriage: a Study of the Gains from Merger. Cambridge: Cambridge University Press.

Miller, E. 1977. Risk, uncertainty and divergence of opinion. *Journal of Finance,* September.

Mueller, D.C. 1969. A theory of conglomerate mergers. *Quarterly Journal of Economics* 83, November, 643–59.

Mueller, D.C. ed. 1980. *The Determinants and Effects of Mergers.* Cambridge, Mass.: O.G. and H.

Mueller, D.C. 1986. *Profits in the Long Run.* Cambridge: Cambridge University Press.

Nerlove, M. 1968. Factors affecting difference among rates of return on investment in individual common stocks. *Review of Economics and Statistics* 50, August, 312–31.

Newbould, G.D. 1970. *Management and Merger Activity.* Liverpool: Guthstead.

Ravenscraft, D.J. and Scherer, F.M. 1986. *Life after Takeover.* US Federal Trade Commission Bureau of Economics, Working Paper 139.

Rhoades, S.D. 1985. *Power Empire Building and Mergers.* Lexington.

Schleifer, P. 1986. Do demand curves for stocks slope down? *Journal of Finance,* July, 579–90.

Shiller, R.J. 1979. Do stock prices move too much to be justified by subsequent changes in dividends? *American Economic Review* 71(3), June, 421–36.

Singh, A. 1971. *Takeovers: Their Relevance to the Stockmarket and the Theory of the Firm,* Cambridge: Cambridge University Press.

Singh, A. 1975. Takeovers economic natural selection and the theory of the firm: evidence from the post war UK experience. *Economic Journal* 85(339), September, 497–515.

Steiner, P.O. 1975. *Mergers: Motives, Effects, Control.* Ann Arbor: University of Michigan Press.

Summers, L.H. 1986. Does the stock market rationally reflect fundamental values? *Journal of Finance,* July, 591–601.

Winter, S.G. Jr. 1964. Economic 'natural selection' and the theory of the firm. *Yale Economic Essays* 4(1), Spring, 225–72.

Winter, S.G. Jr. 1971. Satisficing, selection and the innovating remnant. *Quarterly Journal of Economics* 85, May, 237–61.

Yarrow, G.K. 1985. Shareholder protection, compulsory acquisition and the efficiency of the takeover process. *Journal of Industrial Economics* 34, September, 3–17.

Term Structure of Interest Rates

BURTON G. MALKIEL

The term structure of interest rates concerns the relationship among the yields of default-free securities that differ only with respect to their term to maturity. The relationship is more popularly known as the shape of the yield curve and has been the subject of intense examination by economists for over fifty years. Historically, three competing theories have attracted the widest attention. These are known as the expectations, liquidity preference and hedging-pressure or preferred habitat theories of the term structure.

THE EXPECTATIONS THEORY. According to the expectations theory, the shape of the yield curve can be explained by investors' expectations about future interest rates. This proposition dates back at least to Irving Fisher (1896), but the main development of the theory was done by Hicks (1939) and Lutz (1940). More recent versions of the theory have been developed by Malkiel (1966) and Roll (1970; 1971).

Suppose, for example, that investors believe the prevailing level of interest rates is unsustainably high and that lower rates are more probable than higher ones in the future. Under such circumstances, long-term bonds will appear to investors as more attractive than shorter-term issues *if* both sell at equal yields. Long-term bonds will permit an investor to carn what is believed to be an unusually high rate over a longer period of time than short-term issues, whereas investors in shorter bonds subject themselves to the prospect of having to reinvest their funds later at lower yields than are expected. Moreover, longer-term bonds are likely to appreciate in value if expectations of falling rates prove correct. Thus, if short and long securities sold at equal yields, investors would tend to bid up the prices (force down the yields) of long-term bonds while selling off short-term securities, causing their prices to fall (yields to rise). Thus, a descending yield curve with short issues yielding more than larger ones can be explained by expectations of lower future rates. Similarly, an ascending yield curve with longer issues yielding more than shorter-term ones can be explained by expectations of rising rates.

265

Under the assumptions of the perfect-certainty variant of the expectations theory, there are no transactions costs, and all investors make identical and accurate forecasts of future interest rates. The theory then implies a formal relationship between long and short-term rates of interest. Specifically, the analysis leads to the conclusion that the long rate is an average of current and expected short rates. Consider the following simple two-period example, where only two securities exist (a one-year and a two-year bond), and investors have funds at their disposal for one or two years. Let capital Rs stand for actual market rates (yields), while lower-case rs stand for expected or forward rates. Prescripts represent the time periods for which the rates are applicable, while postscripts stand for the maturity of the bonds. Thus, $t, R, 2$ indicates today's two-year rate, while $t + 1, r, 1$ stands for the expected one-year rate in period $t + 1$.

If investors are profit maximizers, it follows that each investor will choose that security (or combination of securities) that maximizes his return for the period during which his funds are available. Consider the alternatives open to the investor who has funds available for two years. The two-year investor will have no incentive to move from one bond to another when he can make the same investment return from buying a combination of short issues or holding one long-issue to maturity. If such an investor invests one dollar in a one-year security and then reinvests the proceeds at maturity (i.e. $(1 + r, R, 1)$) in a one-year issue next year, his total capital will grow to $(1 + t, R, 1)(1 + t + 1, r, 1)$ at the end of the two-year period. Alternatively, if he invests his dollar in a two-year issue (and leaves all interest to be reinvested until the final maturity date in two years) he will have at maturity $(1 + t, R, 2)^2$. In equilibrium, where the investor has no incentive to switch from security to security, the two alternatives must offer the same overall yield, i.e.,

$$(1 + t, R, 2)^2 = (1 + t, R, 1)(1 + t + 1, r, 1). \tag{1}$$

Thus, the two-year rate can be expressed as a geometric average involving today's one-year rate and the one-year rate of interest anticipated next year.

$$(1 + t, R, 2) = [(1 + t, R, 1)(1 + t + 1, r, 1)]^{1/2}. \tag{2}$$

If equation (2) holds, then the holding-period return for the one-year investor will also be the same whether he buys a one-year bond and holds it to maturity or buys a two-year bond and sells it after one year.

In similar fashion, the rate on longer-term issues must turn out to be an average of the current and a whole series of future short-term rates of interest. Only when this is true can the pattern of short and long rates in the market be sustained. The long-term investor must expect to earn through successive investment in short-term securities the same return over his investment period that he would earn by holding a long-term bond to maturity. In general, the equilibrium relationship is,

$$(1 + t, R, N) = [(1 + t, R, 1)(1 + t + 1, r, 1) \cdots (1 + t + N - 1, r, 1)]^{1/N}. \tag{3}$$

The expectations theory can be extended to a world of uncertainty and it can account for every sort of yield curve. If short-term rates are expected to be lower in the future, then the long rate, which we have seen must be an average of those rates and the current short rate, will lie below the short rate. Similarly, long rates will exceed the current short rate if rates are expected to be higher in the future.

THE LIQUIDITY-PREFERENCE THEORY. The liquidity-preference theory, advanced by Hicks (1939) concurs with the importance of expectations in influencing the shape of the yield curve. Nevertheless, it argues that, in a world of uncertainty, short-term issues are more desirable to investors than longer-term issues because the former are more liquid. Short-term issues can be converted into cash at short notice without appreciable loss in principal value, even if rates change unexpectedly. Long-term issues, however, will tend to fluctuate widely in price with unanticipated changes in interest rates and hence ought to yield more than shorts by the amount of a risk premium.

If no premium were offered for holding long-term bonds, it is argued that most individuals and institutions would prefer to hold short-term issues to minimize the variability of the money value of their portfolios. On the borrowing side, however, there is assumed to be an opposite propensity. Borrowers can be expected to prefer to borrow at long term to assure themselves of a steady source of funds. This leaves an imbalance in the pattern of supply and demand for the different maturities – one which speculators might be expected to offset. Hence, the final step in the argument is the assertion that speculators are also averse to risk and must be paid a liquidity premium to induce them to hold long-term securities. Thus, even if interest rates are expected to remain unchanged, the yield curve should be upward sloping, since the yields of long-term bonds will be augmented by risk premiums necessary to induce investors to hold them. While it is conceivable that short rates could exceed long rates if investors thought that rates would fall sharply in the future, the 'normal relationship' is assumed to be an ascending yield curve.

Formally, the liquidity premium is typically expressed as an amount that is to be added to the expected future rates in arriving at the equilibrium-yield relationships described in equations (1) through (3). If we let $L, 2$ stand for the liquidity premium that should be added to next year's forecasted one-year rate, we have

$$(1 + t, R, 2)^2 = (1 + t, R, 1)(1 + t + 1, r, 1 + L, 2) \qquad (4)$$

and

$$(1 + t, R, 2) = [(1 + t, R, 1)(1 + t + 1, r, 1 + L, 2)]^{1/2}. \qquad (5)$$

Thus, if $L, 2$ is positive (i.e. if there is a liquidity premium), the two-year rate will be greater than the one-year rate even when no change in rates is expected. It has also been customary to assume that $L, 3$, the premium to be added to the one-year rate forecasted for two years hence (i.e. period $t + 2$) is even greater than $L, 2$, so that the three-year rate will exceed the two-year rate when no change is expected in short-term rates over the next three years. In general, the liquidity-premium model may be written as

$$(1 + t, R, N) = [(1 + t, R, 1)(1 + t + 1, r, 1 + L, 2) \cdots$$
$$\cdots (1 + t + N - 1, r, 1 + L, N)]^{1/N}. \tag{6}$$

Assuming that $L, N > L, N - 1 > \cdots > L, 2 > 0$, the yield curve will be positively sloped even when no changes in rates are anticipated.

THE HEDGING-PRESSURE OR PREFERRED HABITAT THEORY. Other critics of the expectations theory, including Culbertson (1957) and Modigliani and Sutch (1966), argue that liquidity considerations are far from the only additional influence on bond investors. While liquidity may be a critical consideration for a commercial banker considering an investment outlet for a temporary influx of deposits, it is not important for a life insurance company seeking to invest an influx of funds from the sale of long-term annuity contracts. Indeed, if the life insurance company wants to hedge against the risk of interest-rate fluctuations, it will prefer long, rather than short, maturities. Long-term investments will guarantee the insurance company a profit regardless of what happens to interest rates over the life of the contract.

Many pension funds and retirement savers find themselves in a wholly analogous situation. A retirement saver who has funds to invest in bonds for n periods will find an n-period pure discount (zero coupon) bond to be the safest investment. It is assumed that if investors are risk averse, they can be tempted out of their preferred habitats only with the promise of a higher yield on a bond of any other maturity. Of course, other investors such as commercial banks or corporate investors will hedge against risk by confining their purchases to short-term issues. These investors will need higher yields on longer-term issues to induce them to invest in such securities. Under this hedging-pressure theory, however, there is no reason for term premiums to be necessarily positive or to be an increasing function of maturity. Under an extreme (and somewhat implausible) form of the argument suggested by Culbertson, the short and long markets are effectively segmented; and short and long yields are determined by supply and demand in each of the segment markets.

EMPIRICAL ANALYSIS OF THE TERM STRUCTURE. The chief obstacle to effective empirical analysis of the determinants of the term structure of interest rates has been the lack of independent evidence concerning expectations of future interest rates. Consequently, the first step in most empirical tests of the pure form of the expectations theory has been to set up some mechanism by which expectations may reasonably have been formed by market participants. Since people usually estimate the future by relying, at least in part, on historical information, this procedure has often involved the generation of forecasts of future interest rates from past values of these rates. Then investigators have sought to determine whether empirical yield curves have been consistent with these hypothetical forecasts and with the premise that investors, in fact, behave as the expectations theory claims. Thus, in essence, two theories were tested jointly: first, a theory of expectations formation and, second, a theory of the term structure. Of course, it is important to realize that any inability to confirm the expectations theory may be due to a failure to specify properly an expectations-forming mechanism rather than a failure of the theory to offer a correct explanation of the shape of the yield curve. Nevertheless, the wide body of evidence we have does suggest a general conclusion.

The expectations-forming mechanisms utilized in empirical studies have been varied and inventive. They have included an error-learning mechanism (Meiselman, 1962); distributed lags on past rates (Modigliani and Sutch, 1966) or on inflation (Modigliani and Shiller, 1973; Fama, 1976); use of ex post data under an assumption that market efficiency and rationality require that ex post realizations do not differ systematically from ex ante views (Roll, 1970; 1971; Fama, 1984a and b); and survey data assumed to reflect the actual expectations of market participants (Kane and Malkiel, 1967; Malkiel and Kane, 1968; Kane, 1983). While affirming the general importance of expectations in influencing the shape of the yield curve, empirical studies have generally rejected the pure form of the expectations hypothesis. There does appear to be an upward bias to the shape of the yield curve indicating that term premiums do exist. But contrary to the liquidity-preference theory, term premiums do not increase monotonically over the whole span of forward rates. Moreover, such term premiums vary over time. In addition, there appears to be seasonal patterns in the forward rates calculated from the short end of the yield curve. While expectations are unquestionably an important determinant of the term structure, it is clear that other factors also play an important role.

TOWARD AN ECLECTIC THEORY OF THE TERM STRUCTURE. The most recent work on the term structure has recognized that many factors play a role in shaping the yield curve. It has also considered the problem of explaining the term structure as one of intertemporal general equilibrium theory. Using the methodology of modern option pricing theory, bonds of different maturities are treated symmetrically with other contingent claims. Cox et al. (1981, 1985) have built such an eclectic model that encompasses all the elements of previous theories in a way that is fully consistent with maximizing behaviour and rational expectations. Expectations of future events, risk preferences and the characteristics of a variety of investment alternatives are all important, as are the individual preferences (habitats) of market participants about the timing of their consumption. Their approach permits the derivation of clear predictions about how changes in a wide variety of exogenous economic variables will affect the term structure. Their model is likely to spawn richer empirical work enabling us to understand better both the expectations-forming mechanism and the varied influences on bond prices.

BIBLIOGRAPHY

Cox, J., Ingersoll, J., Jr. and Ross, S. 1981. A re-examination of traditional hypotheses about the term structure of interest rates. *Journal of Finance* 36(4), September, 769–99.
Cox, J., Ingersoll, J., Jr. and Ross, S. 1985. A theory of the term structure of interest rates.

Econometrica 53(2), Mach, 385–407.

Culbertson, J. 1957. The term structure of interest rates. *Quarterly Journal of Economics* 71, November, 485–517.

Fama, E. 1976. Inflation uncertainty and expected returns on treasury bills. *Journal of Political Economy* 84(3), June, 427–48.

Fama, E. 1984a. The information in the term structure. *Journal of Financial Economics* 13(4), December, 509–28.

Fama, E. 1984b. Term premiums in bond returns. *Journal of Financial Economics* 13(4), December, 529–46.

Fisher, I. 1896. Appreciation and interest. *AEA Publications* 3(11), August, 331–442.

Hicks, J. 1939. *Value and Capital*. 2nd edn, London: Oxford University Press, 1946.

Kane, E. 1983. Nested tests of alternative term-structure theories. *Review of Economics and Statistics* 65(1), February, 115–23.

Kane, E. and Malkiel, B. 1967. The term structure of interest rates: an analysis of a survey of interest-rate expectations. *Review of Economics and Statistics* 49, August, 343–55.

Lutz, F. 1940. The structure of interest rates. *Quarterly Journal of Economics* 55, November, 36–63.

Malkiel, B. 1966. *The Term Structure of Interest Rates*. Princeton: Princeton University Press.

Malkiel, B. and Kane, E. 1968. Expectations and interest rates: a cross-sectional test of the error-learning hypothesis. *Journal of Political Economy* 77(4), July–August, 453–70.

Meiselman, D. 1962. *The Term Structure of Interest Rates*. Englewood Cliffs, NJ: Prentice-Hall.

Modigliani, F. and Shiller, R. 1973. Inflation, rational expectations and the term structure of interest rates. *Economica* NS 40(157), February, 12–43.

Modigliani, F. and Sutch, R. 1966. Innovations in interest rate policy. *American Economic Review, Papers and Proceedings* Supplement, 56, May, 178–97.

Roll, R. 1970. *The Behavior of Interest Rates*. New York: Basic Books.

Roll, R. 1971. Investment diversification and bond maturity. *Journal of Finance* 26(1), 51–66.

CONTRIBUTORS

Douglas T. Breeden Associate Professor, Fuqua School of Business, Duke University, Durham. Batterymarch Fellowship in Finance, 1981–2; Board of Directors, American Finance Association, 1989–. 'Price of state-contingent claims implicit in option prices', *Journal of Business* (1978); 'An intertemporal asset pricing model with stochastic consumption and investment opportunities', *Journal of Financial Economics* (1979); 'Consumption risk in futures markets', *Journal of Finance* (1980); 'Futures markets and commodity options: hedging and optimality in incomplete markets', *Journal of Economic Theory* (1984); 'Consumption, production, inflation and interest rates: a synthesis', *Journal of Financial Economics* (1986); 'Empirical tests of the consumption-orientated CAPM', (with M.R. Gibbons and R.H. Litzenberger) *Journal of Finance* (1989).

Michael J. Brennan Professor of Economics, University of California, Los Angeles. 'Taxes, market valuation and corporate financial policy', *National Tax Journal* 23(4), (1970); 'An approach to the valuation of uncertain income streams', *Journal of Finance* 28(3), (1973); 'The pricing of contingent claims in discrete time models', *Journal of Finance* 34(1), (1979); 'Savings bonds, retractable bonds and collable bonds', (with E.S. Schwartz) *Journal of Financial Economics* 5(1977); 'Evaluating natural resource investments', (with E.S. Schwartz) *Journal of Business* 58(2), (1985); 'Efficient financing under asymmetric information', (with A. Kraus) *Journal of Finance* 42(5), (1987).

James A. Brickley Professor of Economics, University of Rochester. 'The choice of organizational form: the case of franchising', (with F.H. Dark) *Journal of Financial Economics* 18(2), (1987); 'The market for corporate control: the empirical evidence since 1980', (with G.A. Jarrell and J.M. Netter) *Journal of Economic Perspectives* 2(1), (1988); 'Ownership structure and voting on anti-takeover amendments', (with R.C. Lease and C.W. Smith) *Journal of Financial Economics* 20(1–2), (1988).

271

Gregory Connor Professor of Economics, University of California, Berkeley. 'A unified beta pricing theory', *Journal of Economic Theory* 34 (1984); 'Performance theory with the arbritrage pricing theory', (with R. Korajczyk) *Journal of Financial Economics* 15 (1986); 'Risk and return in an equilibrium APT', (with R. Korajczyk) *Journal of Financial Economics* 21 (1988).

Thomas E. Copeland Professor, John E. Anderson Graduate School of Management, University of California, Los Angeles; Finance consultant. *Managerial Finance* (with T.E. Copeland, 1986); 'The effect of sequential information arrival on prices: An experimental study', (with N.F. Chen and D. Mayers) *Journal of Finance* (1987); 'A comparison of single and multifactor portfolio performance methodologies; the value line case (1965–1978), *Journal of Financial and Quantitive Analysis*, (1987); *Financial Theory and Corporate Policy* (with J.F. Weston, 1988); 'A model of stock split behaviour: theory and evidence', *Journal of Economics* (forthcoming); 'Beta changes around stock splits: a note', *Journal of Finance* (forthcoming).

A.D. Cosh Lecturer, Cambridge University. 'The renumeration of chief executives in the United Kingdom', *Economic Journal* (1975); 'The causes and effects of takeovers in the United Kingdom', (with A. Hughes and A. Singh), in *The Determinants and Effects of Mergers*, (ed. D.C. Mueller, 1980); 'The anatomy of corporate control: directors, shareholders and executive remuneration in giant US and UK corporatives', *Cambridge Journal of Economics* (1987); 'Institutional investment, mergers and the market for corporate control', (with A. Hughes, K. Lee and A. Singh) *International Journal of Industrial Organization* (1989).

J.S.S. Edwards University Lecturer, Fellow, St John's College, Cambridge. 'The 1984 corporation tax reform', *Fiscal Studies* (1984); 'Taxes, investment and Q', (with M.J. Kean) *Review of Economic Studies* (1985); 'Inflation and non-neutralities in the taxation of corporate source income', (with M.J. Kean) *Oxford Economic Papers* (1985); *Recent Advances in Corporate Finance* (with J.R. Franks, C.P. Mayer and S.M. Schaefer, 1986); *The Economic Analysis of Accounting Profitability* (with J.A. Kay and C.P. Mayer, 1987); 'Recent developments in the theory of corporate finance', *Oxford Review of Economic Policy* (1987).

Nils H. Hakansson Sylvan C. Coleman Professor of Finance and Accounting and Director, Berkeley Program in Finance. Fellow, Accounting Researchers International Association; Graham and Dodd Award, 1977, 1983. 'Optimal investment and consumption strategies under risk for a class of utility functions', *Econometrica* 38 (1970); 'Convergence to isoelastic utility and policy in multiperiod portfolio choice', *Journal of Financial Economics* 1 (1974); 'The purchasing power fund: a new kind of financial intermediary', *Financial Analysts Journal* 32 (1982); 'To pay or not to pay dividends', *Journal of Finance* 37 (1982); 'Changes in the financial market: welfare and price effects and the basic theorems of value conservation', *Journal of Finance* 37 (1982); 'Sufficient and necessary conditions for information to have social value in pure exchange', (with Gregory Kunkel and James Ohlson) *Journal of Finance* 37 (1982).

Hendrik S. Houthakker Henry Lee Professor of Economics, Harvard University. Distinguished Fellow, American Economic Association; Fellow and Past President, Econometric Society. *The Analysis of Family Budgets* (with S.J. Prais, 1955); 'Can Speculators Forecast Prices', *Review of Economics and Statistics* (1957); 'The capacity method of quadratic programming', *Econometrica* 1960; *Consumer Demand in the United States*, (with L.D. Taylor, 1966); *Economic Policy for the Farm Sector* (1967); 'Growth and inflation: analysis by industry', *Brookings Papers on Economic Activity* (1979).

Chi-fu Huang Associate Professor of Management and Economics, MIT. 'Information structure and equilibrium asset prices', *Journal of Economic Theory* 34 (1985); 'Information structure and viable price systems', *Journal of Mathematical Economics* 14 (1985); 'Implementing Arrow–Debreu equilibria by continuous trading of few long-lived securities', (with D. Duffie) *Econometrica* 53 (1985); 'An intertemporal general equilibrium asset pricing model: the case of diffusion information', *Econometrica* 55 (1987); *Foundations for Financial Economics*, (with R. Litzenberger, 1988); 'Optimal consumption and portfolio prices when asset prices follow a diffusion information', *Journal of Economic Theory* (forthcoming).

Gur Huberman Professor, University of Chicago, Columbia University, CORE, Tel Aviv University. 'Minimum cost-spanning tree games', (with D. Granot) *Mathematical Programming* 21 (1981); 'A simple approach to arbitrage pricing theory', *Journal of Economic Theory* 28 (1982); 'Information aggregation, inflation and the pricing of indexed bonds', *Journal of Finance* 42 (1987); 'Mean variance spanning', *Journal of Finance* 42 (1987); 'Optimality of periodicity', *Review of Economic Studies* 60 (1988); 'Limited contract enforcement and contract renegotiation', (with C. Kahn) *American Economic Review* 78 (1988).

Alan Hughes Chairman, Faculty of Economics and Politics, Cambridge University. Economic Advisor to the Director General of the Office of Fair Trading, 1975–83; Consultant to NEDO on Competition Policy, 1978–9; Consultant to United Nations, World Institute for Development Economic Research, Helsinki, 1987–; Consultant to Advisory Council on Science and Technology, Cabinet Office, 1987–. 'Competition policy and economic performance in the UK' in *Competition Policy* (1978); 'The causes and effects of takeovers in the United Kingdom' (with A. Cosh and Ajit Singh) in *The Determinants and Effects of Mergers* (ed. D.C. Mueller, 1980); 'Competition policy in the 1980s: the implications of the international merger wave' (with D.C. Mueller and Ajit Singh) in *The Determinants and Effects of Mergers* (ed. D.C. Mueller, 1980); 'The anatomy of corporate control: directors, shareholders and executive remuneration in giant US and UK corporations', (with A. Cosh) *Cambridge Journal of Economics* (1987); 'The impact of merger: a study of empirical evidence for the UK' in

Mergers and Merger Policy (ed. J.A. Kay and J. Fairburn, 1988); 'The rise and fall of the Golden Age' (with A. Glyn, A. Lipietz and A. Singh) in *The Golden Age of Capitalism: lessons for the 1990's* (ed. S. Marglin, 1988).

Jonathan E. Ingersoll, Jr. Adrian C. Israel Professor of International Trade and Finance, School of Organization and Management, Yale University. Batterymarch Fellowship, 1981; Sloan Fellowship, 1981; Leslie Wong Research Fellow, 1982. 'A contingent-claims valuation of convertible securities', *Journal of Financial Economics* 1977; 'A re-examination of traditional hypotheses about the term structure of interest rates', (with J. Cox and S. Ross) *Journal of Finance* (1981); 'Optimal bond trading with personal tax', (with G. Constantinides) *Journal of Financial Economics* (1984); 'An intertemporal general equilibrium model of asset prices', (with J. Cox and S. Ross) *Econometrica* (1985); 'A theory of the term structure of interest rates', (with J. Cox and S. Ross) *Econometrica* (1985); 'A theory of the term structure of interest rates', (with J. Cox and S. Ross) *Econometrica* 1985; *Theory of Financial Decision Making* (1987).

Masahiro Kawai Professor, Institute of Social Science, University of Tokyo. 'Price volatility of storable commodities under rational expectations in spot and futures markets', *International Economic Review* 24(2), 1983.

Stephen F. Leroy Department of Economics, University of California, Santa Barbara. 'Risk aversion and the martingale property of stock prices', *International Economic Review* (1973); 'Identification and estimation of money demand', (with Thomas F. Cooley) *American Economic Review* (1981); 'The present value relation: tests based on impliance variance bounds', (with Richard D. Porter) *Econometrica* (1981); 'Expectations models of asset prices: a survey of theory', *Journal of Finance* (1982); 'Atheoretical macroeconomics: a critique', (with Thomas F. Cooley) *Journal of Monetary Economics* (1985); 'Knight on risk and uncertainty', (with Larry J. Singell), *Journal of Political Economy* (1987).

John J. McConnell Professor of Finance, Purdue University. Board of Directors, American Finance Association. 'Returns, risks and pricing of income bonds 1956–1976 (Does money have an odour?)', (with G.G. Schlarbaum); 'Valuation of GNMA mortgage-backed securities', (with K.B. Dunn) *Journal of Business* 54 (1981); 'The market value of control in publicly-traded corporations', (with R.C. Lease and W.H. Mikkelson) 2 (1983); 'Corporate capital expenditure decisions and the market value of the firm', (with C.J. Muscarella) *Journal of Financial Economics* 14(3), (1985); 'Corporate mergers and security returns', (with D.K. Dennis) *Journal of Financial Economics* 16(2), (1986); 'The determinants of yields on financial leasing contracts', (with J.S. Schallheim, R. Johnson and R.C. Lease) *Journal of Financial Economics* 19(1), (1987).

Burton G. Malkiel Chemical Bank Chairman's Professor of Economics, Princeton University. Former President, American Finance Association. *The Term Structure* *of Interest Rates* (1966); *Strategies and Rational Decisions in the Securities Options Market,* (with Richard Quandt, 1961); *Expectations and the Structure of Share Prices* (1982); *A Random Walk Down Wall Street* (1985).

A.G. Malliaris Walter F. Mullady, Sr Professor of Economics, Loyola University of Chicago. 'Martingale methods in financial decision making', *Society of Industrial and Applied Mathematics Review* 23(4), (1981); 'Ito's calculus in financial decision making', *Society of Industrial and Applied Mathematics Review* 24(4), (1983); 'Minimizing a quadratic payoff with monotone controls', (with E.N. Barron and R. Jensen) *Mathematics of Operations Research* 12(2), (1987); 'Asymptotic growth under uncertainty: existence and uniqueness', (with Fwu-Ranq Chang) *Review of Economic Studies* 54 (1987); *Stochastic Methods in Economics and Finance* (1982); *Differential Equations, Stability and Chaos in Dynamic Economics* (1989).

Benoit B. Mandelbrot IBM fellow, IBM T.J. Watson Research Center; Abraham Robinson Professor, Yale University. Fellow, American Academy of Arts and Sciences; Foreign Associate, U.S. National Academy of Sciences; F. Barnard Medal for Meritorious Service to Science, 1985; Franklin Medal for Signal and Eminent Service to Science, 1986; Charles Proteus Steinmetz Medal, 1988; honorary doctorates form the Universities of Syracuse, Boston, State University of New York and Pace University, Laurentian University and the University of Guelph (Canada), University of Bremen (W. Germany). 'The Pareto–Levy law and the distribution of income', *International Economic Review* 1 (1960); 'New methods in statistical economics', *Journal of Political Economy* 71 (1963); 'The variation of certain speculative prices', *Journal of Business of the University of Chicago* 36 (1963); 'Forecasts of future prices, unbiased markets and 'martingale' models', *Journal of Business of the University of Chicago* 39 (1966); 'When can price be arbitraged efficiently? A limit to the validity of the random walk and martingale models', *Review of Economics and Statistics',* 53 (1971); *The Fractal Geometry of Nature* (1982).

Harry M. Markowitz Marvin Speiser Distinguished Professor of Finance and Economics, Baruch College, City University of New York. Fellow, American Academy of Arts and Sciences. 'The elimination form of the inverse and its application to linear programming', *Management Science* 3 (1957); *Portfolio Selection: Efficient Diversification of Investments* (1959); *Studies in Process Analysis* (ed. with A.S. Manne, 1963); *Simscript: A Simulation Programming Language* (with B. Hausner and H.W. Karr, 1963); 'Approximating expected utility by a function of mean and variance', *American Economic Review* (1987); *Mean-variance Analysis in Portfolio Choice and Capital Markets* (1987).

Thomas Marschak Professor, School of Business, University of California, Berkeley. Fellow, Econometric Society. 'Centralization and Decentralization in Economic Organizations', *Econometrica* (1959); *Strategy for RAND: Studies in* *the Microeconomics of Development* (with contributions from R. Summers and T.K. Glennan, Jr., 1967); 'Centralized versus decentralized resource allocation: the Yugoslav 'laboratory'', *Quarterly Journal of Economics* (1978); 'Computation in Organizations: the comparison of price mechanisms and other adjustment processes' in *Decision and Organization* (ed. C.B. McGuire and R. Radner, 1972); 'Restabilizing responses, inertia supergames, and oligopolistic equilibria', (with R. Selten) *Quarterly Journal of Economics* (1968); 'Price versus direct revelation; informational judgements for finite mechanisms' in *Information, Incentives and Economic Mechanisms* (ed. T. Groves, R. Radner and S. Reiter, 1987).

Robert C. Merton George Fisher Baker Professor of Business Administration, Graduate School of Business, Harvard University. President, American Finance Association, 1986; Director, (1982–4, 1987–8); Fellow, Econometric Society; Fellow, American Academy of Arts and Sciences; Leo Melamed Prize, University of Chicago, 1983; Distinguished Scholar Award, Eastern Finance Association, 1989. 'Optimum consumption and portfolio rules in a continuous-time model', *Journal of Economic Theory* (1971); 'An intertemporal capital asset pricing model', *Econometrica* (1973); 'Theory of rational option pricing', *Bell Journal of Economics and Management Science* (1973); 'On the pricing of contingent claims and the Modigliani-Miller theorem', *Journal of Financial Economics* (1977); 'A sample model of capital market equilibrium with incomplete information', *Journal of Finance* (1987); *Continuous Time Finance* (1989).

David M. Newbery Director, Department of Applied Economics, Cambridge University. 'Risk-sharing, share-cropping and uncertain labour markets', *Review of Economic Studies* (1977); *The Theory of Commodity Price Stabilization: a Study in the Economics of Risk* (with J.E. Stiglitz, 1981); 'Oil prices, cartels and the problem of dynamic consistency', *Economic Journal* (1981); 'Commodity price stabilization in imperfect or cartelized markets', *Econometrica* (1984); *The Theory of Taxation for Developing Countries* (with N.H. Stern, 1987); 'Road damage externalities and road user charges', *Econometrica* (1988).

Stephen A. Ross Sterling Professor of Economics and Management, Yale School of Organization and Management. President, American Finance Association; Fellow, American Academy of Arts and Sciences; Associate Editor, *Journal of Finance* and *Journal of Economic Theory*. 'The economic theory of agency: the principal's problem', *American Economic Review* 63(2), (1973); 'The valuation of options for alternative stochastic processes', (with John C. Cox) *Journal of Financial Economics* 3 (1976); 'A simple approach to the valuation of risky streams', *Journal of Business* 51(3), (1978); 'Option pricing: a simplified approach', (with John C. Cox and Mark Rubenstein) *Journal of Financial Economics* 7 (1979); 'A theory of the term structure of interest rates', (with John C. Cox and Jonathan E. Ingersoll, Jr) *Econometrica* (1985); 'The arbitrage pricing theory approach to strategic portfolio planning', (with Richard Roll) in *Financial Analyst's Handbook* (1987).

Ajit Singh Fellow, Director of Studies in Economics, Queen's College, Cambridge. *Growth Profitability and Valuation* (with G. Whittington, 1968); *Take-overs: Their Relevance to the Stock Market and the Theory of the Firm* (1971); 'Take-overs, natural selection and the theory of the firm: evidence from the post-war UK experience', *Economic Journal* 85(339), (1975); 'UK industry and the world economy: a case of deindustrialisation', *Cambridge Journal of Economics* 1(2), (1977); 'The interrupted industrial revolution of the third world: prospects and policies for resumption', *Industry and Development* (1984) 'The rise and fall of the Golden Age' (with A. Glyn, A. Hughes and A. Lipietz) in *The Golden Age of Capitalism: lessons for the 1990s* (ed. S. Marglin, 1988).

Clifford W. Smith, Jr. Clarey Professor of Finance, William E. Simon Graduate School of Business Administration, University of Rochester. Pomerance Prize from the Chicago Board Options Exchange for 'Trading costs for listed options: the implications for market efficiency', (with S.M. Phillips) *Journal of Financial Economics* (1980). 'The interdependence of individual portfolio decisions and the demand for insurance', (with D. Mayers) *Journal of Political Economy* 91(2), (1983); 'Determinants of corporate leasing policy', (with L.M. Wakeman) *Journal of Finance* 40(3), (1985); 'Investment banking and the capital acquisition process', *Journal of Financial Economics* 15(1), (1986); 'Ownership structure and voting on antitakeover amendments', (with J.A. Brickley and R.C. Lease) *Journal of Financial Economics* 15(1/2), (1988); 'Ownership structure across lines of property-casualty insurance', (with D. Mayers) *Journal of Law and Economics* 31(2), (1988); 'Corporate payout policy: cash dividends versus open market share repurchases', (with M. Barclay) *Journal of Financial Economics* 22(1), (1988).

James Tobin Emeritus Professor of Economics, Yale University; Nobel Prize in Economics, 1981; American Economic Association, John Bates Clark Bronze Medal, 1955; Member, President's Council of Economic Advisors, 1961–2; Honorary Doctor of Economics, New University of Lisbon, 1980; Honorary Doctor of Social Science, University of Helsinki, 1986; President, American Economic Association, 1971; Member, National Academy of Sciences, 1972–; Fellow, American Academy of Arts and Sciences; Fellow, American Statistical Association; Fellow, Econometric Society; Phi Beta Kappa; Fellow, British Academy. *Policies for Prosperity* (1987); *Two Revolutions in Economic Policy*, (with Murray Weidenbaum, 1988); *Essays in Economics* vol. 1, 'Macroeconomics'; vol. 2, 'Consumption and Econometrics'; vol. 3, 'Theory and Policy' (1975); *Asset Accumulation and Economic Activity* (1980).

J. Fred Weston Cordner Professor Emeritus of Money and Financial Markets, John E. Anderson Graduate School of Management, University of California, Los Angeles. President, American Finance Association, 1966; President, Western Economic Association, 1962. 'A generalized uncertainty theory of profit', *American Economic Review* 40(1), (1950); 'A test of cost of capital propositions', *Southern Economics Journal* 30(2), (1963); 'Asset expansion decisions in the framework of the capital asset pricing model', *Bedrijfskunde, Tidjschrift voor*

Modern Management 48 (1976); 'Some aspects of merger theory', (with Kwang S. Chung) *Journal of the Midwest Finance Association* 12 (1983); 'The payoff in mergers and acquisitions', in *The Mergers and Acquisitions Handbook*, (ed. Milton L. Rock, 1987).